McFar
Classics

MW00624620

1997

1. Michael R. Pitts. *Western Movies*

2. William C. Cline. *In the Nick of Time*

3. Bill Warren. *Keep Watching the Skies!*

4. Mark McGee. *Roger Corman*

5. R. M. Hayes. *Trick Cinematography*

6. David J. Hogan. *Dark Romance*

7. Spencer Selby. *Dark City: The Film Noir*

8. David K. Frasier. *Russ Meyer—The Life and Films*

9. Ted Holland. *B Western Actors Encyclopedia*

10. Franklin Jarlett. *Robert Ryan*

1998

11. Ted Okuda *with* Edward Watz. *The Columbia Comedy Shorts*

12. R. M. Hayes. *3-D Movies*

13. Steve Archer. *Willis O'Brien—Special Effects Genius*

14. Richard West. *Television Westerns*

1999

15. Jon Tuska. *The Vanishing Legion—A History of Mascot Pictures*

16. Ted Okuda. *The Monogram Checklist*

17. Roy Kinnard. *Horror in Silent Films*

18. Richard D. McGhee. *John Wayne—Actor, Artist, Hero*

19. William Darby *and* Jack Du Bois. *American Film Music*

20. Martin Tropp. *Images of Fear*

21. Tom Weaver. *Return of the B Science Fiction and Horror Heroes*

22. Tom Weaver. *Poverty Row HORRORS!*

In the Nick of Time

In the Nick of Time

Motion Picture Sound Serials

by

William C. Cline

McFarland & Company, Inc., Publishers
Jefferson, North Carolina, and London

Front cover: A publicity still from *Brick Bradford* (Columbia, 1948), one of the most popular science fiction serials.
Back cover: Robert Wilcox and William Newell battle a robot in *Mysterious Doctor Satan* (Republic, 1940).
Frontispiece by Jim Scancarelli

The present work is a reprint of the library bound edition of In the Nick of Time: Motion Picture Sound Serials, *first published in 1984.* **McFarland Classics** *is an imprint of McFarland & Company, Inc., Publishers, Jefferson, North Carolina, who also published the original edition.*

British Library Cataloguing-in-Publication data are available

Library of Congress Cataloguing-in-Publication Data

Cline, William C.
   In the nick of time.

   Filmography: p.
   Includes index.
   1. Moving-picture serials—History and criticism.   I. Title.
PN1995.9.S3C57   1997   791.43'75   83-22231

ISBN 0-7864-0471-X (paperback : 50# alkaline paper) ∞

Manufactured in the United States of America

McFarland & Company, Inc., Publishers
  Box 611, Jefferson, North Carolina 28640

Contents

Prologue

It seldom happens more than once in a lifetime, and it is difficult to describe: To anyone who has experienced a similar sensation, detailed explanation is not necessary; to one who has not—and may never—no amount of explanation would be sufficient. It happened to me on a Saturday morning over forty years ago in a darkened theatre in Concord, North Carolina. By a normally routine and insignificant occurrence I was suddenly and positively confronted with a happening that would literally affect my life.

At that time there was at the Paramount Theatre each Saturday a gathering similar to others in thousands of movie houses all over the country. They were held under many names and designations—Matinee Jamboree, The Popcorn Club, The Mickey Mouse Club, Comedy Carnival, Cartoon Jamboree, Saturday Circus, etc. The Paramount's was called the Popeye Club since that cocky little sailor was by far the most popular cartoon character in our town. For several years there was never a Club gathering without the showing of one or more of those deliciously hilarious Popeye cartoons introduced on the screen by displaying the title and credits from behind the sliding doors of a cartoon ship's poopdeck. Along with Olive Oyl, Wimpy and Bluto, the little one-eyed fighter drew cheers from the kids and wistful smiles from any adults present. On the same program there were booked a half-dozen or so other cartoons featuring such favorites as Mickey Mouse, Donald Duck and Betty Boop (and a series known as Stone Age Cartoons with no particular star), a two-reel comedy with the Three Stooges, Edgar Kennedy, Clark and McCullough or Our Gang, a Western picture and the "real attraction" for many—The Serial.

Though only eight years old, I was not a complete stranger to the movies. I had been taken to the theatre occasionally by my sister Louise, but during the Depression the purchase of movie tickets had to be considered carefully and selectively, and our infrequent trips had been to see pictures with her favorites—Joan Crawford, Bette Davis, Clark Gable, Claudette Colbert, Cary Grant, et al.—which did not at the time mean very much to me. Until that fateful Saturday morning, my attitude toward the movies in general was rather noncommittal. Then it happened.

My next older brother Al, who was then 12 and much more the "man-of-the-world"—with cinematic tastes that ran more to Buck Jones, Tim McCoy, Tom Mix and Hoot Gibson—had yielded to something fine in his nature and allowed his kid brother to tag along with him and his pals to the regular Saturday morning roundup of "hombres," "buckaroos" and "yahoos" at the Popeye Club. Because of what happened I have always reserved a rather special spot in my memories for him and that morning. Under different circumstances I might have encountered the movie serial and met it with a far different response, but that particular morning I was "one of the fellers" and intensely interested in understanding what they understood, liking what they liked.

On the way to town, all the excited talk among the guys was about a character referred to as the "main player" and known in the film as the "Eagle," and what each boy would do to a villain named Jason Burr if he could be the "Eagle" for just five minutes. I could not really imagine what a man called "Eagle" would look like, nor the type of person this Burr might be to invite such ill will from such a nice bunch of guys as my brother's pals, but I was anxious to find out. From a psychological standpoint, I entered the theatre set up for a definitive experience, and I was not disappointed.

From the descriptions by the boys I had not learned that the "continued" we were going to see had a title other than "the Black Eagle" nor had I been told how it would start. So when the screen seemed to explode with exciting music and a shot of a group of riders galloping headlong toward the audience, and the words *The Vigilantes Are Coming* appeared, I knew I was going to see something special, something I had never seen before, even something the others had not seen or they would have tried to describe it better. From that moment I was "hooked."

I was aware that the story had already started because the other boys knew about it from previous Saturdays, and for an instant I felt slightly cheated. But after the announcement of the chapter title, the figures of the "Eagle" and other leading characters (including the ruthless General Burr) appeared in succession on the screen with brief written narratives of what they had done in the foregoing episodes, and I was brought up to date. (It was during this synopsis sequence, with which I was subsequently to become so familiar, that I learned the meaning of the old expression, "cheer the hero and hiss the villain," for that is just what happened. As each player appeared, there could be no doubt about what the kids thought of him. They responded audibly.)

As much as I was stunned by the opening of the chapter, picked up and carried along with the story, and thrilled by the daring exploits of the dashing "Eagle" against the hateful General Burr, I was totally unprepared for the climax: The "Eagle" had pursued a gang of Burr's henchmen to a large mine and was fighting valiantly against overwhelming odds when a giant guillotine-type rock crusher was started and began ominously rising and falling with crashing blows, seeming to boom louder and louder as the fighting carried the "Eagle" closer and closer to its relentless pounding. As was intended — and along with all the other kids in the audience — I clenched my fists and squirmed and twisted (using my instinctive version of "body English") to try and keep the struggling hero away from the ever-increasing threat of the smashing rock crusher. But the sheer force of superior numbers mercilessly pushed him back and back until he was stretched out under the great stone slab. Down it came as the music in crescendo reached an almost unbearable peak — and the screen went dark! The scene was replaced with a stark printed announcement that the next chapter would be shown the following week.

I suddenly realized that I was perched on the very edge of my seat, holding on for dear life to the back of the seat in the next row. I could hardly believe what I had just gone through. It was truly incredible to me that any such excitement as that could exist. Though only a child, I had survived several close calls with danger — such as just being missed by a car I had not seen, and once nearly drowning before being pulled to safety by the hair of my head — but those things had happened fast and were over before I could become scared. I had never been through the excruciating emotional tensions of apprehension, dread, hope and fright of the last few minutes. Now I would have to wait a whole week to know what would happen. And, though assured by my brother and the others that the good old "Eagle" would escape unharmed, I secretly held my doubts until I could see for myself.

This was the beginning, and although I would see many movie serials and be thrilled by many more dashing heroes and hundreds of hair-raising climaxes and escapes, I was never again to have that same particular tingle of pure excitement that I had experienced that special morning. The subconscious quest for it that kept me returning week after week and serial after serial eventually led me into a twenty-year active participation in the business of exhibiting motion pictures in the Carolinas and an insatiable interest in the movie industry that has continued for more than forty.

In order to be as close to movies — and especially serials — as possible, I became at about 12 or 13 what was known around the local theatres as a "stooge." The theatres employed teenagers and young men as ushers, doormen, popcorn machine operators, candy vendors, marquee changers, billboard pasters, leaflet distributors and any other jobs that might come up in the day-to-day operation of a small-town theatre. These employees were on the payroll and received wages, but occasionally felt the need to use other boys to help them (Tom Sawyer style) to carry out their duties. The boys they engaged to help were the "stooges." Their compensation was free admission to the movies, and in those days dimes and quarters for tickets were not easy to come by. Concord had four theatres then: The Cabarrus (named for the county) which had a four-a-week schedule — a top picture from a major distributor on Monday and Tuesday, another on Thursday and Friday, and "B" pictures on single Wednesdays and Saturdays; The Paramount (my base) which ran top pictures from several of the majors second-run on Monday and Tuesday, another on Wednesday and Thursday, and first-run Westerns from those companies on Friday and Saturday with shorts and first-run Republic serials; The Pastime, which played first-run product from Columbia, Republic and Monogram (including Columbia serials); and The State, with second-run features from all companies on the Monday-Tuesday and Wednesday-Thursday changes, and first-run Universal serials with the Westerns on Friday and Saturday. One of the bonus features of being a "stooge" was that free entry to all of the town's theatres was usually extended to the "stooges" of each. This gave me access to far more output than I could have possibly paid for.

From "stooge" at the Paramount I moved into a paying job at the Cabarrus, changing the marquee four times a week for $2.00 (take home: $1.96) and then progressively through all of the salaried jobs up to assistant manager (except projector operator, which I did not want because it was too confining) before switching to another phase.

In 1949 I became a booker in an independent theatre agency in Charlotte, North Carolina, operated by H.D. "Hank" Hearn and D.H. "Max" Reinhardt and known as Exhibitors Service. Later the name was changed to Max Reinhardt Enterprises, Inc., when Hank moved to Florida to open an office. With Hank, Max, and former RKO salesman Clay Jessup, I helped buy and book pictures for an average of sixty independent theatres in North and South Carolina for the next ten years. From 1959 to 1962 I was the Charlotte office manager for Allied Artists, and briefly worked as a booker for United Artists before leaving the business. After thirteen years away from it, I then came back in 1976, and became associated with Frank Lowry at Carolina Booking Service, once again buying and booking films. Since Frank's retirement in 1982, I have operated the agency with the help of my associate, Mrs. Dessie Guyer.

What had started as a routine Saturday for everybody else back in 1936 had become through the viewing of a motion picture serial the day that set my course for the next forty years. During all that time — without my realizing it — I have been preparing this book by relegating to memory every fact and impression I could gain of as many serials as I could see — and now the time has come to write it down. To many observers and students of the motion picture industry the serial has not seemed important enough to bother with, since it has been only an "added attraction." But the millions of "grown-up kids" who will recall the time when they first became interested in movies through an experience similar to mine know that the "continued" deserves examination. If in the lives of many movielovers it was not always the "big shot" of their entertainment, it was at least the "trigger."

Introduction

Having had its beginning in 1912 with the Edison Company's release of a series of films titled *What Happened to Mary?* (which was just that — a series rather than a serial — but with a continuing main character and general story line), the serial as a form of motion picture entertainment began to take shape as it would eventually be during the period from 1913 to 1915. Following up the loosely connected series of completely separate episodes with the same central character came the 1913 production of *The Adventures of Kathlyn*, which consisted of 13 episodes, each complete in story but — unlike the others — all related to each other and following a *direct* plot line. Then during the next two years came the serials of Pearl White and Helen Holmes, which added to the suspense by leaving the lovely heroine in mortal danger at the end of each episode, and the story not completed. Through the years to follow, one of the favorite devices used to accomplish that suspense was to close out the chapter with the star hanging suspended from a cliff, a ledge, a rooftop or an airplane, with the antagonists applying unmerciful pressure upon her to let go, thereby introducing for the serial a descriptive term that still holds its meaning today — the "cliff-hanger" — and is also used to describe a desperate, suspenseful situation in real life.

As a unique form of entertainment that gave the moviegoer something to talk about between episodes and come back to week after week, the serial grew in popularity and became a mainstay for theatres in the years preceding and following 1920, when the pioneer producers of the feature-length film were experimenting and developing ideas, techniques and subjects that would be attractive to the growing public market. Theatre men felt that if a feature was booked that had questionable drawing power, the day might be saved by the continuing interest of his patrons in a good, tight, action-filled serial. And quite often this was true.

Fortunately for the motion picture business as a whole — but not for the serial itself — as the quality of features continued to improve with each

1

passing year, and motion picture producers became more aware of what types of stories and stars would go over best with the public, people became more content to patronize pictures which could be viewed complete in one sitting, and theatre men no longer needed the serial quite as much as before. By 1930 the continued picture had outlived its initial usefulness. It had become an "extra added attraction" and would remain so for the rest of its natural life.

Most of the written histories of the movies and their growth that I have encountered were written after 1930 — after sound came in and made a substantially different medium of the motion picture. By that time the silent film as an entity was an "open-and-shut-case." Since there were to be no more silent pictures made, the time from the beginning of the motion picture to the advent of sound became a period that could be viewed as a whole, and was thus designated as an "era." As an object of study and historical examination, that period — the era of the silent film — was subsequently viewed from the standpoint of the importance of the feature picture rather than the serial. The feature had grown to the position of central prominence in the industry and faced a brilliant future as the unquestionably accepted foundation for a firmly established, thriving and growing entertainment medium. And despite the movie industry's temporary setback by the Depression — the same as all other industries — the passage of time confirmed the dominant role of the feature and the relegation of the serial to the status of permanent "extra added attraction."

This is as it should be. Primary attention should be given to the things of primary importance. However, somewhere along the line it seems that someone could have given the serial whatever recognition it was due for the role it had played in the development of the silent film (and was still playing in the industry), but nobody did for three decades. Only within the past several years has a serious history of the serial been produced, and it came as a long-awaited and lovingly presented treatise, tracing the development of the cliff-hanger from its conception to its greatest crossroad — the advent of sound. But there it stopped, leaving the challenge to complete the story to someone else.

Unfortunately, no one picked up the gauntlet. The serial as a considerable topic of literary or historic interest had not nearly as much appeal as the more popular feature, so time continued to slide by without any real notice of it. Apparently the serial was dead for many, including historians of the latter-day sound era, for they have chosen to ignore it.

But with so much required for its creation, with so many people involved in its making, and with so many moviegoers who can trace to one their first interest in movies, the motion picture serial deserves proper recognition as a distinct and unique phenomenon of the industry. The chapterplay cannot be ignored any longer simply because most film historians view it as trivial. Trivial or not, it existed. Serials not only provided their particular variety of entertainment for the action-minded, they also served as training ground for some of the industry's most competent craftsmen and leading performers. Many talents discovered for, or honed by, their involvement in the production of serials later became valued contributors to feature motion picture and television production — and continue so. Top-rank actors of note have included in their lists of credits roles in the cliff-hangers of the thirties and forties, and a number of television's enduring favorites have their thespic roots buried in the fertile soil of action-by-episodes production.

Since I am not a historian, but one of the inheritors of the serial in its new form, I felt that it should no longer be ignored. Instead, I chose to examine it and see what it had become after it ceased to flourish as a major, accepted part of the industry. For it did indeed survive the changeover to sound and became an entertainment form for purely action fans (who love action for action's sake) and a whole new segment of the population — the kids. (Perhaps it was for this reason that critics and historians chose to no longer acknowledge openly that the serial had any significance, for in those days of the Great Depression and subsequently through World War II, kids were still expected to be seen and not heard and had no influence in economic matters. Today, on the other hand, entire industries — toys, games, records, and major portions of the advertising and clothing industries — depend directly upon attracting the attention of kids and young adults for their success.)

So, in the context of analyzing an entertainment form that had evolved into one appealing mainly to hard and fast action buffs and children between eight and 16, and acknowledging the fact that as such it deserves proper attention as the builder of future audiences for the more sophisticated feature films, let us proceed to the task of determining about the movie serial since 1930: what it was, who the people were who made it what it was, and — as much as we can with a layman's knowledge — how they did it.

1

Anatomy of a Cliff-Hanger

The serial — possibly more than any other form of motion picture — was a pure concoction. Beginning with the knowledge that its main appeal was to be to children and unsophisticated adults, the creators of the continued pictures had no delusions of having to produce films with artistic integrity or dramatic authority. They knew that their job was to put "in the can" a certain number of reels containing enough action, suspense and mystery to satisfy the appetites of their followers. With that done their mission was successful, and they could move on to another. To accomplish the mission, certain basic practices and elements were adopted and used over and over again.

Any successful concoction has a formula — a prescribed inclusion of various ingredients with set regulations and directions as to their use. The proper use of the ingredients and the regulations governing them produces a satisfactory and acceptable result. Failure to properly apply them naturally results in failure. The basic ingredients of a good serial — already clearly ordained in the silent form — consisted of a Hero, a Heroine, a Villain, his Henchmen, a Prize, and the Perils. These were mandatory. Without any one of them the project was doomed to failure from the start, so all serials had these ingredients for sure. Optional additives (highly desirable for peak flavor and enjoyment) were to make the Hero or the Villain — or both — a mystery figure whose identity was revealed only in the final episode, to give the Hero an able and compatible Assistant, to place in jeopardy a likable Pawn (a kindly professor or an eccentric inventor), and to surround the protagonists with a substantial cast of believable Solid Citizens. With all the mandatory elements present and any combination of the optional additives success was assured. (And the sound serial eventually added two things that made it even more different from the silents and set it on a new course — musical scoring with sound effects and the professional career stuntman. These additions gave the new serial form the adaptability to again become unique — and it did.)

4

The Hero (with whom the audience was to identify) had to be immediately recognizable as a stalwart of Truth and Right. There could be no questionable aspects to his character. Knowing in the first chapter that they had a long way to go together, the audience expected the hero to be trustworthy and dependable. They had to be able to believe that he was smart enough and daring enough to undertake what they knew was going to be a rough job. His bravery and courage had to be—from the opening scene on—a matter of accepted fact. Otherwise, because of the twists and turns that normally took place in the course of a twelve-to-fifteen-chapter serial, there would have been no reason to bother with it. And his honesty was the first assumption. No action fan could give proper attention to regaling the forces of evil if he was going to have to worry about the hero's character too. (When it became necessary to deal with underworld elements in any way other than to mete out justice, he could always assume a disguise. But that was all right, as he would have the audience in his confidence.)

The Heroine of necessity was pretty. Heroes didn't go around trying to rescue girls who weren't. (But if she were too pretty, you knew he had better watch out. She might be a spy planted in the hero's camp to corrupt him.) To be useful in the story, the heroine must be vulnerable. Her father (uncle, brother, guardian) would have had to be abducted by the villain and be under pressure to reveal secrets that would directly affect her safety. She could not be too necessary to the plot, however, or she might tend to get in the hero's way. She should be very anxious and willing to help, but not too effective. Her role was usually that of catalyst. There were exceptions, of course, and we will discuss them later on.

The serial from its beginning would have been impossible without an appropriately menacing Villain. His function in the formula was to provide the reason for there to be any story at all. He was the "threat"—to the hero, to the heroine, to national security, to society at large. More often than not—except during the war years when he was an enemy spy— the villain was presented as a determined and ruthless madman bent upon carrying out a scheme for wealth, power or revenge at any cost. The methods he used were altogether vicious, cruel and heartless. No attempt was ever made to lend justification to any of his acts. He was pure evil, and as such to be wholeheartedly resisted and completely defeated. As he gave no quarter, he was expected to receive none. To give credence to the authority of his menace, the villain was depicted of necessity as an intelligent man. Brute strength was a part of his total armory, but the real danger lay in his ability to conjure up plots that would unquestionably draw the hero and his forces into dangerous situations before they realized it was being done. Then their courage and versatility had to be brought into play to combat the villain's line soldiers—the Henchmen.

What can one say about the serial henchmen? Any student or constant observer of the sound serial almost certainly came to the conclusion that the real spice of the whole thing was the manner and means employed by the henchmen in attempting to carry out the plans of the villain. More often than not — and especially if he were a mystery figure — the villain himself was not involved in direct contact with the hero until the last chapter. Symbolically, as the protagonist of evil, he was on a comparable level with Law and Order as such — or society as a whole. He was the threat and society the threatened. Therefore, as the active agent for the villain, the henchman was in effect his "hero," directly pitted against society's active agent, the Law and Order hero. Consequently, the real contest as shown by the action on the screen resulted from the clashes and battles between the hero and the henchmen. The henchman thus assumed proportions in the formula much larger than the casual fan would suspect. As the parallel of the hero, he also had to be loyal, resourceful, singleminded and daring — only in the interest of evil rather than good.

The Prize was the underlying cause for all the concern. A map, a secret paper, a weapon, a chemical formula or whatever, it was the basic requirement for making the villain's scheme work. With it, the villain would muse ominously, his mammoth and complicated plan would work without a hitch — he would certainly become the wealthiest or most powerful man on earth — but without it, he would scowl, his beautiful and intricately conceived plan would fail utterly, and he would have to go back to being a discredited professor, a hack inventor, or a second-rate tyrant. The prize, of course, must be important and secret, very valuable and accessible — preferably portable, so it could be loaded into cars, wagons, trucks, boats, trains or planes (thus precipitating those highly accelerated chases that were standard parts of any good serial's action). To heighten suspense, the prize should change hands at least several times to tease the villain and motivate the hero.

The truly distinctive ingredient that positively identified the serial as a separate storytelling form was the open-end climax to each chapter — the Perils. As a means of provoking the moviegoer to return the following week, it was discovered early in the silent days that nothing worked quite so well as having the main player involved in a seemingly futile situation — staring into the jaws of death or teetering on the brink of destruction — at the end of each episode. In Pauline's days these were called the "perils" and that name — like the designation "cliff-hanger" — also continued to serve to describe a unique and provocative suspense technique. In order to accomplish their intended purpose, a serial's perils had to be diabolically conceived, insidiously perpetrated, destructively fatal, and seemingly inescapable.

The optional ingredients were always present to some degree, but if used extensively they had to be used carefully so as not to over-season or distract from the final result. The Assistants served as liaison between the front-line hero and his base headquarters, for manning the radio to relay messages, driving the car or wagon so the hero could fire shots at fleeing henchmen, doing the "leg work" of running down clues and reporting them to the hero for use in planning further strategy, and occasionally getting involved in a scrape along with the heroine so the hero could dash to their rescue. The Pawn was required to pose opposition to the villain within the span of every couple of episodes at least, and receive in return a veiled threat of what would happen to him or his daughter (niece, sister, ward) if he did not continue to work for the villain to perfect his discovery for the miscreant's despicable purpose. And the Solid Citizens — the policemen, district attorneys, government officials, other scientists, bankers and industrialists — formed the society counterpart to the villain. They gathered periodically to voice the urgency and seriousness of the situation, express their support of the hero, and reaffirm their full confidence in his ability to prevail. Some of filmdom's finest character actors took these roles, and often from this group came the secret villain when he was a mystery figure.

The molding of all these ingredients into a plausible and suspenseful chapterplay resulted from the use of a definite cycle, which was the pattern of most serials and the framework upon which could be built stories that might otherwise wander aimlessly and lose all interest. Where the cycle was ignored, that was almost inevitably the result. Always in the first chapter the existence and master plan of the villain were revealed to the audience and the first step taken toward the realization of that plan. This gave the hero an indication that there was dirty work afoot and alerted him that something would have to be done to try and prevent further catastrophe. There would be a theft, a kidnapping, a murder, or a wave of destruction the nature of which gave him an inkling of what to expect and what type preparations to make. While following up his first clue, initial contact with the henchmen was made and the hero would find himself in dire peril. It would seem that all was lost before it began, as relentlessly death in some form closed in on him at the end of the episode.

From chapter two to seven or eight, the villain's scheme was embellished and further revealed as he began weaving and spinning subplots and side-maneuvers to secure the necessary materials and tools to complete it, and to sidetrack (or otherwise disengage) the hero from his persistent pursuit.

As the action continued from chapter seven or eight to ten or twelve (in a fifteen-chapter story), it began to appear that the scheme would succeed in spite of everything the hero could do. Even though he had followed up every clue and thwarted the villain's henchmen at every turn, they somehow would have managed to squeak through with enough success to provide him with hope and fuel for further machinations.

But in ten and eleven (or eleven to thirteen), the tide would begin to turn. The hero's dogged persistence would begin to pay off and the villain would be checked in all directions. It would have then become apparent that his plan just might fail if he didn't rid himself of his meddlesome adversary. So he would decide to turn his attention directly to the task of eliminating the hated hero and setting in motion a final desperate effort to culminate his grand design.

Aside from the first chapter, the last two were always the most meaningful and exciting. By that time the hero and the villain would have sized each other up and each would be concentrating wholeheartedly upon how best he could overcome his opponent. They both knew they were on a collision course and that victory or defeat was in sight. It was in these last two episodes that the final burst of speed in the race for the prize produced a complete victory for the hero and ignominious defeat for the villain. This was justice's finest hour.

The responsibility for creating something new with each succeeding story while remaining true to the basic proven formula was that of the writers. Usually working in teams of three or four, they would take a general story line centered around some new and dangerous threat, mix in the elements of a successful continued adventure, each then develop one or more aspects of the cycle, and together hammer out a polished, complete screenplay to be turned over to the director, the actors and the technical staff for use as a blueprint for the physical production.

From the standpoint of form, the serial is vastly more like life than any other type of storytelling. Life is episodic, without clear-cut beginnings and endings—except for the *initial* beginning and the *ultimate* end—and provides throughout its course the contrasts of the continued story: peaks of victory and elation and valleys of defeat and despair. There are setbacks and revelations of hope, utter futility and sudden bursts of effectiveness. Just as we did not know what awaited the hero in next week's episode of our favorite cliff-hanger, we have no way of knowing what tomorrow's chapter of life holds for us. The continuing hope that everything will turn out all right—and the basic inquisitiveness of human nature—is what keeps us persistently coming back for more.

2

In Search of the Ammunition

Realizing that the extremely stylized action serial must have stories and characters which would be readily adaptable to the basic formula and highly attractive to the newly developing audience, the studios producing them sought material from many sources. One of them was indefatigable and seemingly inexhaustible, providing some of the most resounding successes throughout the sound era — the legends of the early American West. *The Great Train Robbery* was the first motion picture to tell a story, and although filmed in New Jersey — about as far East as you can get — was a Western. Soon after the serial became fully established as a movie form — and following the smashing success of the early entries starring the lovely young heroines — Westerns began to emerge as the perennial favorites of this field also. And it is most appropriate that the generally accepted "bridge-over" release between silent and sound serials (having been released in both versions) was Universal's *The Indians Are Coming* — a Western. This film is credited with reviving interest in what seemed to be a dying form of entertainment. Through the determined efforts of director Henry MacRae and the pioneer sound technicians at Universal, proof was presented that a fast-paced action story that would satisfy the most avid fan could be produced with sound. For the first time a serial received full "uptown," first-run treatment by playing the Roxy in New York and following in key houses for full runs all over the country.

In the early days of sound, the producers continued to rely heavily on the frontier legends, well-known adventure novels, and ideas derived from them, along with ideas suggested by actual experiences of real-life explorers and adventurers in the news, and the reports of modern scientific inventions and discoveries. Using the characters and plot lines of the action-oriented novels and working in the new scientific techniques and exploits of the renowned heroes of the day, the writers were able to complete exciting stories with authentic and contemporary flavor. Throughout the remaining years of the era, these sources would continue

9

to be of importance in the writing and developing of new projects, but in the middle thirties there began to emerge two new sources of ideas and material that would eventually provide some of the most graphic examples of the changed character of the movie serial since the end of the silent era. These were Radio series and newspaper Comic strips.

From *The Indians Are Coming* in 1930 to *Flaming Frontiers* in 1938, Universal produced a number of their finest Westerns using as inspiration the combination of frontier legends and popular novels. *The Indians Are Coming* was based on the book *The Great West That Was* by William F. Cody, renowned frontier scout who was better known as Buffalo Bill, the name given him by writer Ned Buntline during the Indian wars. From the same novel they produced *Battling with Buffalo Bill* the next year, and the basic plot of the book — the conflict between the pioneers in their great Western migration and the native Indians in defense of their hunting grounds — was the foundation for many other Western serials and features.

With Peter B. Kyne's memorable outdoor adventure story *The Tie That Binds* as a source, two other outstanding serials were adapted by Universal during that period. In 1932 the writers came up with a screenplay titled *Heroes of the West* based on Kyne's book, and in 1938 developed another story from it called *Flaming Frontiers*. In the meantime, turning to W.C. Tuttle's *Redhead from Sun Dog*, they released an outstanding chapter film called *The Red Rider* on the heels of another Peter B. Kyne adaptation titled *Gordon of Ghost City* — both starring Buck Jones.

W.R. Burnett's exciting *Saint Johnson* was turned into the fast-paced 1937 thriller *Wild West Days*, but interestingly the main character as played in the film was not the Saint Johnson of the novel, but a frontiersman named Kentucky Wade. The last of the Louise Lorraine serials released by Universal (*The Lightning Express*, costarring Lane Chandler) back in 1930 had been an adaptation of the famous novel about the legendary railroad detective in the early West — Frank H. Spearman's *Whispering Smith Speaks*.

Quite possibly the most famous of all characters to come alive from the pages of adventure fiction is Tarzan, the incredible jungle man of the Edgar Rice Burroughs novels. Silent serials about this fabulous lord of the jungle were produced many years before sound, features have been made regularly up to the present, and a series depicting the legendary ape man's adventures was begun on television in 1966. If not the most famous character to come from a writer's imagination, he at least seems to be the most durable. In the thirties, three sound serials were released with Tarzan as the hero: Universal's *Tarzan the Tiger* was based on the novel *Tarzan and the Jewels of Opar* and was released in both silent and sound versions in the very last days of 1929. Frank Merrill had the title role and was supported by Natalie Kingston. Three years later Principal Pictures released *Tarzan the Fearless* with Larry "Buster" Crabbe, a bright young award-winning swimming star. The third Tarzan serial was filmed on an expedition to Guatamala and released in 1935. Considered by many to be the best of all the Tarzan chapter films, *The New Adventures of Tarzan* starred a handsome, lean and muscular actor named Herman Brix, who played a serious and very intent ape-man. So sweeping was the scope of this story that two feature-length versions were edited from it, *The New Adventures of Tarzan* and *Tarzan and the Green Goddess*.

Another character created by Edgar Rice Burroughs was featured in two serials by Republic studios in the early forties. His novel *Jungle Girl* was adapted for the screen and released as a continued picture in June 1941. The leading character — a lovely, civilized young girl named Nyoka who lived in the jungle like Tarzan — was also the central figure in a sequel titled *Perils of Nyoka* the following year.

Ivory Trail, the popular jungle tale by Talbot Mundy, was brought to films by Universal as *Jungle Mystery* in 1932, and Otis Adelbert Kline's widely-read *Jan of the Jungle* reached the serial screen in 1935 as *Call of the Savage*.

An expedient in the creation of new stories with familiar characters was the writing of sequels to a well-known original using the same leading character. Such was the case with Nyoka. Another was Sax Rohmer's delightfully satanic Dr. Fu Manchu. Made famous by novels and earlier feature films, Rohmer's classic evocator of evil was made the villain in a 1940 Republic production called *Drums of Fu Manchu* and brought due recognition to a fine young actor named Henry Brandon. Universal, in a variation of this technique, had combined several stories by Burt Standish using his famous teen-age athlete as the central hero and released *The Adventures of Frank Merriwell* in 1936. (The most overworked character in this practice in serials was Zorro, the dashing, romantic creation of author Johnston McCulley. Republic released no less than five serials from 1937 to 1949 with the name Zorro in the title, and a sixth in 1954 with the Zorro character using another name.)

Other widely-read action novels were transformed into chapterplays also, and many stand out as fine examples of the value of good stories to the creation of good serials. When Columbia entered the cliff-hanger field in 1937, one of their first productions was a screen adaptation of a first-rate aviation story by William Byron Mowery titled *The Silver Hawk*. It was released that year as *The Mysterious Pilot*. Three years later they re-made the classic story *The Green Archer* by Edgar Wallace, which had previously been used by Pathé in 1925 as a Walter Miller–Allene Ray vehicle. Two thrilling sea stories based on novels were released as cliff-hangers subsequently — *Haunted Harbor*, based on a Dayle Douglas story of intrigue and murder on a remote island, and a semi-historical science-fiction fantasy titled *Mysterious Island*, based on Jules Verne's *The Isle of Mystery*. The former was released by Republic in 1944 and the latter by Columbia in 1951.

As popular as the heroes of books were, cliff-hanging really hit its stride in the thirties and forties when serials began showing the exploits of champions from radio and the comics. Many of the form's greatest favorites came from the then-new medium of radio. Millions of avid fans who had been required to visualize only in the mind's eye what a particular character looked like were now treated to the movie reincarnation of that character, and in very few cases were there any disappointments.

Although — like the earlier film series — they were presented as complete, independent episodes, the radio series from which came the popular movie serials featured the same central characters and a basic, immediately recognized, and continuing situation. Both into and out of that situation could be thrust many plot twists, topical incidents and sociological statements. It was natural to adapt such a concept into a continued picture. From its inception to the advent of television, much of radio consisted of series embracing drama, adventure, comedy, mystery and romance, and today's television programming follows the same pattern. From the adventure series on radio, serial producers acquired characters and material with which to work that resulted in some of the most interesting and exciting projects of the entire sound era.

Two similar characters with different backdrops came to the movies from the pen of Fran Striker via radio. They had become household friends without anyone really knowing what they looked like, and the movie screen gave them real images, so that they became even more meaningful as entertainment heroes. In 1938 Republic electrified the action market by presenting a fifteen-chapter serial called *The Lone Ranger*. Unlike the radio version — in which it was known that the Ranger was the sole survivor of a cowardly ambush who remains masked at all times, except for occasional disguises to infiltrate enemy positions — the first film presentation gave the moviegoer five young heroes from which to choose the authentic one. Instead of all the rangers being slain in one ambush, they were killed one-by-one performing acts of great heroism until there was only one left — the *real* Lone Ranger. So great was the success of the picture that the following year Republic rushed into release a sequel called *The Lone Ranger Rides Again*. In the second one there was only one Lone Ranger and the audience knew who he was. The other characters in the story did not know, however, and much of the suspense involved the constant threat of his identity being discovered. That same year, the other Fran Striker character was made the hero of a Universal release bearing his name as the title — *The Green Hornet*. The similarities were marked: As The Lone Ranger appeared in the early West masked and dedicated to a fight for Law and Order, riding a silver-white stallion of great speed and stamina, using silver bullets as a trademark, and being assisted by an Indian companion named Tonto, so The Green Hornet operated in a modern-day setting, also masked and fighting for Law and Order, riding in a specially constructed and equipped high-powered automobile, using the hornet symbol as a trademark, and being assisted by an Oriental companion named Cato. The deliberate parallel was obvious, yet both became action favorites and remain so today.

In the golden age of radio, *Gang Busters* had an almost hypnotic influence on its millions of listeners. When the time came each week for the popular series "based on true cases in the files of law enforcement agencies throughout the country," all activity for the action fan stopped abruptly and he figuratively became glued to his set. The stories presented were dramatizations of actual cases and were designed for action and suspense by the program's originator, Phillips H. Lord. Universal brought it to the screen as a serial in February 1942 with an excellent cast of fine actors — in the same tradition as the radio show.

From 1940 to 1950 other radio heroes were also brought to life on the movie screen — favorites of the young "blood-and-thunder" fans such as *Captain Midnight* (Columbia, 1942), *Hop Harrigan* (Columbia, 1946) and *Jack Armstrong* (Columbia, 1947). All of these were action series on the Mutual network. Columbia also adapted *The Sea Hound* from radio in 1947 and *Captain Video* in 1951 from a television series.

Based on stories in Street and Smith's *The Shadow Magazine* and regular series on the Mutual network, Columbia produced *The Shadow* in 1940 and *Chick Carter, Detective* in 1946. As a radio series *The Shadow* was the epitome of mystery and suspense dramas. The secret of Lamont Cranston and the enigma surrounding his ability to "cloud men's minds" so they could not see him were of enduring appeal to the fans of intrigue and the supernatural. To transform this character to the screen with all of his mysterious aura intact would have been almost impossible, but Columbia did an admirable job of trying. The choice of Victor Jory for the title role was most perceptive, as he visually and audibly conveyed the required image of Cranston (and the "man of mystery") more credibly than any other actor of that time that can be brought to mind. An interesting facet of the Columbia screenplay was that both the hero and the villain were masked men of mystery. The arch-villain was known only as The Black Tiger until exposed in the final episode. Furthermore, since The Shadow was none too popular with the police, there were for them *two* villains in the piece. So, at any given time in the proceedings, the characters in the film couldn't be absolutely sure who was "us" and who was "them." This feeling also pervaded many of The Shadow stories in the magazine until unraveled at the end, so for the audience the result was perfectly compatible and a pure delight.

A close relative of the radio series was the newspaper comic strip. Its very nature made it more adaptable to movie serials, however, because the essence of its being was the daily and weekly continuation of the plot. With each installment, a small part of the story was revealed along with background, reaction, and a promise of the next bit to come. To get the entire story, a reader had to see the strip every day.

Comic strips have been called the "teasers" of the newspapers. Whether or not the reader cared particularly about current news or other regular features of the paper that were complete in themselves — articles, specialty write-ups, columns, editorials, etc. — he was provoked into buying a paper each day in order to keep up with the comics. This is true even today, and will probably continue so long as there are newspapers. No other regular feature is more durable than the comics, including the sports page and the women's section. As "teasers," the comics serve the newspaper industry as the serials have the movie industry since the silent days. It was natural that the two would merge and bring some of the comics' most outstanding successes to the action film market.

Chosen to pioneer this new association of entertainment media were strips with wide popular appeal, larger-than-life characters, scientific and mysterious backgrounds, and suspense-sustaining stories. Eventually nearly all of the adventure-type strips from the nation's leading papers were transformed to the screen in serial form, and many of the near-adventure and sometime-adventure comics reached the movies as features (*Joe Palooka, Charlie Chan, Li'l Abner, Prince Valiant*, et al.) along with scores of others depicting comedy, drama and romance. There is a perennial interest in comics by the American public, and the movie serial enhanced that interest for the young and action-minded.

This primary source of inspiration for cliff-hangers in the thirties and forties, however, produced an interesting paradox. The using of comic strips as the basis for stories and familiar characters was a mixed blessing to the serial form. They provided some of the very best of the continued pictures released, and these linger in the memories of the buff as representations of the true nature of the genre. At the same time — by assuming an identity with comics in such an irrevocable way — the serial became the movie counterpart of the "funnies." Then, as the strips became more and more in the public mind an entertainment for the kids, so did the serial. Now, when it is again seemly for an adult to admit that he reads and enjoys the comics — and when they have apparently regained their place in society by being propelled into the dubious realm of popular art — the serial is not here to enjoy the same fruits of rejuvenation. It has been replaced by the very thing that it started out to be — the series — only in television instead of the movies.

In line with the reincarnation of comic strips as pop art, it can be noted that several attempts have been made to bring about the same thing with serial characters — but without success. Following the flash success of a number of complete, one-sitting showings of Columbia's 1943 *Batman* several years ago, a television series featuring the "caped crusader" and Robin, the Boy Wonder, was produced by William Dozier and shown on a major network. Soon after it was followed by another Dozier-produced series featuring The Green Hornet. *Batman*, played in the spirit of pop art — with tongue-in-cheek self-deprecation and reverse snobbery — was a financial success. *The Green Hornet*, which was presented in straight dramatic style as an action mystery series in the tradition of its former presentations, was not accepted by the exponents of pop art and was ignored by action fans who thought it would be the same type of thing as *Batman*. It lasted only one season. In comparing the two attempts as a parallel of the chances of reviving the serial in today's entertainment context, the natural conclusion is that the conditions necessary for bringing about such a revival do not exist in either movies or television.

But the conditions for success in transferring comic strips to the serial screen did exist in the middle thirties. Action strips had an avid following among adults and kids alike. Not yet having been confronted with the realities and horrors of World War II, the public still had a taste for broad, unabashed, fist-slinging, head-knocking action. The proficient use of sound and music to help set desired moods in the movies had progressed for over five years. So the wedding of the stark, two-dimensional picture statement of the comics and the fast-paced, un-adultered free movement of the action serial form was almost inevitable.

Even though Tarzan was depicted in a cartoon strip also, his real status was as a character in the novels of his creator, Edgar Rice Burroughs. So, for the sake of this discourse, Tarzan will not be referred to as a comic strip character. However, in deference to his influence on later characters created by cartoonists, it is needful to say that most of the comic strip heroes transferred to the screen had a marked resemblance to the ape-man in purpose and personality construction. The jungle hero was the first of the "super-heroes" by reason of his great physical stamina and daring personal feats. It is a tribute to his preeminence that most of them were created along the same pattern as he, but that few of them are remembered for their human qualities as well — as he most certainly is.

Having thus qualified the role of Tarzan, the first sound serial based on a popular cartoon strip was Hal Forrest's *Tailspin Tommy*, released by Universal in October 1934 with Maurice Murphy in the title role, Noah Beery, Jr., Patricia Farr, and a cast of supporting players that included several former stars of the silent era. Prior to its release there had been other flying serials with similar action and scenes of as good or better quality, but the fact that the hero was called by a name that they all knew and liked gave a special thrill to moviegoers, and it became a box office success. (When I first mentioned to him a couple of years ago my intention to begin research on serials, my good friend Hugh McDonald, a former Metro-Goldwyn-Mayer sales representative in Charlotte, immediately recalled *Tailspin Tommy* as his first memory of a serial as a boy. For a brief moment he grinned, inwardly recalling other thrillers of that time, got a faraway look in his eye, then gently shook his head as if to clear away a slight wave of nostalgia, and remarked that those were the days when a boy could get a real thrill from the movies. Since then I have mentioned my project to a number of people old enough to remember, and was touched by the similarity of the reactions. All were about the same, the only difference usually being in the title of the serial that each first recalled.)

The following year after *Tailspin Tommy*, Universal released its sequel, *Tailspin Tommy in the Great Air Mystery* — this time with Clark Williams, Noah Beery, Jr., and the lovely Jean Rogers — and in March 1936 released the first science-fiction, space serial based on a comic strip and thereby set the pattern for all that were to follow. It was Alex Raymond's *Flash Gordon*.

Alexander G. Raymond was an art department employee of King Features Syndicate when they decided to hold a contest to select an artist for a new daily adventure strip to be called *Secret Agent X-9*. Raymond won the assignment in spite of the submitted entries of a number of more noted artists. Later, the syndicate laid plans for a fantastic space-oriented strip about life on other planets. After one rejection, Alex Raymond redrew his conception of the idea and submitted a proposed Sunday page. It was accepted and *Flash Gordon* was born. Soon afterward he relinquished the job of drawing *Secret Agent X-9* to another artist and concentrated his full attention on the new strip. It became one of the most popular comic strips of all time, mainly because of the detailed, painstaking artwork of young Raymond. At the beginning, he was advised by veteran cartoonists that it was foolish to waste so much time in drawing so carefully, as the public would not appreciate the effort. They contended that all that was necessary to convey the cartoon strip story idea was the flat, two-dimensional style. In spite of the advice, Raymond continued to fill his strip with the detailed lines, shadings and depth perspective that made his work the outstanding, durable and respected strip it came to be.

When Universal brought *Flash Gordon* to the screen, the job of adapting it into an exciting, quality continued picture was given to veteran serial producer Henry MacRae and director Frederick Stephani, who also shared in the writing of the screenplay. Along with Stephani, the credit for the script belongs to three of the most prolific of serial writers — George Plympton, Basil Dickey and Ella O'Neill. The result was a classic modern cliff-hanger and the mold for all future space-fantasy adventures:

Opening with the terrifying discovery by leading scientists that an unknown and uncharted planet was hurtling headlong toward the Earth, the first chapter, *The Planet of Peril*, found the world's people resigning themselves to certain doom — with one exception. Flying to join his father for the end, young athlete Flash Gordon met lovely Dale Arden on the plane, and when it crashed in the lonely countryside they encountered and joined forces with Professor Zarkov, the one man who had not given up. He planned to rocket to the onrushing planet in his recently completed spaceship to try and find a way to prevent the collision. Rather than passively wait for their demise, Flash and Dale decided to go with him. On the planet — called Mongo — the three were confronted by the evil emperor Ming, the Merciless, who planned to conquer the Universe, starting with the destruction of Earth.

For the next twelve episodes Flash, Dale, Dr. Zarkov and new-found allies Prince Barin (the deposed real ruler of Mongo) and Thun, the Lion King, faced all sorts of perils from Ming and his forces — King Kala of the underwater world, King Vultan of the Sky City, and Ming's beautiful but deceitful daughter, Princess Aura. Finally successful after a veritable "field day" of fistfights, animal attacks, ray gun battles and aerial dogfights with smoke-belching spaceships, the trio of Earth people — by then veteran space travelers — were able to head home with new hope.

Once again a serial had been produced that was worthy of the first-run, "A" theatre treatment in large cities all over the country as well as the small towns and rural communities. Such was the popularity of the Flash Gordon strip that the entertainment pages of many metropolitan news-papers — including some that did not even carry the strip — contained half- and three-quarter-page feature stories publicizing the release and local openings of the first episode, accompanied by many illustrations showing scenes from the movie and sketches by artist Raymond depicting key highlights of the film. Stills and drawings of such outstanding special effects as the Sky City suspended in midair supposedly supported by atomic-powered rays, the gruesome and horrible prehistoric monsters of Mongo, and the futuristic weapons and rocket-propelled spaceships were used generously, along with pictures of the principal characters so well known to everyone by then.

The acceptance of *Flash Gordon* led to not just one, but two sequels based on his exploits — *Flash Gordon's Trip to Mars* in 1938 and *Flash Gordon Conquers the Universe* in 1940. In each of them the basic char-acters (Flash, Dale, Zarkov and Ming) were retained and utilized in plots similar to the first: The threatening force in *Trip to Mars* was a huge "Nitron" ray lamp trained on Earth by Ming to alter the elements of the atmosphere and cause great waves of destruction and death; and a mysterious plague known as "The Purple Death" was perpetrated by Ming in *Conquers the Universe* for Flash and Zarkov to deal with. As always, they did manage to deal with it and emerge victorious.

From 1936 until they stopped making serials in 1945, Universal released chapter films based on an array of well-known comic strips. Many of them, like *Flash Gordon*, were syndicated and thus widely-read. So the market for each new production was preestablished and presold. Just six months after the release of *Flash Gordon*, the film version of another science-fiction strip came out. Captain Eddie Rickenbacker's famous aviator-detective-scientist hero became the central figure in the fantasy serial bearing his name as its title — *Ace Drummond*. During the next ten years, the studio released 12 more cliff-hangers based on nine well-known strips, including the three Gordons. In 1937 there were three: Alex Raymond's *Jungle Jim*, King Features Syndicate's *Radio Patrol* by Eddie Sullivan and Charles Schmidt, and *Secret Agent X-9*, which was then drawn by Leslie Charteris. (*X-9* was made again and released in 1945 — the last comic strip-based serial produced by Universal.)

Will Gould's mystery strip about Chinatown and the Tong wars was brought to the screen by Universal in 1938 along with another action strip by the elder of the cartooning Young brothers: *Red Barry* offered Larry Crabbe in the title role in one of the few serial roles he ever played in plainclothes (as Tarzan, Flash Gordon, Buck Rogers, et al., there was some appropriate costume to wear as identification, but as Gould's square-jawed detective hero he appeared in a suit and hat), and *Tim Tyler's Luck* was the work of Lyman Young, whose brother Chic was the creator of *Blondie*. Lyman had two action strips going for King Features at the same time and on the same Sunday page — *Curley Harper* and *Tim Tyler's Luck* — and both enjoyed wide fame as top-notch adventures. It is a mystery why the former was never made into a movie.

Universal's 1939 comic strip offering has become the unofficial symbol of man's effort to conquer space. *Buck Rogers*, which was thoroughly digested and enjoyed as high adventure by the youth of the time while mildly tolerated by knowing adults as absolutely and utterly fantastic and unbelievable — and therefore harmless — was the most popular strip of its kind. Dealing with interplanetary warfare of the future, such amazing and destructive weapons as death rays, rocket pistols, paralyzing guns and disintegrating machines were introduced by artist Lieutenant Dick Calkins. Rocketships, antigravity belts and space helmets were standard equipment and produced a tremendous sale in the toy market. The Universal special effects men reproduced all of these in a fast-paced cliff-hanger about the efforts of Buck's archenemy Killer Kane to rule Earth completely, and the attempts of Buck's forces to prevent the takeover by enlisting the planet Saturn as an ally. (As evidence of the strip's belying the criticism of its early detractors, science has produced — in less than three decades — the "bazooka" (a rocket weapon), the mace spray device (a paralyzing weapon), the rocket-propelled air-suspension pack (an antigravity device), the laser beam (a death ray) and "Apollo" (the rocket-powered spacecraft which has actually landed human beings on the Moon), now making the ideas of Calkins seem prophetic rather than fantastic. In announcing these scientific inventions over the years, one of the favorite expressions of the news writers has been, "Shades of Buck Rogers!"

The last two cartoon strip characters to be presented by Universal in the early forties were topical military heroes of the sea and air. With the war raging in Europe and America's involvement apparently inevitable, the role of the Navy in the defense of United States shores was uppermost in the minds of the government and the public. Begun in 1934 as a way of depicting life in our sea forces to American youth, Lieutenant Commander Frank V. Martinek's *Don Winslow of the Navy* took on new meaning with America's actual entry into World War II. Up to that time, Martinek had drawn on his own experiences as a World War I Naval officer, newspaperman, G-Man, author and businessman for his *Winslow* stories. During the war, *Don Winslow of the Navy* (which was approved by the Navy Department) became a means of telling the American public the story of our "first line of defense" — its ideals, traditions, motives and heroic exploits. Its presentation as a Universal serial in October 1941 — just before the infamous attack on Pearl Harbor in December — was one of the most timely contributions of the serial field. Its sequel a year later, *Don Winslow of the Coast Guard*, proved the popularity of the first one and included many actual battle scenes taken from newsreels made in the early months of the war. *The Adventures of Smilin' Jack*, based on the strip by Zack Mosley, was released in August 1942 and dealt with the Chinese effort against the invading Japanese. Jack was portrayed as a sort of one-man "Flying Tiger" who had enlisted himself on the side of the Chinese in repelling the invader. Not particularly true to the spirit of the strip — as most of the other Universal serial versions had been — this seemed to be a quick attempt to get a story on the screen about a topical subject, and could have had almost any flyer with any name as a hero. Even though there was the *Don Winslow* sequel and the *Secret Agent X-9* remake to come after it, *Smilin' Jack* was the last comic strip hero to be adapted for serials by Universal.

During the same period from 1936 to 1945, Columbia and Republic released between them seventeen serials based on twelve comic strips — roughly the numerical equivalent of the output of Universal alone. After 1944 the comic strips were used by Columbia exclusively, as Universal soon discontinued serials and Republic turned to original screenplays and sequels based on characters in its earlier successful productions. Because of the outstanding acceptance of continued films based on adventure strip heroes, this period from 1936 to 1945 has become known to serial buffs as the "golden age." This is especially true when referring to those produced by Republic studios.

Republic Productions, Inc., came about in 1935 as the result of a merger between four independent producing companies — one of which was Mascot Pictures, an organization well-known in the serial field since it was begun in 1927 by producer Nat Levine. Mascot had established itself as a first-rate provider of quality serials, and that reputation also became Republic's. Its use of comic strips for cliff-hangers included only six different ones, but from them came ten serials that stand above practically all of those produced by the other companies in well-paced stories, expertly planned and executed action sequences, convincing special effects and well-written, exciting musical scores.

Even though both Columbia and Universal made more comic strips into serials, Republic is usually thought of as the comic hero company because of two major acquisitions—Dick Tracy and Captain Marvel. With Chester Gould's jut-jawed detective as the hero, Republic made four chapter thrillers from 1937 to 1941 that have been unexcelled in the action field, and with *The Adventures of Captain Marvel* in 1941 pioneered a completely new type of screen champion—the SuperHero.

The first samples of an adventure strip titled *Plainclothes Tracy* were submitted to the *Chicago Tribune-New York News Syndicate* in 1931 by a young cartoonist from Oklahoma named Chester Gould. At a time when gangland crime was at its peak, at the height of prohibition when "fixers" and "go-betweens" flourished and it was hard for a good citizen to know who could be trusted, here was a comic strip about a completely honest cop—one who could take care of himself in the daily battles with the underworld, who could dish out just as much as the crooks, and do it better. Using the latest methods and innovations for crime detection, he always managed to win out over crime even though he made human errors just as anyone else and got into some pretty cold-chilling situations as a result. The syndicate changed the title from *Plainclothes Tracy* to *Dick Tracy* and accepted the strip for its papers, thus starting what has been a fifty-year love affair between Tracy and his public. In the thirties *Dick Tracy* was the leading detective adventure strip on the market. In 1984 it is *still* the leading detective adventure strip, and has been every year in between.

Following the tremendous success of Universal's initial adventure strip adaptations, Republic released *Dick Tracy* as its first comic strip cliff-hanger in March 1937: Tracy's adversary was an unknown disguised villain who affected a dragging clubfoot and was known alternately as The Lame One, The Unknown One and The Spider. He was the leader of a nefarious gang of felons called The Spider Ring. A huge aircraft in the shape of a wing—with no fuselage—was used by The Spider's henchmen and provided a futuristic slant without being overly fantastic. A most memorable touch was included by introducing in the film a brother for the famous detective and then having him kidnapped by the gang, changed in personality by one of The Spider's evil tricks, and placed in charge of the ring's henchmen with orders to destroy Dick. Their fatal reunion in the last chapter—as the transformed brother, Gordon, returned to his true personality while he lay dying after an automobile crash—brought lumps to young throats all over the land. This was one of the few moments of real emotional drama ever attempted in serials and it gave Tracy (as portrayed by young Ralph Byrd) a human quality not found in the majority of action heroes—the same quality Chester Gould had given his two-dimensional comic strip Tracy.

There followed in 1938 the first of three sequels to *Dick Tracy*: Released in September of that year, *Dick Tracy Returns* presented as the villain a twisted gangster called Pa Stark, who had trained his sons as criminals and led them in various crooked schemes to grab power and wealth. The father-son relationship of the villain and his henchmen—and the not-too-veiled similarity in names—revealed an obvious parallel to the infamous real-life gangster Ma Barker, who also led her family to a violent end at the hands of law enforcement officers after a career of crime and lawlessness. Taking advantage of the rising popularity of the dauntless detective, Republic followed up again the next year with another Tracy thriller, *Dick Tracy's G-Men*. In that one Tracy worked closely with the federal government to seek out and capture a notorious mastermind known as Zarnoff, who had worked out elaborate and intricate plans for his henchmen to "bring him back to life" after seemingly being executed at the State Penitentiary. After his "miraculous" return to the living, he resumed stealing government secrets and inventions to sell to a foreign power. It goes without saying that *Dick Tracy's G-Men* proved victorious in the end. The fourth and final Tracy serial, *Dick Tracy vs. Crime, Inc.*, was released during Christmas week 1941 and provided suspense in the true Republic tradition. Tracy's antagonist was an unknown villain known as "The Ghost," who wore a rubber-like contour mask over his head and had the means of making himself invisible. His trademark, left at the scene of each of his crimes, was the thumbprint of an executed criminal named "Rackets" Reagan, who had been captured and executed through the efforts of detective Tracy. One of his motives in carrying out his lawless campaign—along with the wealth he accumulated—was to exact vengeance upon Tracy for the downfall of Reagan, who had been his brother.

In any listing of serials released after 1930, the four Dick Tracy adventures from Republic must stand out as classics of the suspense detective thrillers, and the models for many others to follow.

In 1938 and 1939 a new type of champion burst upon the comic strip scene and has been a source of controversy between publishers and parent-teacher organizations ever since. Claiming that they are fantastic and unbelievable and a bad influence on the imaginations of youngsters, the groups have attempted to censor and even prohibit this type of comic strip. Publishers, contending that they are no worse than—and possibly not even as bad as—the fairy tales and legendary folk heroes sanctioned by schools and child educators as desirable literature, have continued to create, publish and propagate all sorts and kinds of the new breed known as superheroes.

The pioneer in comics for this new type of crimefighter was *Superman*, who first appeared in *Action Comics* magazine in June 1938 and almost immediately had a host of would-be imitations, simulations and near-duplications to follow. One of these sparked a lawsuit by the originators of Superman and eventually was removed from the comics market, but not before becoming the first comic strip superhero in continued pictures as the title character in a Republic thriller in 1941. (Interestingly, although he was the original comic strip superhero, Superman himself was not featured in a live-action movie until seven years later, when in July 1948 Columbia released the first of two chapter films about the "man of steel.")

In the wake of Superman's extreme initial popularity, Fawcett Publications (a rival of Superman's DC Publications) introduced as the lead character of their new *Whiz Comics* magazine a handsome, baby-faced strongman in red leotards with a yellow sash-belt, yellow boots, a lightning-streak symbol on his chest and a short cape reminiscent of a guardsman's jacket thrown over his shoulder, with the grandiose monicker of *Captain Marvel*. In this guise he was able to do any of the things that Superman's creators could have him do—fly, fight, lift huge weights, resist bullets and crush objects with his bare hands—but, unlike Superman, he was not always the same strong, invincible champion. In his alter-ego he was a young lad named Billy Batson, a reporter for a radio network whose curiosity and "nose-for-news" led him into countless scrapes and encounters from which there seemed to be no escape. The incredible power to become Captain Marvel was given to young Batson by an ancient mystic named Shazam, who had picked him for the gift because of his purity of heart and honesty of purpose. To become the muscled he-man he needed only to repeat the name of his mentor, Shazam, and he was magically transformed in a cloud of smoke.

Republic chose action and Western favorite Tom Tyler to play the lead in their proposed adaptation of this new strip because of his magnificent physique and athletic ability, and in a remarkable stroke of casting—because of his physical resemblance to the drawn character—assigned young Frank Coghlan, Jr., to play Billy Batson. In order to present the origination of Captain Marvel in a new, unique way—somewhat different than the strip's version, which had Billy simply wander into an abandoned subway tunnel and meet old Shazam—the opening chapter was set in a mysterious region of Siam known as the Valley of the Scorpion, where an expedition uncovered the fabulous Scorpion machine, which could—through the alignment of powerful lenses placed in its claws—turn ordinary stones into gold or serve as a disintegrating death ray. While other members of the expedition entered the forbidden rooms to confiscate the golden Scorpion and divide the lenses, Billy refused to join in the desecration and went to another part of the excavated tombs where he was confronted by Shazam and given the power to become Captain Marvel. From that scene on the action abounded as he rescued members of the expedition from harrowing brushes with death, fought off the attempts of a gang of criminals to steal all of the golden Scorpion's lenses, and pursued their leader, an unknown master villain who had assumed the name The Scorpion and set out to secure the contraption and all the lenses for himself. At the end, when the Scorpion machine and the lenses were all recovered and returned to Siam, the villain was revealed as one of the members of the original expedition and met his doom by the very weapon he had hoped to control. After destroying the infernal machine, Captain Marvel metaphysically reverted to the person of Billy Batson, apparently to return no more — another departure from the strip. Whether intended or not, the termination of the Marvel character prevented any logical sequel.

Using another character from *Whiz Comics*, Republic a year later came up with an outstanding wartime cliff-hanger about the efforts of foreign agents to secure government secrets and commit sabotage. The title character of *Spy Smasher*, although not a superhero and very human, dressed and acted like the most invulnerable of them. In the winter of 1943 Republic released their final serial featuring a superhero of the comics — *Captain America* — to close out for the duration of the era their reliance upon the cartoon pages for colorful stories and figures, two of which had given them respectively a new star and a studio tradition.

The main staple and finest product of the Republic studios were their series Westerns. Stars of the genre such as Gene Autry, Roy Rogers, Bob Steele and Tom Tyler were joined by another in 1940 as a result of his starring in *The Adventures of Red Ryder*, a twelve-chapter serial based on the popular comic strip by Fred Harmon. From the character he played in that production, new star Donald Barry also retained the nickname that has remained with him since. Throughout his career in Western films he was billed as Don "Red" Barry. In later years, Republic filmed a number of feature Westerns based on Harmon's cowboy and two more famous stars, Bill Elliott and Allan Lane, played the renowned redhead for that studio. A decade afterward, lanky actor Jim Bannon played the part in a series for Eagle-Lion, and on radio the voice of Reed Hadley portrayed Little Beaver's "big buddy."

The sixth comic strip hero to be transformed by Republic was the legendary Zane Gray creation *King of the Royal Mounted*. In their continued version he was the personification of the popular Mountie tradition, "he always gets his man," and went on to defend Law and Order and the security of the North American continent in the twelve-episode sequel two years later. After America's entry into World War II, *King of the Mounties* pitted Sergeant King against a triumvirate of Axis agents consisting of a Japanese admiral, a German SS officer and an Italian count. From these two serials — as from those of other types they produced during the golden age — Republic later made and released a number of counterparts using scenes, action shots — even complete sequences — originally filmed for the prototypes. They also found success with the phrase "King of the...." and released no less than four "Kings" of other professions — *King of the Texas Rangers*, *King of the Forest Rangers*, *King of the Rocketmen* and *King of the Carnival* — and even reissued their very first release, *Darkest Africa*, under the title *King of the Jungleland*. So greatly did the phrase impress the Republic "brass" that their leading Western star, Roy Rogers, was summarily crowned "King of the Cowboys." In that vein it could be said without too much fear of contradiction that in the sound era Republic was itself the "King of the Serial Makers."

Counting the well-known masked heroes The Spider and The Shadow (who appeared in comics as well as radio and the pulps) and Hop Harrigan of both comics and radio, Columbia Pictures Corporation adapted into serial heroes more comic strip characters than either Universal or Republic. No less than fourteen different strips were brought to the screen by Columbia, including three of the most famous of the superheroes — Superman, Batman and The Phantom.

After their entry into the cliff-hanger market in the thirteenth year of their existence, Columbia executives quickly followed Universal and Republic to the daily and Sunday newspaper comic pages for characters and story material that could be readily adapted to the serial format. *The Spider's Web* was released in October 1938 and followed seven months later by King Features' *Mandrake The Magician*. Both productions had in the title role Warren Hull, who was later to star in the Columbia sequel *The Spider Returns* and portray still another well-known hero for Universal in *The Green Hornet Strikes Again*. Also, both serials had an unknown villain for suspense — The Octopus in *The Spider's Web* and The Wasp in *Mandrake*. (As a matter of fact, ten of Columbia's first fifteen chapterplays had mysterious, masked villains.)

In 1940 Columbia presented *Terry and the Pirates*, one of the most respected of all the comic strips, as a fifteen-chapter serial. Admired for its authenticity and painstaking attention to detail, Milton Caniff's popular strip had a following among adults as well as kids. Also, he did not hesitate to include in his stories pretty ladies drawn from life (Caniff was one of the few cartoonists to use human models for his characters, thus achieving a realism that escaped the others). He even designated one beautiful creature to be the perennial adversary of heroes Terry Lee and Pat Ryan — the deadly Dragon Lady.

Terry and the Pirates was especially suited to screen adaptation since artist Caniff had begun the strip using motion picture techniques. His panels were varied in perspective and designed to bring out particular aspects of the story continuity in the balloons — long shots to include the central characters of each episode and establish the background, medium shots with balloon dialogue to move the story along, semicloseups to bring out and feature a character's delivery of a line, and full closeups to magnify facial expressions and close out everything else. These are the same variations in photographic composition used to produce the same results in a motion picture. So it might be said that a *Terry* reader was watching a *still* movie scene when he read the strip, and bringing the strip to the screen was more like a transplant than a transformation.

One of Columbia's cliff-hangers produced a belated and unexpected twist in human nature a couple of decades ago. Around the country — and particularly in many college towns — exhibitors were booking and playing an attraction that packed the houses and retained the audiences for more than four hours. Not a new major feature picture nor even a double bill, the attraction was the aforementioned continuous showing of the full 15 episodes of a twenty-two–year-old serial — *Batman*. For the youngsters who comprised the major portion of the audience for each *Evening with Batman and Robin*, the fascination was a perennial one. Since it had been made more than a generation before their first adult awareness as teenagers and college students, and since it represented a mode of entertainment since outgrown by the public in general, they found it to be funny. Just as young people in the fifties had found quaint the "jitterbug" and the "big apple," and teenagers of the forties chuckled at the "Charleston," vaudeville and silent movies, and as swains and flappers of the twenties had giggled at the antics of the Gay Nineties, these kids of the sixties were subconsciously holding up a "relic" to ridicule. And they proclaimed it something called "camp," which was in turn scoffed at by the youth of the seventies. So be it.

But in 1943 when *Batman* was released by Columbia, when it had been designed and produced for kids who took their comic strip heroes straight, when in the midst of a world war and any story upholding the defense of America found a sympathetic reception, the press releases proudly proclaimed it a "Super Serial," and so it was. Created by a young cartoonist named Bob Kane — and unique in comic strips for its eerie, supernatural flavor — *Batman* was first seen in the May 1939 issue (No. 27) of *Detective Comics* magazine, a DC publication, and soon became one of the top favorite superheroes of young comic fans — outdistanced only by the same publisher's fantastic success *Superman*. When Columbia negotiated to acquire the rights for a continued picture, they made it their largest-scale serial production to date and gave it a publicity campaign worthy of a major feature. In 1966 when I went to see *An Evening with Batman and Robin* (for a much different reason than the "camp" followers), I counted more than two dozen well-known featured players from action and Western films — each also a veteran of serials — giving even the most minor roles all the enthusiasm and drive they had learned to project in so many former "knock-down-and-drag-out" adventures. It was easy to recognize the reasons for the current generation's critical abuse — stilted performances by some of the principals, out-dated fashions (broad-brimmed hats, padded shoulders and wide lapels), and corny dialogue (the lines having grown more corny by much repetition through the years) — but also easy to remember a time in the late forties when I had felt the same way about a fifteen-year-old rerelease called *The Hurricane Express*, and I breathed a sigh for the callowness of youth.

In this first of the two Columbia thrillers based on Bob Kane's characters, the villain was a Japanese spy known as Dr. Daka and was portrayed by J. Carroll Naish, one of the most versatile actors on the screen. Six years later in the 1949 sequel *The New Adventures of Batman and Robin*, there was a return to the more conventional serial villain—the mad scientist bent on world conquest. A hooded electrical genius calling himself The Wizard was revealed as a male nurse attending the invalid inventor of a top-secret remote control machine. One of the studio's busiest supporting players, Leonard Penn (who was later a leading director), had the role of the villain-nurse.

Columbia released the second of their "big three" superhero cliffhangers in December 1943. A property of *King Features Syndicate* and created by Lee Falk and Ray Moore, *The Phantom* was then as it is now the comic strip with "a mixture of active ingredients." As any comics reader knows, the hero of the strip is an unknown masked leader of a tribe of pygmies who live deep in uncharted jungle. From his headquarters in the Skull Cave, and with the aid of his great stallion Hero and ferocious wolf-dog Devil, the mysterious champion "goes forth in answer to distress calls" not only into the jungle but to danger points all over the world. While in civilization he assumes the name "Mr. Walker," a derivative of the natives' designation for him (The Ghost Who Walks) and wears a trench coat and slouch hat, with dark glasses to cover the narrow eye mask which he never removes. Not superhuman—but seeming so by being the descendant of a long line of former "Phantoms" who have passed the challenge from generation to generation—he is a mixture of Tarzan, The Lone Ranger and Superman, combining characteristics of each but retaining a mystique all his own. In contrast to many of the other so-called "superheroes," Falk and Moore managed to gain a considerable following for The Phantom with girl fans by giving him a continuing love interest. Although dedicated to a fight for order and justice in his jungle domain, no small amount of the champion's thoughts are always shown to be on a lovely athletic young woman named Diana Palmer, who is also constantly dreaming of her handsome and daring lover whom she sees only intermittently because of the demands on his time and energies. To the regular reader there is no doubt that from a union between Diana and The Phantom will come the next inheritor of the legend and challenge. This gives the girls a stake in the strip's future and the boys a logical hope that the good fight will continue.

Columbia selected to portray this enigmatic-but-human mystery man the same actor who had played Captain Marvel for Republic earlier, and with Tom Tyler in the unique costume of The Ghost Who Walks, there was a visual recreation that was almost uncanny. There had been some small criticism in boyhood circles that Tyler had not looked too much like the beefy, baby-faced Captain Marvel, but as The Phantom he appeared to be the original instead of the copy.

After *The Phantom* Columbia produced ten additional serials based on nine different comic strips. Except for the two Superman adventures in

1948 and 1950 and the Batman sequel in 1949, they were not superhero adaptations. The remaining seven came from a variety of strips that were acquired soon after becoming fairly well-known in comics — and other media — and ranged from the trials and tribulations of a female news-hound — *Brenda Starr Reporter* — to the Earth-to-Moon-and-back-again science-fiction exploits of a latter-day Flash Gordon type — *Brick Bradford*. Included were a couple of Westerns (*The Vigilante* and *Tex Granger*), two pretty good airplane adventures (*Bruce Gentry* and *Blackhawk*), and a return to the jungle for Buster Crabbe (as Thunda, *King of the Congo*). Altogether, more than one-third of Columbia's 57 serials were based on comic strips — or characters appearing in them as well as other media.

If asked to characterize the serial makers by their use of radio and comics as sources of material, it could be said that Universal was the pioneer, Columbia the most prolific, and Republic the most memorably proficient. And, turning from the use of novels as a primary source to these two media, the serial became different in content from what it had been in the silent era while remaining the same in format. Even the original stories and screenplays thereafter took on the flavor of the radio-comics influence, and it continued to pervade to the last.

3

The Six Faces of Adventure

Having secured appropriate properties, adapted them to the requirements of the serial format, arranged for actors and actresses to play the
parts, and outlined the broad plan for achieving the desired result of an
appealing, salable chapterplay, the studios then gave the reins to the
single most important craftsman on any production — the director. Just as
on any other dramatic project, the director of a serial had the responsibility of transforming — through the art of the cameraman, the words of
the writers, the skills of the technicians and the talents of the performers
— the various ingredients into a finished product. And the completed
picture then took its place in the market as one of the types of cliff-
hangers then currently popular with the public.

Because of their existence primarily as action and suspense-
provoking films, serials were generally pretty rigidly classified into six
basic categories or types. The three most prevalent of these — Westerns,
mysteries and jungle stories — having more universal appeal continued
from silent to sound as the most popular, enhanced by the added spice of
the radio series and comic strips. The other three types — costume, aviation and science-fiction — were of a specialized nature and not generally
as dependable for a steady flow of stories. They provided some popular
and well-made chapterplays from time to time, but could not serve as
staples for repeated and continued output as did the first-mentioned three.

Probably the best remembered of the half dozen or so costume serials
was Universal's *Pirate Treasure* because of its eerie and haunting background and the work of Richard Talmadge, one of the greatest of the
stuntmen. Released in 1934 and billing Talmadge as "the King of the Daredevils" in a "whirlwind of action," the advertising displayed liberally
colorful cuts of great sailing vessels, half-buried treasure chests, hand-to-
hand cutlass duels between eye-patched and ear-ringed pirates, and the
familiar and picturesque buccaneers' costumes (silky shirts, wide belts
with huge silver buckles, turned-down seaboots and three-cornered hats).

A swashbuckler in the true sense, it was one of the serial makers' rare ventures into the world of the cutthroats and privateers, and now stands as the genre's best example of the type.

Four years later Columbia released *The Secret of Treasure Island*, the studio's third serial and first of five costume chapterplays. In it a modern-day hero named Larry Kent locked in mortal combat with a ghostly, unknown villain dressed in buccaneer's garb who purported to be the spirit of a long-dead pirate guarding the elusive secret of the buried treasure. Although not a period piece, it exuded the mores and moods of the traditional piratical setting well enough to qualify for the type. The action was well paced and lively. Well received by the fans, it served as notice that Columbia had entered the serial business to stay.

It was six years before Columbia again released a costume chapterplay. This time it was *The Desert Hawk*, a Middle East "Western" that had its hero swashbuckling through a triple role. Playing twin brothers involved in a palace-desert web of intrigue, he also became the mysterious figure known as The Hawk when the script called for direct action. A top-notch athlete — star Gilbert Roland — was superbly convincing as the dashing Hawk, and made memorable an otherwise routine thriller.

Subsequently, Columbia was responsible for three more costume epics — none of which was particularly outstanding, but all having incidental interest: In 1946 — apparently to use the costumes and sets from some of the studio's most costly features — producer Sam Katzman ground out a cliff-hanger called *The Son of the Guardsman*, which featured a Robin Hood-type hero set upon avenging the dreadful wrong done his father by the current usurper of local authority (familiar?). Somewhat better was his 1949 production *The Adventures of Sir Galahad* because of the more dashing and romantic image of the late George Reeves (who later became television's Superman) in the title role as the diligent and courageous aspirant to knighthood. The final costume serial to reach the nation's screens was perhaps the most faithful to the buccaneer tradition since *Pirate Treasure*. Columbia's *The Great Adventures of Captain Kidd* in 1953 gave the few remaining serial fans one parting taste of the Spanish Main and the broad, sweeping saga of pirates bent upon grabbing and holding fabulous treasure. A generous helping of seafaring action made possible by excerpts from Columbia's features and the studio's special effects department gave this last costume effort a unique flavor for which it is fondly remembered.

There were only six sound serials that could be classified as costume epics — out of the more than two hundred released after 1930 — but in any commentary on the form they must be included for their own merit.

Far more popular — but still not extensively utilized by the serial makers — were the aviation stories. This is not to say that air adventure was not sufficiently portrayed, for the opposite is true. Most good modern-day action serials included airplanes and sky thrills, for in the

thirties (the years following the wondrous flight of Charles Lindbergh and
the subsequent mushrooming of aerial development) America was greatly
air-minded and the serial producers did not fail to take advantage of the
phenomenon. But not too many aviation stories per se were to hit the
market as compared to the other types. Some of those that did appear
stand out sharply because of their impact on the young fans, and for that
reason are worthy of note.

With the single exception of Mascot's *Mystery Squadron* in
1933—which was Western star Bob Steele's only venture into cliff-
hanging—Universal and Columbia were the only studios to produce
specifically airplane-centered continued stories. None of the independents
undertook aviation serials, nor did Republic—even though most of its
jungle and mystery productions (notably the Dick Tracy series) contained
very good sequences of air action and depended upon airplanes for a large
part of their tempo. Universal's eight flying serials came in two distinct
phases, and Columbia's six were spread out over a fifteen-year period.

In those early thirties airplanes were thought of mostly as thrill
machines because of the risk involved in the basic act of going up in one.
Stories of their use as aerial weapons in World War I added to the
conception. The "dogfights" depicted in Howard Hughes' *Hell's Angels* left
an indelible impression on the minds of moviegoers, and for years to
follow served as the only image many people had of this strange new
mode of travel. Outside of their potential as war machines, most were
conscious of the airplane's usefulness only as an aerial racer or in its
growing role as a carrier of mail. Consequently, most stories involving
planes and aviators were about speed meets or getting the mail through.

Universal's first chapter film on the subject came in 1932. It was
appropriately titled *The Airmail Mystery* and included such sky-minded
chapter titles as "Pirates of the Air," "The Aerial Third Degree," and the
final episode's twist on a famous cliche, "The Mail Must Go Through."
The action was very good for that time and it helped set the pattern for
the other air serials and features to follow. The next year the studio
presented *Phantom of the Air*, and then came the two famous Tailspin
Tommy adventures that were the forerunners of the great comic strip
cycle. For the time being that concluded Universal's active interest in air
thrillers, and it was not revived until six years later when a renewed
public interest in aviation just before World War II led them to produce
four air serials in succession.

The first was *Sky Raiders* in 1941. With America's involvement in the
war becoming more certain every day, this modest entry pointed to the
sky as a potential major battleground of the conflict and proved prophetic. The following year—when America's participation in the fighting
was a reality—came *The Adventures of Smilin' Jack* and the third serial
venture of the reluctantly intrepid Dead End Kids titled *Junior G-Men of
the Air*. The fourth came in August 1943 with the release of *The Adven-*

tures of the Flying Cadets, which featured Bobby Jordan (one of the original members of the Dead End group), Robert Armstrong (of *King Kong* fame) and Eduardo Ciannelli, the erstwhile villain of the earlier *Sky Raiders*. After *Cadets* there were no more air serials from Universal.

Columbia produced their six aviation serials within a period of 15 years, but—like Republic—many of their productions of other types included air scenes and depended upon air travel for action background. Their second chapterplay—*The Mysterious Pilot*—was the first of the six. Its Canadian wilderness backdrop for a story of murder and retribution almost demanded the liberal use of airplanes to keep the plot moving, and the hero's streamlined fighter "The Silver Hawk" more than filled the bill. It was involved in no less than seven of the 14 hair-raising chapter endings that left the audience gasping for the safety of Captain Hawks and his lovely heroine.

Thirteen months later the studio released *Flying G-Men*, its second attempt at aerial cliff-hanging, and featured a masked hero known as The Black Falcon. The daring and resourceful *Captain Midnight* of radio fame (who was in reality accomplished aviator Captain Albright) had his cinematic day in the 1942 Columbia release of the same name. His adversary in the film was the same perennial villain of the radio series—a sneaky enemy spy named Ivan Shark—who plotted to steal a newly invented range finder developed for the United States government. In the subsequent land and air action, Shark very nearly succeeded in his plan, but was finally thwarted by the intrepid Midnight.

After *Captain Midnight*, four years passed before Columbia invested in another aviation serial. This time the popular *Hop Harrigan*, Jon Blummer's *All-American Comics* feature, was the subject and producer Sam Katzman adapted the widely-followed Mutual radio series of the same title to the serial format to come up with a fairly action-filled cliffhanger. Though older and more mature-looking than Blummer's drawings of Hop, William Bakewell made a convincing enough hero and the action was well paced, making this chapterplay as convincing and successful as it was meant to be. Playing Hop's young associate, Jackie Nolan, was Robert "Buzz" Henry, a youngster who was already known as an accomplished horseback rider and student of the art of professional stunting. "Buzz" continued his acting career playing small parts in serials, Westerns and action features, but became more adept in the field of stunting, eventually rising to the status of action director, creating such wild, acrobatic fight choreography as that found in the *Our Man Flint* and James Bond films of the sixties. Also in *Hop Harrigan* was the very pretty young Jennifer Holt, following father Jack and brother Tim into action films. Usually cast as the female lead in series Westerns, Miss Holt appeared in only two serials, both of which were airplane stories—*Hop Harrigan* and Universal's earlier *Adventures of the Flying Cadets*.

The final two air serials from Columbia, as previously noted, were also based on comic strips. *Bruce Gentry* was adapted from the *New York Post Syndicate* strip and starred Tom Neal in the title role in 1949. In 1952 Kirk Alyn exchanged his Superman costume for the dashing military uniform of *Blackhawk*, "Freedom's Champion." Based on the *Blackhawk Comics* magazine feature drawn by Reed Crandall and Charles Cuidera, this last of the aviation serials abounded in international intrigue, sabotage, plane crashes, midair explosions, a beautiful girl spy and a smashing secret weapon. The hero, known simply as Blackhawk, was surrounded by the famous International Brotherhood of the strip—Chuck, Olaf, Stan, Andre, Hendrickson and Chop Chop—a colorful group of crime and sabotage fighters who had become nearly as well-known as the hero himself. Their persistent efforts in both the United States and Mexico to prevent a highly dangerous electronic ray gun and a new fuel compound from falling into the hands of enemy spies provided the type of action dear to the hearts of comics readers and action fans.

Just as the science of aerodynamics led to the opening of the space age—and had contained the promise of that eventuality from its very beginning—so the aviation serial portended the later introduction of the space and science-fiction story as the basis for chapter films. Contributing to the development of highly imaginative and fantastic productions were the rapidly expanding and technically fascinating innovations of radio and television in particular, the use of electric and electronic energy in general, and the much speculated-upon (but little-known) new physics of rocket and jet propulsion. Having tasted the miraculous first fruits of these marvelous twentieth century discoveries, scientists could and did prophesy eloquently what the future could bring. Writers then translated these prophesies into fiction stories telling of the effects these incredible developments might have on man, whose basic nature does not change. These translations have resulted in many articles, short stories, novels and screenplays that have taxed the average person's ability to comprehend. And yet, because of the later revelation of harnessed atomic power, many of the predictions of the scientists and writers of forty years ago not only have become possible but have been accomplished within their own lifetime. Thus, the science-fiction story has been redelegated from innocuous and imaginative fantasy into the almost credulous herald of things to come. As such the limits to story possibilities are almost boundless.

The advent of science-fiction serials came without doubt with *Flash Gordon*. Even though earlier continued pictures used electrical gadgetry, radio and crude forms of television, none had assumed the futuristic and outright space-oriented stance that it did. Within five years of its release, six of the 14 science-fiction serials to come were produced, including its own two sequels and *Buck Rogers*.

The other two science-fiction chapter films of the prewar era were Universal's *Ace Drummond* and Republic's *Undersea Kingdom*, neither of which was an outright space serial (in the mold of *Flash* or *Buck*), but both of which dealt with offbeat, unusual themes. The creator of *Ace Drummond*, Captain Rickenbacker, called upon his own experiences as an aviation pioneer and also those of his associates and contemporaries in writing a strip that was one of the most topical and advanced of its day. Filled with odd-looking weapons, strange electrical machinery and laboratory devices, the serial made from it exuded the futuristic aura of *Flash Gordon* combined with the eerie mystery of Baron Frankenstein's castle laboratory. *Undersea Kingdom* dealt with the legendary sunken world of Atlantis and qualifies as a "science-fiction" serial by virtue of the pseudoscientific nature of its concept and the weaponry and gadgets employed. It combined the daring, foolhardy bravado of ancient warring factions (in uniforms reminiscent of the Romans) with a smattering of ultramodern scientific devices, and resulted in a totally unbelievable — but visually enjoyable — twelve-chapter madhouse chase. (The scramble was climaxed by a general call-up of the entire United States Fleet to combat the villain's menacing attempt at world conquest by the use of a giant ray gun based in a large metal tower ominously rising out of the ocean's depths from the crumbling Atlantis.)

From late 1940 until the middle of 1945 there were no science-fiction serials released. Even though there continued to be much emphasis on scientific inventions and secret weapons, the underlying motive for their development almost always seemed to be the war effort, which was far too real and intense to be overshadowed by such imaginative fantasy as science-fiction. It was as if there had been a subconscious moratorium on fantasy for the duration.

The first of the postwar science-fiction cliff-hangers was released in August 1945 by Republic. *The Purple Monster Strikes* concerned the arrival of a mysterious, scaly-cowled figure from Mars known only as the Purple Monster who murdered — and then took on the physical appearance of — a renowned scientist. He then proceeded to carry out a plot to weaken Earth's defenses and make arrangements for an impending invasion of this planet by Martians. Needless to say the plot was thwarted eventually, and the Monster was destroyed trying to rocket homeward to trigger the invasion.

Some years later, when Republic began utilizing full scenes and sequences from earlier productions to reduce costs, the visual image of the Purple Monster (as portrayed by Roy Barcroft) was rejuvenated three times to fit in with the scenes borrowed from that original: Gregory Gay wore the cowl in *Flying Disc Man from Mars* in 1950; Barcroft again donned the costume in 1952 to play the King of the Moon in *Radar Men from the Moon*; and later that year it was worn by Lane Bradford as a space visitor named Marex in *Zombies of the Stratosphere*. (With an assistant, Marex had come to Earth with a plan to explode a giant, strategically-placed H-bomb which would dislodge Earth from its orbit and destroy all life, thus making it available for occupancy by the inhabitants of his own dying planet.)

Columbia produced only three serials that could be termed specifically science-fiction films. Like Universal and Republic, many of their projects incorporated science-oriented gadgetry, but were not science-fiction per se. Their first was *Brick Bradford*, which had the popular hero traveling back and forth to the Moon — not by the accepted means of a spacecraft or rocket ship, but through a "Crystal Door" perfected by a Dr. Tymak — and there battling an embittered queen and an ambitious prime minister who were jealous of their kingdom on the Moon and guarded it against trespassers from Earth. Having as its locale both the Earth and the Moon, this fifteen-chapter adventure could use the standard thrill-makers such as fistfights, explosions, automobile chases, etc., and also use the gimmicks of science-fantasy to produce offbeat and extraterrestrial action (as sort of "icing for the cake").

Brick Bradford was a mediocre serial that enjoyed a wide audience, but Columbia did not make another science-fiction chapter film until three years later when they followed up the immediate and widespread popularity of the television character known as *Captain Video* with a fifteen-episode production. That one also used a combination of present-day military trappings and futuristic weapons and ray guns to appeal to the younger generation who had come to expect that sort of thing in their action shows on television. The third and final science-fiction entry by Columbia came in 1953 with the release of *The Lost Planet*, in which the hero was a space traveler named Rex Barrow. Except for the hero's identification, this was essentially a sequel to *Captain Video*, and even used some of the scenes from it, although *Video* was still in release in subsequent runs. By that time, however, it was rather academic whether or not one serial resembled or duplicated another, as television was rapidly taking over the production of films which normally would have been created for this medium, and they all had a tendency to look alike. (As pointed out earlier, the major difference was that the television series were complete episodes within themselves and did not use the cliff-hanger technique. Science-fiction has had by far a better airing on television than it ever had in the movies because of the new medium's requirement for large amounts of material on any given subject.)

Much more popular and widely-produced as serials were stories with a jungle background. Because of their picturesque settings and thrilling shots of fights between ferocious and deadly wild animals, jungle films were favorites beginning in the silent days. It is appropriate that the first talking jungle serial was a Tarzan story, since Edgar Rice Burroughs' famous ape-man was a pioneer and had become the standard for the type. *Tarzan the Tiger* was released in both silent and sound versions — like *The Indians Are Coming* — because many of the theatres in the country had not as yet equipped themselves for the presentation of sound films. (As mentioned, this was not an unusual practice during the earliest years of the era.) *Tarzan the Fearless* is notable for the fact that it was one of the poorest motion picture adaptations ever made of an ERB story — but this was not altogether the fault of the producer and director. During that period there was much necessity for improvisation and experimentation, and the most capable filmmakers in trying to handle both the visual and audio techniques sometimes failed to measure up to the standards of either. This changed with the acquiring of familiarity with the bulky and temperamental new equipment. In that sense of technical inadequacy then, *Fearless* was not a success when compared to those made only for silent films and the later ones made after good techniques in sound reproduction were developed.

A far better production was *The New Adventures of Tarzan*, which presented a different concept of the jungle hero. In this film he was shown as a combination of the traditional heroic ape-man, a daring soldier of fortune, a probing detective, and a somewhat more credible human being — in contrast with some previous presentations of him as a veritable jungle superman with not much intellect. It is to be pointed out that the legends of Tarzan enjoyed much greater success with the public in feature form than in these efforts by the serial producers. As a result there has been a much more careful and conscientious history kept of the character which has made such an impact on every medium of entertainment.

Beginning with *Tarzan the Tiger* Universal produced nine jungle serials in the final fifteen years in the field. In addition to the previously mentioned *Jungle Mystery*, *Call of the Savage*, *Jungle Jim* and *Tim Tyler's Luck*, there was the action-packed *Danger Island*, starring Kenneth Harlan, and the remake of *Perils of Pauline*, starring Evelyn Knapp, during the thirties.

Two of Universal's last efforts in cliff-hanging were jungle serials. In 1945 they released *Jungle Queen*, the story of a young woman involved with wartime intrigue, Nazi spies, British agents and American adventurers, all trying to sway the population of a particular area of the jungle to their side in the great conflict which held the world's attention at that time. Although well-enough produced, it often became bogged down with complicated plot twists, psychological debates and confusion as to who was on whose side, and what was really being accomplished. The title referred to a mysterious young supernatural beauty who could walk through flaming walls of fire and who brought warnings of disaster. Her many appearances throughout the action saved the lives of the principals on various occasions, but her real character and existence were never quite fully explained. One can only recall the image of her fiery appearances — often just "in the nick of time."

Their final offering in the jungle field was *The Lost City of the Jungle* in 1946, which featured Russell Hayden (Hopalong Cassidy's former sidekick) and the renowned character actor Lionel Atwill.

Columbia began its venture into continued pictures with a jungle thriller. For their first release they presented Frank Buck, the dean of big game hunters—known for his slogan, "Bring 'Em Back Alive"—in *Jungle Menace*. Although prior serials had featured great animal trainer Clyde Beatty, and there had been the presentation of actual scenes made on safari in *Across the World with Mr. and Mrs. Martin Johnson,* this was an outstanding milestone. Frank Buck had captured the imaginations of all America by his daring exploits as an authentic big game hunter of heroic proportions. And to have him as the star of their first entry in the market was a "feather in the cap" for Columbia.

Except for the 1943 release of *The Phantom,* it was then eight years until Columbia released another jungle serial—*Jungle Raiders* in 1945— and three years to the next. In 1948 Don McGuire was featured in *Congo Bill* and, while there was nothing unusually significant about this film, it is significant that McGuire later became a writer and director of some reputation. He is written up in a trade almanac with screenplays such as *Meet Danny Wilson, Willie and Joe Back at the Front, Walking My Baby Back Home, Three Ring Circus, Bad Day at Black Rock* and *Artists and Models* to his credit. Directorial credit is given for *Johnny Concho* and *The Delicate Delinquent,* etc. In subsequent years he established himself as a writer, director and coproducer of a number of television series, notably the Jackie Cooper series *Hennesey.*

In the late forties Buster Crabbe again contributed to the type with *The Sea Hound* and *King of the Congo.* In between the two he portrayed another Captain Silver type of hero in *Pirates of the High Seas*—all for Columbia. Although rating the classification of sea story, the latter chapter film took place mostly in jungle terrain on uncharted islands— presumably in the South Pacific—and would thus qualify also as a jungle serial. Columbia's final effort was *The Adventures of Captain Africa* in 1955. An obvious remake of *The Phantom,* it contained many stock shots from the earlier release and at times seemed almost like a repeat run.

Prior to the merger that terminated its identity, Mascot Pictures released *The Lost Jungle,* starring Clyde Beatty, in 1934. After consolidating with other companies and becoming Republic, the new studio released as its first serial under the new banner another Clyde Beatty thriller titled *Darkest Africa.* Some of the finest photography of Beatty's animal training techniques ever seen were numbered in this production, and the special effects technique was devised which gave the appearance of flight to a gang of henchmen known as the batmen of Joba. These were the troops of a secret lost city headed by an evil high priest named Dagna. The destruction in Chapter 15 of this lost city was a picturesque example of the technique of miniaturization that was to play such a large part in all subsequent Republic serials and help give them their own unique flavor when compared to the productions of the other two major companies. Of course, all the companies used the technique to some extent, but it was the technicians at Republic who refined its use and enabled that studio to gain the position of being the Number One serial producer of the time.

Republic's jungle release the following year has the distinction of being the only one produced in the sound era with 14 chapters. Most of them ran for either 12 or 15 episodes, with some being limited to 13 (apparently to coincide with the number of weeks in a year), but for some reason the producers made *Robinson Crusoe of Clipper Island* only 14.

From 1936 to 1945 Republic released at least one jungle chapterplay every 12 to 18 months. Several of them became popular favorites of the young moviegoers and are still remembered with nostalgic pleasure.

In 1938 young serial star Herman Brix was featured in a twelve-chapter adventure titled *Hawk of the Wilderness*, based on the book by William Chester. The hero was obviously another derivation of the Tarzan character, but with several differences. At first glance Kioga appeared to be more an American Indian with blonde hair than a jungle hero of the Tarzan stripe. Around his head he wore a thin band in the Indian tradition, his clothing consisted of long trousers reminiscent of buckskin pants, and—unlike Tarzan—he wore moccasins rather than attempting to race through the jungle barefoot. In the final episode, the poignant scene of the burial of Kioga's native friend Kias—who had been brutally murdered by the evil witch doctor Yellow Weasel—was another of the very few successful attempts at drama in serials, and for its rarity remains memorable.

In doing research for this project and questioning many people who could remember the first decade of the sound era, the one character whose name was invariably mentioned was Nyoka—a tribute to the durability of a character who easily could have been sidetracked by circumstances. The year Republic introduced her in *Jungle Girl* was not the greatest of all years for a new personality to stand out, as that was also the year in which *The Adventures of Captain Marvel* and *Dick Tracy vs. Crime, Inc.,*— two of the most outstanding of all the cliff-hanger favorites—were released, but the beautiful young Nyoka did manage to make her mark, and has stood out in the minds of most serial fans ever since.

When Republic rushed to the market its sequel the following year, it was to take advantage of the initial impact made by Frances Gifford in the role. However, Miss Gifford was preparing to move on to greater things in features at MGM, so the studio cast Kay Aldridge in the role. As a result of her ensuing popularity she graced some of Republic's better chapter thrillers for the next several years.

In 1944 Republic released two consecutive jungle serials and wound up for the time being their interest in the type. In May *Tiger Woman* introduced Linda Stirling in her first featured role, and three months later the studio put out *Haunted Harbor*, their final jungle serial for nine years. Adapted from the Dayle Douglas book, the production was a fifteen-chapter jungle-horror-mystery-sea story that incorporated all the cliff-hanging tricks Republic could muster, including a rigged sea monster that rose from the depths of a lagoon, emitted great roaring sounds, and kept the native population in a continual state of fright.

After the nine years passed — and using many of the scenes from the earlier productions — the studio came up with three final jungle stories before the end of the era: *Jungle Drums of Africa* in 1953, *Trader Tom of the China Seas* in 1954 and *Panther Girl of the Kongo* in 1955. In the latter the greatest writing problem seemed to be how to lead the heroine and her hero from one place to another in order to utilize the scenes borrowed from *Jungle Girl*. The story concerned the efforts of a demented scientist to perfect a discovery that could enlarge living creatures to the point of invulnerability. Using native crabs, he was able to produce gigantic, ugly monsters that hissed and threatened but never quite seemed to harm anybody. All in all, the jungle serial had reached its peak by 1950, and was in a declining phase from which neither it nor the form ever recovered.

As the most popular and dependable type of story for the serial makers, there was a toss-up between the Westerns and the mysteries — with the nod for total number going to the Westerns. Actually these two types were really the foundation for all serials, because in them every element of the action plot per se is included — the Western's broad, bigger-than-life, sweeping attack upon the problems of pioneers and frontiersmen, and the mystery's intrigue, suspense and fear of the unknown.

Since some of the greatest successes in the serial field were Westerns, their particular place in the history of the form is unique. Respected as an appealing background for the telling of exciting stories in all forms of visual entertainment, every conceivable plot and premise were translated into its idiom to produce dramas with new outlooks. As a result, Westerns themselves became — like the serial — categorized and typed, reduced to basics by the flattery of repeated use.

No matter how long you have been going to the movies — nor how many Western films you might have seen — each has fallen into one of seven basic story types which can be labeled: "Covered Wagon," "Iron Horse," "Civil War," "American Indian," "Western Empire," "Lawman," and "Desperados." Many good Westerns have combined the elements of two or more of these descriptive categories to present a more exciting plot, but still had as a central theme or premise the telling of a tale in one of the basic areas. Several ambitious projects have tried to encompass all or most of the basic types in a broad plot of epic proportions. A few (notably MGM's *How the West Was Won*) succeeded; most did not. The same is true of Western serials. Many were well-produced and memorable; others were not, having been filmed only for the purpose of providing immediate but temporary thrills without much substance.

Of the most memorable quality Western serials, possibly the best was *The Lone Ranger*. Essentially fitting first into the "Lawman" category because of the establishment of the leading character as a man of frontier Law and Order—a ranger—this release also contained elements of two more categories. During the post–Civil War period known as the Reconstruction, a band of renegades (similar to the infamous Quantrill's Raiders) were terrorizing the West under the leadership of a murderous villain named Jeffries. The Lone Ranger, with the aid of the other four young lawmen, pledged the defeat of Jeffries and his ruthless band of outlaws and finally accomplished it—but with the sacrifices of the four young heroes. So, in telling that story the film was also partly a "Civil War" and partly a "Desperado" type.

The Lone Ranger Rides Again emerged as a different type altogether. Laid in a place called the San Ramon Valley, the story dealt with the fight between a powerful cattleman and empire builder and a group of homesteaders who had come West by wagon train and settled in the area. After a series of criminal attempts by the nephew of the cattleman to rid the valley of the unwelcome "nesters"—including robbery, arson, assault and murder—the homesteaders were legally settled in their homes and the ruthless villains routed by The Lone Ranger. This, then, was an "Empire" Western.

People trudged West for other reasons than to homestead. In fact, they journeyed West for every imaginable reason, and their human motives and reactions to the challenges they met provided stories of deep emotion, adventure and tragedy. When many banded together in covered wagons and formed wagon trains, the resulting migration gave serial makers background for a number of exciting and successful screenplays.

Outstanding in the category of "Covered Wagon" Westerns was an early Republic offering, *The Painted Stallion*. Concerning a wagon train to Santa Fe which included among its ranks Davy Crockett, Jim Bowie and Kit Carson—along with Clark Stewart, the film's fictional hero who was on the way to represent the United States government in a trade relations pact with the new Mexican government—it featured a mysterious Indian girl who appeared riding a handsome stallion at moments of crisis. With the aid of her straight-to-the-mark whistling arrows, the wagon train was protected and its mission completed. The band of renegades that had tried to destroy it many times was vanquished.

A wagon train also figured prominently in *Custer's Last Stand*, the independent chapterplay from Stage and Screen. Borrowing some background from history—but largely using historical characters Calamity Jane, Wild Bill Hickok, Buffalo Bill and Sitting Bull in a purely fictitious situation—the story rambled through a series of loosely connected plots and subplots, and led to the defeat of Custer at Little Big Horn by Sitting Bull and the allied Indian nations. Boasting one of the largest casts of speaking characters of that time, it was well-received by action fans regardless of its lack of rigid historical adherence, and is representative of the "American Indian" category.

Just as they did in the opening and development of the real West, railroads played an important part in the Western serial. The challenges encountered by small bands of men trying to push Westward the lines of transportation and communication were many and diverse. Threats from the elements, natural terrain and mounting construction problems were compounded by the menacing resistance of ferocious Indians defending their land and by greedy, unscrupulous men who tried to prevent the opening of the West. The Westward thrust of the railroad thus personified all of the efforts of the early pioneers to establish and maintain permanent links to the Eastern part of the country.

Called "The Iron Horse" by the Indians, the railroad became the symbol to them of the entire menace of the Westward advance of homesteaders, pony express riders, stagecoach lines and telegraph poles. And the serial makers found in the legends and tales surrounding the growth of those efforts ample material for a number of interesting films. Typical was the 1940 Universal entry *Winners of the West*. Fresh from a series of B Westerns at Warner Brothers (in which he starred as a singing cowboy), Dick Foran took the lead as a daring and courageous troubleshooter whose job it was to bring the road through on time. Despite the many efforts of the master villain and his despicable crew, he finally was able to bring it off.

To the very end of the era, periodic railroad stories always seemed to please action fans, and never failed to contain an extra momentum provided by scenes of onrushing locomotives "hell-bent for destination." There is a built-in aura of suspense which seems to go with trains — time schedules, the seemingly endless stretches of track through forests, over mountains and across vast plains, and the twitches of wondering what lies over the next rise, around the next curve, or in the next tunnel.

Columbia favored the "Iron Horse" theme (and one of its variations) in its Westerns in the fifties. *Roar of the Iron Horse*, an outstanding release of 1951, featured a buckskin-shirted champion of the railroad. And in a closely related theme — this time concerning the pony express and stagecoach travel — *Cody of the Pony Express* presented a hero working desperately for the prevention of an unscrupulous and criminal monopoly-grab by villains seeking to control an entire territory by taking over all transportation facilities within it. Supposedly predating his great fame as an Army scout and Indian fighter, a young pony express rider named Bill Cody was portrayed as a sort of cohero in the venture.

Even if not the central theme, the railroad and its Western development was the underlying motivation of other Western serials. For example, the intended routing of the Santa Fe line through the territory prompted the villain in *The Adventures of Red Ryder* to begin a reign of intimidation and death to gain control of all the land comprising the potential right-of-way. And, although essentially a gangster film with a Western backdrop, *Zorro Rides Again*, released by Republic in 1937, centered around the scheme of a master criminal to seize control of the fictitious California-Yucatan line. (One of serialdom's most memorable stunt scenes was shot in this film during the exciting race between a train just hijacked by the gang and a fleet of huge transport trucks led by the intrepid Zorro. Doubling for the hero in the black, silver-trimmed outfit of the Latin crimefighter, the dean of American stuntmen, Yakima Canutt, galloped his horse at full speed along the dirt shoulder of the highway, pulled abreast of the cab of the leading truck, and without apparent effort swung himself from the saddle to the running board of the speeding truck. One miscalculation by Canutt, the driver of the truck, or the horse, could have been disastrous but, as executed, the stunt was a thing of beauty. Later, Canutt was to repeat the stunt a number of times as part of his repertory.)

The growth and spread of other modes of transportation and communication such as mail and telegraph service — as well as the already-mentioned pony express and stagecoach lines — accounted for some exciting footage along the way. For typing purposes they could be lumped together under the general heading of "Iron Horse" because of the similarity in themes. In addition to *Cody of the Pony Express* there was Universal's 1942 *Overland Mail*, and *Daredevils of the West*, from Republic in 1943, pitted the hero against a frontier speculator who tried to keep a fledgling stagecoach line from spanning the unopened Comanche Strip.

Not too many serials used as a central theme the Civil War itself, but many depicted circumstances and events that supposedly took place in the West leading up to and following the war years. During the war most of the military action took place in the East, and the states and territories of the West contributed men, materials and money to the two sides. Consequently, much background espionage and intrigue took place in the West, and many stories of courage and heroism involved men who returned from the fighting to their homes on the frontier.

One such was the main character in a Republic Zorro sequel in 1947 titled *Son of Zorro*. Jeff Stewart, a descendant of the legendary hero, returned from his duties as a cavalry officer after the Civil War to find his hometown overrun by crooked politicians who had taken advantage of the war to levy unfair taxes and bleed the people of their earnings. Assuming the Zorro identity of his famous ancestor, he set about to right the wrongs and return justice to the area.

The Civil War produced another breed of veterans that also figured prominently in the history of the Western United States for a generation following the conflict. These were renegades who had fought during the war for the side that would pay the most or allow the most looting and profiteering. In serials these were the men who became the villains. Men such as Quantrill, the Daltons, the Youngers, and other graduates of Quantrill's Raiders, were portrayed as scavengers attempting to continue their pillaging and slaughter for gain on the frontier.

Not always were the so-called "outlaws" shown to be criminals, however, even though history dealt less kindly with them. In features as well as serials, Jesse James and his brother Frank were often shown as misunderstood victims of the times, and in several were even played as the heroes. (As a matter of fact, Republic produced three with Jesse as the central hero: *Jesse James Rides Again* in 1947, *The Adventures of Frank and Jesse James* in 1948, and *The James Brothers of Missouri* in 1950. In the first one, Jesse appeared in a dark business suit of the era and, in the finest heroic tradition, managed to rout a gang of raiders terrorizing the area. The second one, released 13 months later, teamed Jesse and Frank as repentent fugitives who wished to repay their gang's victims by reviving a supposedly played-out silver mine and giving them the profits. The third, with a new team of actors playing the brothers, was a quick warm-over of the first two.)

Other "outlaw" and "renegade" types were destined to be the heavies in most pictures about the Civil War aftermath. They weren't as lucky as Frank and Jesse. Notable as particularly ruthless or nasty were the gangs who were in business just for the money and meanness of it. The Black Raiders, led by the unknown Pegleg in Columbia's *Overland with Kit Carson*, seemed to revel in each opportunity to drop a boulder upon, explode a wagon containing, or dispatch from a cliff the helpless form of the valiant Carson.

Outlaw rule was the prime factor again in their *The Valley of Vanishing Men* in 1942. To operate a secret mine deep in the bowels of a mountain cavern — accessible only through secret doors in the back of an abandoned livery stable in an old ghost town — a greedy and brutal criminal kidnapped unsuspecting citizens and chained them to a giant grist wheel watched over by a whip-wielding slave driver. After many trials, the hero succeeded in rescuing his abducted father and squelching the vile desperadoes.

In the late thirties and early forties, Columbia produced several "Desperado" serials with much gusto and bravado, but later aimed their Western projects to more modern settings or specialized themes such as Indians, railroading, etc. One of their earlier ones dealing with a power-hungry outlaw gang was *Deadwood Dick*, in mid-1940. The gang, led by an unknown fiend called "The Skull," was challenged by a courageous newspaperman who also fought as the masked avenger Deadwood Dick.

Universal's considerable contributions to the "Desperado" type came mostly in the thirties with a steady stream of action films starring Tom Tyler, Buck Jones, and Johnny Mack Brown. Their last one came in 1944 as *Raiders of Ghost City*. One of the last half dozen or so serials to be released by them, this was not a particularly noteworthy production, but had a good cast and slick production values. It came off quite well.

Although herds of cattle and buffalo usually figured prominently in the pictorial action, serials did not dwell very much on the economic value of buying and selling livestock and running ranches. Baronial empires (such as television's celebrated Ponderosa) were represented — if portrayed at all — as backdrops for more sinister activities, or were inserted as trapping to suggest the villain's appetite for opulence. The empires aspired to in continued pictures were more of the political and dictatorial brand, suggesting control over territories rather than acreage, and the quest for power rather than just money.

In *The Vigilantes Are Coming* the entire California territory was the goal of General Burr. To accomplish his desire to be actual dictator of the region, he imported an army of Cossacks from Imperialist Russia and preyed upon the rich mines and fertile lands of the Spanish settlers of the area. He was thwarted finally only by the efforts of a group of vigilantes inspired and led by the masked Eagle, a combination of The Lone Ranger and Zorro.

The hope of partitioning Texas in 1875 motivated the villain — a mysterious traitor known as Matosca — to foment an Indian war in Universal's *The Scarlet Horseman*. Failing to gain by that, the villain then activated a scheme to kidnap the wives and daughters of influential Texas senators and force them to cede as ransom a large territory called the Staked Plains to a tribe of Indians controlled by the traitor.

Often used in Westerns as a pawn in some greedy scheme such as Matosca's, and most frequently portrayed as a wild, bloodthirsty savage, the American Indian was seldom shown as he actually was — a primitive but proud man, mindful of his heritage and steeped in its lore, familiar with hardships, pain and death, and utterly confounded by the new breed of man from the East. He could not understand why the intruder insisted upon forging deeper and deeper into the wilderness, but was not content to pass through and leave it as it was. Instead he brought trailing after him strange vehicles filled with stranger objects, and people who built permanent wooden dwellings and actually lived in them. As others came, the dwellings were built closer together and became known as forts and towns. The suspicion and hostility created by this clash of mores and concepts became the basic cause for the fiercely violent uprisings and wars that resulted between the two societies.

For many years after the silents were gone, the movies continued the same stereotype presentation of the American Indian, using him in their stories as the chief roadblock to Western expansion and primary adversary of the Western pioneer. Only rarely did a story appear that treated him as a human being with problems matching those of the relentless pioneer. Then, as some measure of understanding began to creep into screenplays, the emphasis was switched to the idea that most Indians were simply people like everyone else — whose main interests were to feed and care for his own — and that the Indians who were villains were the renegades just as were the white men who were villains.

An early advocate of this new idea was the late Buck Jones, who starred in four serials for Universal from 1933 to 1936, and one each for Universal and Columbia in 1941. In his Western features as well as the serials, Jones adhered to the principle that the Indian was not just a violent, savage animal, but a man who reacted to provocation and would fight tenaciously when threatened.

In *White Eagle*, the Columbia release, his hero role was that of a man who believed himself to be a part-white Indian brave who fought valiantly against a renegade gunrunner for the preservation of peace between the Indians and white pioneers. (His last film before his tragic death in a Boston nightclub fire was *Dawn on the Great Divide*, a covered wagon story for Monogram. Although not an expensive or pretentious picture, it was a poignant, moving story about the trials of a small wagon train pressing Westward against overwhelming odds. In it the Indians were portrayed as brave defenders of their world against a menace they did not comprehend but had to resist.)

During the middle and later forties, several attempts were made to depict the Indian in a better light, and by 1950 the time was right for the climactic role of Cochise in Twentieth Century Fox's classic film *Broken Arrow*. As the proud, stubborn chief, Jeff Chandler brought dignity to his character and gave moviegoers a completely new concept of the bedeviled and beleaguered red American.

Republic's *The Phantom Rider* in 1945 had helped lead the way by exposing the scheme of a villainous Indian agent to take advantage of the ones whose interests he was supposed to be fostering. With the help of a colorful figure known as The Rider, who wore a mask and a striking chief's headdress, the Indians were finally rescued from the crooked agent.

Columbia's *Black Arrow* the year before had revived an interest in Indian Westerns that had lain dormant since before the war and, following *The Phantom Rider*, the one remaining such adventure was Columbia's *Son of Geronimo* in 1952, which ended on a note of brotherhood and understanding after 15 episodes of conflict between the races. The frontiersman's main antagonist was such because of mistrust and suspicion which grew out of ignorance and misunderstanding. This was the tragedy of our country's Westward growth, and the motion picture — including serials — finally became aware of it.

The Indian stands out in history as the West's most tragic figure; the frontier lawman emerged as its most heroic. More tales and legends have been spun about this breed of Westerner than could have been lived out in the history of the Western world, yet most of them supposedly took place during a brief period of about thirty to thirty-five years, from the close of the Civil War to the end of the nineteenth century. Of course, the answer is that most of the stories are repetitions, variations and expansions of the same few exploits that brought fame to the best-known handful of law officers in the West during that period. Serials delved profusely into the rich reserve of legend.

By the time motion pictures with sound were accepted as common-place, Mascot and Universal had already produced serials extolling the virtues of various sheriffs, marshals and scouts such as Kit Carson, Bill Hickok and Buffalo Bill Cody, following the trend set by the silents. This continued right on through the entire era.

Columbia's fourth serial was grandly titled *The Great Adventures of Wild Bill Hickok* and introduced a new Western star who was thereafter to be known as "Wild Bill" because of his identification with the role of the famous lawman. A year later the studio cast him in the title role in *Overland with Kit Carson*, and again he played a famous lawman, but the "Wild Bill" stuck so they made a series of Western features with him in the continuing role as Hickok.

Episodes taken from the experiences of other reputed lawmen such as Wyatt Earp, Bat Masterson and Pat Garrett have been embellished and incorporated into literally hundreds of short stories, magazine features, novels and screenplays to the point that the facts about who did what, when and where, have become obscured by the sheer volume of fiction based on them. Imaginary lawmen have been created as composites of all these men and have become almost as legendary as the real ones. The most famous is television's Matt Dillon of the weekly CBS series, *Gun-smoke*.

History reveals that the real-life lawmen were only human — with mortal weaknesses such as cowardice, greed and lust — but motion pictures did not seem to notice that too much. In movie Westerns the lawman was all good; his adversaries all bad. It made for neater climaxes, when the sheriff had to exercise his "right" to gun down a lawbreaker. Had he manifested a human weakness — or the bad guy a streak of decency — complications of motivation, cause and effect might have arisen — something that a good action story could well do without. The consequence was a steady flow of action for the sake of action, and the single, un-deviating lesson that Good must overcome Evil because it is nicer. This conformed with the direct, unsophisticated approach of the serial, so most of the form's Westerns came with the hero clean-shaven and smartly clad in his white hat — no questions necessary, and none asked.

Some of the most dashing heroes were the "masked-avenger figures" such as the aforementioned Lone Ranger, Zorro, Deadwood Dick and The Scarlet Horseman, who by their occultistic trappings struck fear into the hearts of their quarries. More carnal — but no less daring — were the "police-figures" of fictional stories who were bound somewhat by the restrictions of legal tradition and law enforcement regulations. They could not take refuge in hidden identities, secret hideouts, and the wreak-ing upon criminals of "an-eye-for-an-eye" retribution. Instead, their activities had to be legal (as well as daring) and their motives just (as well as indignant).

An adaptation of a popular poem by Robert W. Service was the forerunner of a category of action serials that must be classified as Westerns (because of their locale) though they were essentially detective or police stories. They featured dauntless individual lawmen rather than squads or teams of law enforcers, thereby qualifying them as stories of frontier lawmen. The Royal Canadian Mounted Police furnished a colorful hero for Universal's *Clancy of the Mounted* in 1933, which was the production based on Service's poem.

The screen adaptations of the popular Canadian police hero created by Zane Grey were to be the standard for all others to follow. Republic's *King of the Royal Mounted* in 1940 introduced to the action fans the valiant Mountie sergeant who fought courageously to protect his beloved Canada from the espionage plots of its cunning and determined wartime enemy, and *King of the Mounties* in 1942 continued the tradition.

That same year Columbia submitted the first of its two Mountie adventures — *Perils of the Royal Mounted*. The hero, a Sergeant MacLane, did battle against a crusty, hardened gang of raiders and hijackers out to corner the fur market in frontier country. Their other Canadian frontier cliff-hanger came in 1954 when Jock Mahoney donned the red and blue for 15 chapters of action and stunts (his forte) in *Gunfighters of the Northwest*.

Universal's only other sound serial about the Canadian Mounted — *The Royal Mounted Rides Again* — came pretty close to being the weakest chapter film they ever made. An excellent cast seemed wasted as they plodded through a routine story that wandered aimlessly and provided almost no suspense.

Two later entries by Republic included some very good action scenes, but compared to the two "Kings" were not particularly outstanding. As a matter of fact, some sequences of the earlier films were quite obviously inserted into the later ones and reduced their credibility. Nevertheless, *Dangers of the Canadian Mounted* in 1948 and *Canadian Mounties vs. Atomic Invaders* in 1953 presented attractive enough "police" heroes, and the stories moved along in the traditional Republic manner.

Though there have been in recent years a number of features made in Spain, Italy and Yugoslavia using Western stories, cowboy clothes and horses, the Western is uniquely American. As such it has understandably become the primary expresser of the American literary culture. It has been said that even when Hollywood filmmakers produce biblical and historical epics, Middle East desert stories of adventure and intrigue, war films, and even love stories, they all come out somehow as Westerns. And the makers of serials were no exceptions.

Since mystery and suspense are the indispensable elements of the cliff-hanger, it is almost redundant to classify particular productions in a category so singularly designated. By their nature all serials were of the mystery and suspense type. Only the backgrounds were different.

However, for the purpose of identification and separation from the easily recognizable specialty types already mentioned, chapterplays centered around police investigation, espionage and sabotage, intrigue and the supernatural are herewith included under the general heading of "mystery" serials.

The dictionary defines the word *mystery* as: 1. secret; something that is hidden or unknown; 2. thing, person, or situation about which there is something unexplained that arouses curiosity or speculation. This is the essence of the cliff-hanger. From the very beginning it was hoped that by leaving something hidden or unexplained, or by showing a sympathetic character in a crisis with the outcome in question, the resulting curiosity would force the viewer to return. This was accomplished in many ways: What could happen if some evil mastermind were able to secure the weapons and equipment he required for his scheme was a primary provocative theme. (Not so much what he was doing, but what he might be able to do elicited the moviegoer's interest.) Why a criminal genius might want some seemingly commonplace or worthless item also sparked many a quest by the hero. The nagging uncertainty from week to week whether the provocateur might bring off the next job somehow before being out-maneuvered by the good guys was always present, and in itself became the mystery in some films. And by far the favorite device was the inclusion of the unknown villain. Masked and garbed in some outlandish, fetishistic outfit, or secluded in some hauntingly funereal place and shown only as a menacing shadow or an ominous, disembodied voice, the portrayal of the villain as a mystery figure served two purposes in the heightening of apprehension and suspense. Added to the natural curiosity about the culprit's real identity was the human tendency to shrink from that which is distasteful and dreadful. The villain's choice of a particular symbolism was thus designed to instigate fear to throw his adversaries off guard.

The emphasis on the mystery serial continued undiminished from the silents to sound, and then right on to the end. In the first year of full sound, Universal released *The Jade Box*, starring Jack Perrin and Eileen Sedgwick. Although not of first-rate technical quality, as compared with previous silent classics, it showed that the addition and synchronization of music and some dialogue could be beneficial to the mystery film, and led to others of the type which fared much better. The following year *The Spell of the Circus* sported a full sound track and featured Francis X. Bushman, Jr., in a mystery story of the Big Top. Universal's last chapter thriller to contain only ten chapters was *Fingerprints* that year — also a mystery.

The year 1932 saw no less than four mystery serials from Mascot and Universal, including two involving railroads in modern settings — Universal's *The Lost Special*, a Sir Arthur Conan Doyle story, and Mascot's *The Hurricane Express*, with a masked crook known as The Wrecker.

The Whispering Shadow in 1933 marked the debut in chapter films of the leading mystery star of his generation. Universal's classic *Dracula* established Bela Lugosi as the foremost exponent of the weird and supernatural, and he became known as the personification of evil and cunning in dozens of features and serials for the next decade. His portrayals exuded an eerie, haunting discomfort which was to audiences both repulsive and fascinating. The only serials that were successful as supernatural pieces per se were the ones in which Lugosi appeared.

As the master magician Chandu and his alter ego Dr. Frank Chandler in *Return of Chandu* for Principal Pictures in 1934, Lugosi established another character remembered even now. In this feature-serial production, he performed acts of magic for which no attempts at explanation were made. None were necessary, as his image and demeanor made them seem credible. (This art eluded other performers, so not too many stories involving magic and the supernatural were attempted.) His portrayal of the demented genius Victor Poten in *Shadow of Chinatown* was an example of the aura he cast as a sinister individual. In that 1936 production for Victory Pictures and Sam Katzman, Lugosi so exuded the hate that Poten was supposed to feel for both the Oriental and Caucasian races (he being an outcast Eurasian) that it did not seem implausible at all for him to attempt one final act of vengeful hate in the anticlimactic banquet scene in the final episode. Completely foiled in his scheme to close the Chinatowns of the West coast and paralyze the importing industry of China in favor of an illegal European firm, betrayed by a woman who had been his employer and ally, on the run from the Law with no hope of ever rebuilding any effectiveness as a scientist or inventor, and believed dead in a runaway car crash, he refused the chance to escape to other parts and returned instead to try and murder those responsible for his downfall. Disguised as a waiter, he infiltrated the celebration banquet of the victorious hero and the grateful Chinese merchants. Before he could successfully poison the party's wine and destroy all his enemies at once, he was discovered by the hero and turned over to the police.

In Republic's 1937 *S.O.S. Coast Guard* and Universal's 1939 *The Phantom Creeps*, Bela Lugosi demonstrated his mastery of the technique of providing mystery by depicting a villain so utterly sinister and unpredictable as to defy rationality.

A fascinating example of the mystery created by speculation as to what a master criminal might be able to do with certain weapons or devices he desired was Republic's 1940 classic, *Mysterious Doctor Satan*. From its opening scene (the cold-blooded assassination of a noted criminologist) to the ironic climax (Dr. Satan's destruction at the hands of his own monstrous mechanical creation), the total threat of world conquest (the "mystery" element) hovered in the background as a calamitous implication. The piercingly malevolent countenance of the superb actor Eduardo Ciannelli set the tone. As Dr. Satan, with his head slightly lowered, his eyes blazing under clenched brows, his voice hissed out in clipped, accented syllables his plan to create an army of mechanical robots with which to conquer and control the world. In order to do it he needed the means of controlling the machines from a distance. Stealing such a device — a remote control panel — and then seeing its main control tube destroyed by the hero (a young man in a heavy hood-mask known as The Copperhead), Satan subsequently put his henchmen through all the paces in his devious and persistent attempts to again secure the control device.

Whether or not any of his schemes would succeed then became the essence of the mystery. Foiled in an attempt to salvage the panel from a yacht he had caused to be sunk, the evil doctor kidnapped a friend of the hero and made him into a walking bomb by placing an explosive harness on him which would go off if removed, hoping to blackmail the control panel's inventor into surrendering the vital tube. Then he kidnapped the inventor himself and tried to force him to duplicate the device under hypnosis. This would have succeeded but for the need of additional amounts of the control cell's key substance — a mineral called Tungite. Dr. Satan had the only known supply stolen and, learning the location of a deposit of the mineral ore, set up an elaborate mining operation, took over a smelter plant, and trucked the stuff to it. All along the way, the hero was right on his heels preventing the full completion of any of the mad genius' plans, but falling just short of stopping him altogether. At last the mechanical robot was captured by the good guys and Satan's job became trying to recover it. In so doing, he led The Copperhead and law enforcement agents to his lair, where he met his end in a last-ditch attempt to murder his adversaries.

Usually an ambition such as Dr. Satan's to rule the world, or at least control a part of it for personal gain, was the motivation of the pre-World War II serial villain. With the advent of the war, he was depicted mostly as an agent of the Axis powers, with the defeat of America his main purpose. In that context, the battle of wits as a mystery inducer took on a noble and patriotic connotation.

Universal released a succession of patriotically oriented mystery serials in the early forties, as did both Columbia and Republic on a lesser scale. Most of the chapter films from all three companies were generally geared to the nation's mounting concern over the European war situation and the part America would eventually have to play in it, but a small number were produced specifically to exploit that concern.

From a successful series of features which had begun several years before with the Samuel Goldwyn filmization of Sidney Kingsley's hit play *Dead End*, the famous Dead End Kids turned to cliff-hangers and starred in three of Universal's early entries in the spy and intrigue mystery field. Prior to Pearl Harbor, there was *Junior G-Men*, in which the gang of young toughs became involved in a search for the Army Colonel father of their leader, played by the gang's real leader, Billy Halop. They were persuaded to become members of the Junior G-Men and worked with regular federal agents to uncover a ring of spies known as the Flaming Torch gang. The following summer, *Sea Raiders* was released. Here the kids found themselves besieged by the harbor police on one side and a gang of foreign agents on the other. Led by a supposedly respectable industrialist from his headquarters aboard an anchored yacht, the criminal gang known as the Sea Raiders tried desperately to wreak sabotage and steal government secrets, including plans for a new type of torpedo boat designed and built by the brother of one of the kids. Reconciling themselves with the police, the boys then became their allies and were instrumental in routing the vicious spy ring. Following America's entry into the war, the third chapterplay of the series starring Billy Halop, Huntz Hall, Gabriel Dell and Bernard Punsley, was presented. In *Junior G-Men of the Air* the kids were joined by Gene Reynolds, Frankie Darro and Frank Albertson as additional members of the Junior G-Men who teamed up with a federal agent against an international Axis spy ring known as the Order of the Black Dragonfly.

The Great Alaskan Mystery contained wartime intrigue in a Yukon locale, and *The Mystery of the Riverboat* was laid in the bayou country of the lower Mississippi, with secret oil deposits on apparently worthless land as the motivation. They comprised two-thirds of Universal's 1944 output. Neither was an outstanding contribution to the genre, but both had all the necessary ingredients and were graced by good casts.

Universal's last two mysteries each contained the primary ingredient of a successful mystery serial — an unknown master criminal — and thus are remembered with more favor by the avid fan. *The Master Key* was a diabolical enemy agent bent upon ruining the economy of the United States by flooding the world market with phony gold, and *The Mysterious Mr. M* a greedy gang leader who sought to steal and sell industrial and military secrets to the highest bidder.

Except for *The Monster and the Ape* (which was strikingly similar to *Mysterious Doctor Satan*) and *Holt of the Secret Service* (a straight, hard-fighting action story about an undercover Secret Service agent and a counterfeit ring), all of Columbia's mystery serials had unknown master villains and a group of supposedly respectable citizens from which to select a suspect. Republic also favored this device, but with several notable exceptions. During the war, two mystery serials pitting Allied agents against foreign spies — with the top villain known by the audience — took their places as excellent examples in which the "mystery" grew out of the suspense provoked by tactical action and reaction. *G-Men vs. the Black Dragon* (the title of which practically tells the story) and *Secret Service in Darkest Africa* (whose villain — a Nazi spy disguised as an Arab chieftain — was known to the audience but not the players) were both well-made topical dramas with highly capable and professional casts.

The postwar mystery serials not involving unknown characters for suspense all pretty much followed the same idea — unscrupulous international agents trying to secure top-secret plans and inventions for sale to the highest bidding "foreign power" — with each attempting some unusual twist to achieve a degree of individuality. *The Black Widow* in 1947 utilized a beautiful woman as the chief villainess. Operating as a fortune-teller (with a deadly poison sting concealed in her clients' interview chair), she was able to extract secrets from people sent to contact her. In *G-Men Never Forget*, the top gangster assumed the identity of the police commissioner (his physical double) and proceeded to direct the fight from both sides — until exposed by the hero. And in *The Invisible Monster* in 1950, the writer used all the trappings of a mystery figure — a long, flowing robe of black, a hood with black mesh covering the face, and a light-beam device to produce invisibility — and then proceeded to reveal his villain's identity to the audience in the first episode. From there on the only mystery left was wondering what methods the "Phantom Ruler" would employ to utilize the talents of the four foreign "specialists" he had smuggled into the country.

Without question, those mystery serials that kept the audience guessing — along with the cast of players — the true identity of the unknown villain (or hero) were the most effective and most successful. Few of us have ever forgotten the enthusiasm we felt in explaining to fellow serial lovers our pet theory concerning which particular professor (or lawyer, government official, scientist, inventor, archaeologist, banker, policeman, technician, businessman or butler) just had to be the Scorpion (or The Octopus, The Ghost, The Claw, The Voice, The Wrecker, The Rattler, The Dragon, Pegleg, Don Del Oro, Dr. Vulcan or Captain Mephisto). We were sure we had detected a slight gesture or voice inflection that certainly betrayed our favorite suspect, and we held fast until either proved wrong by his violent elimination, or right by his eventual exposure. Unfortunately, many later serials diluted their own mystery potential by utilizing a completely different actor for the mystery figure than any of those playing suspects, so that audience speculation was made academic. With no visual or audible clues, anybody's guess was as good as anybody else's.

Even so, some of the more imaginative and striking mystery figures still provided an extra measure of spine-tingling excitement and remain in memory as the integral element of suspense in a given film.

It is difficult to remember one of the best mystery serials ever released without immediately bringing to mind its colorful, unknown villain, The Lightning. Republic's *The Fighting Devil Dogs*, by virtue of a stirring musical score, magnificent editing, imaginative writing, and a very able cast headed by two personable leading men, stands as one of the best mystery cliff-hangers ever made, in spite of the fact that it was also apparently one of the least costly — using a number of clips from newsreels and other serials, and two chapters devoted to flashbacks of its own story. The archcriminal of the piece was out to conquer whole nations by the use of a fiendish aerial weapon called an "electrical thunderbolt," which could electrocute all life within its impact radius. His costume — designed to personify the electrical devices he used to carry out his mad scheme — was all black and trimmed with jagged lightning symbols. It consisted of loose-fitting black shirt and trousers cupped by a broad black belt at the waist, black protective gloves covering hands and forearms, and shiny black boots below the knees — all enveloped by a flowing, jet-black cape which swirled dramatically when the wearer strode across the scene. To cover his face he wore a black, helmet-like mask with a lightning-streak-designed visor and narrow, slanted eye-slits. His hand weapon was a small, cylindrical pistol which emitted electrical charges, and his calling card a metallic object in the shape of a lightning bolt. With his oily, diabolical henchman Gould leering at his side, The Lightning waged his dark campaign from a secret headquarters on a Pacific island and the flight deck of his giant Wing aircraft (the same one used in *Dick Tracy*), until finally unmasked in Chapter 12. Marine officers Tom Grayson and Frank Corby (Lee Powell and Herman Brix) were the heroes responsible for his ultimate downfall.

Each of the mystery characters affected similar trappings or symbols in keeping with whatever garish image he chose to project. Some, like The Scorpion in *The Adventures of Captain Marvel*, followed the main theme of the story itself, while others — such as The Voice in Republic's *Government Agents vs. the Phantom Legion* and The Skull in *Deadwood Dick* — assumed enigmatic but not necessarily relevant appellations, seemingly for the purpose of merely concealing their true identities and thus providing suspense. (Except for its visual shock effect and a vague connection with a mysterious one-handed sea captain who had been defrauded by his primary target victims, the cloaked villain with the claw-like appendage in Columbia's *The Iron Claw* could have masked himself and become known by any name he chose, and still served his real purpose — to function as a respected member of society while secretly carrying out his criminal scheme.)

A most striking and visually fascinating villain was the title character of Republic's *The Crimson Ghost*. Covered by a stark shroud and hood — except for the facial opening — the outsize replica of a leering skull concealed the wearer's face while jolting a confronter with fright. Again, the affectation had no connection with the plot other than to shield the true identity of the criminal, and the voice used was not that of the actor who was later found to be the villain. Rather than the voice of Joe Forte, who played the man supposed to be the "Ghost," the sonorous tones emanating from the skull-mask were easily recognizable as those of I. Stanford Jolley, the veteran actor of many Westerns and serials (who, incidentally, played another character in the serial who became a victim of the "Ghost").

A variation of this theme was used in *Manhunt of Mystery Island* by Republic in 1945. The suspects were the four owners of a small, private island in the Pacific supposedly once the base for a legendary pirate known as Captain Mephisto, common ancestor of the group. Purported to be reincarnated and again using the island as headquarters, he conducted a terror campaign to secure control of the world's industrial capability to gain the power he coveted. By use of an elaborate electronic gadget, one of the owners was able to restructure his physical appearance and take on the features of the dreaded pirate and pursue his sinister plan in that guise. In practically every episode, a shadowy figure was seen emerging from a small dressing room and stepping up to a throne-like seat not unlike a prison electric chair. From a shot of a hand turning a valve on the front of the chair between costumed legs, the camera followed its movement to the chair arm where it pressed a switch. There followed a high-pitched whine like that of a huge turbine generator, and a slow pan shot from a long, overhead glass cylinder containing a steady series of electronic arcs, down to the grimly rigid face of Roy Barcroft, who portrayed Captain Mephisto. The hand — by then having obtained a skull-like tattoo — would move again to the valve and turn it back, gearing down the machinery. The "mystery" was which of the owners thus turned himself into the erstwhile buccaneer. It was entirely guesswork because of the use of Barcroft as the transformed villain, and the criminal's true identity was revealed only by the process of elimination.

In a reverse switch of the practice, Republic had employed the "stand-in" technique to conceal the identity of its hero (rather than the villain) in *The Masked Marvel* in 1943. Supposedly one of four young investigators trying to stop a Japanese saboteur, the masked hero dressed in a light, double-breasted business suit and a fedora hat, wore black gloves and a skin-tight, rubbery-looking black mask that covered his entire face except for the mouth and chin. Here, too, the fact that the masked character was neither of the suspects — but another actor altogether — was quite obvious to the discerning fan. It was especially apparent in the fight scenes, during which the easily recognized, fluid motion of one of serialdom's most proficient stuntmen clearly identified the tall, spindling hero as Tom Steele, veteran fight double for practically every serial leading man at Republic for a decade and a half. And, though this might have proved disappointing to some in thwarting any success at the guessing game, the sheer delight of seeing a hero jump right into his own fights without the sometimes disconcerting transition to a double was enough to justify the deception to the avid buff. The moment of truth in Chapter 12 — when the actor who was supposed to have been the Masked Marvel all along appeared in the scene with the mask on, and then removed it to disclose his identity — became almost anticlimactic (and maybe just a little embarrassing) when the audience instantly recognized the young investigator wearing the mask *before he took it off!* Regardless of the ruse, *The Masked Marvel* holds a place as one of the finest mystery serials released, because of the outstanding work by its team of able stunt-men, headed by the lanky Steele.

Just as serials of all types contained the basic ingredient of mystery (i.e. suspense), the mysteries also contained the elements of the other types. The primitive urgency for "survival of the fittest" of the jungle stories, the relentless drive and unmitigated resistance of the Western pioneers and the determined Indians, the bold recklessness of the buccaneer legends and adventurous costume epics of the days of knight-hood, the daring bravado of aviation's sky heroes, and the fascination of imaginative gimmickry and fantasy of the space and science-fiction yarns, all provided usable embellishments and motivations for the thrillers known specifically as mystery serials.

And therein lies the essence of the serial. Not concerned with comedy, romance, music and drama per se — yielding those themes to other capable hands — the serial makers provided the natural piquancy of curiosity, the fundamental involvement of suspense and anxiety, and the basic entertainment of excitement and thrills.

4

The Plotters of Peril

In a past issue of the Charlotte *Observer* there appeared an article headed "Compound X May Halt Cancer." Two biologists had reported a discovery that appeared to stop the growth of cancer cells and might some day lead to development of a drug which would inhibit their growth altogether and effectively conquer the disease. Their use of the term "Compound X" for this secret substance brought to my mind another "Compound X" from a Republic serial released forty years ago. That substance was the "prize" in *King of the Royal Mounted*, and was supposed to have the power to cure infantile paralysis. More important to Canada's wartime enemy, it also contained certain magnetic properties which could make the explosive mines they used more effective against the British fleet. Knowing it to be available only from a mine in Caribou, Canada, they sent one of their top intelligence officers to promote a steady flow of the material from the Caribou mine. Sergeant King, of the Royal Mounted Police, set out to stop the plan—and therein lies the tale.

In the course of his effort to salvage control of the vital substance for its humanitarian use and to capture the enemy agents, Sergeant King had used a direction finder in Chapter Three to lead him to one of the gang's hideouts—an old sawmill—where he was overpowered by the spies and left in the path of a whirring steel-tooth saw, which seemed sure to sever him bodily. That situation was only one of the "perils" concocted for the purpose of leaving the audience breathless and compelled to return for the next episode to see the good Mountie's miraculous escape. Before the final episode, which saw the destruction of the foreign agents, King had to face at various times entrapment in a blazing forest fire, falls into a boiling cauldron and from a high dam, the threat of gunfire through a wooden door and being blown to bits in a warehouse explosion, crashes in a car, a train, a motorboat and an airplane, and death in the jaws of a massive bear trap. The purveyors of these predicaments and creators of the catalytic prizes were the writers—the weavers of webs and plotters of perfidy.

Those responsible for the developments in that particular thriller were Franklyn Adreon, Sol Shor, Barney Sarecky, Norman S. Hall and Joseph Poland. All prolific serial men, a list of their credits would include some of the greatest ever filmed and would stretch from Sarecky's work in silent films with Nat Levine up to Adreon's direction of the final five cliff-hangers from Republic in 1954 and 1955.

For Adreon those five releases culminated a seven-year career as associate producer of the studio's chapter films after two years of writing following his return to the field after a six-year absence for World War II. During his career as a serial writer, Adreon also penned many of Republic's Westerns and action features. In Barney Sarecky's earlier days at Mascot, he variously received credits as production supervisor, associate producer and producer, as well as writer. He then became very active at Universal where he contributed to their serial output in the late thirties in much the same capacities. (Notable were his efforts on the Flash Gordon trilogy, *Radio Patrol* and *Buck Rogers*.) This came after he supervised Republic's first two continued pictures in 1936. He returned to that studio in 1939 for *Zorro's Fighting Legion* and helped write three of the four they released in 1940, including *King of the Royal Mounted*.

Sol Shor's episode writing was confined to Republic from 1938 to 1950 (except for the war years); while Norman S. Hall had already written for Universal; and Joseph Poland's career included all three studios and ranged from Columbia's *Mandrake the Magician* and Universal's *Scouts to the Rescue* in 1939 through Republic's 1946 *The Purple Monster Strikes* and back to Columbia, where he coauthored the second *Batman and Robin*, the second *Superman*, and concluded with *Captain Video* in 1951. His credits embraced many of the golden age classics at Republic. Norman S. Hall's credits include *Ace Drummond*, *Jungle Jim*, *Radio Patrol*, the second *Flash Gordon* and *Buck Rogers*. Both Hall and Poland were natives of Connecticut and received experience as newspaper and magazine writers there and in New York, and both had served in the armed forces – Hall in the AEF field artillery, and Poland in the United States Air Force.

It was natural for these men to write for the new medium when it came along. And for Barney Sarecky, with so much experience as a production executive as well, television provided new opportunities for more than just writing. Following his career during the forties as the man in charge of Monogram's Western output (producing the Johnny Mack Brown and Jimmy Wakely series), he became a producer for the successors of the serial – television series – and engineered, among others, *Terry and the Pirates*.

These five men were part of a select group of less than two dozen writers who formed the nucleus for practically the entire output of the three major producers of serials. The others were Ella O'Neill, Basil Dickey, Sherman Lowe, Morgan B. Cox, Joseph O'Donnell, Jesse Duffy,

Harry Fraser, Royal K. Cole, Arthur Hoerl, Ronald Davidson, William Lively and George H. Plympton. Joined from time to time by other less prolific serial writers — and on various projects with each other — this group accounted for a large percentage of all screenplays and a great many original stories during the heyday of the cliff-hanger. They were a versatile lot and came from a diversity of backgrounds.

William Lively, a native of West Virginia and son of a judge, had military academy training, experience in vaudeville, musical comedy, dance band directing, advertising, newspaper reporting, publicity promotion and magazine writing — all of which gave him a keen awareness of what the public would like and buy, and helped him in penning imaginative situations for the plots he worked on. In addition to serials, he wrote many Western and action stories and was an assistant director. Robert E. Kent (*The Spider's Web* and *Flying G-Men*) was born in the Panama Canal Zone, educated in New York, became a commercial artist, violinist and orchestra leader, newspaper feature writer, radio producer, talent scout and author of several novels. His chief contribution to Columbia Pictures is a long list of features (rather than serials), and at one time he adapted Columbia films into novelizations for a news syndicate. Ronald Davidson, one of the few serial writers who was a native Californian, had been a rancher before going into the motion picture business.

The one thing most of the writers shared in common was their background of long careers in theatrical and motion picture enterprises. Sherman Lowe received education at the University of Utah in his native state, and also at the University of Pennsylvania. After Army service in World War I, he entered motion pictures and wrote for all kinds of films for theatrical release and television. Joseph O'Donnell was in his early twenties when he joined Pathé in New York as a writer and studio manager. He went to Hollywood via Puerto Rico (where he was production manager for associated exhibitors) and became a story editor and free-lance writer, penning many Westerns and action films. Jesse A. Duffy, from Owensboro, Kentucky, wrote gags and worked on many comedy short subjects and series features for Darmour Productions, and when Larry Darmour took over serial production at Columbia in 1940 following Jack Fier, Duffy joined Morgan Cox, John Cutting and director James W. Horne in turning out one of that year's best-remembered chapterplays, *The Green Archer*. Three years later, he moved to Republic where he wrote chapter stories until 1948. Harry Fraser — like colleague Albert DeMond — left the New York area where they were born for greener fields in California. Both wrote college stories, action and Western yarns, as well as serials.

Since many early talking serials were based on novels and other written sources, credit for the stories often went to the author of the book or to the director. The writer was given credit for continuity or dialogue. Thus, early Universal releases such as *Detective Lloyd*, *Battling with*

Buffalo Bill and *Danger Island* are recorded as written by Henry MacRae, with dialogue or continuity by Ella O'Neill, Basil Dickey and George H. Plympton. Later, credit was more accurately designated as Original Story and Screenplay credit. It was for screenplay credit that most of the serial writers were engaged, although in many cases they were responsible for both.

At Universal the sound era began with a veteran writer from the silents working on nearly every project. For five years, every serial released by that company listed credit for either dialogue or screenplay to Ella O'Neill, and in the following two years, six out of eight releases used her words. With Dickey, Plympton and George Morgan, she rounded out the basic Universal writing team from 1930 to 1936. Directors Henry MacRae and Ford Beebe collaborated with the group on a number of stories the first two years, but after that their credits were confined to direction. In 1932 Joe Roach helped with *Heroes of the West*, and in 1933 Harry Hoyt contributed to two of the four screenplays turned out by the team. One or two projects each were aided by writers Het Manheim, Charles Goddard, Jack Foley, Jack Nelson and Vin Moore up to 1934, and 1935's output contained the work of Nate Gazert, Edward E. Repp, Robert Rothafel, Nat Eddy, Raymond Cannon and Robert Hershon.

In 1936 the writing assignments were split up so that one team did not have to produce all the stories. That year Plympton, O'Neill and Dickey scripted *The Phantom Rider* for Buck Jones, and with director Frederick Stephani wrote the sensational *Flash Gordon*. Maurice Geraghty joined them for *The Adventures of Frank Merriwell*, and a new team for Universal turned out the fourth screenplay: Wyndham Gittens from Mascot, Ray Trampe and Norman Hall (who had worked on *Tailspin Tommy* with Dickey, O'Neill and Moore) began a four-year association writing the screenplay for the serial version of Rickenbacker's *Ace Drummond*. As before, other writers joined the two basic teams and added touches from time to time, but the bulk of the writing came from the veterans. Leslie Swabacker and Herbert Dalmas pitched in on the second *Gordon*; Paul Perez contributed to *Flaming Frontiers*, and Irving Crump and Joe Poland assisted on *Scouts to the Rescue*. Plympton and Dickey did three in 1939 and all four in 1940, with help by an assortment of one-time assignees whose serial writing experience began and ended almost at the same time.

The last six years of Universal's cliff-hangers after 1940 saw most of the scripts coming from Plympton, Morgan B. Cox, Paul Houston and Griffin Jay. Occasional work by well-known serial men Lowe, Poland, O'Donnell, Vic McLeod, Barry Shipman and Ande Lamb added spark to various projects, but many of the writers assigned to work with the veterans (Al Martin, Maurice Tombragel, Dwight Babcock, Jack Natteford and Luci Ward) chose to go on to bigger and better things in features after a brief taste of episode writing. Martin, who worked on

Gangbusters with Plympton, Cox and McLeod, became a prolific television writer as did both Tombragel and Babcock, who had helped with
The Great Alaskan Mystery and *The Master Key* respectively. Natteford,
who was married to Luci Ward, also assisted on *Key*. Miss Ward's sole
contribution was on *Raiders of Ghost City* with Morgan Cox.

Typical of the "prizes" invented for their outstanding lineup of
chapter dramas was the mysterious ring bearing an almost illegible
Spanish inscription in *The Adventures of Frank Merriwell*. The ring, en-
trusted to Frank by his missing father, was the key to a vast treasure in
gold, and eventually led to the fortune and the return of the elder Merriwell. Tempting all who would covet them, the crown jewels of a country
friendly to the United States became the much-sought-after prize of a
mysterious international jewel thief known only by the name "Brenda" in
1937's *Secret Agent X-9*. Assigned to recover the stolen gems, X-9 was also
successful in disclosing the identity of the wanted man.

Nothing less than military and political control of two planets rested
upon the shoulders of *Buck Rogers*. Awaking from a state of suspended
animation in the 25th century A.D., Rogers and his pal found the Earth
conquered by a master criminal named Killer Kane. To regain control for
the decent citizens in exile, an alliance was sought with the planet Saturn,
and finally produced victory over Kane and his forces. On a smaller
scale — but closer to understandable reality — power was also the prize in
The Jungle Queen. Symbol of control over a key tribe in the African
jungle was a strange and mysterious sword which contained a closely
guarded secret. There to try and secure the sword, and thus stir up the
tribe to their own ends, were agents of the Nazi high command. The
beautiful, enigmatic Queen Lothel, aiding two Allied agents in thwarting
the Nazis' plans, managed to foil their schemes and preserve the sword's
secret.

In concocting their perils, the Universal writers were not to be excelled. After thirty years in silent and sound form, they had used every
conceivable twist and angle, and had shown the others the way. One of
the most pictorial of those classic endings was obviously taken from a
newsreel, but remains to this day in many minds as the epitome of total
destruction dealt swiftly and completely: Drawn to a condemned building
on a ruse, the hero did not know that the building was rigged for
demolishment by the demented villain. When the time came for the
detonation (with the hero apparently inside), the explosion came as a
shock. Instead of blowing apart, as scenes using miniatures usually
pictured it, the building trembled violently, seemed to burst at the
corners, and then simply crumbled in a heap of rubble at its own base.
Professional explosives men probably would not be surprised, as no
doubt that kind of blast is the result of a special technique for using high-
powered explosives in confined areas; but to the eye of a nonprofessional
moviegoer it was almost traumatic. Unlike the in-again-out-again plotting

of dangers for the sake of danger that later became predominant in the cheaper remakes and quickies that closed the serial era, some of Universal's perils were so deeply ingrained in the story that no separation could be made without destruction of an entire plot sequence. Such a one was the peril bridging chapters Two and Three of *Flash Gordon Conquers the Universe*: On an expedition to the frozen kingdom of Frigia on the planet Mongo, in search of an element known as "polarite," which could combat the emperor Ming's "purple death," Flash, Dale and Barin were trapped in an avalanche of snow and ice caused by the aerial bombing of Ming's "death squadron." As the episode ended, the avalanche was crashing down relentlessly on the helpless victims. At the beginning of Chapter Three there was no sudden, incredible miracle to snatch them from the jaws of danger. Instead, the avalanche subsided, and there was quiet. It seemed that here, finally, death had actually claimed a hero. There was an eerie feeling of finality — a fine moment created by directors Ford Beebe and Ray Taylor — and drama that was rare in the form. A twelve-year-old could almost believe that the unbelievable had happened. (It's strange how a feeling like that can live for forty years.) Then Flash and Dale were shown to be badly shaken but unhurt, slowly reviving, and Prince Barin still knocked out, apparently more seriously injured but alive. And it was clear that they were all still in danger of being frozen in the unbearable cold. After finally establishing radio contact with Flash and learning they were still alive, Dr. Zarkov organized a rescue party which trudged over the vast wasteland by the light of magnesium torches to reach the helpless group. The pinpoints of light piercing the darkness and the echoing cries of the rescuers induced throat-gripping anxiety until the cries were heard by the stranded trio and they realized rescue was in sight. The situation had consumed nearly half of Chapter Three and was an integral part of the plot. In the hands of able directors, the Universal writers' screenplays produced many such memorable sequences.

When Republic began, original story credit was given for six of the first seven serials — John Rathmell and Tracy Knight for *Darkest Africa* and *Undersea Kingdom*, Maurice Geraghty and Leslie Swabacker for *The Vigilantes Are Coming*, Morgan Cox and George Morgan for *Dick Tracy*, Cox and Ronald Davidson for *The Painted Stallion* and *S.O.S. Coast Guard* — then original story *and* screenplay credit recorded for Cox, Geraghty and Barry Shipman for *Robinson Crusoe of Clipper Island*. Thereafter, credit was just for either screenplay or original screenplay.

The nucleus of the Republic writing department from 1938 to 1943 consisted of Barry Shipman, former child actor and world traveler, Ronald Davidson, Joseph O'Donnell, William Lively, and the five mentioned before (Adreon, Shor, Hall, Sarecky and Poland). Others, including Lois Eby and George W. Yates (*The Lone Ranger*), Rex Taylor (*Dick Tracy Returns, Hawk of the Wilderness* and *Daredevils of the Red Circle*), Arch B. Heath (*The Adventures of Captain Marvel*), Alfred

Batson (*Jungle Girl*) and Taylor Cavan (*King of the Mounties*) con- tributed their services, but — like the team at Universal — the veterans who formed the nucleus are the ones who made the studio's product what it was. This period has become known as Republic's "golden age," the time when the studio released one success after another, and each one became a standard of its type. The combination of directors William Witney and John English, the musical scores of Cy Feuer and Mort Glickman, and the output of this writing team made it possible.

In 1943 Basil Dickey and Jesse Duffy left Columbia to fill gaps left at Republic by the departure of Lively, Hall and O'Donnell, and Royal Cole teamed up with the Republic group while still writing for Columbia, too. Grant Nelson started with Republic that year and worked on the six next releases, including *The Masked Marvel* and *Captain America*. The former benefited by George Plympton's work (his only contribution at Republic) and the latter had no less than seven top writers assigned, including Harry Fraser in his only credit at the studio.

From 1944 to 1950, the basic team of Dickey, Duffy and Poland were joined at various times by a succession of writers such as Alan James, Albert DeMond, Lynn Perkins and Robert G. Walker, with return stints by Sarecky, Shor, Cole, Lively and Adreon. During that time, Ronald Davidson succeeded W.J. O'Sullivan as Associate Producer until 1947 when Mike Frankovich, former pro football and baseball star turned radio announcer, was elevated to that position. He piloted four of Republic's 1947–48 schedule — *Jesse James Rides Again, The Black Widow, G-Men Never Forget* and *Dangers of the Canadian Mounted* — before going on to a diversified international career in motion pictures and television that led to his status as the top producer at Columbia (and one of the most successful in the entire industry). Former marine Frank Adreon followed Frankovich as Republic's serial producer, and presided over the final one-third of the studio's serial history. In 1950 Davidson wrote *The Invisible Monster* and continued as the sole writer of Republic serials thereafter.

The screenplays turned out by these men were some of the genre's finest, and covered a wide range of imaginative situations. The central plot motivations (the prizes) varied from the temptations of power that lured the villains in *Drums of Fu Manchu, Mysterious Doctor Satan* and *Manhunt of Mystery Island*, to the very human lust for revenge, the desire for wealth, and the determination to commit sabotage. The perils to the good guys were sometimes tributes to the fertile imaginations of the scriptwriters and challenges to the cameramen and special effects men:

Seeking revenge upon a former employer who sent him to prison for embezzlement, an escaped convict known by his number — 39013 — set out in *Daredevils of the Red Circle* to wreck the enterprises of his former boss and then kill him. When defied by three young athletes who had per- formed on an amusement pier destroyed by the criminal, he then vowed to exterminate them, too. Disguised as the industrialist he had kidnapped, the vicious 39013 always had access to the heroes' plans and very nearly succeeded in his scheme before being victimized by one of his own murderous traps in Chapter Twelve. The memory of the demented villain awaking in the rumble seat of the heroine's roadster (where he had been placed unconscious by one of his henchmen), realizing it to be the one he had ordered wired to explode at seventy miles-per-hour, and screaming unheard above the noise of the wind and motor to the unsuspecting driver as he urged it to the fatal mark and resulting conflagaration, never fails to come to mind when I hear the term, "poetic justice."

From the pens of Shipman, Adreon, Davidson, Shor and Taylor came perils devised by madman 39013 such as those climaxing chapters One and Three. In the first, the vengeful convict had learned of the near completion of his hated adversary's newest project — an underwater tunnel from the mainland to a nearby pleasure island — and plotted to have it sabotaged on its opening day. As a caravan of dignitaries entered one end, explosives were set off at the other, flooding the tunnel with a massive wave of water. On a motorcycle, the hero raced furiously to warn the lead automobile containing the heroine and chief of police as the mountain of water crashed relentlessly behind him. Two chapters later, as the daredevil trio investigated a mysterious death in the industrialist's garage, the evil avenger forced a deadly gas through the sprinkler system which threatened to overcome the courageous group. Quick thinking resulted in the almost ridiculously simple solution of smashing through the locked doors with the host's big sedan to reach fresh air.

As mentioned, revenge against those who brought about the capture, conviction and execution of his gangster brother was the obsession of a supposedly respectable citizen in *Dick Tracy vs. Crime, Inc.* To carry out his plan of vengeance, no less than three prizes were coveted by the master criminal — a shipment of gold bullion, a top secret aerial torpedo, and a bogus "diary" of his brother's which turned out to be an almost-successful lure concocted by Tracy. One of the episodes devised by writers Davidson, Hall, Lively, O'Donnell and Poland employed two perils for the hero in a wild, relentless chase after The Ghost. Racing through a crowded harbor after the fleeing criminal in Chapter Five, the speedboat carrying the detective was drawn between two large steamers that were gradually moving toward each other and would surely crush the tiny craft. (This was a stock shot lifted from an earlier Tracy film, and the hero escaped predictably by diving into the water and swimming under one of the larger ships to safety on the other side.) In further pursuit, the villain was again located by Tracy and his men but became invisible and got away after cutting a rope which sent a load of lumber crashing down on the battling detective. As might be suspected, the writers also devised a narrow escape for the dauntless Tracy so that he might carry on until eventually victorious.

Great wealth, next to great power, was the strongest attraction of all to the villains of the chapterplays. More plots dealing with hidden treasure, vast fortunes and schemes to secure them were rolled out than on any other motivation. Gold bullion on a sunken yacht was the fatal fascination for the villain Kane in *Haunted Harbor*, and he set out to prove there was nothing he would not do to gain it, including the rigging up of the hideous, mechanical sea-monster that he caused to rise out of the lagoon to terrify and frighten away any intruders, thus giving him time to continue his search. One of the more chilling perils to the hero (who had owned the sunken schooner containing the gold) was the climax of Chapter Five: Having decided to check out the haunted lagoon for a possible clue to the villain and the sunken fortune, he had gone there with the island doctor's daughter to investigate. Attacked by the monster, he dived overboard with a knife to battle the beast. A terrific underwater explosion rocked the harbor and his limp, apparently lifeless body floated to the surface. Luckily, we learned the following week, he had only been stunned and was revived to fight another day.

Oil rights in the vast, unexplored jungle domain of the legendary white goddess known as *The Tiger Woman* was the prize to be gained in the 1944 release bearing her name as its title. This time writers Cole, Davidson, Dickey, Duffy, Nelson and Poland sent an oil company engineer to develop their jungle fields within a stated deadline or lose the rights. On the scene to prevent the development and thus secure the oil rights for his "employers" was a smooth heavy who also had a personal side interest. Believing the Tiger Woman to be an heiress to a vast fortune and the sole survivor of the plane crash that killed her parents, the crook hoped to secure proof and use it to get control of the fortune for himself. In the first chapter an oft-used device was employed to intensify the threat of death implied by the impending peril: Having captured one of the bad guys, the natives strung him up by the wrists over a vat of molten liquid in their temple. In the execution ceremony, the drums announced by increasing their tempo the approaching fatal moment. When they reached fever pitch, the rope was cut and the henchman dropped screaming into the pit. Later, the hero became their captive and through a misunderstanding faced the same fate. As the Tiger Woman raced through the jungle on horseback to rectify an erroneously-sent death message, the drums in the temple beat a relentless crescendo of doom for the suspended hero. Having already witnessed one execution by the same method, the audience knew only too well what to expect and felt every beat of the drum bringing it closer, until the tempo was reached that meant certain death. As Chapter Two opened, the Tiger Woman succeeded in reaching the temple just "in the nick of time," and the game was on for 11 more episodes.

During the war, the security of the United States was the prize. Various enemy agents whose sole intended purpose was the destruction of the nation's resources and facilities by acts of sabotage continued to inflict upon those heroes who would resist them all the dangers and perils theretofore threatened by villains with more personal ambitions. In a way this was more adaptable to ·the serial format, for it gave a wider range of possibilities for the writers to create action for its own sake. On the very heels of America's entry into the war, when the public's awareness of the espionage and sabotage efforts by its enemies was most keen, Republic released *Spy Smasher*. Adapted from the brand-new strip in *Whiz Comics* magazine and written by the team of Davidson, Hall, Poland, Lively and O'Donnell, the story dealt with an attempt by the Nazis to flood the United States with counterfeit money so extensively that the economy would be undermined and virtually collapse. Side prizes of a secret bombsight, a gold shipment and a powerful ray gun — all potential weapons for the enemy's arsenal — were employed to create a very tight and fast-moving screenplay. (One highly pictorial touch was the sight of the hero in full fighting costume zipping along on a high-powered motorcycle, photographed from the rear of the famous Republic camera truck.)

A sabotage effort from the oriental branch of the Axis powers was the central concern of government agents the following year in *G-Men vs. The Black Dragon*, by the same team of writers. In it, a top Japanese agent of the infamous Black Dragon Society — whose sworn purpose was the utter destruction of the United States — was smuggled into Los Angeles in a state of suspended animation. Revived, he set up headquarters and proceeded to direct a sabotage campaign of terror and destruction beginning with the burning of vital ships by use of a special chemical in their paint, then attempts to blow up Boulder Dam's power system, wreck a train carrying Army equipment, steal a top secret robot-controlled plane, and destroy the plans for a new television camera. Fought every step of the way by a team consisting of an American special investigator, a British secret agent and a member of the Chinese secret service, the wily Japanese spy was finally tracked down and trapped in a devastating explosion of a motorboat and the submarine he was desperately trying to reach for escape.

To cash in on the popularity of famous jungle explorer Frank Buck, and to get established in the lucrative action serial field, Columbia assigned producer Jack Fier and director George Melford to the task of putting together their first chapterplay in 1937. The result, *Jungle Menace*, was the product of the brain power of eight men, including Melford himself. The story was by George Merrick, Arthur Hoerl, Dallas Fitzgerald and Gordon Griffith, and the screenplay was written by George Rosener, Sherman Lowe, Harry Hoyt and Melford. Merrick and Rosener followed up with the next two — *Mysterious Pilot* and *The Secret of Treasure Island* — with L. Ron Hubbard and director Elmer Clifton contributing to the latter. Merrick wrote no more after that, and Rosener's last serial credit was *The Great Adventures of Wild Bill Hickok*. Writers

Charles Powell, G.A. Durham, Tom Gibson and Martie Ramson — like Fitzgerald and Griffith — were not to make their mark with serials, and wrote for just the few beginning ones. Also, Robert E. Kent would write his two and depart for greater things. Basil Dickey and George Plympton from Universal joined Kent and Ramson for *The Spider's Web*, and Dickey followed up with Kent and Sherman Lowe for *Flying G-Men*, and Joe Poland and Ned Dandy for *Mandrake the Magician*. Poland and Dandy then scripted *Overland with Kit Carson* with Morgan Cox, and *The Shadow* with Joe O'Donnell.

In 1940–41 George Morgan, Wyndham Gittens and Morgan Cox supplied the experience and were joined in brief stints by John Cutting, Jesse Duffy and Lawrence Taylor, and in one-shot assignments by Mark Layton, Joseph Levering, Arch Heath and Charles Condon. Dickey and Plympton were again engaged by producer Larry Darmour for *The Iron Claw*, following up Plympton's return to Columbia for *The Spider Returns*. They also turned out *Holt of the Secret Service* and *Captain Midnight* for him with Gittens. Dickey completed two more for the 1942 schedule — *Perils of the Royal Mounted* and *The Secret Code* — with Duffy, Scott Littleton, Louis Heifitz, Leighton Brill and Robert Beche, before moving over to Republic as a key member of their writing department.

The year 1943 saw two of Columbia's most famous serial productions from a new producer, Rudolph Flothow. Victor McLeod and Leslie Swabacker worked on both of them — with Harry Fraser on *Batman*, and with Morgan Cox and Sherman Lowe on *The Phantom*. Swabacker and Lowe then completed the 1944 schedule for Flothow, joined by Jack Stanley and Leighton Brill for *The Desert Hawk* and Royal Cole for *Black Arrow*. Lowe and Cole wrote Flothow's fifth and final — and possibly best — serial for early 1945 release — *The Monster and the Ape*.

Sam Katzman became Columbia's serial producer in 1945 and immediately engaged veteran Universal writer George Plympton, who then worked on 28 of the next 32 productions as either story or screenplay writer (the final four were turned out by him singlehandedly). With Plympton as the continuing member, the Katzman writing team consisted of Ande Lamb, Harry Fraser, Royal Cole, Lewis Clay, Arthur Hoerl and Joe Poland, with scattered assignments to Swabacker, Lowe, Condon and David Mathews.

The full array of possible prizes was brandished by the Columbia storytellers — from a grim murder secret held by the heroine in *The Mysterious Pilot* (for which the villain went to any extreme in attempts to abduct her) to the less complicated fortune in gold (with which to stock an army for territorial conquest) sought by the heavy in *Blazing the Overland Trail* — and the perils and pitfalls planned for the downfall of the good guys took a backseat to no one.

Two of the lures to villainy were classic prizes sought in literature through the ages — wealth in the form of Spanish treasure, and power in the form of King Arthur's famous sword, Excalibur: With an old map as a guide, Captain Silver and the crew of *The Sea Hound* engaged in jungle island and sea adventures against a villain known appropriately as The Admiral in search of a sunken galleon supposed to contain a vast cargo of Spanish treasure. (In the 1947 release, the heroine at one point was threatened in a way unique to jungle serials. Attempting to free an ally from a staked pit, Captain Silver left her alone for a moment and she promptly fell victim to a giant man-eating plant! As the plant's tendrils closed in about her throat, the chapter ended with the familiar voice of good old narrator Knox Manning admonishing the audience that they "don't fail to see the next exciting episode of *The Sea Hound* at this theatre next week!" Needless to say, Silver arrived the following week in time to cut away the deadly plant.) The hero of *The Adventures of Sir Galahad*, having allowed himself to be overcome and his charge (the coveted Excalibur, sword of invincibility) stolen, vowed its recovery in the 1949 production written by Plympton, Clay and Mathews, and set out through a maze of political and military intrigue to retrieve and return it to King Arthur and claim his right to knighthood. Close calls with death in the forms of burning, beheading, trampling, crushing, impalation, falling, torture and suffocation in quicksand seasoned the lad for his ambitious goal, which of course he eventually reached.

The potential power contained in the control of destructive weapons motivated a large number of the villains in the Katzman era. A disintegration machine that could destroy entire cities by sound vibration was the aim of the evil Luthor in *Atom Man vs. Superman*. To perfect it he needed a substance known as plutonium. Also, to combat the indestructible Superman, he sought radium to make synthetic Krypton, the only element to which the superhero was vulnerable. Along the way, he used a smaller variation of the disintegration machine to reduce a human to his basic atoms and reassemble them again in any other location he chose. To make that gimmick work there was a small activated coin which traded hands a few times. It was not uncommon for Katzman serials to contain several key prizes rather than just one, and an assortment of weapons and pseudoscientific devices (nearly all familiarly similar to those in earlier films) was displayed in a succession of colorful continued pictures that lasted for nearly eleven years: An electronic ray gun and a secret fuel known as Element X kept the heroes of *Blackhawk* busy combatting criminals and saboteurs with names like Boris, Laska, Olaf and Bork. A similar ray gun and a secret motor, inventions of a depraved criminal called the Chief Pilot and an eccentric inventor named Dr. Tobor (robot spelled backwards), made life interesting for *Hop Harrigan* and his friends. And exploding flying discs, a fantastic remote-control machine and an antiguided missile ray caused much concern on the part of *Bruce Gentry*, *Batman and Robin* and *Brick Bradford*, to name just a few.

Columbia's writers over the years gave new polish to the tried-and-true perils of the silent films, and even came up with a few new ones. Memorable are a handful of classic situations which were repeated many times but always managed to elicit wide-eyed apprehension from a new crop of kids every few years. One such inveiglement — almost guaranteed to make young viewers want to cry out a futile warning to their brave, unsuspecting hero — was the climax of Chapter Two of *The Iron Claw*: Having kidnapped the heroine, the mystery man fled from the good guys in a wild nighttime automobile chase over mountainous roads. Well ahead, but fearful of being overtaken, the Claw stopped his car and quickly set up a strange mirror device at the far point of a sharp curve. As the hero's vehicle careened around the turn, his own headlights reflected in the mirror and gave the instant illusion that another car was bearing down on his. Swerving to avoid the apparent collision, the car left the road and plunged over an embankment. To a lad of 13 that seemed like a fiendish thing to do, yet there was also a flashing twinge of appreciation for what seemed a devilishly clever deception. Even now, the scene comes to mind when the expression "dirty pool" is heard. *The Shadow* found himself in a well-known predicament in the 1940 chapterplay: Trapped by his adversary in a small, cell-like room beneath a trapdoor through which he had fallen while investigating a clue, the masked hero was taunted by the villain from a loudspeaker in the room. When the realization began to come that he was at the mercy of the criminal (in itself bad enough), worse befell. The walls of the room began to move together, threatening a crushing end for the crimefighter. This was a favorite peril-device, as it played on two very common fears — being closed in and being physically hurt — and it was used often. A variation of that danger ended an episode in the 1943 *Batman*. Supposedly concealed in a long, coffin-like box which was delivered to the lair of the evil Dr. Daka, the comic strip hero apparently became crocodile bait when the box was dropped through a trapdoor by the cunning villain into a pit containing several of the huge, hungry creatures, and split open.

Also apparent victims of vicious or fear-crazed animals (like the crocodiles) were many other heroes and heroines of Columbia serials — ranging from jungle attacks by lions, tigers and leopards to cattle stampedes such as the one in Chapter Nine of *Deadwood Dick*. Twice in the 1940 remake of *The Green Archer* the hero was attacked by huge, vicious dogs in scenes of terrifying fright, and both times rescued by the timely intervention of the phantom bowman.

The independent producers also contributed much to the storehouse of exciting plots, prizes and perils. Mysterious documents known only as the "Caswell papers" and a strange black coin coveted by several factions kept things moving in the Weiss-Mintz release *The Black Coin* in 1936. Dallas Fitzgerald, who later wrote for Columbia and Universal, wrote the screenplay with Eddy Graneman, Bob Lively and director Albert

Herman. He also did the words—in league with Leon D'Usseau—for director Herman again that year in the serial version of Arthur Reeves' Craig Kennedy thriller, *The Clutching Hand*. A formula for making synthetic gold induced a great deal of intrigue and action before it was learned that the formula was phony and a cover-up for its inventor, who turned out to be himself the mysterious villain of the title. A statuette called the Green Goddess contained a fortune in gems and plans for a secret weapon in *The New Adventures of Tarzan*. Charles F. Royal wrote the screenplay. And a magic arrow, the key to the location of a medicine cave containing a cache of gold, figured in events leading up to a historical massacre—according to writers George Durham, Eddy Graneman and Bob Lively—in the Stage and Screen production of *Custer's Last Stand*.

Danger of death can come in a myriad of ways, and the hardy breed for which the imaginative scribes of serialdom wrote survived them all. They say that the pen is mightier than the sword, and that is true. In the case of the motion picture cliff-hanger, there would have been no sword but for the pen—and the penmen. And to one of them must go a dubious distinction:

Having written the first sound serial and the last; having written every type of story produced; and having written for all three major producers of the genre, with over six dozen stories or screenplays to his credit; the title of "Dean of sound serial writers" must go to George H. Plympton. (His colleague on so many ventures, Basil Dickey, would share the honor except for longevity. They were together in 1930 and ran neck-and-neck for twenty years. Dickey's last credit was *Federal Agents vs. Underworld, Inc.*, for Republic in 1949, and Plympton went for seven more years at Columbia to the very end.) In many ways he was the typical example of his fellow writers. Born September 2, 1889, in Brooklyn, New York, he was educated at Cooper Union. His trade biography states he was a "trouble-shooter" for the telephone company in 1909 and in the lumber business from 1910 to 1913. In 1914 he joined Vitagraph as a writer, when serials were just being born. Except for service as an officer in World War I, he continued to write for motion pictures from then on, and for television when it came along. Aware of his responsibility to his community and nation, Lieutenant Plympton moved up in rank to Captain Plympton of the California State Guard during World War II and remained active in the American Legion, as well as the Masonic Lodge. Not only did he span an era, but he helped greatly to make it what it was. And the products of his work—and that of all his fellow craftsmen— while trivial to many, will be remembered fondly for decades to come by the kids who rode the edges of millions of theatre seats since the early 1930's, thrilled by the exploits that sprang from the imaginations of George Plympton and the others of that versatile group of unsung artists —the cliff-hanger writers.

5

A Cheer for the Champions

Inherent to the broad, sweeping adventure tales and intricate, intriguing mystery stories so used of the movie serial was the hero and/or heroine. Defined as the most important person in a story, play or poem (by the use of words and expressions such as "bravery," "great deeds," "noble quality," "daring courage," "valor," "gallantry," "intrepidity," "magniloquent" and "grand"), the character or characters so designated had to be cast with actors and actresses who could project visually and dramatically these attributes to the satisfaction of a peculiarly discerning audience. The standards for acceptance were very rigidly forged, and any attempt to deviate was met with cautious doubt — if not outright suspicion. There were just certain things the action fan expected in his heroes, and to measure up the actor chosen to portray one had to have at least one or two of those qualifications. Of course, the more the better.

One selected to carry the banner vicariously for the next twelve or fifteen weeks for the thousands of would-be champions of justice in theatres across the nation had to be a likeable fellow. No sourpuss, grump, malcontent or axe-grinder could engage the loyalty of those seeking an earnest battle from the lists. A modicum of intelligence was required so that the craftiness of the villain could be dealt with, but it was more important to be rugged and brave, since most threats from the bad guys were physical and taxing rather than devious. Handsomeness — although not required — was highly advantageous as it made identification with the hero much more palatable. Versatility was important in showing that the hero was an accomplished man, capable of trust. To earn that trust from an audience right away, the actor had to be believable. This was particularly true of one playing a superhero from the comics or a familiar character from a well-liked radio series. Those who were not credible did not last long. Finally, to endure the rigors of battle certain to face him, the hero of necessity was athletic. Even with others filling in for him in scenes involving personal danger, an actor portraying the hero was required to account for himself creditably as a man of action in those shots in which he was recognizable as a combatant. A nonathletic thespian had little chance of doing this, and could soon be exposed as an histrionic fraud.

Immediately well-liked — and typical of the affable and engaging young leading men — was Warren Hull. Featured in four of the best-remembered chapterplays of the late thirties — all based on well-known heroes from magazines, comics and radio — this well-groomed, smiling and ruggedly handsome actor became famous in radio and television as well as motion pictures. Perhaps the highlight of his later television career were his years as host of one of the medium's most popular quiz shows — *Strike It Rich* — during which his name became a household word as the man who smilingly gave the money away — even if the answers were not just exactly right — when the contestant's cause was a good one. His first appearance as a serial "main player" was in 1938 as the pulp magazine mystery hero in *The Spider's Web*, in which he portrayed a triple role. In costume of black slouch hat, black mask and flowing black cape, he was the enigmatic Spider. Out of costume, he played the alter ego of the masked crimefighter, socialite Richard Wentworth. His third role was as a one-eyed hoodlum known as "Blinky McQuade," an identity Wentworth assumed when he wanted to go prowling in underworld haunts in search of clues. Early the following year, he appeared in the title role of *Mandrake the Magician* (minus the strip character's famous moustache), and in 1940 was featured again as a masked hero in *The Green Hornet Strikes Again*. Returning to Columbia for his fourth and final role as a serial hero, he again portrayed The Spider in the 1941 sequel *The Spider Returns*.

Republic had a leading man who was also extremely well-liked for his good-natured, disarmingly friendly manner. With a smile and a wink, Robert Livingston played the hero with a deceptively loose abandon that made the audience wonder sometimes if he fully realized the seriousness of the task. They needed have no fear, for Bob always came through in a crisis, retaining the lighthearted charm that later became the trademark of "Stoney Brooke," the character he so ably vivified in the Three Mesquiteers Westerns. A native of Quincey, Illinois, the man who played The Eagle in *The Vigilantes Are Coming* and the masked hero in *The Lone Ranger Rides Again* had also been a writer, and was to rack up some sixty picture credits and many appearances in television series before retiring from acting.

A big, open-faced grin (reminiscent of William Holden and Fred MacMurray) belonged to Lewis Wilson, who portrayed Bruce Wayne in the 1943 *Batman*. Unfortunately for action filmgoers, that was to be his only appearance in a serial.

A likable fellow who survived no less than six slam-bang serial hero roles was something of a paradox. Soft-spoken, with a face that more rightly belonged to a mild-mannered insurance agent than an action hero, Dennis Moore projected that rarely portrayed type of leading man in chapterplays — the put-upon hero. He seemed to be drawn into the fight against his wishes because of his bland manner, but bravely set his course in spite of the fact. And for it, we admired his spunk. This image was misleading, however, as his biographical sketch revealed he was anything but bland.

A native of Texas (he was born Dennis Meadows in Forth Worth), a veteran of the dramatic stage and stock theatre, a commercial pilot for four years, and a physical education director, the handsome young man was well-qualified to play the rugged leading man. His first episodic encounter was with the threat of *The Raiders of Ghost City* in 1944. Next came the cofeatured leading role (shared with Milburn Stone) in *The Master Key*, followed by his confrontation with the title menace of *The Purple Monster Strikes* in 1945. Again sharing the lead (this time with Richard Martin), Moore was then featured in *The Mysterious Mr. M* in 1946. Nearly a decade later, he returned to Western serial roles at Columbia in *Perils of the Wilderness* and *Blazing the Overland Trail*, the last continued picture ever released.

Donald Barry made only one serial, but it led to a career in Westerns and features that spanned forty years. Following the popular hit *The Adventures of Red Ryder* in 1940, Barry retained the nickname "Red" from the title role and was billed by Republic for several years in a succession of highly profitable Westerns as Don "Red" Barry. With a jaunty carriage and high-pitched, husky voice that clipped out his lines in an unmistakably authoritative tone, the swaggering young hero brought to mind as much as anything else a confident, self-assured gamecock.

(The audiences liked the aggressiveness of the young actor, but his demeanor was not always so appreciated offscreen. In a discussion with George "Gabby" Hayes in 1949 — while he was in town for a personal appearance — Barry's name came up, and the grizzled old thespian gave me his personal assessment of the young man some thought of as brash. He said that the fiery Texan had earned a reputation among some of their contemporaries as being arrogant and somewhat belligerent because of a short temper and apparent egoism, but that he had seen beyond those very human shortcomings an actor of considerable stature and a human being of quality. Of Don Barry, "Gabby" said simply, "We get along fine. I like him.")

Born Donald Barry de Acosta in Houston, Texas, he retained the first two names for his career in motion pictures, which has included — in addition to his serial — features, Westerns and television. During World War II, he traveled overseas to entertain troops while he was one of the top ten money-making Western stars. One of his finest portrayals was in the 20th Century–Fox tribute to the armed forces in 1944 — *The Purple Heart* — and since then he has played in numerous roles in major motion pictures (MGM's *I'll Cry Tomorrow*, Warners' *Seven Men from Now*, etc.) as well as television (*Batman* for laughs, *Wild Wild West* as a villain, etc.). A proficient performer, he has portrayed many characters well.

There was an aura of wisdom and human understanding about Harry Carey, Sr., which bespoke intelligence. Not a handsome man by physical standards, he projected a feeling of trust and confidence in his screen roles that gave an impression that he had a good mind as well as a good heart. His three starring sound serial roles — *The Vanishing Legion*, *The Devil Horse* and *The Last of the Mohicans* — were memorable for the quality he injected into them. From Universal's *Graft* in 1915 (a twenty-chapter thriller) to his character roles in major features (including the above chapterplays for Mascot), his hallmark was the image of a decent man who could think straight. So the serial audience took him to their hearts as an accepted hero.

In a more urbane way, Kent Taylor also projected the image of the intelligent hero. In his lone serial appearance in *Gangbusters*, he and co-star Robert Armstrong illustrated well the calm, deliberate and analytical skills of the efficient law officers they were supposed to be. A native of Nashua, Iowa, where he was born Louis Weiss in 1907, Taylor was featured in dozens of feature motion pictures and starred as Boston Blackie in television. In all of them he displayed keen perception and a knowledgeable air, but is remembered for none of them any more fondly than as the dynamic hero of *Gangbusters*.

Of the rugged, rough-and-tumble heroes, none was more so than Jock Mahoney. A big, handsome fellow and an accomplished stuntman — having taken the licks and spills for many leading stars — he was a natural for serial stardom as a hero. Born Jacques O'Mahoney in Chicago in 1919 and educated at the University of Iowa, where he excelled in swimming, basketball and football, he was a United States Marine Corps fighter pilot instructor during World War II. Entering the bone-crushing stunt field, Mahoney established a following of substantial size among action fans as Charles Starrett's double in the "Durango Kid" series, even though he received either supporting billing or no billing at all. All the kids knew when "Durango" went into action it was really Jock and not Starrett providing the thrills. From Jacques to Jack to Jocko to Jock, and from O'Mahoney to Mahoney, Columbia's then-new action star played the lead in *Cody of the Pony Express*, *Roar of the Iron Horse* and *Gunfighters of the Northwest* before going on to stardom in big-budget Westerns and action features at Universal, two television series — *The Range Rider* and *Yancey Derringer* — and as the movies' thirteenth Tarzan.

A key member of the "John Ford stock company" (which included such action veterans as Ward Bond, John Wayne, Victor McLaglen and Paul Fix), former salesman, reporter and movie extra, Grant Withers acquitted himself admirably as a battling hero in Mascot's *The Fighting Marines* and Universal's *Radio Patrol* (sharing honors with Adrian

Morris), and again for Universal as the title hero of *Jungle Jim*. Also a big man, Withers could convey a look of grim determination as a hero, or what could best be described as a glower for heavy roles — so he played either with ease. From Pueblo, Colorado, with a military background, he became identified with some of the movies' outstanding action films as a leading player and supporting actor. In fight scenes he was always in the thick of things, providing his share of thrills.

Tom Neal made the character Jack Stanton in Republic's *Jungle Girl* memorable in the face of great odds. With its emphasis on the unfamiliar existence of a female lead, the film could have very easily relegated the male hero to a supporting role, but the aggressive and positive manner with which he portrayed Stanton kept Neal established firmly in the foreground of the action. As the strange sight of a Tarzan-type girl riding astride an elephant or swinging gracefully through the trees gave the audience a new kind of thrill, it was the fighting, struggling conventional hero that eventually saved the day. His rugged determination and fighting spirit were later displayed again in *Bruce Gentry*.

Experience as a stage actor, professional football player and coach at Notre Dame (where he received his education) helped Harry Albershart of Mishawaka, Indiana, convince serial fans of his qualification to portray the best-known literary exponent of the adage, "he always gets his man." Known later to movie audiences as Allan "Rocky" Lane, he became popular as the famed title hero of Republic's *King of the Royal Mounted* and its sequel. Following them with *Daredevils of the West* and *The Tiger Woman* in 1943 and 44, "Rocky" went on to greater fame and designation as a Top Ten Western Money-maker as Red Ryder in the Republic Series he inherited when Bill Elliott was elevated to major picture stardom by that studio. One of the most ruggedly handsome of all serial heroes, Lane is remembered by action fans chiefly for his four cliff-hangers, in spite of his credits in dozens of features and Westerns. And he wasn't a bad actor, either. It was his modulated, expressive delivery that led to his unbilled fame as the voice of "Mister Ed," the talking horse, on television.

To have a handsome face was not a stringent requirement for an actor to play a serial hero, but it didn't hurt. One who qualified well in that department was Kane Richmond. With a strong chin, chiseled features and clear, piercing eyes topped by a wide brow and shock of well-groomed, wavy hair, he kept many a young female fan returning each week to sigh at his good looks. That was just a bonus for them, though. Fortunately, he also brought all the other attributes of a good cliff-hanger champion to his roles, which kept the boys interested as well. Starting in the film business as a salesman using his own name of Fred Bowditch, the young Minneapolis athlete first appeared in motion pictures in 1930 at the age of 24 in Universal's twelve-film *Leather Pushers* series. From those he moved on to leading roles at MGM, Fox and Columbia for several years, and in 1935 the first two of seven chapter-hero roles—*The Adventures of Rex and Rinty* for Nat Levine and *The Lost City* for Regal. During the late thirties he appeared in a number of Universal episode thrillers in a variety of supporting roles and also was featured in many action and dramatic features. Kicking off a second stint of serial hero roles that stretched up to 1947, Richmond took the lead in *Spy Smasher* in 1942. Again at Republic he headed the cast in the 1944 thriller *Haunted Harbor* and then joined Sam Katzman at Columbia for his final three chapterplays. Katzman starred him in his first two releases for the studio in 1945—*Brenda Starr Reporter* and *Jungle Raiders*. Then, following his starring roles in three 1946 mystery features as The Shadow for Monogram, Richmond culminated his serial career back at Columbia in *Brick Bradford*; the production that served as the forerunner of a spate of science-fiction thrillers from Katzman and his rivals at Republic.

A handsome, wavy-haired hero in three mystery cliff-hangers was Charles Quigley. A stage actor educated at the American Academy of Dramatic Art, the young man from New Britain, Connecticut, who was to become one-third of serialdom's most colorful acrobatic triumvirate (*The Daredevils of the Red Circle*) first appeared in motion pictures in 1935 in a Tom Keene Western. From then on he was featured in a number of pictures of many different types, ranging from the mystery and adventure yarns of a famous Oriental detective (*Charlie Chan's Secret*, Fox 1935) to a country and western musical (*National Barn Dance*, Paramount 1944) and including first-rank comedy from a famous radio program (*Duffy's Tavern*, Paramount 1945). Along the way he starred as the hero in *The Iron Claw* and *The Crimson Ghost*.

Robert Lowery played romantic leads in more program pictures than probably even he can remember. But later in television it was his lot to be cast mainly as a suave villain because of his by-then matured good looks. In 1945 he was the hero of *The Monster and the Ape*, desperately trying to corner the menacing villain. Just six months before its release, he had played in Universal's *Mystery of the Riverboat* as the scion of an old New Orleans family involved in a real estate deal swirling around some seemingly worthless bayou territory (actually containing oil) and a riverboat owned by his girl's father. (This part may have helped serve as background for his later roles as the riverboat-saloon gambler type on television.) Born Robert Lowery Hanks in Kansas City, he dropped the last name for his career, which varied from orchestra singer to superhero via little theatres and the aforementioned feature films. His role as a superhero came in the 1949 sequel to *Batman*. In *Batman and Robin* he portrayed the "caped crusader" and his alter ego, Bruce Wayne.

Another tall, handsome leading man in two serials became (for a while) television's Lone Ranger, but relinquished the part after a time and wound up in supporting roles. In 1947, John Hart was starring as *Jack Armstrong*, the All-American Boy, in Sam Katzman's serialization of the famous radio series. The early fifties found him playing The Lone Ranger in the syndicated television series prior to the return and permanent establishment of Clayton Moore in the role; and in 1956 Hart helped close out the serial era in the title role in *The Adventures of Captain Africa*. All during that time it was not at all unusual to see Hart crop up in a Western, a serial or television film in a minor part as one of the gang, part of the crowd, or a walk-on in a single scene — often unbilled and unexpected, but always noticeable because of his striking good looks.

Robert Kellard left a lasting impression on serial fans as Corporal Tom Merritt, Jr., in *King of the Royal Mounted* when in the last chapter he knocked out fellow-captive King in the torpedo room of an escaping enemy submarine, ejected his unconscious form through an empty torpedo tube to safety, and then blew up the submarine to prevent its escape, killing all the villains in one heroic, sacrificial gesture. He is remembered for this scene most vividly, even though in his three other serial roles he portrayed the hero rather than the secondary assistant. Just six months earlier he had appeared as Allan Parker in *Drums of Fu Manchu* for Republic. Then, after playing in Columbia's *Perils of the Royal Mounted* in 1942 (billed as Robert Stevens), the broodingly handsome young man returned to the surname Kellard for feature roles and his final serial, *Tex Granger*.

In the early fifties, following the successes of *Brick Bradford* and *King of the Rocketmen*, Republic produced for television a series of twelve 26-minute science-fiction adventures with a new hero named "Commando Cody," who used the "Rocketman" flying suit in his exploits. Also at that time one of the most popular television heroes for the kids was the intrepid Captain Video. Out of these grew the career of Judd Holdren, a young actor with the noncommittal good looks of a TV newscaster or commercial announcer. When Sam Katzman secured film rights to the popular series *Captain Video and the Video Rangers*, he cast young Holdren as the hero because of his Cody portrayal and released *Captain Video* in December 1951. He appeared in another Katzman release 18 months later, that time in an original sci-fi-thriller *The Lost Planet*, as space hero Rex Barrow. In the meantime, he returned to Republic to play a Commando Cody-type hero (with Rocket flying suit, et al.) in *Zombies of the Stratosphere*.

One of Katzman's most unusual leading players did not fit the accepted mold at all. With curly blond hair, a boyish twinkle in his eye and a neat cleft in his well-shaped chin, Richard Crane had played in many features — usually as a student, a young serviceman or romantic interest — before trying a cliff-hanger. His playing a daring serial hero seemed somewhat incongruous at first, but then the role he was to play was not one usually associated with serials, either. Columbia had secured film rights to Jules Verne's *The Isle of Mystery*, and Katzman was planning it as a fifteen-chapter film. As an escaping Civil War Union Army officer who became involved with futuristic beings from the planet

Mercury on a deserted island in 1865, the story's leading character, Captain Harding, had to look like a man of the past as well as the future. The athletic but youthful-looking Crane filled the bill just right, and *Mysterious Island* became one more of Katzman's long string of winners. Two years later, when another out-of-the-ordinary role was called for — that of young British naval officer Richard Dale in *The Great Adventures of Captain Kidd* — Katzman again engaged Crane for the part and came up with serialdom's final pirate film.

In the title role as the colorful buccaneer Captain William Kidd was John Crawford, one of the few versatile actors who could be equally convincing as a good guy or a bad guy. Usually performing in a supporting role as either an assistant or a henchman, *Captain Kidd* was his most memorable role, and it was most fitting. Kidd himself was a paradoxical figure in the annals of naval history. A hero of King William's War against the French and Indians, he went to London in 1695 for a commission from the Crown to hunt down and arrest all pirates of the high seas. Instead of doing that, he apparently became one himself and subsequently was convicted and hanged for his crimes, which had become legendary. History contains much doubt about the extent of Kidd's actual guilt and raises the question of the fairness of his trial and execution — and around that doubt was written the character portrayed by Crawford. The serial ended with the conclusion that he was misjudged, though history records he was a convicted criminal. The casting of good-bad guy John Crawford lent credence to the theory and left young audiences still wondering.

Another actor who could "switch-hit" from hero to bad guy with ease was Harry Lauter, who continued doing the same thing in television. Conversely appearing in a *Tarzan* episode for NBC as a scraggly, brutal hunter and a frightened, victimized bar and grill operator in a *Green Hornet* stint for ABC, he could evoke animosity or sympathy equally well. Serial-wise, Lauter's hedge-hopping goes back to the early fifties, when he appeared as a tight-lipped henchman in *Flying Disc Man from Mars*. Deciding the grimly determined visage of the handsome young man could also be used on the good side, the studio cast him as hero Bill Henry's aide in *Canadian Mounties vs. Atomic Invaders*, then elevated him to "main player" in *Trader Tom* and *King of the Carnival*.

Lauter thus followed in the tradition of versatility previously exemplified by veteran thespian Reed Hadley. This literally tall, dark and handsome actor has played as a matter of fact a variety of roles including "doctor, lawyer, Indian chief," as well as hero, villain, lawman and thief. He was the only actor to play the *original* Zorro in a serial (*Zorro's Fighting Legion*), then turned right around and played the villainous leader of a mountain tribe in *Adventures of Captain Marvel* the next year. His deep, enunciative voice forebodingly gave the documentary flavor to Fox's classic spy film *The House on 92nd Street*, and was Red Ryder on the radio. He played lawman Wild Bill Hickok in Warners' *Dallas*, was shot in the back by his own man in Lippert's *I Shot Jesse James*, and played a down-and-out, has-been sheriff rejuvenated by Rory Calhoun in an episode of the latter's television series *The Texan*. Himself a Texan, born in Petrolia, the man with the imposing glare and take-charge manner worked as a floorwalker while gaining acting experience in little theatre productions, then played in stock companies before moving into motion pictures and radio. His ability as a narrator was utilized profusely in television, and he did dozens of documentary jobs for that medium, while also starring in two adventure series — *Racket Squad* and *Public Defender*.

A hero-turned-villain-turned-hero-again became one of the genre's most prolific leading men. Matched in number of hero roles by very few cliff-hanger stars — and exceeded by perhaps only one — Clayton Moore also appeared as the villain's top henchman in two serials and very nearly stole the spotlight from the hero in those. The first of his eight hero stints was in *Perils of Nyoka*, in which he was billed second to the heroine but still managed to establish himself as a leading man with a future. Following the close of the war, Republic completed one of its more popular mystery serials, *The Crimson Ghost*, with Moore cast as Ashe, chief lieutenant of the unknown mystery villain. Since The Ghost was not seen, the henchman Ashe was for practical purposes the primary adversary of hero Charles Quigley. The running battle of wits and fists between those two gave that chapterplay a quality of action long remembered by ardent fans. The following year, Moore starred as the hero in *Jesse James Rides Again* for Mike Frankovich, and followed with leading roles in *G-Men Never Forget* for him, and *The Adventures of Frank and Jesse James* and *The Ghost of Zorro* for Frank Adreon before becoming television's original Lone Ranger in 1949. After the first season, Moore was replaced by John Hart as the "masked rider of the plains," but the replacement was temporary. Realizing the public liked Moore in the role better than Hart, the producers reassigned him to the part, and there he continued through many years of television and two major color features for the movies. In the meantime, he had starred in *Son of Geronimo* for Columbia and been featured in his second henchman's role (as Graber in *Radar Men from the Moon*) at Republic. His last two serial roles came in 1953, the year before he starred in the first of the two major features. Co-starring with Jock Mahoney, he completed *Gunfighters of the Northwest* at Columbia and wound up his serial career back at Republic with *Jungle Drums of Africa*. After that, the role of The Lone Ranger consumed all of his time — with production and promotion tours — and he became to an entire generation of young Americans the personification of Fran Striker's great hero.

To convincingly portray such a famous figure as The Lone Ranger, Clayton Moore had another quality which was vitally essential in an actor cast as a hero — believability. The kids could accept him without reservation simply because they could believe that maybe he really *was*

The Lone Ranger. Part of this was due to the fact that he never appeared in public in costume without the mask, and was never billed as actor Clayton Moore except in the official credits of the films. But it was also the result of his complete submersion into the character and his startling physical resemblance to the collective image conceived by the millions of radio listeners.

The first motion picture Lone Ranger, Lee Powell, had also possessed believability. Although his serial career was a short one, he is remembered as the hero of two of the period's most outstanding successes. In addition to *The Lone Ranger* he costarred as Lieutenant Tom Grayson in *The Fighting Devil Dogs*, and both of these 1938 releases have to be included on any list of the ten best sound serials of all. The next year he appeared in a major supporting role in Universal's *Flash Gordon Conquers the Universe* and then left the serial field. From an ill-fated series of Westerns at Grand National (only one film was completed before the company expired), he embarked on a brief tour of personal appearances billed as "The Lone Ranger of the Movies," but was forced to discontinue it on legal grounds. Returning to Western features at the newly formed Producers Releasing Corporation, Powell costarred in six releases with Bill "Cowboy Rambler" Boyd and Art Davis, displaying again the quiet but forceful manner that gave his roles the strength of credibility. When the war came, he enlisted in the United States Marine Corps. and achieved the grade of sergeant. He was killed in action on the island of Tinian on July 29, 1944, at the age of 36.

Robert Kent took on a formidable adversary in *The Phantom Creeps* for Universal in 1939. Dr. Alex Zorka, played by Bela Lugosi, was determined to rule the world, but the tenacity and courage of young Kent's hero thwarted and eventually smashed his plan. A good-looking fellow, he could easily have been "just another pretty face," but his intense, sincere manner lifted his portrayals above that. His was the only seemingly sane characterization in a cast of mixed-up "kooks" in his role as police investigator Bob Stewart in Columbia's *Who's Guilty?* in 1945. All the others in that complicated melange of victims and suspects, accusers and schemers, seemed lost in a swirl of plots, counterplots and crossplots that none of them could understand. Only the hero seemed capable of a sensible thought, and it was he who eventually unraveled the mess. Not as complicated was his role in *The Phantom Rider* the same year for Republic. Cast as a dedicated frontier doctor come to minister to the needs of the reservation Indians, he assumed the identity of a legendary mystery figure with a hawk-face headdress and grim-visaged life-mask covering his face to flush out and bring to justice a band of renegades who were exploiting them. In features and Westerns, Kent also made a convincing villain by applying the same determined and serious effort into convincing an audience of his evil intent.

One of the finest actors ever to grace the serial screen was Victor

Jory. So authoritative were his booming, rich voice and steely, incisive eyes that when he delivered a line of dialogue one was almost compelled to believe what was said in spite of himself. Although more widely known as an actor of depth in feature films, the two serial roles of this former New York stage writer and performer made fans of youngsters who were captivated by the melodramatic force of the quasi-Shakespearean bearing he often conveyed. This was something new to the action fan. Perfectly suited for the Jory technique was the dual character of Lamont Cranston and his alter ego, The Shadow, in the 1940 Columbia release. In *The Shadow* he was charming and witty as the playboy criminologist Cranston, modulating his cultivated tones to elicit a mood of disarming affability while prying some secret or piece of information out of an unsuspecting dupe, but was sinisterly impelling and dominating as the black-caped man of mystery. Not many actors of that day could have carried it off as convincingly as Victor Jory. Later the same year, he starred in the remake of the Edgar Wallace classic *The Green Archer* playing the part of hero Spike Holland, a private detective. From Dawson City, Alaska, where he was born in 1902, Jory went to the University of California for his education, won a boxing and wrestling championship promoted by the National Guard, and moved East to the New York stage. Entering motion pictures in 1932, he began a career the spanned fifty years. In the same year he starred in his serials, Jory also appeared in a small but memorable part that helped propel him into a lengthy career of villain and tyrant roles. In the most successful motion picture of all time, *Gone with the Wind*, he played the carpetbagger who married a "poor white trash" unwed mother previously helped by Scarlett O'Hara's mother and returned to Tara for a cynical "visit," only to be spat upon by the unreconstructed Scarlett. His reaction was so vehement that the scene became a stand-out in a picture filled with classic scenes. My own best remembrance of the man whose credits lists dozens of major motion pictures and practically every dramatic series in television (including *Manhunt*, in which he starred) is a scene from Warners' *South of St. Louis*, a 1949 release. A swaggering, boasting renegade bully who had incurred the wrath of star Joel McCrea and his two partners, Zachary Scott and Douglas Kennedy, Jory noisily barged into a crowded saloon, ordered up drinks, and loudly began to laughingly proclaim what all he had done and was going to do to the "three bell" partners McCrea, Scott and Kennedy. Midway in his tirade, he suddenly became aware that all eyes were not on him and turned to see the three ranchers nonchalantly stationed just inside the door, ominously watching and listening. The change in his expression from raucous, sneering scorn to disbelief, bewilderment and fear was as if an invisible hand had passed over his face, remolding the emotions from one to the other as it moved. Even in his seventies, Victor Jory still dominated any scene in which he participated.

So believable in the screen role he originated that it affected his entire career was Ralph Byrd, the movies' Dick Tracy. A mature-looking 27 when he first appeared as the comic strip detective in Republic's *Dick Tracy* in the winter of 1936–37, the young actor played the part to the hilt, giving his portrayal such unbridled, exuberant enthusiasm that the resulting excitement was contagious. The serial fans loved him immediately, and to them forever thereafter he *was* Dick Tracy. Even though he would star in three more chapter films as other characters — Jerry Sheehan in *Blake of Scotland Yard*, Terry Kent in *S.O.S. Coast Guard*, and the title role in *The Vigilante* — and would appear in numerous features in supporting roles, his name would never again be mentioned to a serial fan without an immediate identification with Tracy being made. In the following fifteen years, Byrd played the square-jawed, dedicated lawman three more times for Republic, twice for RKO Radio Pictures — *Dick Tracy's Dilemma* and *Dick Tracy Meets Gruesome*, both 1945 features — and finally in a 1951–52 television series for Snader TV Productions. Partially responsible for his success as the famed plainclothes detective was his pronounced physical resemblance to the character. Except for the beak-like nose, which was added to the character later and became a sort of trademark (the original Tracy had a strong but less prominent proboscis), Byrd was a dead-ringer for the Gould characterization. His firm jaw, full, cleft chin, thin-lipped mouth, high cheekbones and piercing eyes, along with a straight, noticeable-enough nose, gave the impression that his might have been the face the cartoonist had in mind when he first drew Tracy. In addition to the physical similarity, Byrd also projected the intense dedication to law and order associated with the strip hero. His was an all-business, no-nonsense demeanor that wasted no time on things not directly related to the case at hand.

(This quality became even more apparent when I met and talked with the actor while he was appearing at the Paramount in Concord in the middle forties. Seeming unusually nervous, Byrd found sitting still quite difficult, was up and pacing when he stayed in a room, darted in and out of his dressing room between shows, and often went to the outer lobby to greet entering patrons — even allowing himself to be ganged up on for questions and autographs on the sidewalk outside. It was as if he could hardly wait to get on with the business of making Ralph Byrd known to every citizen in town. When he did pause for a few minutes for a cup of coffee in the theatre office or to apply makeup just prior to a stage appearance, the talk was of pictures, roles and stories; never of social interests, political beliefs or other activities. For a long time afterward, Concord remembered the day Ralph Byrd was in town and often asked us at the theatre when they would be able to see him in a picture again.)

A native of Dayton, Ohio, veteran of community theatre and radio prior to motion pictures, the personable and extremely believable serial star was married to actress Virginia Carroll and they were the parents of a daughter. His untimely death of a heart attack in 1952 ended a career in action films that had spanned 17 years and had literally given life to one of the most famous pen-and-ink characters of all time.

Not all of the leading men in serials continued in hero roles for several reasons. Some simply did not make it with action fans because of a lack of one or more of the requirements for full acceptance. Others moved on to different types of parts in features and radio. And some felt steady work in continued pictures would restrict their ambitions to become known in major productions. For whatever reason, most of those who moved on left some memorable mark on the genre by their solo performances:

Gordon Jones had originated the role of The Green Hornet for Universal and then became a top character actor portraying affable cops, tough-guy-with-heart-of-gold comic sidekicks, glib cab drivers and good-natured pugs. Tom Brown, who was Smilin' Jack for the same studio, became the perennial brash young man in dozens of features, often playing student types and cocky young rookies in service and military films. Robert Wilcox — alias The Copperhead in *Mysterious Dr. Satan* — appeared in several low-budget features while still in motion pictures, usually as a romantic lead. Dick Purcell, who had gone from the stage to films and made his way through a host of B action thrillers and mysteries at Warners and Monogram before starring in *Captain America* for Republic, might have become a leading serial hero but for his unexpected death in 1944 just several months after completing that serial. Marten Lamont was a suave, urbane hero in *Federal Operator 99*, but did not make any more serials after that 1945 release for Republic. The same year, Richard Bailey turned in a creditable job as the hero in their *Manhunt of Mystery Island*, but then began appearing in minor roles in important feature films, mostly cast as an Army officer or government official. Bruce Edwards, a big (6 feet, 6 inches) rugged-looking actor, was featured in *The Black Widow* in 1947 and — like Larry Thompson, another husky and handsome hero type who played in *King of the Forest Rangers* a year earlier — had been presented as a possible contender for serial stardom, but did not stay in the genre. In 1948 associate producer Mike Frankovich cast tall, sombre-faced Jim Bannon as the hero in *Dangers of the Canadian Mounted*, but Jim's prominence was to come later in detective and spy films for Columbia, and as the famous redheaded cowboy Red Ryder in a color series at Eagle Lion. Richard Webb, who became typecast in features as an F.B.I. agent and federal official, delivered a convincing portrayal as a hero of that stripe in *The Invisible Monster* in 1950. Others who contributed only one leading role in serials but were quite active in action features were Paul Kelly (The Black Commando in *The Secret Code*), Robert Scott (of *Black Arrow*), Russell Hayden and Richard Martin (heroes respectively in *The Lost City of the Jungle* and *The Mysterious Mr. M*), George Turner (*Son of Zorro*), Keith Richards (*The*

James Brothers of Missouri), Richard Powers (*Desperadoes of the West*), George Wallace (*Radar Men from the Moon*), Bill Henry (*Canadian Mounties vs. Atomic Invaders*), Myron Healey (*Panther Girl of the Kongo*) and Richard Simmons, television's *Sergeant Preston of the Yukon*, (*Man with the Steel Whip*). Walter Reed, readily recognized for his countless appearances in features and television in character roles, was featured as the hero in two for Republic in 1951—*Flying Disc Man from Mars* and *Government Agents vs. the Phantom Legion*—but also found his major calling elsewhere.

By far the most popular actors of all as serial heroes—and also the most prolific—were the athletes. Although all of them had to be athletic to endure the physical demands of the many action scenes involving the hero, those who stood out were the men who were obviously trained athletes, who made the most difficult human effort seem easy. Now, these were men a young boy could identify with! Many of those already mentioned were fine athletes as well as bearing the other qualities attributed to them, just as the actors we think of as outstanding athletes also possessed many of their characteristics. The distinction is made to recognize that pictorially the performances of the athletes were aesthetically more adroit. Since the role of serial hero was broad and exaggerated, it was invariably more pleasing to see it portrayed by one who could expand in physical effort sufficiently to meet the requirement. This was best done by the trained athlete. A small handful of leading men were eminently qualified to represent that type of hero.

In any discourse on athletic prowess, the role of the most famous of all fictional athletes must be included. Superman was the creation of two young men named Jerome Siegel and Joseph Shuster, who wrote and drew the strip respectively. He has appeared as a drawn character in comic books, newspapers, magazines and propoganda leaflets and in motion picture and television animated series, and has been portrayed by actors Kirk Alyn and Christopher Reeve in movies and George Reeves on television. The personification of the bigger-than-life exaggerated hero, it was natural to build a serial around his exploits, so producer Sam Katzman did so in 1948 and again in 1950. Both times he cast as the "man of steel" young Alyn, who resembled as much as anyone could the handsome Superman, and who possessed the coy wit expected of his alter ego, Clark Kent. Alyn had gone to Hollywood with experience on the Broadway stage and had already appeared in Republic's *Daughter of Don Q*, in which he costarred with Adrian Booth, and was cast for another by that studio, *Federal Agents vs. Underworld, Inc.* In addition to those four, he was also to star in another for each studio, bringing his total to six hero roles in as many years. As a federal agent assigned to set up a radar defense warning system, he appeared in Republic's *Radar Patrol vs. Spy King* in 1950, and portrayed another comic strip hero in the 1952 *Blackhawk*. When produced on the screen as a feature movie and as a series on television, Superman was portrayed by George Reeves, a superbly built athlete who had previously starred in *Adventures of Sir Galahad* and had appeared in numerous features, including a bit part in *Gone with the Wind* (as one of Scarlett O'Hara's suitors) and a major role (as Claudette Colbert's lover) in Paramount's *So Proudly We Hail*. Reeves was from Woodstock, Iowa, and had experience in little theatre groups and many Hopalong Cassidy Westerns before appearing in such features as *Till We Meet Again, Winged Victory, Samson and Delilah, The Good Humor Man* and *From Here to Eternity*. His career was cut short by untimely death.

A veteran of silent Westerns whose first all-talking film was a serial became one of the most prolific of the genre's heroes. Tom Tyler — real name, Vincent Markowski — made his debut in MGM's *Ben Hur* in 1924 as an extra, hired because of his muscular physique, which he had developed by weightlifting. Born in Port Henry, New York, and reared in Detroit, Michigan, the son of a factory worker, Vincent worked his way across the country to Los Angeles to try for a movie career. After *Ben Hur* he appeared in *The Only Thing*, an Elinor Glyn feature, before going to FBO studios to star in Westerns. His first was *Let's Go Gallagher* in 1925 and was followed by some twenty-five others for FBO during the next four years. Eight silent releases for Syndicate Pictures in 1929–30 preceded his first serial, *Phantom of the West* for Mascot, that same year. After several more all-talking Westerns back at Syndicate, Tom then portrayed the legendary Colonel William F. Cody, complete with moustache, goatee and long, flowing hair, in Universal's *Battling with Buffalo Bill* in 1931. For the next eight years, the young veteran continued to ride, fight and shoot his way through dozens of Westerns for Monogram, Monarch, Reliable, RKO (formerly FBO) and Victory, while starring in three more serials for Universal — *Jungle Mystery* in 1932, and *Clancy of the Mounted* and *Phantom of the Air* in 1933. Then came several nonhero parts to attest to his ability as an actor. He made a vivid impression as the villainous Luke Plummer in John Ford's masterpiece *Stagecoach* in 1939, and followed with non-Western roles in *Gone with the Wind, Brother Orchid* and *The Mummy's Hand* (as Kharis, the mummy). Tyler was 37 years old when he made *The Adventures of Captain Marvel*, but still possessed one of the finest physiques in Hollywood. His striking performance as the red-clad superhuman remains in thousands of minds as the most memorable serial hero of all time — bar none. So successful was that film that Republic immediately put Tyler into their Three Mesquiteers series as costar with Bob Steele and comic Rufe Davis, to capitalize on his popularity. The resulting productions proved to be among the all-time top money-makers of all the studio's Westerns. Tom's final serial role was as the title hero in *The Phantom* for Columbia, a characterization that was even more vivid than *Marvel* but slightly less memorable. With a total of seven serials to his credit, Tom Tyler stands as one of the most prominent stars of the continued picture, and deserves his place among the leaders.

Ray Corrigan began his screen career as an action star in 1936. The 28 year old native of Milwaukee, Wisconsin, who had changed his last name to Corrigan from Benard, was one of the original costars of *The Three Mesquiteers*, the first of a long line of Westerns that would affect the careers of several of Hollywood's leading Western stars including Tyler, Steele, John Wayne and the other costars of the series — Robert Livingston and Max Terhune. The same year, he starred as "Crash" Corrigan in *Undersea Kingdom*, Nat Levine's second serial under the new Republic banner. His handsome physique and uninhibited enthusiasm for his role overcame some unsuitable dialogue, and he justified the rather ostentatious name of "Crash" sufficiently as to make it palatable. So well did he make it stick that it stayed with him throughout his acting career. He also appeared as Captain Fremont, an American Army officer, in *The Vigilantes Are Coming*. The following year he starred in his only other serial role in which he was recognizable. As Clark Stewart, representative of the United States government to Mexico, he was the hero of *The Painted Stallion*, one of the best Western serials ever released. In other chapter films thereafter, Corrigan played an important but not easily identifiable role — as a gorilla! Dressed up in a specially designed suit, he appeared without billing as one of the most hideous-looking jungle primates on film. While he continued to star as one of the Mesquiteers — and later at Monogram in an imitation of that series known as The Range Busters — Corrigan kept an "ace in the hole." Securing some of the most picturesque real estate in California, he made it available to movie and television producers for location filming at some highly attractive rates. His ranch, known as Corriganville and containing landmarks and scenery so often photographed for a variety of Westerns and outdoor action films, thus became familiar to millions of fans across the country, and is famous today as a tourist attraction.

Tarzan, the supreme human athlete, has had many faces and forms on the screen — from the barrel-chested primitive ape-man of Elmo Lincoln in 1918 to the thin, literate, urbane jungle hero of Ron Ely fifty years later. One of the most fondly remembered by genuine Edgar Rice Burroughs buffs was the sinewy, articulate, graceful Tarzan of Herman Brix in 1935. Prior to Brix, seven actors had played the jungle champion in 12 motion pictures, none of which had been filmed in a real jungle, and neither of which had presented Tarzan as Burroughs had created him: an educated English Lord who lived in the jungle by personal preference. When plans were made to take an expedition to Guatamala to film an on-the-scene jungle chapterplay, the title role was given to Brix, and the resulting physical feats of that superb athlete have never been surpassed since. Eminently qualified to play such a coveted and demanding role, Brix was a star athlete in his own right. A native of Tacoma, Washington,

Herman had achieved the status of all-American football star at the University of Washington and was a shot put champion in the 1932 Olympics. His performance in *The New Adventures of Tarzan* stands as one of the best. Quickly becoming very popular as a result of it, Brix signed with Sam Katzman to be featured in the Bela Lugosi thriller *Shadow of Chinatown* in 1936 and moved over to Republic to star in *The Fighting Devil Dogs* and *Hawk of the Wilderness* in 1938 and *Daredevils of the Red Circle* in 1939, all of which benefited greatly from his magnificent athletic abilities. In an effort to seek a new career in features, Brix changed his name to Bruce Bennett in the early forties and appeared in such outstanding films as *Sabotage, The More the Merrier, Sahara, The Man I Love, Dark Passage* and *Treasure of the Sierra Madre.* He was quite successful as a featured player in many motion pictures, and later in character parts in television dramas. But to serial fans he never really became Bruce Bennett. He was always the stalwart Herman Brix — our favorite Tarzan, the good Kioga, one of the best Marines there ever was, and one-third of the most unforgettable team of daredevil serial heroes who ever leaped from a burning building "in the nick of time."

If there could be a crown for "King" of the sound serials, it would rest rakishly on the head of Clarence Linden Crabbe, better known as "Larry" and best known as "Buster." Not only did his career as a serial hero span the entire sound era of the form, he also starred in more of them than any other actor, and created for the screen more different characters from other media than anyone else. The going rate for the other leaders in the hero business was from three-or-four (Lane, Livingston, Mahoney, Quigley, Kellard and Hull) up to six-or-seven (Richmond, Brix, Byrd, Tyler, Moore and Alyn), and Crabbe starred in nine. (If you count the two in which he played a bad guy, only Clayton Moore surpassed that number with ten, but he played the hero in only eight.) Barry, Lane, Neal, Hart, Wilson and Kellard (Stevens) portrayed one character each from comic strips or radio; Alyn, Tyler, Richmond and Byrd each played two; and Hull accounted for three. Buster Crabbe created no less than six: Tarzan, Flash Gordon, Red Barry, Buck Rogers, Captain Silver and Thunda. And, although his good-humored, ingratiating manner and dashing bravura were evident in every appearance, each character stands out in retrospect as different and unique. When he was two years old, Buster's family moved to Hawaii from Oakland, California, where he was born in 1909, and it was there he grew up, developing his athletic skills to the point of near-perfection. While in high school in Honolulu, he became an outstanding boxer and was winner of the light heavyweight championship of the city — a talent that later made his convincing screen fights seem so realistic. His major forte, however, was swimming, and he excelled in that sport so highly that he was chosen to compete in the 1932 Olympics at Los Angeles. Young Crabbe returned to California to break several world swimming records in those games, and was spotted by movie talent scouts who were immediately impressed by his handsome features and magnificent build. He was signed by Paramount Pictures and quickly put to work in the H.G. Wells thriller *Island of Lost Souls*, which starred Charles Laughton and Bela Lugosi. Then he was cast as a jungle hero similar to Tarzan in Paramount's 1933 release, *King of the Jungle*, which was followed by a succession of Western and action roles for that studio that began a considerable fan following for the young athlete. In the meantime, he was loaned out to producer Sol Lesser to star as Tarzan himself in the Principal Pictures release *Tarzan the Fearless*, which was designed to be shown as either a feature or a twelve-chapter serial. Following a variety of action and college sports roles for his home studio, Buster was loaned out again in 1936, this time to Universal for the thirteen-chapter fantasy *Flash Gordon*. Such was his impact as a serial hero that Universal immediately began work on the first sequel in order to cash in on Crabbe's popularity. No sooner was that done than they began work on another popular comic strip property to star the famous young man – Will Gould's Chinatown detective, *Red Barry*. Switching to yet another space hero, the studio then starred him as *Buck Rogers* in their futuristic twelve-chapter cliff-hanger and released it in 1939. A year later came the third chapter thriller based on Alex Raymond's great comics creation – *Flash Gordon Conquers the Universe* – and by then Buster Crabbe was firmly established as the outstanding serial hero of the decade. Turning to Western stardom, he signed with Producers Releasing Corporation in 1941 and subsequently ground out over forty films with his bearded sidekick, former Keystone Kop Al "Fuzzy" St. John. In 1947, Sam Katzman contracted with Crabbe to appear in his modern-day pirate adventure *The Sea Hound* as the popular Captain Silver, and the result was so satisfactory that 36 months later he was again on movie screens in a follow-up similar to it called *Pirates of the High Seas* (the only serial in which he did not portray an already known character from comics or radio). His final serial role before going on to independent production in television and subsequent major studio features again was as Thunda, *King of the Congo*, for Katzman and Columbia in 1952. By that time, Buster Crabbe had a son who was well on the way to being grown; and he and Cullen (nicknamed "Cuffy") starred in the television series *Foreign Legionnaire*, along with popular Western comedian Fuzzy Knight, thrilling yet another generation of action fans who would remember with a smile the grinning, friendly face atop the big, muscular build, striding confidently through another adventure, firm in the knowledge that his cause was just and his purpose right.

Requirements were no less stringent for the actresses who would play the heroines. Even though in most serials (as in most Westerns and B action features) the heroine was secondary to the hero, she was expected to possess those qualities of courage, bravery and daring that the hero exhibited, as well as those of attractiveness and vulnerability peculiar to her sex. In order that she appear worthy of the effort they knew would be spent by the hero (and for her to deserve his ultimate obeisance and companionship), the action fans expected complete loyalty and unqualified support for him from the heroine. Given that, they obligingly gave her in return the same degree of concern and anxiety as the hero during her moments of peril and danger. As pointed out, there were notable examples of a reversal of this concept — *Perils of Nyoka, Zorro's Black Whip, Daughter of Don Q,* etc. — where the heroine was the chief (or at least equal) activist for the good side. To satisfy all these requirements primarily or secondarily — there were also definable attributes sought in actresses being considered for a heroine's role.

It was mandatory for her to have presence — to be noticeable. Due to the melodramatic nature of the serial, there was a challenge to the heroine not to be subdued and relegated to the background by the deliberate and intensive emoting required of the male principals. Since she was not usually given the main story line to convey, the best chance for the heroine to stay in the game was to have a screen presence strong enough to pervade the scene without appearing to dominate it. In many cases this was accomplished not by great beauty (although most of the serial heroines were extremely good-looking girls) but by an earnest enthusiasm for the plans of the hero, which registered well with the mostly quite-young action fan who wanted to see the plan gotten on with. A pretty actress, of course, drew more attention than one who was not, so physical appearance was very important; but the image projected had to be wholesome and natural rather than sensual and sophisticated. Fortunate was the young lady who could project both, however, for occasionally there was a call for a villainess, and it was just those qualities of sensuality, mystery and sophistication that immediately tagged a female as "bad." Serial heroines were a durable lot, and they needed to be. Their trials and tribulations are the ones most vividly remembered and most often constituted the tests that proved the mettle of the heroes.

To match the crown of the "King" — if there was one — would be a jewelled, feminine replica for the sound serial's "Queen," and it would perch prettily atop the head of Linda Stirling. A beautiful, long-limbed model from Long Beach, California, the tall slim girl born Louise Shultz was one of the most prolific of the serial heroines, with no less than six releases to her credit — all at Republic — all filmed within a short three-year span. Tested without a camera by producer William O'Sullivan, director Spencer Bennet and stunt expert Yakima Canutt on the basis of her fame as a model, the lovely Linda was hired in 1944 to star in *The Tiger Woman* after the veteran filmmaking trio were satisfied that she moved and walked, ran and jumped, and mounted and rode a horse in a visual manner well enough to be accepted by action fans. Accepted she was, and immediately. Not since Nyoka several years before had the serial audience been treated to such a delight as a beautiful, lively, activist heroine, and they loved her right away. So pleased was Republic at her impact that they quickly went into production on *Zorro's Black Whip* with Linda starred in the lead role (the "main player") as "The Whip," a masked hero in the tradition of Zorro, whose descendant she was by implication. Employing charm and feminine wiles rather than disguise and subterfuge to conceal her identity, and using a long black whip and jiu jitsu instead of a gun and fisticuffs in her encounters with the bad guys, Linda created a unique and memorable champion — a female hero — and is still remembered today for it. Less flamboyant but no less impressive were her successive cliff-hanger roles. As the niece of the professor whose body was comandeered by the cosmic villain in *The Purple Monster Strikes*, Linda struggled side-byside with hero Dennis Moore to hunt down and stop the menace from space. In *Manhunt of Mystery Island* she played the daughter of a kidnapped scientist being forced to work for the piratical Mephisto, and in her efforts to free him became involved in as many of the action scenes as the hero. Again she stood out in a cast dominated by the imposing visage of the title menace in *The Crimson Ghost*, and was then gracing the sets of *Jesse James Rides Again* when her serial career was abruptly altered by that perennial terminator of feminine careers — marriage. During the filming of that production, Linda was wooed, won and wed by writer Sloan Nibley, and her screen appearances thereafter were few — especially after the arrival of her sons Chris and Tim. Although brief by comparison with some others, her career had a definite impact upon serials in the mid-forties, and assuredly qualified her as the form's "Queen" — the latter-day "Pauline." Of the characteristics necessary in a heroine, Linda Stirling possessed all — presence, wholesomeness, beauty and versatility — and any single one would have been sufficient in her case.

Perhaps the most typical of the heroines with presence was pert, vivacious Peggy Stewart. One of the busiest actresses in Hollywood, she was already a veteran of many Westerns and features while still just a young girl. Her bright, crisp articulation of lines, usually delivered from an open stance with her chin tilted upward — some of her leading men were pretty big fellows — demanded the attention of audiences and gave her roles more distinction than had sometimes apparently been intended by the writers. Except for her serious, intent demeanor, she might have been described as saucy. A very athletic young lady — having been a swimming champion at age ten and a horseback riding instructor at 14 — the dark-haired beauty from West Palm Beach, Florida, projected a naturalness in the outdoor surroundings of action pictures and serials that was immediately discernable by the audience. They could see that she belonged where she was. So natural was it to see her in that context that, despite her obvious capability to portray more dramatic roles, she was typecast as an outdoor girl. All of the four serials in which she was featured were Westerns: In the first, *The Phantom Rider* (Republic, '45), she played a young schoolteacher aiding the mysterious hero in a fight to lift oppression from a tribe of Indians whose children were her pupils. Two years later she appeared as a small town postmistress in *Son of Zorro*, and the next year as the heroine in *Tex Granger*. Finally, she was featured as the daughter of a frontier pony express relay station owner in *Cody of the Pony Express*. Meanwhile, her list of credits in features and Westerns grew into the dozens—all action and Western epics of the outdoors. After each, the moviegoer was aware when he left the theatre that he had once again seen that pretty little saucy brunette, whether he remembered her name or not. And when television came, Peggy Stewart began to charm new millions.

A different type of girl—but also one who defied relegation to the background—was the irrepressible Veda Ann Borg. She appeared in only two serials but she made them hum with her glib audacity. In *The Shadow* she portrayed a somewhat surprising Margot Lane. Where the pulp stories had described Lamont Cranston's confidante as a lovely, urbane and sophisticated young woman with just a touch of titillation, Miss Borg portrayed her as a somewhat brash, hintingly cynical, but completely dedicated ally of the mystical hero. *The Shadow* was released on her 25th birthday—January 1, 1940—when she was a four-year veteran of motion pictures, and her performance foreran the type of roles that would become her forte in features. When she appeared in her other cliff-hanger venture five years later, her role as Cora, the ill-fated accomplice of villain Charles King in *Jungle Raiders*, was more nearly like those with which moviegoers had by then come to identify her. Hard, biting and sarcastic in tone, completely merciless in manner, with her expressive eyes glaring hatred, she made a convincing villainess. The beautiful, blonde Boston girl who had earlier been an artists' model so personified the established type that she made a perfect gangster's moll, wisecracking prison inmate, cynical chorus girl, or just sarcastic, gum-chewing broad. When she appeared in a scene, one thing was certain: Veda Ann Borg did not go unnoticed.

For still different reasons, other serial heroines exemplified the trait of presence and established for themselves a memorable niche in the minds of the cliff-hanger addicts. Because of her no-nonsense, matter-of-fact grasp of the problems facing the two heroes she aided in her only serial appearance, and her unstinting contribution to their solutions, Irene Hervey is an inseparable part of the memory of Universal's *Gangbusters*, one of their finest chapter films. A fine actress, Miss Hervey's career continued on in featured roles in movies and into television drama, with many different portrayals even later as a mother or favorite aunt. (More pertinent to latter-day audiences was her real-life role as mother of singing star Jack Jones and husband of another singing star of the forties and fifties, Allan Jones.) In two of Republic's best episodic adventures, blonde, handsome Louise Currie stood out by projecting much the same type of earnest and conscientious involvement. With a superhero and an unknown villain to compete with in *The Adventures of Captain Marvel*, and with no less than four leading heroes vying for attention in *The Masked Marvel*, it would have been easy for a girl to be all but invisible. Instead, Miss Currie not only carried a large part of the plot in both serials but managed even to save the hero from death a couple of times. Ramsay Ames could not be ignored in a scene no matter what the other cast members might be doing. Tall and slim, with features almost unbelievably perfect, topped by a fashionable hairdo, her presence on screen was felt by everyone in the audience—the men and boys from sheer appreciation, and the women and girls possibly from envy. The New York beauty, educated at Edgewood Park and the Hillhouse School of Dancing, had been featured in several pictures at Universal and Monogram when she was signed by Republic for two serials in 1947. *The Black Widow* provided a supporting role for her and in *G-Men Never Forget* she was the featured heroine. The same year she played the female lead opposite Ralph Byrd in *The Vigilante*.

Others who are fondly recalled for their appearances as heroines are also admired for sheer durability: In the early thirties, Cecilia Parker withstood all sorts of dangers and gave Tom Tyler, Frank Albertson and Clyde Beatty almost unlimited opportunities for "nick of time" rescues in *Jungle Mystery*, *The Lost Special* and *The Lost Jungle*. During the same period, the pretty, wide-eyed beauty who was so charming she caused one of her "heroes" to fall in love with her and propose, graced five cliffhangers at Universal and Mascot. Lucile Browne costarred with Tom Tyler, Kenneth Harlan, James Flavin, Bob Steele and Bob Custer in *Battling with Buffalo Bill*, *Danger Island*, *The Airmail Mystery*, *The Mystery Squadron* and *The Law of the Wild* respectively from 1931 to 1934. It was Flavin who became her real-life "leading man." At Universal Allene Ray and Louise Lorraine continued careers during that time that had started in silent films, and at Mascot, Dorothy Gulliver and Edwina Booth were the charmers. In the forties it was Pamela Blake, playing in serials from all three companies (*The Mysterious Mr. M* at Universal, *Chick Carter* and *The Sea Hound* at Columbia, and *The Ghost of Zorro* at Republic), who provided for her heroes the numerous risks they took with seeming aplomb. In the fifties it seemed that almost the entire output of Republic was designed to destroy two girls—Aline Towne and Phyllis Coates. Between them they accounted for seven of the last 12 serials from that studio. It was during that time of decline when most releases were remakes of earlier successes—with most of the action scenes actually lifted in clips from the earlier films—so the girls weren't in all that much danger. Still, to a segment of the audience who did not see the earlier releases, the Misses Coates and Townes represented all that was expected of the heroine. Probably the best known of Phyllis Coates' three was *Panther Girl of the Kongo*, in which she played a Nyoka-type heroine with many stock shots from *Jungle Girl*. Columbia's *Gunfighters of the Northwest* and Republic's *Jungle Drums of Africa* were the other two. Miss Towne appeared in five quickies, all at Republic: *The Invisible Monster*, *Don Daredevil Rides Again*, *Radar Men from the Moon*, *Zombies of the Stratosphere* and *Trader Tom of the China Seas*.

Just as many actors had tried their hands at heroics in cliff-hangers and then moved on to other things, so did the actresses. The credits are filled with the names of those who graced the serial screen only once, and then no more. For some it was just as well. For others, one stint as a heroine was simply a histrionic challenge, a stepping-stone to bigger things, or a final fling at unabashed melodrama.

Entrenched in cinematic history as the frightened young bride of the demented Baron whose creation became his nemesis in the classic feature *Frankenstein*, and as the recipient of James Cagney's famous grapefruit-in-the-face bit in *Public Enemy*, Mae Clark romped with apparent enjoyment through one of Republic's last cliff-hangers with any originality to it. Opposite Tris Coffin in *King of the Rocketmen*, she played a reporter whose chance snapshot of the flying hero became the central motivation for three of the serial's 12 episodes. The bright candor projected by the lovely veteran of musical comedy, vaudeville and motion pictures was a refreshing note in an otherwise routine proceeding. In 1941 Evelyn Brent had made her sole appearance as a heroine in a serial. Well known for her roles in action and mystery films in England and the United States and as a villainess in Universal's *Jungle Jim*, Miss Brent played a pretty Secret Service operative assisting hero Jack Holt in his undercover effort to expose a counterfeit gang in *Holt of the Secret Service*. The same year, Columbia also featured two other young hopefuls in one-time stints as heroines, whose chief activity seemed to be gasping at the backs of their hands. Mary Ainslee appeared as the hero's girl friend Nita Van Sloan in *The Spider Returns*, and Dorothy Fay provided the romantic interest for super Western star Buck Jones in *White Eagle*, his last cliff-hanger.

Nell O'Day, the rancher's pretty blonde daughter in many a Western feature, graced Columbia's *Perils of the Royal Mounted*, and dark-eyed Carmen Morales sought the aid of the valiant Bill Elliott in recovering her kidnapped uncle from *The Valley of Vanishing Men*.

Republic had also sought to find a winner among some of their young thespians, and finally did with Kay Aldridge, after a series of acceptable but not outstanding appearances by some lovely girls: Lois Wilde added to *Undersea Kingdom*; Maxine Doyle prettied up *S.O.S. Coast Guard*; and Helen Christian had her railroad saved by John Carroll in *Zorro Rides Again*. Eleanor Stewart suffered the dismay of learning her father was the villain in *The Fighting Devil Dogs*; Jill Martin flew away into the sky with *Hawk of the Wilderness*; Lita Conway walked into the pines hand-in-hand with *King of the Royal Mounted*; and Ella Neal helped to exonerate The Copperhead in *Mysterious Doctor Satan*.

At Universal during the thirties there was a succession of them following the reigns of Allene Ray, Louise Lorraine and Lucile Browne: Patricia Farr, Gloria Shea, Marion Schilling, Muriel Evans, Joyce Compton, Diana Gibson, Betty Jane Rhodes, Catherine Hughes, Eleanore Hansen, Louise Stanley and Dorothy Arnold are names that appeared only once in Universal serial advertising but more often in that of features. In the forties the names were Claire Dodd, Mary Field, Marjorie Weaver, Marjorie Clements, Wanda McKay, Daun Kennedy and Janet Shaw. Others in the forties went on from an appearance in a serial to become well-known feature players and starlets during and after the war. Two of them — Carol Hughes and Anne Gwynne — appeared in *Flash Gordon Conquers the Universe*, and then had the leads in a variety of musicals, comedies and thrillers at Universal. Elyse Knox played in some of that studio's most popular features after being Don Terry's beautiful leading lady in *Don Winslow of the Coast Guard*, and became the bride of real-life football hero Tom Harmon. Marjorie Lord, Jeanne Kelly, Helen Parrish and Kathryn Adams also cringed in fright for one sitting before going on to bigger things.

In the fifties there was a new crop — such lovelies at Columbia as Virginia Herrick, Karen Randle, Gloria Dea, Eileen Rowe, Vivian Mason, Joanne Rio, June Howard, Eve Anderson and Norma Brooks; and at Republic Jean Dean, Mary Ellen Kay, Susan Morrow, Barbara Bestar and Fran Bennett — each of whom contributed her part to the role of serial heroine but for various reasons did not come through as did others who made more indelible marks.

One young actress who did make a vivid impression in a single appearance was Constance Moore. As Wilma Deering in Universal's *Buck Rogers*, her impellingly attractive appeal helped to persuade the time-displaced aviator and his sidekick to join forces with her and Dr. Huer in their fight against Killer Kane in the 25th century. A singing star of radio and the New York stage, the lovely Miss Moore projected on screen that necessary quality of the deserving heroine — passive importunity — which could only exude from a demeanor of wholesome honesty. After meeting her, Buck and Buddy were in the game to the bitter end.

This disarming trait in a heroine snared many a big man in the serial game and was not a minor factor in the appeal of several other young actresses who aspired to inherit the mantle of Pauline. Dorothy Short used it to advantage with Noah Beery, Jr., in *Call of the Savage*, and again with Dave O'Brien in *Captain Midnight*. Iris Meredith secured the assistance of the legendary scout Kit Carson in tracking down the evil Pegleg in *Overland with Kit Carson* by appealing to his protective instincts without actually saying so. She did it again in *The Green Archer* when she was instrumental in involving the hero in the affairs of Garr Castle, where her sister's husband had evidently been done in and replaced by his evil brother. As Nita Van Sloan (the first) in *The Spider's*

Web, she was a beautiful and valuable helper. Kay Hughes served as inspiration to two of Republic's earliest heroes — Bob Livingston in *The Vigilantes Are Coming* and Ralph Byrd in *Dick Tracy* — by demonstrating her willingness to assist in any way possible their efforts to restore law and order.

Anne Nagel stood by the hero steadfast, wholesome and true in four hectic and action-filled chapter films — as Miss Case in both *Green Hornet* episoders, a railroad pioneer in *Winners of the West* and as the Black Commando Paul Kelly's confidante in *The Secret Code* — in addition to building a very busy career in features. Born Ann Dolan in Boston, the pretty, wide-eyed young charmer began her screen career in 1933 following her graduation from the Notre Dame Academy in Boston, and went on to play in a number of action and mystery films for the next two decades. She was the romantic interest in the film which brought the famous "touchdown twins" of West Point to the screen. Glenn Davis ("Mr. Inside") and Felix "Doc" Blanchard ("Mr. Outside") starred in Film Classics' *The Spirit of West Point* on the heels of their fabulous performances on the great Army team of the mid-forties, and Miss Nagel provided lovely support. With her disarmingly open manner, she immediately secured sympathy for her plight from an audience and motivated any hero to ply his best efforts on her behalf.

Perhaps the most quickly remembered serial heroine of all for that trait of guileless wholesomeness was Kay Aldridge, the second Nyoka. In all three of her featured cliff-hanger roles for Republic she projected the image of the deserving young daughter of a kidnapped or murdered pioneer or man of science struggling valiantly against all odds to continue his work. With her clean-cut, symmetrical beauty and round, imploring eyes, she enlisted without much difficulty the full cooperation of heroes Clayton Moore, Allan Lane and Kane Richmond in *Perils of Nyoka*, *Daredevils of the West* and *Haunted Harbor*. Although in only three films, the lovely former Powers model closely trails Linda Stirling for the imaginary honor of being Republic's "Serial Queen."

It was true of serials as it always has been of features that the real, basic requirement for a leading lady was the possession of photogenic beauty. It is not the purpose here to catalog the names of the young women who have become stars not because of acting ability but by reason of natural physical endowments. They are legion. Suffice it to say that all of us are aware that it is better to watch a pretty girl do something than a plain one. And in action films the emoting talent of the heroine usually could not have been less important. As pointed out, the image was the thing. However, there were those who appeared occasionally possessing both beauty and talent, and they are the most kindly recalled.

Frances Gifford, the first Nyoka, was one of these. Borrowed especially for the part from Paramount Pictures where she was under contract, the gorgeous young woman was cast by Republic in the title role of Burroughs' *Jungle Girl* and became, by virtue of that one role, an inseparable part of the total serial tradition. No man who was a boy in 1941 and saw Miss Gifford as the lovely Nyoka can deny that he was just a little bit in love with her. Varied roles in a number of later features failed to erase the memory of that beautiful, wavy-haired girl in the brief jungle costume, riding high on the neck of a huge elephant or gamely grappling with the heavies to try and gain the initiative for the dashing hero.

Just several years before, a young actress with one of the prettiest countenances ever to appear in a chapterplay had reigned at Universal, playing the heroine in six of that studio's outstanding mid-thirties cliff-hangers. Perhaps best remembered as the beautiful Dale Arden in the first two Flash Gordons, Jean Rogers had already become dear to the chapter addict's heart as the damsel-in-distress in *Tailspin Tommy in the Great Air Mystery* in 1935 and *The Adventures of Frank Merriwell* in 1936; and between the two Dale Arden stints was also featured as John King's inspiration in the futuristic *Ace Drummond* and as Scott Kolk's leading lady in *Secret Agent X-9*. After the prolific feat of starring in three of Universal's four serial releases in 1936, followed by *X-9* and *Trip to Mars* in 1937 and 1938, she bowed out of serials for good, to the collective disappointment of all those who can still close their eyes and see her wide-eyed scream as she was about to be attacked by a creature called a Tigron in the labyrinthine caverns of Mongo.

Maybe not to the degree of Miss Rogers or Miss Gifford, but certainly to a great extent, did some other very pretty ladies contribute to the overall mystique of the serial heroine. Such lovely creatures as Ruth Mix and Dorothy Gulliver in the middle thirties, Lynn Roberts, Frances Robinson and Joan Barclay in the late thirties, Joyce Bryant, Jan Wiley and Helen Talbot in the early forties, and Joan Woodbury, Noel Neill and Lois Hall in the postwar forties, were typical of the continuous parade of beautiful young actresses who kept alive the image of the plucky, determined young lass fighting gamely beside her man for "what was right."

Miss Mix appeared in all three of the independent cliff-hangers released by Stage and Screen Attractions in 1936 — with Ralph Graves and Dave O'Brien in *The Black Coin*, Jack Mulhall in *The Clutching Hand*, and as one of the large cast in *Custer's Last Stand*, which also included Dorothy Gulliver. Miss Gulliver had previously been featured with Tom Tyler in Mascot's *Phantom of the West* and was the leading lady of the legendary Harold "Red" Grange in *The Galloping Ghost* for the same producer. In *Shadow of the Eagle* for Mascot, she had appeared as John Wayne's leading lady.

Lynn Roberts played in the classic *The Lone Ranger* and as Gwen in *Dick Tracy Returns* the same year at Republic. She was also billed in Gene Autry and Roy Rogers Westerns as Mary Hart. Frances Robinson played opposite Buster Crabbe in Universal's *Red Barry* as "Mississippi," and appeared the same year as the heroine in *Tim Tyler's Luck* for that company. Miss Barclay was the female lead in both of Sam Katzman's Victory Pictures releases. As a young newspaper reporter in *Shadow of Chinatown*, she helped bring down the mad Victor Poten, and as Hope Mason, niece of the famed Inspector Blake, she assisted Ralph Byrd in uncovering the menacing Scorpion in *Blake of Scotland Yard*.

Joyce Bryant appeared in two of Columbia's 1940–41 entries — as the lovely Normandie Drake in the screen adaptation of Milton Caniff's *Terry and the Pirates* and as Pat Benson, niece of one of the suspects in *The Iron Claw*. A slim, striking blonde, Jan Wiley appeared as June Chandler in *Dick Tracy vs. Crime, Inc.*, at Republic in 1941 and in two for Universal in 1945 — *The Master Key* as reporter Janet Lowe, and as the romantic interest in *Secret Agent X-9*. Helen Talbot's was a haughty, challenging beauty and was used to great advantage in Republic's somewhat uncharacteristic 1945 serial *Federal Operator 99* — uncharacteristic because of its use of a very sophisticated and urbane team of villains (portrayed by George J. Lewis as a frustrated pianist turned to crime, and Lorna Gray as his beautiful "confidante") and an obviously cultured, polished hero, Marten Lamont. Miss Talbot gave this unusual chapter film just the proper touch. More standard was her portrayal of Marian Brennan in *King of the Forest Rangers* the following year.

Joan Woodbury was a natural for her single-shot role in serials. For his initial entry as Columbia serial producer, Sam Katzman was planning a screen version of Dale Messick's popular comic strip *Brenda Starr, Reporter*. He needed a beautiful, flame-haired actress with a comedic wit and sense of timing to accurately portray the vivid, dynamic Brenda, one who could convince an audience she was the leading character in a suspense and action drama but leave the necessary fighting and brawling to a more suitable male hero. His choice was Miss Woodbury, who was already a veteran of just such roles in a string of action and mystery features for Columbia and Monogram. With Kane Richmond as the male hero, she managed to carry the story from one episode to another in fine style, leaving herself in jeopardy just enough to require his services as a rescuer each week. One of the most strikingly beautiful of all serial heroines, the vivacious Miss Woodbury salvaged by her beauty and charm what might have been Katzman's greatest fiasco except for *Who's Guilty?*

Katzman could pick them, though, as evidenced by his later selection of Lois Hall as the Lady of the Lake in *The Adventures of Sir Galahad* and as Buster Crabbe's girl friend in *Pirates of the High Seas*. He also selected the cute and saucy Noel Neill to be Lois Lane in his epic production *Superman* in 1948. She followed that up in the same role two years later in the sequel and, in the meantime, played the heroine in *The Adventures of Frank and Jesse James* and *The James Brothers of Missouri* at Republic. In television the attractive, flippantly audacious Miss Neill was *in fact* Lois

Lane to millions of youngsters and continues to become her to millions of new ones each year, as the reruns of *Superman* go into countless numbers.

For many of these girls it was true that their faces were their fortunes (since acting ability was a secondary virtue), and if Helen of Troy indeed had the "face that launched a thousand ships," then these girls could each boast of launching several dozen highly perilous adventures in their own modest ways.

It would be criminal to close a discourse on serial heroines without the mention of one very versatile and unforgettably beautiful young woman. The inclusion in a serial's cast of Lorna Gray gave the promise of more than the standard portrayal of the loyal ingenue, for that young actress was equally capable of playing convincing heroines with unusual depth or slinky, seductive villainesses with guile and predatoriness. Miss Gray was particularly adept at playing both types alternately and being completely accepted as either. Following her first two roles as heroines at Columbia—as Babs McKay in *Flying G-Men*, and Anne Butler in *Deadwood Dick*—she moved over to Republic to portray the beautiful and crafty Vultura in *Perils of Nyoka*. As Charles Middleton's cohort in crime, she proved a cunning adversary for the lovely Nyoka and created a new image for herself as a scheming villainess. Completely reversing herself again, the talented former vocalist from Grand Rapids, Michigan, appeared next as an assistant to the district attorney in *Captain America*. Then it was back to villainy again as the lovely Lorna teamed up with George J. Lewis to menace *Federal Operator 99*. Her final serial in 1946 found the dark-haired beauty in the starring role but with a new name. For a new start in features, the gorgeous young thespian took the name Adrian Booth, and so billed appeared in a number of outstanding action and dramatic pictures for Republic. It was under her new name that she was starred in the title role as *The Daughter of Don Q*, sharing heroic chores with Kirk Alyn.

In my neighborhood there were two expressions of fond recognition for the hero and the heroine. The hero to us was "the main player," and the heroine was called simply "the girl." By whatever name, they were the "good guys" and it was they with whom we identified. Continuing the tradition of "cheer the hero, hiss the villain" begun in the silents, these were the people we cheered. No home team or favorite champion ever experienced fiercer loyalty or extracted greater empathy from their fans than these stalwarts. Today it is not possible to witness any such phenomena. Heroes are passé. Law and Order are suspect terms. Gallantry is folly. But, it was nice while it lasted.

6

Guardians of the Sword

"There is nothing in the world so pleasant as for an honest man to be the squire of a knight-errant that seeks adventures."

So spoke the faithful Sancho Panza to his wife upon returning from his journeys with the venerable old hero of Miguel de Cervantes' *Don Quixote de la Mancha*. And since that writing of those tales (which has become recognized as the first modern novel), the heroes of countless other novels, stories, plays and motion pictures have had their Sanchos. The subhero (or vice-champion, or assistant-to-the-chief-good-guy, whichever designation suits your thinking) served several needs in the telling of a continued story. Since the purpose of the hero was usually pretty grimly fixed — the saving of society from a dreadful threat of some kind — not much margin for levity was granted him, so an assistant was sometimes engaged to furnish a few laughs. Also, as brave and resourceful as a hero was recognized to be, many jobs simply required more hands than his to master, so a straight, serious assistant hero was used. And in situations created by particular circumstances, people with particular talents or characteristics had to be employed — a "specialist," if you will. For whatever reason he was selected, the assistant had to be someone with as many of the qualities of the hero as possible, but one who could function in the secondary role.

In the first decade or so of sound serials there was a wide use of secondary principals for comic relief. In Westerns they were usually called the "sidekick," and the term became accepted in other types of films as well. Some of the motion picture industry's best-known and well-liked character actors filled those parts and thus provided the very few light moments to be recalled in the cliff-hangers. Many also served in the dual capacity of providing some comedy relief along with serious support in dramatic and action sequences.

Coming immediately to mind as a "sidekick" of repute during the thirties is the crusty, wizened old Raymond Hatton. His almost cynical lines were delivered with an impudent acerbity that belied his subsequent actions. His humor was almost mordant, but the seasoned action fan knew that his bluster was a facade to conceal the fact that he was at heart an incurable softy who could be counted on to come through in the clutch. Appearing much older than his actual age, the fortyish native of Red Oak, Iowa, usually portrayed an old former Army trooper recounting his days of glory or a grizzled hunter-trapper-scout who had been everywhere and done everything. Best remembered for his costarring roles in Westerns with Buck Jones, Tim McCoy and Johnny Mack Brown, Hatton appeared in such serials for Mascot, Universal and Republic as *The Three Musketeers, Rustlers of Red Dog, Jungle Jim* and *The Vigilantes Are Coming*. One of his few "heavy" roles was as the henchman Gasspon, one of the villain Khan's followers in *Undersea Kingdom*.

Almost exclusively a comical sidekick was Sid Saylor. The lean, goggle-eyed blusterer who could not control a wild "adam's apple," had appeared in a series of comedy shorts for Universal and became well-known for rube-like character parts in major features such as *Little Miss Broadway, Union Pacific* and *Abe Lincoln of Illinois*. In 1934 he made his initial appearances in two serials at Mascot — *The Lost Jungle* and *Mystery Mountain*. The Chicago actor's third serial role came 11 years later when Sam Katzman signed him to play Chuck Allen, a none-too-smart hero's foil in *Brenda Starr Reporter*.

Before becoming so closely identified with Gene Autry as the bumbling Frog Millhouse, and then a top money-making Western star in his own right, the likable, rotund Lester "Smiley" Burnette gave serial fans some chuckles in the middle thirties. His credits include roles in *The Adventures of Rex and Rinty* and *The Miracle Rider* for Mascot and *Undersea Kingdom* and *Dick Tracy* at Republic. Burnette created a unique image as the well-meaning but inept detective Mike McGurk in the latter, furnishing an almost exact antithesis to the briskly efficient Tracy as played by Ralph Byrd. Pursuing the ready audience acceptance of his image, the jocular comedian from Summum, Illinois, who had performed as a one-man radio station prior to his movie career, continued to develop his considerable talents for rural slapstick alongside such Western heroes as Sunset Carson and Charles Starrett in the forties, and continued in similar characterizations in television. At the time of his death he was a central figure in the CBS comedy series *Petticoat Junction*, playing one-half of a team of bucolic train engineers who operated the irrepressible Hooterville Cannonball. Rufe Davis (formerly a "Mesquiteer") was the other half.

The charm of Fuzzy Knight was his anxious determination to be helpful despite his sometimes uncontrollable stammer. It seemed that the harder he tried to say something, the worse it got, until he finally had to give up and phrase it another way. An imploringly sensitive actor, he created an unforgettable movie vignette in Paramount's *Trail of the*

Lonesome Pine as the lonely mountain man strolling through the trees singing "Twilight on the Trail," and later repeating it sobbingly through his tears at the funeral of his young friend, a small boy who had been killed while playing in the cab of a steam shovel blown apart by dynamite. The lovable, husky-voiced partner of Johnny Mack Brown and Rod Cameron in many Universal series Westerns was born Forrest H. Knight in Fairmont, West Virginia, and performed in all phases of show business before his career in motion pictures. His serial roles were both for Universal — *Oregon Trail* in 1939 and *The Great Alaskan Mystery* in 1944. To a subsequent generation he was known as Buster Crabbe's buddy in television's *The Foreign Legionnaire*.

Solo jobs as a sidekick were performed by many veteran character actors in various Western serials, and most of them were creditable. One in particular bears mention. The unlikely casting of Slim Summerville in such a part at first might seem incongruous. The tall, gangly man with the jowly, hangdog look of utter discomfiture seemed to belong more in caricaturistic comedies playing a put-upon schoolmaster or much-abused public servant than in a rough-and-tumble action serial such as *The Valley of Vanishing Men*. But after a few episodes his worth began to show. Involving kidnapped men forced into slavish captivity, it was a grim tale. Ordinary comedy relief would have seemed pretentious. So the solution was to insert into the proceedings the completely outlandish character "Missouri" in the person of Summerville. That quiet, gentle soul with his downcast eyes and bird-like gestures was so pitiful in his hopeless pleas to be left out of things unpleasant that it jerked one away completely from the mood of ominous dread cast by the rest of the film.

Quite opposite from the "Casper Milquetoast" image cast by Summerville was the cocky brashness projected by such personable young "second bananas" as Eddie Quillan, Billy Benedict and Eddie Acuff. Always ready with a wisecrack, even in the tensest moments of danger, the alert, irreverent, boastful characters typified by these three personified the quirk in human nature that causes one to assume a false facade of confidence when in reality he is scared to death — the feeling that a small boy has as he whistles nonchalantly but very loudly while passing a graveyard on a windy night. This bravado when stacked up against the depicted bravery of the hero produced a comedy of contrasts and served to ease the conscience of the viewer, who was thus given middle ground to occupy in the matter of his identification with courage. If he secretly felt that he wasn't as dauntless as the intrepid hero, he could at least be certain that he was made of sterner stuff than the hapless sidekick.

Especially adroit at conveying the feeling of apprehensive involvement in heroics was Quillan, the bug-eyed, very nervous and jumpy buddy of hero Kane Richmond in *Jungle Raiders*. Almost from the time of his birth in Philadelphia, Eddie was in show business. His parents were Sarah Owen and Joseph Quillan, vaudeville professionals who provided young Eddie his first stage experience performing in the family act. So inherent with the stage was his background that in movies when the story called for a brash vaudevillian, the first thought was to get Eddie Quillan. His other serial credits were for comedy cohero roles in *Mystery of the Riverboat* and *The Jungle Queen.*

Billy Benedict portrayed the same type of assistant hero for Republic. Because of his youthful appearance and shock of unruly hair that appeared to be snow white on film, he was always cast as a teenager. In *The Adventures of Captain Marvel* he was Billy Batson's antithesis as the fumbling, awkward "Whitey" Murphy, and in *Perils of Nyoka* he was known as "Red," right hand man of hero Clayton Moore. Bill also appeared earlier in Universal's *Tim Tyler's Luck.*

Eddie Acuff began his serial chores as Tom Neal's buddy Curly in the first Nyoka film, *Jungle Girl.* His performances as a supporting hero were more serious than comic, but it was he who delivered any wisecracks in the proceeding. In *Daredevils of the West* he played the part of Red Kelly, foreman of a roadbuilding gang, and was involved in a great deal of the action along with hero Allan Lane. His third serial role — as Spud Warner in *Chick Carter Detective* — was more like those he played in features than the other two. In it he was a fast-talking newspaper photographer, partner of reporter hero Douglas Fowley, who in the final episode unknowingly turned up the cliff-hanger's "prize" — a $100,000 diamond — from his own pocket where it had been concealed in a handkerchief throughout the entire serial. That anyone could be that seemingly stupid was easy to believe after watching Acuff's masterful performance as a witless stooge.

Another serio-comical performer in serials was Walter Sande, a fine character actor and veteran of many features and television productions. In *The Iron Claw* he appeared as "Flash" Strong, a newspaper photographer buddy of Charles Quigley; and in the Don Winslow serials at Universal he played the hero's aide, Red Pennington. In all of them his breezy, lighthearted manner offset the required intensity of the "main player." But in a tight squeeze he was all business and saved the day on many occasions. His subsequent career included a variety of featured dramatic roles, notable among which was the continuing role as the Scandinavian-American farmer and father of Inger Stevens in the television series *The Farmer's Daughter.*

Perhaps the early sound serial's chief exponent of the serio-comical sidekick was Noah Beery, Jr. From the early thirties up to the war he was featured in ten serials — all but one as the hero's good buddy, trusted right arm, squire, court jester, you-name-it. Born in New York City the son of famous silent star Noah Beery, the young thespian appeared in silent films as a child and because of an amiable quality similar to that of his popular uncle Wallace Beery (and not unlike that of humorist Will Rogers) developed his screen image into that of a likable, self-effacing young character actor as he grew to manhood. This led to the type of parts in which he excelled as the good guy's best friend in serials for Mascot (*The Three Musketeers, Fighting with Kit Carson*) and Universal (*Heroes of the West, The Jungle Mystery, Tailspin Tommy* and *Tailspin Tommy in the Great Air Mystery, Ace Drummond, Riders of Death Valley* and *Overland Mail*). In the latter, his famous father played the villain. His sole nonsidekick role was as the hero in *Call of the Savage* when he was only 19 years old.

The straight assistant — or cohero — was not employed to be funny but to be a real and ready asset to the good side. These roles were very often filled by men who later came into their own as leading players, or at least continued to get costarring credit in Westerns and features. In several instances they were played by older character actors who portrayed scientists or professionals more knowledgeable than the hero but subservient to him in importance to the story. This combination of experience and daring, brain and brawn, made for some interesting hero-teams, the most memorable of which was the Dr. Zarkov–Flash Gordon duo of the Universal trilogy. And some were more reminiscent of a reverse Don Quixote–Sancho Panza relationship, where the young hero was the foolhardy "knight-errant" and the older assistant was the faithful plodder-with-wisdom. When the coheroes ideally were brave young men with a good helping of wisdom, the results were far more satisfactory.

Dave O'Brien was a cohero who became a leading player. In *The Black Coin* for Stage and Screen in 1936 the young man from Big Springs, Texas, played Terry Navarro, an agent for a shipping company who got involved with a plot to use the company's ships in a smuggling scheme. The other hero was a federal agent played by Ralph Graves, but it was O'Brien who endured most of the perils. In *The Secret of Treasure Island* for Columbia he had the supporting role of Jameson and again became a cohero in *The Spider Returns*, playing the part of Jackson, The Spider's trusted right hand man. Then, in 1942 for the same studio, he portrayed the legendary radio hero Captain Midnight in the serial of that title. The same year he appeared in several of the fabulously funny Pete Smith shorts for MGM and costarred with Bela Lugosi in the Monogram feature *The Devil Bat*. Bringing into play his Texas background, Dave then costarred in a series of "Billy the Kid" Westerns with Bob Steele at PRC, followed by a series with Jim Newell and Guy Wilkerson in which they were billed as "The Texas Rangers." He continued to appear in numerous features in supporting parts, but it was his exposure as the hapless hero of the Pete Smith comedies that set his future career. At the time of his death in 1969, Dave was a top television comedy writer on the wacky *Red Skelton Hour.*

A fine supporting actor who unfortunately did not rise higher was Richard Fiske, who played The Spider's man Jackson in the first screen version of the mystery man's adventures, *The Spider's Web*. His credits as an assistant hero included roles in *Overland with Kit Carson*, *The Flying G-Men*, *The Shadow*, *The Green Archer* and *Perils of the Royal Mounted*. His lot was the same as many others who turned in faithful jobs as the hero's legman, headquarters contact, copilot or general handyman, and was then not heard from again. Ralph Byrd had such a helper (in lieu of the comic strip's Pat Patton) in each of the four Dick Tracy serials, and each time he was played by a different actor. In the first three the character was known as "Steve," and was played respectively by Fred Hamilton (*Dick Tracy*), Michael Kent (*Dick Tracy Returns*) and Ted Pearson (*Dick Tracy's G-Men*). In the fourth, *Dick Tracy vs. Crime, Inc.*, the character's name was changed to "Billy Carr" and was played by Michael Owen.

Other young would-be leading men who served in the shadow of the hero included such actors as William Newell, Rick Vallin, Scott Elliott, John Compton, House Peters, Jr., Wilson Wood and John Spencer, and teenage sidekicks such as Sam Edwards ("Chuck" in *Captain Midnight*), Sumner Getchell ("Tank" in *Hop Harrigan*), George Offerman, Jr. ("Stuff" in *The Vigilante*), Joe Brown, Jr. ("Billy" in *Jack Armstrong*), Tommy Bond ("Jimmy" in the *Superman* duo), Robert "Buzz" Henry (*Hop Harrigan, Son of the Guardsman* and *Tex Granger*) and Ralph Hodges (*The Sea Hound, Bruce Gentry* and *Mysterious Island*).

Character actor Clancy Cooper performed the task of supporting the hero in two cliff-hangers and illustrated perfectly the manner of the "old pro." As patrolman Pat Flanigan in *The Secret Code*, he served as liaison man between supposedly discredited undercover hero Paul Kelly (The Black Commando) and federal authorities. Tough-sounding but gentle, Cooper appeared in many features in similar roles as a policeman, cab-driver, merchant seaman and a variety of other hardworking types. In *Haunted Harbor*, his only other serial role, he portrayed a sailor named Yank who helped the hero escape from prison and vindicate himself of a murder charge. His partner-and-also-aide to hero Kane Richmond was Marshall Reed, a handsome actor who has had a long career sub-sequently in supporting roles in serials and features and in television, playing mostly plainclothes policemen. He was a regular on *Dragnet* as a coworker of Jack Webb and Harry Morgan.

William Bakewell has a string of credits reaching back to silent films, and at this writing still appears in television dramas. A versatile actor, he has played as many different types of roles as a handsome, square-jawed, serious-faced man can play — from rugged hero to whiningly obeisant hotel clerk. A native Hollywoodian, he was born when that town was struggling to become established as the nation's filmmaking center. After graduation from Harvard Military Academy, young Bakewell entered motion pictures as an extra in 1925 and since has appeared on Broadway and in so many films it would be difficult to name them all. Among his serial credits are the roles of Tom Banning in *Jungle Menace* and the title role in *Hop Harrigan* for Columbia, and the supporting roles of Ross in *King of the Mounties* and Ted in *Radar Men from the Moon* at Republic.

The outstanding example of the older specialist assisting the younger hero in the aforementioned role of Dr. Zarkov in the Flash Gordon serials. As played by veteran actor Frank Shannon, the character remained true to the Alex Raymond concept and portrayed Zarkov as an alert, wily and pragmatic captain played against the sometimes hasty, ill-considered daring of Flash, the physical and brusque young lieutenant. Afterward, Shannon did not again match his key roles in the Gordon trilogy and reverted to straight character parts in subsequent serials—a small bit in *Batman* and the "girl's father" in *The Phantom*. Similar to the Zarkov characterization were several other notable roles played by older coheroes. Herbert Rawlinson played the title role of former inspector Sir James Blake in *Blake of Scotland Yard*, but the real hero was the young inventor, Jerry Sheehan, played by Ralph Byrd. The same was true of the Sir Nayland Smith and Allan Parker roles (William Royle and Robert Kellard) in *Drums of Fu Manchu*.

The most famous of all sidekicks is probably the Lone Ranger's Indian companion, Tonto. And he is representative of that genre of colorful assistant who was dreamed up to complement—by comparison or contrast—an equally colorful hero. The Green Hornet's Kato, the Cisco Kid's Pancho and Batman's Robin are all examples. These were characters concocted by their creators to provide fealty to otherwise basically lonely people—the completely dedicated champions. It was not that these heroes actually needed any help in their work, but that they seemed less than human without someone to be personally concerned about, and have concerned about them. They also provided vulnerability for those otherwise indomitable creatures who operated incognito by being the only ones who knew their true identities, and thus being susceptible to capture and torture by the current enemy, with unwillful disclosure of the secret a dreaded possibility. It was inevitable that they became so closely identified with the hero that they were just as well-known.

Tonto in the serials was an Oklahoman (from Muskogee) named Victor Daniels—but you never saw him billed that way. Moving from cattle ranching to mining, from boxing to rodeo performing and finally to movie stunt work, this man of many abilities entered pictures in 1929, and for the next quarter-century was a fixture as an Indian brave in the Hollywood Western. When *The Lone Ranger* was being planned, the natural choice was this young athlete who had become known as Chief Thundercloud. He repeated the role in the sequel and thereafter, even though he appeared in dozens of films as various Indian characters, he was always "Tonto" to the serial fan of the thirties.

As for Keye Luke, it is more difficult to say whether he is better remembered by action fans as Kato in the two Green Hornet serials or as the "Number One Son" of the beloved Oriental sleuth Charlie Chan in many films of that famous detective's adventures. Certainly by more sophisticated filmgoers he is remembered for his distinguished career in major motion pictures and on the stage. Born in Canton, China, and educated in Seattle and at Washington University, the talented young man worked as an artist for a West Coast theatre chain and for RKO Radio Studios, and also served as a technical adviser on films about China. Then came his career as an actor, which included roles in such productions as *Oil for the Lamps of China, King of Burlesque, The Good Earth, International Settlement* and *Dragon Seed*, to name just a few. His serial roles in addition to Kato were all in Universal films — *The Adventures of Smilin' Jack, Secret Agent X-9* and *The Lost City of the Jungle*. (And, as if it were not enough to be undecided about whether Kato or Chan's Number One son is my favorite Luke role, I had the privilege of seeing him as the delightfully confused Wang Chi Yang in Rodgers and Hammerstein's *Flower Drum Song* on Broadway. His portrayal of a Chinese gentleman of the "old school" surrounded by a family who were rapidly becoming totally modern American was so charmingly engaging that a new favorite was added.) Luke's paintings have been widely exhibited, illustrating his exceptional talent as an artist as well as an actor.

For the colorful Batman, Columbia provided two actors for their two productions, and likewise employed two "Robins." In 1943 the Boy Wonder was portrayed by Douglas Croft, who became well-known to movie audiences by playing the central figure in film biographies "as a boy." (One of his most notable was *Pride of the Yankees*, in which he played the famous baseball great, Lou Gehrig, "as a boy." Gehrig "as a man" was Gary Cooper.) For the 1949 *Batman and Robin*, Columbia selected a young athlete named Johnny Duncan for the role of Batman's assistant.

In less flamboyant form the serials also utilized coheroes of various nationalities and specialized abilities in comparable parts. In addition to Keye Luke, the natural choice for a Chinese cohero, there were also available for Oriental roles such fine thespians as Philip Ahn (Hong Kong Cholly in *Red Barry* and Prince Tallin in *Buck Rogers*), Al Kikume (Lothar in *Mandrake the Magician*), Allen Jung and Victor De Camp (Connie and Big Stoop in *Terry and the Pirates*) and Roland Got (Chang in *G-Men vs. the Black Dragon*). When a French ally was needed for *Spy Smasher*, there was Franco Corsaro. And when the script called for a Spanish or Mexican cohero, Republic's immediate solution was Duncan Renaldo.

Renault Renaldo Duncan was born in Camden, New Jersey, shortly after the turn of the century, and was educated in Versailles, France. An artist as well as a thespian, he painted portraits when he was a teenager and was an art director at the same time he performed as an actor and producer in New York. When he wrote, he used his own name, Renault

Duncan, but when he acted, he was billed as Duncan Renaldo. All that talent led him to motion pictures where he also became a cameraman and director, and wrote and collaborated on stories and screenplays. His acting credits include major features *Bridge of San Luis Rey, Trader Horn, For Whom the Bell Tolls, Jungle Flight* and *Valiant Hombre.* In Republic serials he was a Mexican bandit (Zomarro in *The Painted Stallion*), a trusted retainer (Renaldo in *Zorro Rides Again*), a rancher-turned-deputy (Juan Vasquez in *The Lone Ranger Rides Again*), a border policeman (Pedro Garcia in *King of the Texas Rangers*), a French legionnaire (Pierre La Salle in *Secret Service in Darkest Africa*) and an oil engineer (Jose Delgado in *The Tiger Woman*). His sole Columbia billing was a featured role in *Jungle Menace.* Renaldo's handsome features and crisp, businesslike accent bespoke a man who was in every way qualified to be the main player, so his selection as a cohero gave the fan an extra measure of excitement. Greater fame came to him as a Western star when he succeeded Warner Baxter and Gilbert Roland as the popular Cisco Kid in movies, and then became the best known of them all in the role when the character moved into television. His "Pancho," Leo Carillo, although a major Mexican star below the border, had also seen service as a serial "sidekick" in *Riders of Death Valley.*

And then there were the kids. Lee Van Atta played Junior in *Dick Tracy* and Billy Norton in *Undersea Kingdom.* Manuel King was Clyde Beatty's little helper in *Darkest Africa*, and Jerry Tucker played Junior in *Dick Tracy Returns.* Tommy Cook was Little Beaver in *The Adventures of Red Ryder* and Wakimba in *Jungle Girl*, and Jackie Moran played Buddy Wade in *Buck Rogers.* A raft of kids headed by Jackie Cooper were the *Scouts to the Rescue*, and we've already discussed the Dead End variety.

There was one "kid" costar in serials who was the most famous of them all: Several seasons back on the Red Skelton television show, there was a recurring character in the "silent spot" — Red's pantomime skit — who looked awfully familiar. The character was a little old gray-haired lady in a black dress and shawl, stooped and bent, who became the unwitting victim of Skelton's brand of comic mayhem and went sprawling and tumbling in some of the wildest pratfalls imaginable. At length it became evident that this was no "old lady" but a cleverly disguised stunt-man instead. Then, by George, as "she" came into closer view and grew more familiar, it was obvious that under that shawl and black dress was former kid star Frankie Darro!

Young Darro played in six of Nat Levine's Mascot serials from 1931 to 1935 and in one each for Columbia and Universal after that. His earliest costar was the famous canine hero Rin Tin Tin in *The Lightning Warrior.* The same year he appeared with Harry Carey and Edwina Booth in *The Vanishing Legion* and the next year with Carey in *The Devil Horse.* In 1933 he teamed up again with Rin Tin Tin, Jr., for *Wolf Dog,* and wisecracked his way through *Burn 'em Up Barnes* in 1934. His final Mascot role was with Gene Autry in *The Phantom Empire*. Subsequently he appeared mostly in features as a smart alec newsboy, a glib-talking jockey, or a tough young punk in gangster films. His only serial role at Columbia was in *The Great Adventures of Wild Bill Hickok* in 1938, and at Universal he appeared with the Dead End Kids in *Junior G-Men of the Air*. The following years saw him in a succession of costarring and supporting roles in features and television, usually involving action and stunt work such as the Skelton stint. (An interesting note about the "little old lady" is that "she" was also played by ace stuntman David Sharpe, himself a pretty well-known cohero.)

Without his "Sancho Panza" — cohero, assistant or sidekick, as you prefer — many a "main player" would have been diminished in stature and effect, and would have had to go for entire plots without uttering the immortal line, "you stay here and guard the prisoner, and I'll head 'em off at the pass!"

7

The Masters of Menace

What is beauty without ugliness? Wherein lies the glory of a bright, sunny day without the contrasting gloom of black night? And of what value are truth and honor and good without the recognition of their antitheses — deception and treachery and evil? As we know, genuine appreciation of anything depends upon the contemplation of its opposing alternative. It was upon that precept that the entire serial form was based. Exultation in the acquisition of a valued prize could only be felt after the dejection of seeing it in the enemy's possession; the relief of escape could result only from an encounter with mortal danger; heroism could grow only from facing the challenge of foul villainy. And to lend credibility to the heroics there had to be the proper perpetration of that villainy. To accomplish it, the makers of serials turned to the real "pros" for their arch-malefactors, and the audience gratefully responded.

Because of the wide use of masked and unknown villains, the somewhat elite roster of actors who created memorable roles as evil masterminds of one kind or another is rather exclusive. Without the obvious crutch of mystique provided by a gaudy or supernatural facade, actors who were to portray villains not concealed from the audience had to be able to quickly establish their characters and sustain them for the remainder of the episodes. This was easiest accomplished if an actor had the properly ominous-looking facial features, but could be brought about by those with less malevolent countenances through application of various thespian techniques. Basically, the serial villain had to pose an immediate, recognizable threat to mankind to gain the instant animosity of the audience. He therefore had to immediately project the image of total depravity. If a man looked sufficiently evil, this could be done with an expression — a sneer of contempt or a suggestive grimace. Another actor could accomplish the same thing by a crafty insinuation, a show of arrogance or an outright act of brutality. Quite often the very first thing the villain said or did in the first chapter stamped his character for the remainder of the film. The audience typed him as crafty, arrogant, brutish or just plain mad, and his subsequent actions were all seen by them in that light.

Craftiness, the skill to deceive others, is perhaps the prime requisite of the successful villain. To appear to be one thing when actually something else altogether was what permitted him to function. And this is the hallmark of the character actor.

Take for example kindly, silver-haired Ralph Morgan: He could make you believe he was anything he wanted you to think he was. A distinguished actor of stage and screen, his motion picture career did not equal that of his gifted brother Frank (remembered as the flighty and very phony "professor" in MGM's *Wizard of Oz*), but his portrayals in action films and serials left a legion of fans who thought of him as great, many without ever knowing his name for sure. Possessor of a law degree from Columbia University in his native New York, and highly respected by his fellow thespians, Morgan served as president of the Screen Actors Guild and helped shape it into the force it finally became in Hollywood politics. His first major serial role was as a respected-citizen-who-turned-out-to-be-the-villain in *Dick Tracy vs. Crime, Inc.*, but it was his next a few months later for which he is best remembered as a villain. In Universal's *Gangbusters* he played the nefarious Professor Mortis, leader of a band of criminals known as the "League of Murdered Men." For his "League" he stole the bodies of hoodlums executed by the law and through a mysterious process he had discovered, apparently restored them to life as human robots subject to his own will. His adversaries had to use every known technique of law enforcement (including scientific laboratory investigations, radio triangulation and just plain old-fashioned "legwork") as well as hard-fisted, determined personal action to bring his master scheme for wealth and power to an end. Throughout the film there was a consistent feeling of disconcertion about his Mortis characterization. His dignified, venerable appearance was continuously belied by his viciously threatening manner and hoarsely uttered invective. It was much like seeing a favorite uncle about to tear the wings off of a bird. (That role stands out for me personally as one of the finest ever created for a serial.) Morgan's other two roles were as scientific inventors whose discoveries were the prizes in *The Great Alaskan Mystery* at Universal and *The Monster and the Ape* at Columbia.

Noah Beery, Sr., was the personification of the self-made man — big, gruff, effusively expansive, with a hearty laugh and a friendly slap on the back — until the door was shut. Then the facade fell away as he upbraided a confederate about a failure or grimly began to outline a new plan to do in the hero. Like Ralph Morgan he was the brother of a more famous actor, Wallace Beery, but nonetheless had a distinguished career of his own as a screen actor reaching back to outstanding roles in silent films. In sound serials he appeared in two for Nat Levine at Mascot in the early thirties — *The Devil Horse* and *Fighting with Kit Carson* — two at Republic in the late thirties — as the mercenary tycoon Marsden in *Zorro Rides Again* and the treacherous Ace Hanlon in *The Adventures of Red Ryder* — and one at Universal in the early forties — *Overland Mail*, in which he played another Hanlon type villain and appeared in the same cast with his son. *Overland Mail* was the second time he and Noah, Jr., had appeared together. The first had been *Fighting with Kit Carson* nine years earlier.

Cast in the same mold, but with a continental flair, was Lionel Royce, who at first observation could have been a respected diplomat, statesman or financier. In fact, as a Nazi agent in *Secret Service in Darkest Africa*, he portrayed Sultan Abou Ben Ali, the ruler of a small Arab nation, whose identity he assumed in the first episode. When talking to the good guys, he was suave and reassuring, but when conspiring in secret with his cohorts (as the spy, Baron Von Rommler), he was cold and calculating, spitting out his words venomously. He had previously scored in the villainy department earlier that year in *Don Winslow of the Coast Guard* — also as a Nazi spy.

And, speaking of distinguished actors who contributed to serial villainy as crafty deceivers, mention must be made of one who appeared only once in a chapterplay but left an indelible mark on the character of the type. Known to the public as an accomplished director, with such major films to his credit as *She, The Happy Land, And Now Tomorrow, A Medal for Benny, Miracle of the Bells, Mr. Peabody and the Mermaid, Without Honor, Destination Moon* and *Santa Fe* (to name a few), only the most avid serial fan remembers that Irving Pichel was the wily Zarnoff, who returned from death by lethal gas chamber to plague the intrepid hero in *Dick Tracy's G-Men*. As in the other three Tracys, the choice of a convincing villain was one of the major factors of a successful cliff-hanger. Pichel, Pittsburgh born and Harvard educated, had been a respected Shakespearean actor and had served on the advisory board of the Theatre Guild. He entered motion pictures as a writer at MGM and continued as actor and director.

One of the feature films directed by Irving Pichel starred an actor who is perhaps among the ten best character actors of sound motion pictures. In *A Medal for Benny*, J. Carroll Naish played the very confused and poignantly proud father of a young man who was to receive the Medal of Honor for bravery in World War II. His performance was thought by many to have deserved an Academy Award, but it was not to be. A man of diversified talent, Naish played characters of practically every nationality and caste, from the pathetic little Italian Army deserter (almost left stranded in the desert by Humphrey Bogart's tank crew) in *Sahara* and the supposedly-pixilated but shrewdly urbane French policeman in *Enter Arsene Lupin*, to the stoical, determined Indian chief in the title role of *Sitting Bull*. It could almost be said of J. Carroll Naish that he was to the character field what Lon Chaney had been to the mystery and horror field. Along the way, Naish appeared in two serials. In Mascot's *Mystery Squadron* the veteran of the New York and Paris stage played one of the henchmen of the unknown Black Ace, and in Columbia's *Batman* he played the Japanese spy leader, Dr. Daka. By today's standards his portrayal of the insidious Oriental conspirator in that production is a little ludicrous, as learned by the laughter and ridicule of many during the full-length showing of the serial several years ago to a new generation of youngsters. But in the context of World War II his exaggerated melodramatics and hissing dialect were well-suited to the average moviegoer's concept of the typical Japanese entity, and was accepted as such. At that time, to have played him differently would have defied credibility.

To exemplify the Italian branch of the Axis conspiracy in serials was the lot of Nestor Paiva. Everybody's idea of what the gregarious Italian fisherman (merchant, farmer, laborer) was like, the rotund, open-faced man with the booming, Latin-flavored voice, appeared in dozens of features in such roles, and thus became a type. In Republic's *King of the Mounties* he played Count Baroni, the fascist representative of the Italian dictator who was supposedly his country's top agent in America. But he was constantly being put down by the other two members of the Axis triumvirate — Nazi Marshal Von Horst and the top conspirator, Japanese Admiral Yamata. In *Don Winslow of the Coast Guard* he was cast as the hero's perennial adversary, the Scorpion.

The villains most required to practice guile and trickery were those who operated within the circle of the good guys and who were trusted *prima facie*. They had to cultivate that trust without seeming to be solicitous and had to use whatever information they secured discreetly so as to prevent any backlash of guilt. Good at that kind of intrigue was Leroy Mason, who was suave and glib on the surface but well-schooled in when and where to insert the proverbial knife-in-the-back. His career embraced ten prominent roles as the chief villain (or the top henchman) in sound serials, from RKO's *The Last Frontier* in 1932 to Republic's *Daughter of Don Q* in 1947, and included *Phantom of the Air* at Universal, *Jungle Menace* and *Overland with Kit Carson* at Columbia, and *The Painted Stallion, The Tiger Woman, Federal Operator 99, The Phantom Rider* and *King of the Forest Rangers* for Republic.

Trevor Bardette achieved his deceptions with a demeanor of sincerity. In *Overland with Kit Carson*, so efficacious was his desire to be helpful that it seemed almost impossible that he could be the mysterious Pegleg. And in *Jungle Girl* his assumption of his murdered twin brother's identity brought no trace of suspicion whatever from his niece, Nyoka. As Jensen, a spy leader in *The Secret Code*, Bardette had his most activist role as a villain. In that one, a cops-and-robbers spy thriller with an undercover hero, it was strictly a battle of good guys versus bad guys, with not too much room for deception per se.

One could never be sure about Lyle Talbot. He was just as apt to turn up as a clean-cut hero (the title role in *Chick Carter Detective*) or a deep-dyed villain of the "mad professor" school (Luthor in *Atom Man vs. Superman*), or anywhere between — quite fitting for an actor with the unlikely real name of Lysle *Hollywood*. A versatile thespian, he portrayed a police executive (Commissioner Gordon in *Batman and Robin*), a Canadian Mountie officer (Inspector Wheeler in *Gunfighters of the Northwest*) and an Army commander (Colonel Foster in *Son of Geronimo*), but many cliff-hanger fans prefer to remember his heavy shots. In addition to the redoubtable Luthor, he also played a deadly serious foreign agent twice. In Universal's *Mystery of the Riverboat* he played Rudolph Toller, an unscrupulous agent for a foreign power seeking chemical deposits in the Louisiana swamplands owned by the hero. And in *Trader Tom of the China Seas*, the Air Force veteran, Shriner and Lambs and Masquers member from Pittsburgh, Pennsylvania, played a hard-as-nails spy leader named Barent, whose purpose it was to foment revolution in a vital United Nations protectorate by smuggling in arms and munitions and encouraging native subversion. When Lyle Talbot was a good guy, he was a real good guy; when he was a bad guy, he was all bad; but when either, he was all business.

The lean, wavy-haired, finely chiseled features of James Craven gave him the look of unqualified integrity. To be told that he was a renowned scientist, revered professor or respected statesman was wholly believable. His manner was suave, sophisticated and cultured. He was the picture of a gentleman. Usually, however, he was anything but. For most of his roles, the outward show of charm and grace was merely an integument concealing as cruel and bitter a villain as ever stalked the screen. In his first major heavy role in a Columbia serial, his opening act was to have his own brother kidnapped and thrown into a dungeon so he could seize his inheritance, an ancestral castle estate. As the demented Abel Bellamy in *The Green Archer*, he then engineered attempt after attempt to destroy anyone who threatened his scheme. Just as ruthless and treacherous were his machinations against hero Buck Jones in *White Eagle* while posing as a respectable citizen known as Dandy Darnell. As enemy saboteur Ivan Shark, he next took on the famed *Captain Midnight* and gave that intrepid champion a tough time for 15 weeks. In Republic's *The Purple Monster Strikes*, Craven started out as a professor of astronomy and it looked as if he finally might be one of the good guys, but, alas, no. The Purple Monster — a Martian invader in the person of Roy Barcroft — quickly did him in and commandeered his lifeless body as an earthly disguise. For the remaining fourteen-and-a-half chapters, Craven was thought to be the good Dr. Cyrus Layton, but the audience knew him as really the Monster's alter ego. Finally he was permitted to operate on the side of law and order for awhile. In his next two cliff-hanger roles Republic cast him as a scientist (Professor Clayton in *Federal Agents vs.*

Underworld, Inc.) and an inventor (Professor Millard in *King of the Rocketmen*), but for his final one it was back to skullduggery. As an industrialist named Bryant in *Flying Disc Man from Mars*, Craven reverted to previous type, playing a former Nazi collaborator who threw in with another Purple Monster type (this time played by Gregory Gay) in a plan to soften up the Earth for a Martian invasion. Unsuspected as Bryant, he manipulated the heroes almost as he wished—by employing them as security agents for his plant and sending them on "wild goose" chases—until they caught on to his trickery.

In his own element nearly every villain displayed monumental arrogance. It was a mark of the breed. To be unequivocally certain that his was the master plan of all time and to boast of it to his confederates was the vanity of every supposed criminal genius. A half dozen or so actors so adroitly projected this quirk of the archmalefactor's nature that they can be identified with it. Even though he chose to infiltrate the good side from time to time for a particular purpose, the arrogant villain more often preferred to remain aloof and "call the shots" from the confines of his own domain, so certain was he that his strategy was foolproof and perfect. Played right, this type of villain appeared totally despicable and evoked utter contempt from the audience. And several fellows could surely play him right.

In his feature roles as well as his single serial appearance, George Macready was arrogance personified. A slight backward toss of his head, a disdainful glare aimed down his long, pointed nose left no doubt what his thoughts were concerning anyone unlucky enough to be the subject of his displeasure. And when he spoke it was much like pouring acid into a bowl of honey. A mathematician by education (Brown University), a classical dramatic actor by training (stage roles in *Macbeth, Romeo and Juliet, Lucrece, Barretts of Wimpole Street, Victoria Regina*, etc.) and an art connoisseur by instinct (cooperator of an art gallery with friend Vincent Price), this man of many parts was well-equipped for the roles he so vividly portrayed—the scheming prime minister in gaudy swashbucklers, the feudal land baron in quasi-Freudian Westerns, the haughty politician or militarist in historical and war films, or the pseudo-sophisticate in contemporary dramas. His performance as Professor Ernst in Columbia's *The Monster and the Ape* demanded only a few of the dramatic facets possessed by this talented, capable man, but he displayed them with rare aplomb, giving the serial form one of its choicest villains.

Douglass Dumbrille was also an actor of magnitude who gave the serial some excellent moments. As a minor minion in *King of the Mounties*, the Canadian dramatic artist stood out among the heavies because of his curt, no-nonsense dispatch of the lesser henchmen on assignments radioed to him by the three major villains. Later, in Universal's *Jungle Queen*, he was cast as a Nazi agent sent to the African jungle to foster unrest among the natives and turn them against the Allies. In both films, the authoritative evincing of orders from that haughty, confident man left an image not again recalled until a quarter-century later while watching a telecast of French President Charles De Gaulle as he revealed to his nation and the world what his latest plans were for them.

To fully appreciate the arrogance emoted by Lionel Atwill, one need only see his performance as the village police official in Universal's *Son of Frankenstein*. In the scene in which he visited the newly arrived Baron Frankenstein, son of the monster's creator, and ostensibly welcomed him back while in reality grimly warning him not to resume his father's experimentations, Atwill demonstrated a fierce, determined pride that evoked an unexpected reaction in the mind of the viewer. When he explained the cause of the obvious incapacity of his rigid right arm by relating how the monster on his initial rampage had wrenched it from its socket, and boasted of how he had overcome the atrocity and again become functionally proficient, then followed with an audaciously manipulated salute by the wooden substitute, the immediate effect was stunned incredulity. There was a sudden desire to feel pity or compassion, but that was immediately counteracted by the man's defiant disclaimer of that human reaction. He left as he came, a man of his own with his status made clear. The scene was replete with possibilities for a maudlin or acrimonious tirade, but Atwill left only that feeling due emotional arrogance — the feeling of, "so be it." Because of his continental bearing and the talent to project arrogance, he was in serials almost always cast as a high-ranking foreign spy, presumably a member of his homeland's aristocracy, who stooped to engage in espionage as a penance for his position, or conceivably just for the sport of it. In Universal's *Junior G-Men of the Air* he played such a villain called The Baron, but was made up to appear Oriental. Other credits for Universal were *Raiders of Ghost City* and *The Lost City of the Jungle*, but his best serial role was that of Dr. Maldor in Republic's *Captain America*. As the curator of a museum, he concealed the fact that he was an archcriminal who called himself The Scarab, and was bent upon the revenge murders of all the members of an archaeological expedition he felt had cheated him out of his share of wealth. Their deaths and his acquisition of all their scientific discoveries was nearly accomplished before the fabulous crimefighter, Captain America, finally stopped him.

Sitting upon the bench as a dignified judge in a Perry Mason drama, his kinky grey hair and lined face exuding an aura of judicial austerity, Kenneth MacDonald hardly could be visualized as a cruel, heartless, arrogant leader of a cutthroat band of outlaws by any but those who had hissed at him on the screen in more than a half dozen such roles in Columbia serials. Beginning as Webster, a prime suspect (but not the guilty one) in *Mandrake the Magician*, MacDonald quickly moved to the outdoors to play another decoy (the gambler Winchester) in *Overland with Kit Carson*. Then he came into his own as a villain. As Mort

Ransome in *Perils of the Royal Mounted*, he led an irascible gang of renegades in promoting Indian uprisings, robberies, kidnappings and murder
to block a proposed railroad project until he could grab the franchise for
himself. With his commanding voice and cocky self-confidence he
ordered that bunch of toughs around as if he were certain he could tear
them apart with his own hands, although all of them appeared capable of
just the reverse. His arrogant edictions seemed to be the only language
they understood. In *The Valley of Vanishing Men* he recreated the same
type of ruthless, tyrannical character as the outlaw Kincaid, who ordered
men kidnapped and mercilessly driven to slave in his mine. Next he
became the jungle adversary of *The Phantom*, playing the unscrupulous
Dr. Bremmer, and in *The Desert Hawk* joined in the schemes and
intrigues against the hero as a villain named Akbar. In open spaces again,
he joined Robert Williams and I. Stanford Jolley to form an unholy trio of
gold-seeking carpetbaggers who callously attempted to trigger a bloody
Indian war in *Black Arrow*, and reverted to his previous devilment as a
bandit overlord (but this time with modern devices such as automatic
weapons, cars and a hydroplane) in the Canadian Mounted thriller *Perils
of the Wilderness*, before assuming responsibility on television.

To many the epitome of villainous arrogance in serials was the
portrayal of Sax Rohmer's infamous Oriental Dr. Fu Manchu by Henry
Brandon in *Drums of Fu Manchu*. To properly demonstrate the diabolical
egotism of the famed evil genius, young Brandon employed a glowering
sneer that seemed to defy a confederate or an adversary to so much as
even think anything contrary to his own prognostications. The idea that
he might be wrong or might fail in his sadistic plot was simply not permitted voice. In his search for power, he was impudently certain that de
facto control of the world was rightly his, and that is the way Brandon
played him. Having served as a henchman twice before — as Blackstone
(who was revealed as the mystery leader in the final chapter) in Universal's 1937 *Secret Agent X-9*, and as Captain Lasca, emissary of the
despotic Killer Kane in that studio's *Buck Rogers* — Brandon was well-
versed in the required histrionics of screen villainy, and he packed it all
into his Dr. Fu. The result was a performance that stands alone.

Brute force was the trademark of Fred Kohler, Sr. In the two chapter-
films he made, his brutish snarl and growling invective permeated his
scenes, and the threat of violent action hung at all times in the atmosphere. (His General Jason Burr in *The Vigilantes Are Coming* was so
menacingly foreboding that I actually felt intimidated. Whether it was
because that was my first encounter with unabashed villainy or because I
was only eight years old I don't know, but I never saw Kohler — nor even
his son, Fred, Jr. — in a film after that without immediately recalling the
vicious Burr.) Earlier he had threatened Frankie Darro and Rin Tin Tin,
Jr., in Mascot's *The Wolf Dog*.

Like Kohler, Eugene Stutenroth (also billed as Gene Roth after 1947) was a big man. And, although his roles were not always heavy, his expansive frame and stern, Nordic face lent themselves perfectly to the type of roles that called for a man of blunt, physical force. He played well a brawling seaman, a relentless frontier sheriff or a mean, ruthless criminal. After a string of roles as a minor henchman in Universal serials, he began to garner more important parts at Columbia and Republic following the war. At first in occasional character roles such as Dr. Albour in *Jack Armstrong*, the sheriff in *Jesse James Rides Again*, the marshal in *The Adventures of Frank and Jesse James* and *The James Brothers of Missouri*, and a minor part in *The Black Widow*, he rose to covillain status in *Ghost of Zorro*, sharing chores with Roy Barcroft as a couple of greedy scoundrels intent upon preventing the westward extension of the telegraph. In *Pirates of the High Seas* he played Frederick Whitlock, owner of a small Pacific island and ringleader of a band of cutthroats using a speedy phantom ship to raid shipping on the high seas. Again portraying a pirate (but this time one who is regenerated to the good side before demise), Roth appeared as Captain Shard in *Mysterious Island*. Following two similar roles as space-age brute heavies (Vultura in *Captain Video* and Reckov in *The Lost Planet*), Roth wound up his serial career back at sea, as Nardo Thompson in *The Great Adventures of Captain Kidd*.

Both Kohler and Roth, by virtue of their size and hulking appearance, made excellent villains of the purely brute caste, and were unique for it. Many less physical but more intellectual heavies utilized big, burly guys as henchmen, but only these two rose to top-villain rank.

It is obvious that a naturally evil-looking face would be an asset to an actor aspiring to melodramatic malevolence. By itself, a mean-looking face could qualify one for a role in a quickie serial where the immediate need was for visual antagonism, but such a countenance combined with acting ability could produce screen villains whose images would last longer than those of most heroes.

Lucien Prival exemplified the first contention as Dagna, the high priets, in *Darkest Africa*. Had it not been for a mean and treacherous cast to his features, his portrayal would have been nothing. His acting, which consisted of a rapid, shrill delivery of lines in a monotone, was less than that. It is likely that an earlier performance as Vindhyan, another high priest, in *The Return of Chandu* might have been better, and he certainly came off better in *King of the Texas Rangers*. As Neil Hamilton's dirigible captain, his job was mainly to stand by villain Hamilton and look mean.

An actor possessed of both talent and a lurid expression was Kurt Katch, whose slick bald head and leering eyes foretold of impending dangers for the young Naval officers in *Don Winslow of the Navy*. In his sole serial appearance, Katch played The Scorpion, hero Winslow's archadversary. As mentioned, the role went to Nestor Paiva in the sequel, but Kurt Katch is the Scorpion remembered by most action fans. His thick, guttural accent sent a shiver down the spine when he glared fiendishly at a confederate and gave the order to stop Winslow at any cost. Aside from this cliff-hanger role, Katch is perhaps best remembered as the fiery Khan in the Maria Montez-Jon Hall desert opus *Ali Baba and the Forty Thieves*, in which he gleefully had his minions dance wildly around forty large crocks suspected of containing the intrepid thieves and Ali Baba, and then plunge swords through the drawn skin covers. His rage at discovering the crocks did not contain the thieves was a classic display.

The sight of Charles Middleton rigged up as Ming the Merciless — with the long, flowing dark robe trimmed in slashing designs, topped with a stiff, arched cowl-like collar jutting up from his shoulders to frame his head like a dark, satanic halo — was enough in itself to excite the serial addict (and even give a moment of pause to the jaded moviegoer), but to further enhance the image of evil there was the face of the man: It was long and lean, with the suggestion of a scowl in two vertical wrinkles on the brow directly above the nose, which was long and equine and centered two high, sharp cheekbones over which two narrow eyes smouldered ominously. Around the thin, slit-like mouth, which turned slightly down at each end, there was the long drooping moustache and pointed black chin beard of the infamous emperor of Mongo. When he squinted his eyes, the whole visage took on a threatening, lupine quality. His head was starkly bald for *Flash Gordon*, the first of the trilogy, but a toupee-like black skullcap was added for the others. Having already appeared in minor roles for Mascot (notably *The Miracle Rider*), Middleton came to the front rank of serial villains at Universal with the Gordons and a choice heavy role in the Johnny Mack Brown Western, *Flaming Frontiers*. Then at Republic he left three of the most vivid characterizations in the history of the form for fans to remember in addition to Ming — Pa Stark in *Dick Tracy Returns*, Convict 39013 in *Daredevils of the Red Circle* and Cassib in *Perils of Nyoka*. As a supporting player he appeared in a number of features at 20th Century–Fox during that time, usually playing a sullen farmer, angry townsman or gang member. Following *Perils of Nyoka* he moved to Columbia and played in three undistinguished featured roles — a gregarious cowboy on the town in *Batman*, an Arab merchant in *The Desert Hawk* and an Indian agent in *Black Arrow* — before once again portraying the top villain in his final serial appearance — Jason Grood in *Jack Armstrong*. To many cliff-hanger fans, Charles Middleton rates as the Number One villain of sound serials. He certainly is among the top few.

One of the finest dramatic actors to lend his talents to the movie serial was Eduardo Ciannelli. Trained in medicine at the University of Naples in his native Italy, an accomplished opera singer in Europe, and a respected and successful stage actor in America before going into motion pictures in the thirties, he brought to the screen some of the most polished and distinctive portrayals it was privileged to reflect. Too numerous to list completely, his credits include some of the outstanding feature films of all time: *Winterset* (which he had also done on the stage), *Gunga Din* (as the fanatic Punjabi who jumped into a pit of snakes), *Foreign Correspondent* (as a Nazi torturer), *Kitty Foyle* (in a surprising comedy role as a waiter), *For Whom the Bell Tolls* (as a revolutionist), *A Bell for Adano* (as a discredited town official) and more recently *MacKenna's Gold* (as a wandering old Indian outcast killed for a treasure map). So descriptive of the type were his dark, lined features, expressive eyes and pronounced Neopolitan accent, that he was constantly in demand as a Latin gangster and Mafia chieftain. He played the part dozens of times in minor films and television, but never were the roles completely stereotyped. To each he gave an individualistic touch that set it apart. As the big-shot racketeer who verbally fenced with Spencer Tracy over the fate of James Arness in *The People Against O'Hara*, he betrayed a human uncertainty about continuing to hold his young, attractive wife whom he suspected of infidelity. In *Dillinger*, as one of the conspirators, he was cold and calculating, while as Sophia Loren's father in *Houseboat*, he was stern and unyielding but fair. As the years went by, he was more and more closely identified by a newer generation as the personification of the aging Mafia overlord because of roles such as that in the motion picture *The Brotherhood* and similar ones in *Burke's Law*, *The Man from U.N.C.L.E.*, *The Fugitive*, *I Spy* and *Mission: Impossible* on television. His initial impact on the serial was as the determined criminal scientist in *The Mysterious Doctor Satan*. In a role so susceptible to overacting and scenery chewing, the accomplished Mr. Ciannelli created the exact balance between a wild-eyed lunatic with dreams of world conquest and the brilliant, gifted man of science that Dr. Satan might have been. There was a poignancy in his portrayal that gave the uneasy feeling that this cruel genius was somehow a victim of forces that drove him to evil against his basic desire. Nothing was said or done in the screenplay to indicate it, but the feeling was there, nonetheless. Twice more Ciannelli depicted serial villains — in *Sky Raiders* and *The Adventures of the Flying Cadets* for Universal — and each time he was excellent, but Dr. Satan was his masterpiece.

There was never any doubt about the sanity of the villains portrayed by the maestro, Bela Lugosi. Ever since audiences had trembled in the marrow of their bones at his creation of Dracula in the Universal feature of that name, the very presence of Lugosi in the cast was sufficient to guarantee a performance of eerie, supernatural fascination. Along with Karloff, he was the undisputed master of terror and superstition. Born Bela Lugosi Blasko in Lugos, Hungary, educated at the Theatre Arts Academy in Budapest and trained on the dramatic stages of Europe, the man whose name was to become synonymous with spells, curses and vampires first appeared in America in *The Silent Command* in 1924. There followed one of the most extraordinary careers of any film star in history, in which the principal became an institution so firmly established in the minds of a generation of moviegoers that even after his death his personality lives on — almost as if he actually did continue to live after death. In his failing years he was ravaged by drug addiction, an affliction so terrible in its effect that the horrors he must have endured have vicariously become a part of his legend. His work in serials stands alone as a special kind, parallel to that of his features. Principal Pictures' casting of Lugosi as the mysterious Chandu the Magician in *Return of Chandu* was the only role in which he played a nonvillain. In it he was Dr. Frank Chandler (Chandu), guardian of an Egyptian princess marked for sacrifice by a cult of black magic fanatics who believed her sacrifice would restore to life their comatose goddess Ossana, and that she would then raise their sunken continent and lead them in ruling the world. The first four chapters were released as a feature, and then joined with eight more later to complete a twelve-chapter serial — like other productions in the early thirties. Nat Levine had secured his services for a 1933 Mascot production, *Whispering Shadow*, and Sam Katzman starred him in the 1936 Victory release, *Shadow of Chinatown* — each time as a deranged villain. In Republic's *S.O.S. Coast Guard* in 1937, Lugosi was cast as a mad inventor named Boroff who aspired to perfect a deadly disentegrating gas and sell it to a foreign power; and in Universal's *The Phantom Creeps* two years later, he plotted to rule the world with robots. No other villain, before or since, has managed to leave such an indelible imprint on an entertainment medium as Bela Lugosi did on motion pictures.

And then there was Roy Barcroft.

While Lugosi was incurring the boo's and hisses from avid serial fans as Boroff, an unbilled minor player in *S.O.S. Coast Guard* was learning the ropes for future use. Howard N. Ravenscroft from Crab Orchard, Nebraska, former Army officer, seaman, musician, Oregon rancher, salesman and construction worker, was dutifully going through the paces as a minor henchman and spear-carrier in serials such as *S.O.S.* at Republic and the Flash Gordons and Johnny Mack Brown Westerns at Universal. He later would become the most prolific of the serial villains in the forties — nearly matching the output of Walter Miller and William Desmond after they switched from good guys to bad in the thirties — but not under the name of Howard Ravenscroft.

As Roy Barcroft he piled up credits in a total of 15 Republic serials as a featured lead in a variety of tough-guy roles — two as modern-day pirates (*Haunted Harbor* and *Manhunt of Mystery Island*), two as outer-space invaders (*The Purple Monster Strikes* and *Radar Men from the Moon*), two as gangsters (*Daughter of Don Q* and *Federal Agents vs. Underworld, Inc.*), one as a crooked police commissioner (*G-Men Never Forget*), two as Western sheriffs (nonvillain roles in *The Phantom Rider* and *The Man with the Steel Whip*) and six as a Western bad guy of one sort or another (*Son of Zorro, Jesse James Rides Again, The James Brothers of Missouri, Desperadoes of the West, Ghost of Zorro* and *Don*

Daredevil Rides Again). His characterizations of Captain Mephisto and The Purple Monster rank with the best of the outlandish mystery figures created for earlier chapter films, and he accomplished it without benefit of mask. Except for outstanding acting ability, Barcroft possessed all the characteristics of a successful serial villain: His features were pliable enough to depict the evil of Mephisto or the menace of The Purple Monster, and his bold swagger and nasal, insinuating voice bespoke the arrogance of an Emperor Retik, Supreme Ruler of the Moon. Possessor of a large, hulking frame, he never hesitated to threaten brutal violence, and you believed he would carry it out. And in one of his best performances — the Jekyll-Hyde hypocrisy of his role in *G-Men Never Forget* as the escaped criminal Murkland posing as respected police commissioner Cameron — displayed a craftiness worthy of Noah Beery, Sr. Continuing to play character roles in features and television, Barcroft was seen many times in Western programs such as *Gunsmoke* and *Bonanza*.

Rarely have there been seen villains in feature movies and television like those of the action and mystery serials, for their concept was too broad and exaggerated for the "uptown" films. Features strived for realism, but cliff-hangers pursued suspense and fantasy for the sake of action and thrills. It is this fact that is often forgotten when judgments are made. In its essence, the serial was a moral parody, symbolizing all good versus all evil, and is an anachronism viewed by any other standard.

The villains were fascinating to watch and must have been fun to play, judging from the rush of name actors who clamored to fill the guest-villain shots on the recent *Batman* television series in which the crooks were played in the melodramatic style for laughs — names such as Burgess Meredith, Anne Baxter, Cesar Romero, Victor Buono, David Wayne, Cliff Robertson, Julie Newmar, Ethel Merman, Otto Preminger and George Sanders. As adversaries of a comic strip hero, they would over-act, "ham it up," steal scenes and otherwise engage in an actor's field day: And all in the name of old-fashioned villainy.

8

Emissaries of Evil

" — And to complete the weapon there is a key element I must have. There is a supply at the professor's laboratory that you must get for me. Now, here's my plan: Take some men and — "

" — A shipment of vital supplies that could critically delay our take-over is right now on wagons headed for the valley. They must be stopped at all cost. Now, here's my plan: Get the boys and head them off at — "

" — If they finished that project before the deadline two days from now, it will ruin everything we set out to do. Just to be sure they won't, we'll give them a little surprise. Now, here's my plan: Grab some dynamite at the powder shack and take a couple of good men to — "

" — That blasted meddler has interfered with me for the last time. I want him out of the way once and for all. Now, here's my plan: Pick two or three of your best gunmen and wait for him at — "

Lines like these were delivered through clenched teeth with narrowed eyes glaring hate at some neutral point in the room by the chief villain to his top aide, who in response always nodded his head resolutely to let the boss know he was in full accord. Seldom were they finished. Instead, the words trailed off in a swell of ominous background music and the picture faded to black or dissolved to the location of the proposed skullduggery. Then the real "bad guys" took over — the Henchmen, the perpetrators of the villain's foul schemes, the troops in "Evil's" army.

These were the imminent adversaries of the heroes who posed the immediate physical threat and had to be dealt with by direct confrontation. They were the activists who attempted to put into operation the battle plans formulated by their general, the master villain. This almost always resulted in direct contact with the good guys, and the subsequent action in the form of fistfights, gun battles, automobile chases, motorboat pursuits, stagecoach or wagon runaways, and horseback acrobatics was the meat of the excitement.

Men chosen to play these parts were a tough and rugged lot. Included were the roughest-, meanest-, hardest-looking mercenaries a casting director could find. And in their ranks were found the real he-men of the film business—the stuntmen. Because of the combatant nature of their activities, it is natural to make a comparison with the chain-of-command aspect of an army, for indeed there was a categorical rank-grouping whether intended or not. The villain's right hand man and initial instigator was like nothing so much as a commander's lieutenant, who passed along the orders to a subordinate (the counterpart of a squad sergeant) who would be responsible for the actual implementation of the strategem, using the main body of the gang (privates, if you will) to carry out individual assignments. Also, there were the "specialists"—just as on the side of the good guys—who could project some peculiarly singular dimension to the overall picture. The lieutenants seemed to be a degree more intelligent than the others; the sergeants were just a bit meaner and rougher than the rest; and the privates were primarily "muscle." As circumstances required, of course, these general requirements among feature players were interchangeable.

In a 1914 William S. Hart melodrama titled *The Ruse*, two of the outstanding henchmen of twenty years later had key roles. When hero Hart went to the big city to convert his ore findings into money, the wily broker who immediately laid plans to swindle him was young John Davidson. Later in a nearby bar, Hart was inveigled into a crooked card game by a ne'er-do-well toughie who was played by the grim-visaged Robert Kortman. Throughout the silents and into the forties, both men continued to portray characters of similar stripe, and are well-remembered for their many scurvy deeds.

Excelling in specialty portrayals of strange and offbeat characters— Lin Wing, the Oriental curio dealer murdered after revealing the villain's mission in *The Fighting Devil Dogs*, Tal Chotali, enigmatic and aloof Siamese aide to the Malcolm expedition in *The Adventures of Captain Marvel*, Lhoba, the Taureg chieftain in *The Perils of Nyoka*, and the emperor of Mars in *The Purple Monster Strikes*—John Davidson's most memorable roles as henchmen were for Republic. Two of the most vivid were: Lucifer, sly confederate of The Ghost in *Dick Tracy vs. Crime, Inc.*, and Gruber, Lionel Atwill's aide-de-camp in *Captain America*. His oblong, oval-shaped head, prominently squared jaws and chin jutting out from a thin, spiny neck, gave him a suspiciously serpentine look, easily adaptable to the aura of hostility required of a villain's lair.

The gaunt, skeletal face of Bob Kortman was alone enough to make one shudder. And when a black eye patch was placed on it for his role of "One-eye Chapin" in *The Adventures of Red Ryder*, one of the most colorful and picturesque henchmen in all serialdom was the result. A veteran of dozens of action films and serials in the thirties at Mascot, Universal and Republic—following many more in silent films—Kortman specialized in Western-heavy and mutinous-pirate roles.

Another veteran of silent serials — as were a number of henchmen players in the thirties — was Frank Lackteen. As the treacherous half-breed in *Wild West Days* or the jealous witch doctor Shamba in *Jungle Girl*, he instantly provoked suspicion and distrust because of his long, pointed, rodent-like features. His searing, shifty eyes left no doubt that he was up to no good and should be watched carefully. A face like that was testimony of his value in depicting evil visually in silent pictures. His voice (a hoarse, thickly accented sound) added to the overall image and helped make Lackteen a favorite with Saturday matinee audiences, especially in Universal releases. He is credited with over a dozen serials and countless Westerns during the thirties and forties.

John Picorri's screen presence was the epitome of subvillainy. To a generation of youngsters his was the very face of Evil — the vivification of all that was sly, clever, treacherous and mean. His dark, swarthy features, dominated by a huge, snarling, beak-like nose and burning black eyes, suggested what the devil himself might look like if incarnated. With his head thrust forward by a large, crippling hump on his back, the resulting image was much like that of a vulture perched anxiously await-ing the final gasp of his prey. The memory of his Moloch in *Dick Tracy*, gloating sinisterly while slowly rubbing a nervous black cat, haunted the dreams of many a boy who could hardly wait until the next Saturday to see how Tracy would overcome the latest vile plot of Moloch and The Spider to wreak vengeance upon him. And when Tracy was eventually captured and forced onto the same operating table where his brother had been so viciously transformed, with the leering, oily, deformed madman poised over him holding a deadly-looking hypodermic needle, there was a feeling of impending doom in the hushed audience unmatched by very many other scenes in motion pictures. Having already scored in *Robinson Crusoe of Clipper Island* as the hated Porodu, Picorri next antagonized audiences as Rackerby in *S.O.S. Coast Guard*, and finally (in a repeat of his *Dick Tracy* characterization) as Gould, first assistant to The Lightning and commander of his huge Wing aircraft, in *The Fighting Devil Dogs*.

When the script called for a cringer, the man to get was Jay Novello. As a henchman who fell in battle and was deserted by his accomplices, then realized that he was to be interrogated and possibly blamed for the whole thing, he was expert at depicting sudden cowardness and begging for mercy from the good guys. Cringing on his knees, his rectangular face twisted with fear, he became so pitifully weak that any information he might have known became the hero's for the asking. Adept at portraying a particularly nasty sort of Mexican or half-breed bandit in Westerns, Novello appeared in three outstanding Republic serials in billed roles: as Lewis in *King of the Mounties*, Simms in *Captain America*, and Heinrick in *Federal Operator 99*.

As early in the sound era as *The Hurricane Express* and *Shadow of the Eagle* for Mascot — and for the next two decades at all three serial companies — there was a diminutive, erratic actor who was known by the kids in my neighborhood as "the Weasel." The appellation stuck even when he occasionally played a good guy (Rusty Fenton, ally of the hero in *The Phantom*), because his usual assignment called for the little fellow to strut cockily through the proceedings as a henchman up to the point that a double cross was called for. It was he who then surreptitiously "ratted" on his confederates and was methodically eliminated when they found him out. Short in stature, with a face not unlike a monkey's (wide mouth, high-set nose, round, peering eyes and ears set low on the head), Ernie Adams romped through features, Westerns and serials up to the late forties, almost always playing the type of part that had given him his nickname.

As "specialist" henchmen, easily identified at first sight, these fellows thus became known in the Saturday crowd by such Runyonesque designations as "the evil" (Picorri), "yellowbelly" (Novello), and "weasel" (Adams). And the terms were no more meant derogatorily than were those of the great Runyon in describing his friends. Their use was merely a type of descriptive shorthand, to be employed in the rapid give-and-take of a bunch of youngsters excitedly trying to outdo each other in being the one to remember the most details and relate them faster in the weekly discussions of the most recent episode.

One such favorite — known variously as "the whiner" and "the coward" — was a multitalented veteran. Visually, from the mindless zombie-slave in *Buck Rogers*, the terrified gangster in the Batcave in Chapter Two of *Batman* or the subservient storekeeper-henchman in *The Tiger Woman*, to the egotistical Phantom Ruler in *The Invisible Monster*, Stanley Price was always a minor league minion, usually worked into the plot for some specific reason, such as being forced to provide some clue needed by the hero, and then disposed of forthwith. His other talents were more evident behind the scenes. His voice was heard from time to time dubbed in for a mystery character (The Lightning in Chapter One of *The Fighting Devil Dogs*) or giving background narration. And he has a number of screenplays to his credit as a writer.

The "lieutenants," the top-echelon henchmen, were played by a versatile and diversified lot of thespians. Unlike the specialist baddies, they did not project any immediate images by virtue of instantly distinguishable physical features, although they were established early in Chapter One as the villain's spokesman and chief arbiter. In the case of an unknown mystery villain, the lieutenant often was in effect the actual villain, since he was the uppermost known adversary of the good side and the villain himself a vague nonentity. Such was the role of Tony Dirken, played by Don Haggerty, in *King of the Rocketmen*. His boss, Dr. Vulcan, was only a shadow on the wall whose voice issued orders over a radio. He took no active part in the action until the last few minutes of Chapter Eleven. It was Haggerty who was the villain for all practical purposes up to that point. Where the chief villain was himself an activist, the lieutenant henchman was a faithful right-arm and confidant. This was the relationship most prevalent throughout the serial's history.

Wheeler Oakman doubled as the villain and his own chief lieutenant in *The Airmail Mystery*. In the 1932 Universal sky thriller he was rancher Judson Ward, who donned black leather flying clothes, helmet and goggles to become the treacherous Black Hawk when trying to steal shipments of gold ore from the hero and heroine. Revealed to the audience as the Hawk in the first episode, Oakman then functioned as a villain without mystique for the remainder of the serial, and became for practical purposes the chief lieutenant of a nonexistent personage. Throughout his career as a heavy he played the assistant villain many times (a la Ming's first-in-command in *Flash Gordon's Trip to Mars*), as well as assorted other shady characters in every type of adventure.

Oakman's boss in *Buck Rogers*—the infamous tyrant Killer Kane— was portrayed by another young actor who would become best known as a subvillain. Anthony Warde, a darkly handsome man, might have been able to play hero parts but for the menacing image projected by his swarthy features and husky, slightly high-pitched voice. Instead, he made an effective lieutenant for such villains as the wily Sakima in *The Masked Marvel*, Professor Carver in *King of the Forest Rangers*, the alluring Sombra in *The Black Widow*, Skagway Kate in *Dangers of the Canadian Mounted*, and Nitra and Baroda in *Radar Patrol vs. Spy King*. As a less important but always effective henchman, he appeared in a number of other cliff-hangers—*Flash Gordon's Trip to Mars*, *Dick Tracy vs. Crime, Inc.*, *King of the Mounties*, *The Purple Monster Strikes*, *Brenda Starr Reporter*, *The Monster and the Ape*, etc.—and became a favorite of the serial fans over a period of fifteen years.

The Flash Gordon and Buck Rogers thrillers from Universal served as training ground for a number of would-be heavies like Warde, who determinedly barked out their emperor's orders to each other on mock-up spaceship sets (later the film editors spliced in shots of the miniature ships engaged in toy-like dogfights) in the hope that they would sound mean enough to be picked for bigger roles in the future. One was a young Canadian named Kenneth Duncan MacLachlin from Chatham, Ontario. Educated at St. Andrews College, Toronto, and trained at the Royal School of Infantry at Wolseley Barracks, London, Ontario, he had dropped his surname for billing purposes and had appeared on the dramatic stage before entering motion pictures in 1930. His military training and dramatic background lent authority to his portrayals of officers in Ming's and Kane's legions, and did indeed lead to better parts. His role as Barnett, chief aide to the nefarious Scorpion in the American sequences of *The Adventures of Captain Marvel*, set him up as one of Republic's best known henchmen for the next five years. His teaming with Bud Geary as Roy Barcroft's henchmen Gregg and Snell in *Haunted*

Harbor created a classic example of the type of uninhibited criminality practiced nearly a decade before by Wheeler Oakman and Edmund Cobb in *Darkest Africa*. (As a pair of scoundrels named Durkin and Craddock, they were so crooked they chose to perish in the ruins of Joba rather than give up a final chance at the secret treasure.) And as Brand, right-arm of the colorful Captain Mephisto in *Manhunt of Mystery Island*, Duncan was as mean and despicable as any Jack London first mate ever was. His few departures from the usual henchman role had come earlier when he portrayed hero's assistant Ram Singh in the two Spider thrillers and a futuristic space officer who discovered the inert forms of Buck and Buddy in their downed dirigible in the 25th century in *Buck Rogers*. From serials, Duncan went to Japan in the early fifties where he became a popular star of Westerns made in that country.

Because of his role in *Dick Tracy* as the detective's brother Gordon, who was changed from a decent young man to a vicious, hardened criminal by Moloch's brain operation, Carleton Young became for five years one of the best known henchmen in the cliff-hanger business. Although none came close to matching his Gordon Tracy portrayal, he played minor villains and character parts in a half dozen of Republic's "golden age" serials and several (including *Buck Rogers*) for Univeral. They ranged from heavies in *The Fighting Devil Dogs*, *Dick Tracy Returns*, *The Lone Ranger Rides Again* and *The Adventures of Captain Marvel* to a sheriff in *The Adventures of Red Ryder* and Mexican President Benito Juarez in *Zorro's Fighting Legion*. Following a series of "Billy the Kid" Westerns as Bob Steele's saddle pal Jeff, he appeared in countless major films as an Army officer or professional man. His deep, commanding voice immediately established him as a man of authority, and gave authenticity to his characterizations of lawyers, doctors, government officials, etc. But, for many years when he turned up as one of these in a major production, the serial fan's mind invariably would quietly click with the thought, "it's good old Gordon Tracy." Mine did whenever I saw him on television as a kindly but urbane family doctor or in some similar bit part.

John Merton was Loki, the Number One dacoit, mindless slave of the insidious Oriental genius, in *Drums of Fu Manchu*. He was also Champ Stark, meanest of the five sons of Pa Stark in *Dick Tracy Returns*. In *Zorro's Fighting Legion* he was Manuel, one of the town councilers suspected of being the power-mad Don Del Oro, and in *The Adventures of Sir Galahad* he was the medieval Saxon King Ulric, archenemy of the Round Table's King Arthur. In a dozen or more other chapterplays for Republic and Columbia from the mid-thirties to the early fifties, the square-jawed, glint-eyed, huskily-built Merton was also a Western renegade (Jeffries' assistant, Kester, in *The Lone Ranger*), a big-city gangster (Schultz in *Brenda Starr Reporter*), an English duke (Hampton in *Son of the Guardsman*), a foreign spy chief (Baroda in *Radar Patrol vs. Spy*

King), and even a pawn (inventor Dr. Tymak in *Brick Bradford*). To many he was the ideal Number Two villain. His ramrod-straight bearing and grim expression lent authority to his role as top man of the gang and intermediary to the Chief. As a matter of fact, when he appeared as "just one of the boys" in a Western or action feature, it was then he seemed unconvincing, for there was the nagging feeling in the minds of action fans that he ought to be giving the orders instead of taking them. It just seemed natural.

It was much the same with Cy Kendall. A big, stout, lumbering man, whose first impression of drowsiness or laziness was disarmingly deceptive, he portrayed with finesse the sly, crafty, insinuating gang boss who badgered those around him with guile and deceit, praising them with a sarcastic display of oily supercilious charm, while constantly nagging them with a cynical sneer of thinly disguised contempt. His "boys" never knew what he *really* thought of them, but the audience did. He was so easy to hate that regular serial fans grew to love him. Kendall appeared in several Universal releases, notably as Monroe, the gang lieutenant who turned out to be the unknown master criminal himself in *The Green Hornet*, as Brand, the leader of The Flaming Torch Gang in *Junior G-Men*, and the sinister second villain in 1945's *Secret Agent X-9*. Also an outstanding character actor in features, Kendall contributed tremendously to the image of the top henchman in serials.

Other lieutenants of note could be characterized in general as falling into two categories — the "sophisticate," or somewhat suave and urbane criminal who tried not to mix in too much with the actual combat, and the "roughneck," who took a personal hand in all the meanest and dirtiest tricks the top villain could contrive. Like the boss-heavies themselves, they were played by a variety of actors with different images but the same basic ability to elicit the mistrust and enmity of the action audience.

There is perhaps no better example of the sophisticate than Tristram Coffin. His first serial appearances came within months of each other from Columbia (*Holt of the Secret Service*) and Republic (*Spy Smasher*). As Valden in the former he was the right-arm of gambler Lucky Arnold, who plotted to set up a vast counterfeit operation through his illicit gambling outlets until thwarted by hero Jack Holt, a treasury agent working undercover. In *Spy Smasher* he played a Nazi spy named Drake, first in command of another attempted counterfeit plot by the top German spy in America known only as The Mask. Then came the role of Torrini, an undercover spy for the villains in *The Perils of Nyoka*. After the war came the same type of sneaky roles in *Jesse James Rides Again* and *Federal Agents vs. Underworld, Inc.*, for Republic and *Bruce Gentry* and *Pirates of the High Seas* for Columbia. His sole appearance as a hero was in *King of the Rocketmen* and he appeared in a change-of-pace good guy role as a government official in *Radar Patrol vs. Spy King*. In all of them, Coffin's dignified bearing, articulate delivery and slightly haughty manner gave an indication that he was no ordinary criminal but an intelligent, educated and cultural man who had chosen crime as a profession. The result was a feeling of icy dislike for so callous and impersonal an individual.

I. Stanford Jolley conveyed the grand manner of Shakespearean drama even in his most minor parts. And here was a working actor who played many parts in all kinds of motion pictures — large and small, seen and unseen. From the chief villain ("Dude" Dawson in *Desperadoes of the West*) to a lesser henchman ("Lippy" in *Daughter of Don Q*); as a solid citizen who was really the mystery villain (Professor Bryant/Dr. Vulcan in *King of the Rocketmen*) and the voice of a mystery villain (*The Crimson Ghost*) while playing a totally unrelated character (the minor part of Blackton) in the same story, his assorted roles included an English nobleman (*Son of the Guardsman*), a Western sheriff (*Don Daredevil Rides Again*), a crooked circus manager (*Congo Bill*), and a living robot (*Captain Video*). Since the versatile Jolley often turned up in pivotal but unbilled minor parts in a number of serials, it is almost impossible to put a total number to his appearances in chapter films during the forties. One of his best as a villain's lieutenant was as the scientist Jaffa in *The Black Widow*. It was he who cooked up the deadly gimmicks for villainess Sombra and her aides to try out against the good guys. A popular "dandy"-type villain in scores of Westerns, he continued to perform in television and major features during the fifties and sixties.

A little less classically sophisticated than Coffin and Jolley, but obviously more intelligent than the average henchman, were Robert Fiske, Dr. Daka's lieutenant, Foster, in *Batman* and bad guy of earlier Columbia chapterplays, and Hugh Prosser, a very businesslike, matter-of-fact lieutenant in nearly two dozen cliff-hangers at Columbia and Republic.

Typical of the roughneck henchman lieutenant was swaggering Harry Woods of the Universal Westerns of the thirties. His face screwed into a sneer, he barked orders to his gangs with a threatening nasal twang that is almost impossible to forget. From minor roles in early sound Western cliff-hangers to the top roughneck in *Winners of the West* in 1940, he created a memorable place for himself as a downright "mean, ornery, no-good blackguard" with practically no redeeming personal characteristics. His dark, swarthy, mustachioed face was never seen to laugh nor show any human qualities. And one wondered secretly if maybe the lousy "galoot" wasn't all the time suffering from a toothache or something that made him so cranky.

Much like him was big, rangy Dick Curtis, who almost made a career out of bucking Charles Starrett in his Columbia series Westerns during the forties. Blessed (for a screen heavy) with narrow eyes, high cheekbones with long, vertical wrinkles giving the appearance of scars, and a pointed chin below a slightly pouting mouth over which grew a thin black

moustache, he was naturally equipped visually to portray the lowest type
of rotter and scoundrel the writers could dream up. When time came to
cast the Oriental archfiend Fang in *Terry and the Pirates*, Curtis was the
logical choice. Already a veteran heavy at Columbia (*The Flying G-Men*,
Mandrake the Magician and *Overland with Kit Carson*), he was picked
by producer Darmour and director Horne for the role that would be
carefully scrutinized by the comic strip's followers and action fans as well.
He passed with flying colors.

By virtue of the same (only huskier and more Latin) physical attributes, Robert Barron contributed to a half dozen or so Republic and
Columbia cliff-hangers as a visual example of the swarthy underworld
type. His big part came in *The Sea Hound*, in which he played a ruthless
pirate leader known as The Admiral.

Neither completely suave nor completely savage, yet possessing a
modicum of both, was one of the best known henchmen of the forties at
Republic—George J. Lewis. When last seen he was playing character parts
in television dramas and feature motion pictures—usually a Mexican or
Spanish statesman or dignitary because of his snow-white hair, Latin
bearing and confident manner—but in 1943 he was romping through his
first major supporting role as a spy named Lugo (cohort of the treacherous Ranga, played by Noel Cravat), colieutenant of the villain Haruchi in
G-Men vs. the Black Dragon. In Republic's very next continued picture,
Daredevils of the West, the handsome heavy continued his scurvy activities as a henchman named Turner, this time teamed up with big, burly
William Haade as a ruffian named Barton Ward. Then he was elevated to
"chief" lieutenant Matson in *Captain America*, second in command to the
wily Dr. Maldor and his aide, Gruber. *The Tiger Woman*, *Haunted
Harbor*, *Federal Operator 99*, *The Adventures of Frank and Jesse James*
and *The Ghost of Zorro* all included his name in the cast as the villain's
henchman lieutenant. In the meantime, he also switched over to other
roles, trying his hand at being a hero (Vic Gordon in *Zorro's Black Whip*),
an Indian (Blue Feather in *The Phantom Rider* and "Snake-that-walks" in
Black Arrow) and a hero's assistant (Manuel in *Radar Patrol vs. Spy
King*). Then a dark-haired, good-looking Latin type with a rakish moustache, he displayed little dignity but a great deal of arrogance: For
example, when admonished by chief crooks Leroy Mason and Crane
Whitley in *The Tiger Woman* for allowing one of his gang to be captured
by the heroine's native friends (thus threatening their scheme with
exposure), Lewis scornfully rebuked them by saying he had hired the man
and he would take care of the threat, and besides, the man didn't even
know who he was working for beyond him—quite a stance for a
supposed subordinate.

Lewis' partner in crime in *Daredevils of the West*, William Haade,
was representative of the second rank of henchmen—the "sergeant"
type—in his two serial appearances. Prior to *Daredevils*, his only other

venture had been as the gullible, outspoken gangster Taboni in *Gang-busters*, next in command under slicker, more perceptive Ralf Harolde, who relayed Professor Mortis' orders to Haade and the others for perpetration.

Not too smart (for he didn't need to be) but smart enough to carry out orders (which he had to be), the sergeant was essentially the mob's rallying point, the trigger for the fracas, the voice in the melee shouting,

"Get 'em, boys!"

"Work around behind and move in on my signal!"

"Cover Jake while he gets in closer!"

"Let's beat it, men, we got what we came for!"

His primary qualification was that he appeared just a little tougher and more mercenary than the others, but the job of the minor leader quite often seemed to just alternate among the troops by whim, almost as if the director might have mused, "Now let's see, who hasn't been the leader lately?"

Many of the best known of the battle-line sergeant heavies were men who had either performed in similar roles in silent films or had played heroes when younger and turned to villainy after sound came in. George Chesebro was one of the latter, having appeared as Ruth Roland's leading man in Pathé's *Hands Up*, a 1918 release he left to enter the Army. The Minnesota actor had begun his career in a stock company in Minneapolis when he was 19 and toured the Orient with a musical show while in his early twenties. His motion picture work started in 1915 and continued, except for his Army service in World War I, for over thirty years. During that time he appeared in so many Westerns and continued pictures at every studio that it would be nearly impossible to list them all. For all of the major serial studios — and the independents as well — Chesebro worked in more than three dozen sound cliff-hangers and received billing in about half of them. Typical of his roles was that of Gaspard, a renegade dressed in buckskins and a fur hat, in *Perils of the Royal Mounted*. In his early fifties at the time, his lean, rugged, once-handsome features were lined and tough, and when he "got the drop" on the hero, the audience knew there was real trouble.

Edmund Cobb was another silent film good-guy-turned-bad, having been Neva Gerber's hero in the 1924 Arrow release *Days of '49* and portrayed the legendary Colonel Cody in Universal's 1926 version of *Fighting with Buffalo Bill*, among others. Billed third, behind stars Allene Ray and Tim McCoy, the briskly authoritative Cobb moved into the sound era as one of the principal players in *The Indians Are Coming* and continued as a featured principal throughout the thirties and forties, playing every type of role written for action serials and Westerns, mostly as the minor villain or, in later years, ranchers and sheriffs.

Al Bridge was an outstanding henchman in several of Mascot's Western adventures (*The Devil Horse* and *Mystery Mountain*) and was featured in the late thirties in releases by Universal (*Flash Gordon, Wild West Days*, etc.) and Columbia (*The Great Adventures of Wild Bill Hickok*). His was a slow, sort of snarling drawl that seemed to threaten by insinuation.

Effective in much the same way was Ted Adams, who could switch with ease from Western to gangster-type heavies. Possessing a deadly-serious countenance, Adams never smiled in his screen roles, and almost seemed to resent it when someone else did. A favorite in Westerns as the saloonkeeper-villain, Adams was billed in two Columbia thrillers (*The Mysterious Pilot* and *Holt of the Secret Service*) and three for Republic (*Daredevils of the West, Dangers of the Canadian Mounted* and *King of the Rocketmen*), playing henchmen and regular character parts.

Two of the most prolific ramrod henchmen in all serialdom were visually as different from each other as it was possible to be. Tom London was tall, lean and mature—the type of man who almost seemed to be associated with the bad guys against his better judgment—and Charles King was short, pudgy and volatile, impetuous to the point one wondered if he had any judgment at all. Between them credits were compiled in over fifty cliff-hangers, with only four or five shared. Their billings account for more than twenty percent of all the sound serial titles released.

Although well-exposed in so many continued pictures, King's greater fame lay in series Westerns. As a cocky, loud-mouthed bully, his penchant was for provoking saloon brawls with the hero (who was earnestly trying to mind his own business) and consequently getting the bejabbers beat out of himself, to the great delight of the audience (the kids never seemed to tire of seeing such a one get his comeuppance in so basic a display of poetic justice). Practically every Western he made with Bob Steele at PRC in the early forties (which was quite a few) contained such a scene. The particular sight of the lightweight, ring-trained Steele absorbing the licks of the heavier brawler and then so deftly over-powering his brute strength with boxing prowess was a crowd-pleaser for several years. And, though our neighborhood bunch lavished such picturesque nicknames as those already mentioned on many of their favorite heavies, there was no doubt about who was meant when someone chuckled and smilingly referred simply to "Charlie." It always meant Charles King.

Tom London was 35 years old when he began his screen career in 1917, which accounts for his obvious maturity in roles during the thirties and forties. His first serial credit was in Universal's *The Lion's Claw* in 1918. Several years later he starred in a series of outdoor adventures for them using his real name, Leonard Clapham, but changed it to Tom London in the late twenties. As Clapham he portrayed a young Mountie hero in Universal's *Nan of the North* in 1922, and as London he played the mystery villain The Claw in that studio's *The Mystery Rider* in 1928, going from one extreme to the other. Almost twenty years later, when he again turned up as the unknown villain in Republic's *Son of Zorro,* he was nearly retirement age but still had another decade to go in films and television.

Three years after *Son of Zorro* — in January, 1950 — Tom London came to Concord on a personal appearance tour. Billed as "The Sheriff of Western Movies," we arranged with city officials to conduct a welcoming ceremony during the last show and name him our town's "honorary Chief of Police." I had the pleasure of meeting and talking with him, and when I asked him how many films he had made, the grand old man grinned and in that familiar, hoarse stage whisper of his said, "Bill, I could no more tell you that than I could tell you how many pairs of socks I ever wore. When I'm on call, I go to work and do what the director says, and then I go home. Sometimes they don't even use the scenes in the same film they're shooting, but they turn up in others. All I know is that I've been in a good many." He continued to be in a "good many" films for movies and television up to the late fifties, and had reached 81 when he died in 1963.

Husky Al Ferguson was playing villainous characters such as "Red Fox" as early as 1921, when he appeared in the Warner Brothers release *Miracles of the Jungle* in that role. He continued playing them in a number of memorable silent serials (*Timber Queen, Tarzan the Mighty, Tarzan the Tiger,* etc.) and then in sound for Mascot (*Three Musketeers*), Universal (*The Airmail Mystery, The Red Rider, Flash Gordon,* etc.), the independents (*The Mystery Trooper, The Sign of the Wolf*) and Columbia (*The Spider's Web, Captain Midnight,* etc.), where he joined former silent fellow thespians Reed Howes, Kermit Maynard and Bud Osborne as a henchman in that studio's last two releases, *Perils of the Wilderness* and *Blazing the Overland Trail.*

In the ranks of the henchmen were the authentic men of the outdoors, the kind of men about whom the action and adventure stories were written. Some of them rose to leading status and even stardom, but most of them provided support for the principals by just being for the cameras what they already were in reality. One outstanding henchman of countless Republic Westerns and serials had been a star in the silents and had reverted to his real name in the mid-thirties for a career in supporting roles. Known to Western fans as Wally Wales from 1925 to 1933, Hal Taliaferro had in his life — which began in Sheridan, Wyoming, in 1895 — been a solider in the AEF in World War I and a professional horse wrangler and cowboy before entering motion pictures in 1915 and appearing in Fox Westerns starring Tom Mix. Billed as Hal Taliaferro (pronounced "Toliver") he portrayed Jim Bowie in Republic's *The Painted Stallion* and followed up as one of the heroes suspected of being the legendary masked man in *The Lone Ranger.* As the beared, buckskindressed good guy Cherokee in *The Adventures of Red Ryder,* he played one of the few sympathetic parts to come his way thereafter. In Western features and later serials he earned the image of the rough-and-ready boss henchman, ready to take on any dirty or crooked job the villain might hand him.

One of the best at conveying the same impression of ruthless toughness was Richard Alexander. Appearing miscast in the first two Flash Gordon serials as the planet Mongo's deposed royal heir Prince Barin, the big, burly Alexander seemed much more comfortable in his roles at Republic. As Thorg, the brutish henchman of the crazed Boroff in *S.O.S. Coast Guard*, he gave the hero some pretty bad moments, and as Brad Dace (also known as "El Lobo") in *Zorro Rides Again*, would have succeeded in killing the unmasked hero in Chapter Twelve but for the timely attack of the man-in-black's faithful horse, who trampled him to death against a rock.

When discussing hard, tough bad guys, it would not be proper to overlook Harry Cording. Featured twice as a henchman in Republic and Universal serials, the first performance was a credit to the genre. As Wade Garson in *King of the Royal Mounted*, he personified the single-minded, no-nonsense henchman who set out to complete his orders no matter what the hero might do to prevent it. With two of the most viciously glaring eyes imaginable topping an apparently broken nose above a wide, clenched mouth, Cording was visually equipped to quickly establish the quality of pure meanness in his roles. With a bushy moustache and thick eyebrows that nearly joined at a point between his eyes, the picture was complete. And then when he spoke—in a gutteral growl with an unmistakable cockney twang—the total image of the unquestioning, almost mindless brute with but one intent was firmly stamped. When in Chapter Ten the churlish Garson was killed in a gunfight with the Mounties, the crowd in the Paramount Theatre actually rose to their feet and cheered—a tribute to the performance of a fine actor. Cording's second appearance in a serial was as a murderous ship captain named Greeder in *The Great Alaskan Mystery*. He lasted nearly six chapters before being dispatched by the film's secret weapon.

As in any other field of endeavor, there were several henchmen sergeants who—like cream in a bottle of milk—rise to the top. Cobb, Bridge, King and London were all like that. In the thirties their gangs— the "privates" in the armies of the villains; the troops, the workers, the fodder, as it were—were composed of such stalwarts as Stanley Blystone, Slim Whitaker, Glenn Strange, Harry Tenbrook, Tom Dugan, Ethan Laidlaw, Jack Rockwell and the deliciously sneaky Charles Stevens. In the forties they were Ted Mapes, John Bagni, Ken Terrell, Dale Van Sickle, Al Taylor, Duke Green, Tom Steele, Terry Frost, Fred Graham, Jim Diehl, Rusty Westcoatt, Pierce Lyden, Stephen Carr and Don Harvey. In the fifties the names were Zon Murray, Bob Cason, Nick Stuart, Holly Bane, Sandy Sanders, John Cason, Ed Coch and Mike Ragan. Most of them were stuntmen, trained to give and get the hard knocks of physical combat and fast action.

Spanning all three decades as private, sergeant and lieutenant, was a man in reference to whom the expression "Mr. Henchman" would not be trite. Appearing in the thirties as Carter, one of the gang, in *Zorro Rides Again* and as Slasher Stark in *Dick Tracy Returns*, Jack Ingram was to rack up credits for major supporting roles in over thirty serials during his career—practically all of them playing a henchman. (Notable exceptions: a policeman in *Who's Guilty* and one of the four suspect coowners of the island in *Manhunt of Mystery Island*.) Most of his serial activity was at Columbia, where he received official billing in 27 of their releases from 1940 to 1954. Having been featured in about a half dozen of their early forties productions beginning with *The Shadow*, Ingram hit his stride in 1945 with the part of Kruger in *Brenda Starr Reporter*, and was in the cast of 18 of Columbia's next 24 chapterplays—a record challenged only by stuntmen Tom Steele and Dale Van Sickle during the same period at Republic. During the fifties he played in a score of syndicated film series on television such as *The Cisco Kid*, *The Lone Ranger*, *Annie Oakley*, *Kit Carson* and *Wild Bill Hickok*. So firmly was he typed that the instant he was seen on the screen the audience knew what he would be doing, and settled back to see how he would try it this time.

There are many who said that serials were so formulated and stylized that in seeing one you had seen them all. But that was no more true than saying you had seen all football games when you had seen one. As each game produces its outstanding plays and unexpected variations of action because of the peculiar abilities of the players and the manager's deft use of those abilities, so each serial produced its memorable scenes and un-predicted twists in plot and form, largely due to the director's finesse in manipulating the movements of the henchmen. In simple terms, the continued picture as we knew it just would not have been possible without them.

9

They Who Also Serve

The completely opposite number of the master villain was the planner and mover of ways to provide life's best for people — the Solid Citizen. Portrayed in serials as men of maturity and courage, this category of characters represented the broad spectrum of society's leaders who were involved in the creation of the hardware with which a nation functions, the economy that enables it to grow, the professions that serve it, the governments that guide it, and the agencies that enforce its laws and regulations — the scientists, businessmen, doctors, lawyers, politicians and police. The leaders in turn represented all of us who are engaged in the conducting of life as it is, while searching for ways to make it better. Because of the complexity of so many intents and purposes on the parts of so many different individuals, it was among the citizens that any character deviations could be developed in a serial, if that was desired. It was also among the citizens that the villains who wished to conceal themselves infiltrated.

To play that diverse array of roles, actors who could project qualities of integrity, purpose, substance and dignity were sought. Many were found right in the serial field in the persons of former leading men grown past the age of derring-do but still retaining the other qualifications that had sustained their former heroics. Others were recruited from major features and the dramatic stage. All were handsome, distinguished-looking men with strong bearings and serious demeanors.

Of the many actors who had made the transition from silent to sound, none had more credentials than J.P. McGowan, who appeared in many Universal serials up to the late thirties. In 1914 the Australian-born veteran of the Boer War directed one of the first of the genre's superstars, Helen Holmes, in the series of one-reel action films known as *The Hazards of Helen*. Not a serial by definition, its succession of complete adventures involving Miss Holmes (and later Helen Gibson) as the girl telegrapher who regularly risked her life to keep the trains running, proved a smash

134

hit and established Miss Holmes as a star of the calibre of Pearl White. Later true serials such as *The Girl and the Game, Lass of the Lumberlands, The Lost Express* and *The Railroad Raiders* teamed up the director and his star (who had also become his wife) as hero and heroine as well. McGowan continued to direct such silent greats as Eddie Polo, Marie Walcamp, Elmo Lincoln and Joe Bonomo (and himself occasionally taking major acting roles) after the dissolution of the team and their subsequent divorce. At the entry of sound there was a new breed of directors named Taylor, McRae, Bennet, Hill and Nelson, and McGowan's activity in serials thereafter was chiefly in character roles.

Like J.P. McGowan, by the time talkies took over in the thirties, Francis Ford was already nearly a legend in the annals of cliff-hanging. His silent credits began with *Lucille Love, Girl of Mystery* for Universal in 1914. Directing as well as costarring with Grace Cunard in it, that was the first of four ventures they made together, followed by two with Rosemary Theby and one with Ella Hall. Four more as director with stars Jack Hoxie (*Thunderbolt Jack*), William Desmond (*The Winking Idol*), Jack Perrin (*The Fighting Skipper*) and Joe Bonomo (*Perils of the Wild*) brought to 11 the chapter thrillers produced under his megaphone in the 12 succeeding years. During the early thirties he appeared in such Universal productions as *Battling with Buffalo Bill, Heroes of the West, Clancy of the Mounted* and *Gordon of Ghost City*, and later in Republic's *King of the Mounties*, before becoming a fixture in features as the salty old Irish patriarchal rascal.

James Flavin was the dashing hero of Universal's *The Airmail Mystery* in 1932 but is much better recognized as the gruff-but-friendly Irish cop in scores of feature films. Born in Portland, Maine, the smiling, open-faced man was educated at the U.S. Military Academy at West Point, which accounts for his natural adaptability to a uniform. He moved very quickly from leading-man roles to substantial character parts because of his very distinct projection of maturity and experience — qualities so much required for credibility in those parts.

Also quick to move from the role of hero to that of solid citizen was sober-faced, square-jawed Kenneth Harlan. As the hero he had the lead in *Fingerprints* (the last ten-chapter thriller from Universal) released in December of 1930. He followed that with *Danger Island* in 1931 — again as the hero — and *Shadow of the Eagle* for Mascot in 1932, in which he played a key supporting role. For the next decade in continued pictures, he specialized as police chiefs, G-men, lawyers and judges in scores of features and in chapter films such as *The Mysterious Pilot, Dick Tracy's G-Men, The Mysterious Doctor Satan, Dick Tracy vs. Crime, Inc.,* and *The Masked Marvel.*

Jack Mulhall's was the fast-clipped voice of authority. As the glib racecar-driving hero of *Burn 'em up Barnes*, the indomitable detective Craig Kennedy in *The Clutching Hand*, efficient military man Captain

Rankin in *Buck Rogers*, or the chief of police in *Doctor Satan*, the handsome, gregarious Mulhall was never overlooked in a scene because of reti-
cence. A thespian all his life, beginning with minor juvenile parts in stock
productions in Passaic, New Jersey, and continuing on the New York
stage in juvenile leads up to his film career, pro Jack knew the value of the
brief moments of exposure in any given scene, and he played his bits
accordingly — to the hilt. The result was a long and busy career playing so
many different kinds of citizens they could not all be listed. In only one of
his serial roles was he a bad guy: Deceiving hero Bob Steele for 11
episodes by pretending to be his good friend, Mulhall was exposed in
Chapter Twelve of Mascot's *Mystery Squadron* as the mysterious Black
Ace. A complete surprise to everyone, that revelation to some was more
than just a bit unfair, as clearing all the suspects and ringing in one of the
good guys as the villain was a gambit serial fans were not accustomed to
expecting. In most of his later appearances, Jack Mulhall was the friendly
but briskly efficient policeman personified, inspiring in a generation of
kids a respect for uniformed authority much lacking in present day
mores.

The nonuniformed police executive was ably and aggressively
played in countless features by Joseph Crehan. Salty, sharp and volatile,
the white-haired Crehan played the city official constantly under fire by
the press in *Gangbusters*, the first of his two featured serial roles. In the
second he played Bill Hudson, father of the hero and discoverer of a
powerful ore needed to perfect a new device known as a Peratron in *The
Great Alaskan Mystery*. In both he played the outspoken involved citizen
with grit and determination, as he did in all his roles. Like Flavin and
Mulhall a veteran of the stage, Crehan also had perfected the technique of
making the most of his scenes, and the scenes benefited by it.

So similar to Crehan in demeanor and style that they were often confused with each other by fans was veteran actor Charles Wilson. Also a
brusque, uncompromising man of action, Wilson stood out in many a
film as the officer-in-command arriving "Just in time to tie up the loose
ends," and was featured in just such a role in the 1943 *Batman* as Captain
Arnold, harassed police official who pursued the hero and villains with
equal vigor until realizing whose side "the Batman" was really on. In *The
Spider's Web* earlier for Columbia, he had played a banker who was supposedly kidnapped by The Octopus, the unknown masked villain, but
was actually exposed as the villain himself in Chapter Fifteen.

Selmer Jackson projected to a nation at war the image it wanted to
have of its military leaders — fatherly, patient, kind and understanding,
but also efficient, businesslike and determined to achieve victory. To the
kids who were serial fans in 1942, his minilesson in codes and cryptology
and brief patriotic admonishment at the end of each chapter of *The Secret
Code* were significant vignettes in their overall view of America's role in
World War II. Here was propaganda in its basic form — appealing to

youth to love and support their nation and beware of all its enemies — delivered in the most effective way possible — by a respected authority figure in the person of one of Hollywood's most credible actors. Better known to audiences for roles similar to that one in features, Jackson nevertheless had also played a heavy several years before when he was exposed as the mysterious villain known as H.K. in *Robinson Crusoe of Clipper Island*, and portrayed citizens of various kinds in a number of Universal serials as well.

The picture of the "old school" Army officer-turned-policeman who carried himself in a rigid military posture and conducted his investigations in precise, straightforward ways was Joseph Girard. Quite familiar to millions of moviegoers as famed General John J. "Blackjack" Pershing (a role he played many times because of his uncanny physical resemblance to the revered World War I hero), he was also well-known and liked by action fans as the gruff Inspector Ross in *The Green Archer*, Commissioner Kirk in *The Spider Returns* and Major Steele in *Captain Midnight*. The word best to describe the main characteristic projected by old gentleman Girard would probably be formidable — for he was that.

Less military than Girard or Jackson, but certainly no less enthusiastic about justice and duty, Wade Boteler is remembered for outstanding character roles in several Universal cliff-hangers. In *Red Barry* he played Inspector Scott, staunch ally of the hero, and in *Buck Rogers* played the hero's father, who had the nebulous duty of ordering Buck and his friend to direct upon themselves the gas that held them in suspended animation for five hundred years. His husky, high-pitched brogue was well-suited to the character of Mike Axford, the determined newspaper reporter and avowed enemy of the hero-believed-criminal in both of Universal's Green Hornet productions. His portly frame dressed in a somber business suit and topped by a ludicrous derby hat, the blustering Axford came across as a semiserious, semicomic threat to the Hornet's concealed identity just as he did in the radio series — thanks to the talented Boteler.

Much more serious in nature were the citizens who held political offices or elective positions — the mayors, governors and senators, et al. — and who almost never smiled in private. These were the men who got the heroes involved (along with the influence of the heroines) in the plots in the beginning, the men who first recognized "the threat." Quite often, as a reward for their diligence and awareness, these citizens were among the first to be killed off by the villains. Inventors and scientists could be kidnapped and used or ransomed, but politicans were of no use to an ambitious villain, so usually they were either left alone or quickly dispatched.

The latter was the fate of Charles Trowbridge in *Doctor Satan*. As the governor of a "large Western state," he recognized the villain's threat to society and was about to take measures against him when his own murder became imminent. Before it happened, he was able to relate to his

ward the colorful story of a friend of his, a youth who had fought injustice behind a copper mask — sacrificing himself in the effort — and get
the young ward totally involved in a crusade for retribution by revealing
that "the Copperhead" had been his father. That accomplished, the
governor quickly became Dr. Satan's next victim.

Trowbridge was one of the screen's outstanding players of men of
unquestioned integrity. He portrayed the type in dozens of feature films,
one of the most memorable being his role of Secretary of State Cordell
Hull in Warner Bros.' *Sergeant York*. His scenes escorting the young war
hero about New York and into the new world of a plush, big-city hotel,
explaining as one former farm boy to another those wonders of modern
civilization, held a poignancy and camaraderie still remembered after
forty years. In addition to his role in *Doctor Satan*, Trowbridge also
appeared in *King of the Texas Rangers* and *Captain America* for
Republic.

In the latter film, Trowbridge played police commissioner Dryden
and was allied with another fine character actor, Russell Hicks, who
played the part of Mayor Randolph. Suave, sophisticated and charming,
the urbane Hicks gave the impression of having just given you a friendly
smile without actually doing so. In much demand as a society doctor,
lawyer or judge in features, the accomplished character actor graced the
casts of one other Republic serial and two at Universal — in each using his
Army experience from World War I to good advantage, along with his
Broadway stage training. As Marshal Carleton in *King of the Mounties*,
the Baltimore native helped lead the fight against the enemies of Canada.
In Universal's *Junior G-Men*, he played the kidnapped Colonel Barton,
father of hero Billy Barton, and in *The Master Key* portrayed police chief
O'Brien, whose own trusted secretary turned out to be the unknown
master villain.

Depending more upon hardheaded realism and the direct confrontation of situations than on compassion or charm, William Gould created
two very stern and rock-like citizens for the annals of serialdom. He
appeared many times in similar roles, but his portrayals as Jed Scott,
pioneer leader of the beleaguered homesteaders in *The Lone Ranger Rides
Again*, and as Air Marshal Kragg, defender of the Hidden City exile band
in *Buck Rogers*, stand out as examples of solid, dependable professionalism — the basic quality for actors cast as the citizens. Possessing a
ruggedly handsome face with clear, determined-looking features and a
voice tinged with a Midwestern twang, Gould delivered his lines in a
level, moderate tone that left no doubt of his self-confident authority, and
evoked immediate response from those around him.

This same self-confident, almost arrogant, demeanor was
reminiscent of that displayed by master craftsman Robert Warwick in his
numerous appearances in the sound era. In silent films the imposingly
handsome Sacramento thespian had played leading roles, but with the

advent of sound the more mature Warwick (then in his early forties) turned to character parts. In such ventures as *The Whispering Shadow, The Three Musketeers* and *The Fighting Marines*, he became a substantial part of the Mascot-Nat Levine era, and continued at Republic as the wily Raspinoff, czarist agent behind General Burr in *The Vigilantes Are Coming*. Finally, as MacLeod in *Jungle Menace* for Columbia, he completed his serial activity and concentrated on choice character parts in major features such as *The Palm Beach Story, Tennessee Johnson, Gentleman's Agreement, The Adventures of Don Juan, Mississippi Gambler, Lady Godiva* and dozens more. His dark, brooding features and self-assured manner lent themselves equally well to the portrayal of kindly, benevolent patricians or scheming, grasping villains. Often he was cast as a politician or nobleman — good and bad.

Perhaps the role most associated with Pierre Watkin — one of the most versatile character actors in film history — was that of Perry White, the domineering editor of the *Daily Planet* in the two Superman epics from Columbia, even though he appeared in at least a half dozen other serials from 1947 to 1953. The forceful, aggressive Watkin played the famed "Uncle Jim" in *Jack Armstrong* and Professor Salisbury in *Brick Bradford* prior to his Perry White stints, then appeared in several more for Columbia in various character parts, and finally as an R.C.M.P. official in *Canadian Mounties vs. Atomic Invaders* for Republic — his last serial credit. Watkin was unsurpassed as the bombastic, outspoken executive or the outraged, demanding politician of many a modern, big-city melodrama, and his biting, stinging attack on a subordinate or an adversary left vivid impressions that are still with us. He was not timid.

A less volatile but every bit as stern and driving a Perry White was John Hamilton, who took over the chore of periodically "chewing out" Clark, Lois and Jimmy in the *Superman* television series. With credits dating back to the thirties, the dignified, white-haired Hamilton was no stranger to serials. His respectable, honest-looking face had given him the image of the trusted town banker in several Westerns and had cast him as a renowned scientist in *Flash Gordon Conquers the Universe* and *Captain America*, a U.S. Senator in *Daredevils of the West* and *The Phantom Rider*, a frieght line executive in *The James Brothers of Missouri*, and in *Zorro's Black Whip* — the town banker. Hamilton was typical of the many fine actors whose names were not known to many, but whose faces were as familiar as those of personal friends. Being cast as Perry White changed that somewhat, for the kids then learned his name.

Forbes Murray also had white hair and looked dignified. Except for particular family features, there was a difference between him and John Hamilton only in that Murray appeared slightly more cosmopolitan — like a city banker rather than a town banker. Exuding the assurance that results from wealth and influence, the dapper Murray always gave the appearance that he might have just emerged from a board meeting. In his first cliff-hanger for Columbia, *The Spider's Web*, he played Commissioner Kirk with a flair not normally associated with a policeman, then followed as a suspect named Brewster in *The Flying G-Men* and a pawn named Professor Houston in *Mandrake the Magician*. At Republic he appeared in three releases during the early forties — *Perils of Nyoka* as leader of the archeological expedition, *G-Men vs. the Black Dragon* as a government envoy, and *Manhunt of Mystery Island* as one of the island's coowners suspected of being Mephisto — while also playing similar roles in action and mystery features.

One of the ablest performers of the prominent community leader in Westerns was Lafe McKee. It would be difficult to think of the fatherly McKee as anyone but the heroine's put-upon sire after so many times out in that role. His name appeared everywhere in the early thirties — at Universal (*Rustlers of Red Dog*, *The Red Rider*, etc.), at Mascot (*The Lone Defender*, *Phantom of the West*, *The Lightning Warrior*, *The Vanishing Legion*, *The Whispering Shadow*, *Mystery Squadron* and *The Law of the Wild*), and the independents, too (*Queen of the Jungle*, *Custer's Last Stand*, etc.).

Later years gave the Lafe McKee parts to such grand gentlemen as Russell Simpson (*Wild West Days*), veteran of stock, chatauqua and stage, Eddy Waller (*Flaming Frontiers*), caustic frontier films pro, Tom Fadden (*Winners of the West*), John Elliott (*Perils of the Royal Mounted*), and Francis Ford.

Frequently cast in the same type of parts as community leaders, ranchers, bankers, merchants and sheriffs were such players of distinction as Robert Homans, Nolan Leary, Hooper Atchley, Lloyd Ingraham, Ed Cassidy, Wheaton Chambers and Edward Peil, Sr. The list of actors who played other diverse characters from all walks of life continues with names such as Lloyd Whitlock, Byron Foulger, Harry Strang, Douglas Evans, George Pembroke, Joseph Forte, Kernan Cripps, Robert Walker, Harry Harvey, Patrick J. Kelly, Edward Keane, Emmett Vogan and Jack O'Shea.

In the early thirties the trusted statesman-father figure was personified by Richard Tucker, a distinguished citizen in *Shadow of the Eagle* for Mascot and the concerned father of the hero in *Flash Gordon*; during the late thirties by handsome, aristocratic Edwin Stanley in *Dick Tracy* (finally revealed as The Spider), *Scouts to the Rescue* and *The Mysterious Doctor Satan*; and in the forties by Sam Flint, silver-haired Colonel Grayson (father of the hero) in *The Fighting Devil Dogs*, silver-haired Admiral Corby (father of the heroine) in *Spy Smasher*, silver-haired Horace Black (respected attorney) in *Who's Guilty*, silver-haired Professor Maxwell in *The Crimson Ghost*, silver-haired Dr. Weston in *The Black Widow*, and silver-haired banker Paul Thatcher in *The Adventures of Frank and Jesse James*.

The maestro of the father figures (the venerable patriarch, the good, grey benefactor) was former Shakespearean actor and silent film star, William Farnum. Born on the fourth of July, 1870, at Boston, Massachusetts, he and his brother Dustin were to become nearly as famous as a family acting team as did the Gish sisters and the Barrymores. Dustin was a popular adventure star in silent movies, and William majored in dramatic parts. As Sharad, ruler of Atlantis in *Undersea Kingdom*, or Father Jose, confidant of the Eagle in *The Vigilantes Are Coming*, Father McKim in *The Lone Ranger*, or the revered Colonel Tom Ryder, father of the hero, in *The Adventures of Red Ryder*, the big man with the strong but kindly face gave each performance a touch of distinction and quiet dignity. His presence in a serial lifted it above itself for a moment, and made the audience feel briefly a sensation of quality all too rare in the genre.

To a less sentimental degree, this was also the contribution of Addison Richards—Mr. Sincerity. His long, lean face with the earnest eyes and resonant, reassuring voice held a charisma that was undeniable. Everyone had the feeling watching him that, "given a choice, here is what I would like my boss to be like—persuasive but understanding, exacting but lenient, firm but fair." Throughout a long career in a variety of film roles, the Zanesville, Ohioan, who had approached films in 1933 with experience in community theatre as an actor and director, gave the spark of reality and stamp of credibility to hundreds of scenes simply by his presence. His two serial appearances did not occur until near the end of Universal's activities in the field, but they are memorable for their quality. As Garret Donahue he played in *The Master Key*, one of Universal's final flings at a mystery villain, and later the same year appeared in *The Royal Mounted Rides Again*.

Television viewers remember Stanley Andrews kindly as The Old Ranger, original host of the long-running *Death Valley Days* series. Those over fifty remember him as the ruthless Jeffries in *The Lone Ranger* of 1938. In between those extremes, he was one of the screen's most accomplished character actors, with dozens of feature credits and at least a half dozen in serials. From Jeffries, the diehard villain, he switched to the part of a mine owner killed in Chapter One for his discovery of Compound X in *King of the Royal Mounted*. An Army colonel named Andrews was his role in *Daredevils of the West*, and in *The Adventures of Frank and Jesse James* he was again a miner who was killed early in the story to conceal his discovery of a rich vein of gold. His final serial credit before concentrating exclusively on his television character was in *Canadian Mounties vs. Atomic Invaders* in 1953.

Since the prime suspense factor in continued films was to keep the audience guessing, the normal approach to characters of such obvious integrity as those portrayed by actors like Murray, Flint, Farnum and Richards, et. al, was to include them as suspects when a mystery villain was involved. By placing them in a group which also included obvious suspect types such as lawyers, financiers and industrial promoters, there was planted an element of doubt or lingering suspicion whether the obvious types were really the guilty ones. And often one of the trusted father figures was revealed as the villain to keep the curiosity alive.

It was the lot of some veteran character men to always appear as guilty as sin until the final episode, and then come up "smelling like a rose" when the real culprit was exposed. These men were the real "pros" of the serial game, and many had already been practitioners of the art in the silent days. Others switched over from good to evil, and the sound era even spawned a couple of its own.

Robert Strange enjoyed the distinction of being thought the obvious choice for the villain in one serial because he had just been one in another. *King of the Royal Mounted* was released by Republic in September, 1940. In it, the deliciously sneaky-looking Strange had played John Kettler, the master spy, in a flawless characterization. Six months later, the studio released its masterpiece *The Adventures of Captain Marvel*. Cast as Professor John Malcolm was the same Robert Strange. As soon as it became evident that the unknown, hooded Scorpion was in reality a member of the archaelogical expedition he headed, audiences immediately were prepared to see Strange exposed as that villain because of his superb portrayal of the thoroughly wicked Kettler. When the final episode revealed one of the others as the fiend and cleared him, there was a note of almost disappointment in the kids' reaction. In his third serial role — the heroine's lost father, Professor Henry Gordon, in *The Perils of Nyoka* — the fans were ready to accept him as a good guy at last.

Actors like Robert Strange made the best suspects because you just couldn't be sure of them. John Dilson was another. Bald, middle-aged and mean-looking in the manner of a penny-pinching landlord or shyster lawyer, Dilson's contribution to most scenes was an acidic criticism of any idea the hero might have come up with. This opposition and dissent led to an automatic assumption that the wily Dilson might be the villain trying to thwart the good guys' plans, yet his objections almost always made some sense. So, you see, you couldn't be really *sure*. In three of his four featured serial roles, Dilson was a key suspect, and turned out to be the villain in none of them: In *Robinson Crusoe of Clipper Island*, he was suspected of being the mysterious H.K., in *Dick Tracy* the Spider, and in *Dick Tracy vs. Crime, Inc.*, The Ghost. His fourth featured role was as a character named Howard in *Drums of Fu Manchu*.

As sneaky-looking as was Robert Strange, and as mean-looking as was John Dilson, so was George Eldredge handsome. A big, good-looking man, there was nevertheless a trace of weakness in his demeanor which gave cause for a shudder of fear that he might betray the hero if pressed or tempted enough. In *Hawk of the Wilderness* he invited his own death by breaking away from the escape party to return for forbidden wealth in a deadly, sacred (for the natives) cavern. In later serials for Columbia, he dropped pretense and became a full-fledged villain — Baron Karl Ulrich in *Roar of the Iron Horse*, and Tobor in *Captain Video*.

Robert Frazer was a master at keeping the audience guessing with his glowering expressions and menacing voice. In 1933 he portrayed (wearing the costume and mask) the mysterious El Shaitan in Mascot's *The Three Musketeers*, and was also a character named Major Booth, one of the key suspects (a dead give-away to the discerning fan who would listen). However, Booth turned out to be *not* the real villain at all, but a secret service man, and one of the other suspects was disclosed as the culprit — which was all quite confusing. Later that year, he was suspected of being The Black Ace in *Mystery Squadron* and in the following years played in two more for Mascot — *The Miracle Rider* and *The Fighting Marines* — each time as a prime suspect. In *The Clutching Hand* in 1936, he played a kidnapped scientist who turned out to be his own kidnapper and the villain of the title. In *The Black Coin* he was a rogue named Hackett, who — although not an unknown villain — was an outright scoundrel. A choice suspect in *Dick Tracy vs. Crime, Inc.*, and a villain again in *Daredevils of the West*, Republic utilized fully his talent to be deadly menacing without necessarily being the bad guy. His final serial role — the high priest in *The Tiger Woman* — is a case in point. At first threatening — and very nearly taking — the life of the hero in his zealousness to avenge the heroine, Frazer then became a staunch ally of the good guys when their true mission became known to him and he realized they meant the lady no harm. Such a switch could have been extremely suspect — or even rejected outright — by avid cliff-hanger fans, except for the credibility of a craftsman such as Frazer.

To a handful of character men fell the assignment of playing the scientist-inventor and/or father-of-the-heroine in practically every one of their serial appearances. Subjects of typecasting in its strictest sense, they simply did not play anything else. For a young star this would be anathema, but to a serious character actor it was the way of the cliff-hanger — and a good buck.

George Cleveland (kindly "Gramps" of the *Lassie* television series a couple of decades later) appeared in three such roles in the late thirties: as Blanchard, whose daughter was threatened with violence by the heavies in *The Lone Ranger*, Professor Parker, father of hero Allan Parker in *Drums of Fu Manchu*, and one of the breathlessly awaiting Earth scientists in *Flash Gordon*. A native of Sydney, Nova Scotia, the former stage actor had the physical appearance of a trusted favorite uncle. Never would he have been suspected of being the villain — it would have been almost sacrilege. For nearly thirty years he was practically the accepted symbol of the respected older relative, and the image culminated with his role in *Lassie*. His death in 1963 left much the same void as that left by the passing of such a one in your own family.

The exposing of such a character as the mystery villain added to the overall effect of the classic whodunit *The Fighting Devil Dogs*. As Warfield, a renowned scientist engaged to assist the young Marine heroes in their fight against The Lightning, distinguished but gaunt-looking actor Hugh Sothern projected an image of sincerity and intellectual integrity that made the ultimate revelation of his secret identity tragic as well as triumphant for the good guys. His role as Professor Dodge in *Captain America* five years later was somewhat more satisfying, as he left the scene in Chapter Five with his honor still intact — victim of the mad villain Maldor. Sothern's screen image has been likened to that of a white-haired Abe Lincoln.

Tom Chatterton had been a leading man in silent films circa World War I following a stage career in stock and touring companies, and returned to the stage during the twenties. In 1933 at age 52, he again went West to appear in motion pictures and stayed there to play in a number of Westerns and serials until the middle forties. In serials, his two most prominent roles were both as father of the heroine. In *Hawk of the Wilderness* he played scientist Dr. Munro, leader of an expedition in search of a "scientific treasure" located by hero Kioga's father before being killed in the shipwreck that brought his surviving infant son to the lost island in the North Pacific. In *Drums of Fu Manchu* he was a colleague of George Cleveland's named Professor Randolph (and father of the heroine). When he and Cleveland (Professor Parker) were abducted by the wily Oriental schemer, their offspring teamed up to rescue them and foil the plans of the evil mastermind. Chatterton was a serious-visaged man with a look of dedication tempered with personal concern. Instinctively well-liked by the audience, he was a favorite in Western character parts and appeared often without billing as a merchant or town official. His last serial credit was as a merchant in *Zorro's Black Whip*.

A paradox in this type of role was Nelson Leigh, who played the part of professor-scientist-doctor in several Sam Katzman productions in the late forties. A clean-cut, rather handsome man (but without particularly distinguishing features), Leigh's substance was in his rich, mellifluous voice. In supporting roles in *Brick Bradford* and *Congo Bill*; as Jor-l, father of the "man of steel" in *Superman*; and as King Arthur in *The Adventures of Sir Galahad*, Leigh was adequate but not extremely impressive by cliff-hanger standards. His was a quiet, soft-spoken authority in contrast to the definitive, two-dimensional bravura usually seen in serials. Later in television dramas his manner and technique were more suitably employed. He was notably effective in stories of a religious nature (biblical and modern) and in roles such as the judge in a number of *Perry Mason* episodes. In them his steady, controlled style of underplaying attracted attention and interest.

Variety in nationalities and races was provided by a score of excellent players who, by virtue of outstanding traits immediately identifiable with those of a particular country or genealogical group, projected the image of that distinctive heritage then held by moviegoers. As Keye Luke in his role of Kato established his Oriental identity, and Victor Daniels (Chief Thundercloud) as Tonto personified the American Indian by his physical appearance, so did a host of character actors portray by their facial features and manners of speech the peculiarities of their national and ethnical backgrounds.

J. Farrell MacDonald could not have portrayed a character other than Irish. In *The Hurricane Express* he was the epitome of the "railroad dick"—but an *Irish* railroad dick, mind you—and in *The Lone Ranger Rides Again* his portrayal of Craig Dolan, the unsuspecting dupe of his evil nephew, was a showcase display of the blarney, bluster and bullheadedness that were the trademarks of that grand old "man o' the auld sod." Born in Waterbury, Connecticut, and educated at Yale University, MacDonald had already had a distinguished career on the dramatic stage and in silent films as actor and director before settling down to acting in character roles in the early thirties. Most of his memorable feature-film supporting roles (*Meet John Doe*, *The Great Lie*, *Whispering Smith*, *Fury at Furnace Creek*, et. al) came when he was already past retirement age.

When a French official was needed (*Spy Smasher*, *Secret Service in Darkest Africa*), or a desert chieftain with French background (*The Perils of Nyoka*, *The Desert Hawk*), the call was to Georges Renavent. Another Frenchman, Nigel De Brulier, created the impressive and picturesque high priest Shazam in *The Adventures of Captain Marvel*.

Robert O. Davis (*King of the Texas Rangers*, *Spy Smasher*, *The Secret Code*), William Vaughn (*King of the Mounties*, *Secret Service in Darkest Africa*) and Hans Von Morhart (*Spy Smasher*, *Secret Service in Darkest Africa*) were all much in demand when Germans were required, especially in the early forties during the war.

European and Asian nationalities were almost always portrayed in a serious light—either as honest, straightforward public servants (if they were U.S. allies) or as dedicated, villainous espionage agents (Germans and Japanese). Only in the depiction of North American characters was there any levity exhibited. Mexican, Negro and illiterate Southern characters were shown to be both comic and serious, depending upon the plot requirement.

Multitalented actors such as Leo Carillo, Frank Yaconelli and Nacho Galindo could portray funny Mexicans, but there were also actors like Martin Garralaga, Julian Rivero and Leander De Cordova playing dignified, intelligent Latins. Black dramatic actors Roy Glenn, Sr., Clarence Muse and Napoleon Simpson played straight character parts (albeit mostly as jungle native chieftains) while comedy actors Willie Best (*The Monster and the Ape*) and Snowflake (*Hawk of the Wilderness*, *Daredevils of the Red Circle*) perpetuated the slow-moving, easily-petrified "darkie" image so prevalent at the time. Southern "hillbilly" types were portrayed as ignorant, bumbling louts by Smiley Burnette (*The*

Adventures of Rex and Rinty, Undersea Kingdom, Dick Tracy), a team called Oscar and Elmer (*Dick Tracy, The Painted Stallion*), Roscoe Ates (*The Great Adventures of Wild Bill Hickok*) and Guy Wilkerson (*Captain Midnight*), while in many Westerns leading citizens — and even some of the heroes — were depicted as former Southerners seriously and effectively pioneering the frontier.

American Indians, because of their inexorable image as enemies of the early pioneers, were almost never treated in any way but with deadly seriousness. Although occasionally shown in a sympathetic light, they were never portrayed as lighthearted or comical. Most key Indian roles went to Chief Thundercloud before his emergence as Tonto, and after that to Chief Yowlatchie and Iron Eyes Cody, veterans of most of the Indian Westerns ever made.

Adept at playing more than one of these types — native chief, Mexican, or Indian — were men like Paul Marion (an Indian in *Zorro's Fighting Legion*, modern gangster in *Doctor Satan*, native warrior in *Tiger Woman*), Al Kikume (Polynesian giant Lothar in *Mandrake*, native chief Lutembi in *Jungle Girl*), Jerry Frank (Lion man in *Jungle Girl*, Western desperado in *Zorro Rides Again*), and Rico de Montez (*Tiger Woman* and *Haunted Harbor*).

Allen Jung, best remembered as Connie in *Terry and the Pirates*, was the perennial Oriental (Sato in *King of the Mounties*, Fugi in *G-Men vs. the Black Dragon*), and Ramsey Hill played the British officer in the only way serials ever portrayed them — very stiff and very proper — in *Trader Tom of the China Seas* and *Panther Girl of the Kongo*.

By reason of sheer prolificacy alone, there were two actors who could be characterized as the ultimate cliff-hanger "citizens." However, there is much more than the number of releases they appeared in to qualify Bryant Washburn and Herbert Rawlinson for topmost positions in any list of outstanding actors playing distinguished men in continued pictures. Both were accomplished actors with substantial careers established before sound serials, and both were very earnest about the roles they were given. Dramatically, many of the characters written for chapter films were not developed too deeply. As a matter of fact, some were meant for not much more than "window-dressing" or backdrop. Consequently, some actors went through the motions and provided the required dialogue without any real interest in the result, knowing the kids were not going to be too critical or analytical. In quite a few instances the results were lifeless and inane. But watching Bryant Washburn or Herbert Rawlinson give even a brief, minor part the best effort he had in the spirit of the scene was gratifying to the youthful fan. And even though he was unsophisticated, unanalytical and uncritical, the average young devotee could feel in his guts when a scene was right and when it was wrong. Almost always when Rawlinson and Washburn were up, things were right.

Bryant Washburn came from Chicago via the dramatic stage to become a popular star of silent films. Handsome to the point of prettiness, his penetrating gaze, pencil-thin moustache and deep cleft chin made him a romantic favorite with young women, and he appeared in a number of films as a leading man. In his thirties during the first decade of sound pictures, he projected a maturity beyond his years and turned to character parts, majoring in cliff-hangers. At Universal he turned out creditable performances in some of their most popular releases, including the Tailspin Tommy entries, *Call of the Savage* and *Jungle Jim*. During the same period he was featured in three of the best known of the in-dependents — *Return of Chandu*, *The Black Coin* and *The Clutching Hand*. From 1940 to 1942 he played key supporting roles in two of Republic's finest (*King of the Royal Mounted* and *The Adventures of Captain Marvel*) and in *The Spider Returns* and *Captain Midnight* for Columbia.

As early as 1915, audiences were being fascinated by the charm of Herbert Rawlinson. As scientific criminologist Sanford Quest, a combination Sherlock Holmes-Dick Tracy-Man from U.N.C.L.E., the handsome English actor starred in Universal's *The Black Box* that year and gave the moviegoing public a new type of hero — urbane, charming and obviously cultured, but also alert, resourceful and imaginative. He followed with starring roles in Oliver films' *The Carter Case* in 1919 as detective Craig Kennedy, Rayart's *The Flame Fighter* in 1925 as hero Jack Sparks, and in their *Phantom Police* and *Trooper 77* in 1926. Returning to serials in the middle thirties, the wavy-haired, poised Rawlinson appeared as a key suspect in *Robinson Crusoe of Clipper Island*, as Commander Boyle in *S.O.S. Coast Guard*, and in the title role of Sam Katzman's *Blake of Scotland Yard*. Prominent roles followed in releases at all three serial-producing studios, including Universal's *Flash Gordon Conquers the Universe*, Republic's *King of the Royal Mounted*, *King of the Texas Rangers* and *G-Men Vs. the Black Dragon*, and Columbia's *Perils of the Royal Mounted* and *Superman*. In the meantime, he also appeared in dozens of features playing mostly professional men — lending his own stamp of quality and substance to each part.

These are by no means all of the actors who contributed to the serial as its citizens, but they are representative of the best. These were the people in chapterplays for whom the good guys worked and fought. Without them there could have been, of course, no plots, no suspense, no action. If there be unsung heroes of continued pictures, they would be — as in real life — the Solid Citizens.

10

In the Hands of the Enemy

Kidnapping was practiced without qualms by every villain doing business in continued pictures. There was simply no hesitation whatsoever to stalk, overpower and capture a human being to hold for ransom or extortion. It was so blithely done that it appeared to be one of the lesser crimes of which man is capable. And, because the hero could be counted on to effect rescue in nearly a hundred percent of cases, there was no particularly real concern on the part of the audience for the victim's personal safety. Since this was all make-believe anyway, the capture of a person to gain some particular end became in the formula a ploy, and the victim a "pawn." The question of how quickly and by what means the hero would regain the freedom of the kidnapped then became part of the suspense. The audience did not wonder whether — only how.

Holding the beautiful girl to lure the main player into a trap, or an inventor to coerce his secrets, was a necessary tactic of the villain. Often it became the only way he could move from one failing situation to another with more promise of success. And to be thus used was the chief function of more than one pretty face. Almost every heroine could look forward to the dubious fate at least once in the course of a serial, and many solid citizens also were periodically subjected to it. Therefore, as an aspect of the formula, the role of the pawn took on a meaning of its own, and even created — as did other peculiar aspects of the cliff-hanger — its own unique brand of professional.

Possibly the record for establishing a pawn was the kidnapping of Gus Glassmire in the 1943 *Batman*. Upon his release from prison (for a crime he did not commit), the uncle of heroine Linda Page named Martin Warren (Glassmire) was met at the prison gate by the villain's chief henchman and whisked away to the gang's hideout, where he was to be held for the next 14 episodes, while Batman and Robin tried diligently on behalf of his niece to rescue him.

In Universal's *Buck Rogers*, one of Hollywood's subsequently leading

Oriental actors, Philip Ahn, played a pawn. Billed in that release — and the previous year's *Red Barry* — as Philson Ahn, the young Los Angeles native, a Korean diplomat's son, was featured as Prince Tallen, emissary from Saturn to the tyrannical Earth dictator, Killer Kane. Switching sides after learning Kane's true nature, Tallen returned to Saturn to denounce Kane to his leaders, but was kidnapped and electronically brainwashed by Kane's henchmen in Chapter Six. Controlling his actions, Kane's men very nearly succeeded in duping Saturn into their cause before Buck rescued the prince and restored his mind. Again, in Chapter Eleven, Kane's forces kidnapped the hapless Tallen and demanded Saturnian alliance for his release, but again the Earth people rescued him and ended Kane's threat.

Throughout the Flash Gordon trilogy, the good Doctor Zarkov (Frank Shannon) was regularly being captured and held by Ming for his scientific knowledge. Shrewdly, the crafty Zarkov would give the gullible egotist just enough of a secret to stall him until Flash could again spring him.

In several instances, the pawn became the focal point of a story, providing the motive for involvement by the hero, who might otherwise not have interfered, or becoming the vehicle for the villain's perpetration of his master plan. The former was the case in *Batman* and the latter was true of *Dick Tracy*, in which the villain's chief henchman was in reality a pawn (the kidnapped brother of the hero). In at least one case the villain himself appeared to be the pawn, and in another the pawn was really the culprit. In still another, the pawn was the mystery hero.

The distinguished British actor, Miles Mander, portrayed the kidnapped industrialist, Granville, in *Daredevils of the Red Circle*. To delude the good guys, the real villain (convict 39013, played by Charles Middleton) appeared among them wearing a life-mask of Manders and masqueraded in his identity. Of course, when the life-mask was supposed to be on, Mander himself actually played the role, so in truth two actors (Mander and Middleton) alternately played the villain, and Mander also played the pawn. As already mentioned, in Stage and Screen's *The Clutching Hand* the pawn was really the villain himself. Supposedly missing and believed to be kidnapped throughout the story, Dr. Paul Gironda (Robert Frazer) turned out to be a fake pawn but the real master criminal. He had feigned his own capture and effected the mystery character The Clutching Hand to cover his diabolical schemes. This subterfuge was reversed in Columbia's *The Green Archer*, when the pawn (Michael Bellamy) turned out to be the mysterious Archer. Supposedly imprisoned in the dungeon of his ancestral estate by his vicious brother Abel, the brave Michael ventured forth through secret passages and portals known only to him to save the good guys when needed, and to thwart his demented sibling's plans.

Of all the many actors who played pawns, there were three who almost seemed to make careers of the role. Together their credits stretched from 1936 to 1954 and included over one-third of the entire serial output of Columbia and Republic. Almost always cast in the part of a renowned scientist and inventor who was kidnapped and forced to apply his knowledge to the development of his invention for the villain's benefit rather than society's, these three became nearly as closely associated with the enemies' secret hideouts as did the bad guys. Their ultimate fate never deviated from two possibilities — eventual release and reunion with the heroine (his daughter-niece-ward) or demise by noble self-sacrifice saving the would-be rescuer-hero.

Typical of the role of serial hostage was that of the venerable C. Montague Shaw, one of the three who might be called "professional pawns," in Republic's *Undersea Kingdom*. As Professor Norton, leader of the submarine expedition to the lost city of Atlantis, he was captured almost immediately upon arrival (Chapter Two) and placed under hypnosis by the evil Unga Khan in his "transforming cabinet," and ordered to work on rocket motors that could propel Khan's battle tower hideout to the surface of the upper world. Because of his hypnotic state, Norton in effect became a henchman of Khan, and unwittingly nearly brought about the destruction of the good guys several times. Distinguished and scholarly-looking, the handsome Shaw played featured roles in four more serials for Republic (*Daredevils of the Red Circle, Zorro's Fighting Legion, The Mysterious Doctor Satan, G-Men vs. the Black Dragon*), three at Universal (*Radio Patrol, Flash Gordon's Trip to Mars,* Dr. Huer in *Buck Rogers*) and one for Columbia (*Holt of the Secret Service*) during the next seven years.

In the meantime, Forrest Taylor, the most prolific of chapterplay pawns, was continuing his career in character roles and beginning to gain notice as a "suspect" type as a result of his portrayals of Benson, the shifty-eyed butler in *The Fighting Devil Dogs*, and Anton, the crafty former thief in *The Iron Claw*. In *Terry and the Pirates* as Allen Drake and *The Green Archer* as Howett (both fathers of the heroine), he garnered some sympathy from audiences in 1940 and again in 1942 as Hinsdale in Columbia's *Perils of the Royal Mounted*. In 1944, at Republic, he again portrayed the father of the heroine in *Haunted Harbor*, and was summarily dispatched by the villain in Chapter Four, when it came known he could expose the criminal's real identity. In *Manhunt of Mystery Island* the following year, his role of Professor Forrest was pure "pawn." Already a prisoner of the gaudy Captain Mephisto when the first episode opened, he remained so until the 15th before being rescued by hero Lance Reardon and his niece, Claire. This was a classic example of the pawn providing the motive for the hero's intervention. Asked by his niece to help locate her uncle, criminologist Reardon entered the case and eventually exposed Mephisto, who had hoped to gain control of all world industry by the use of Forrest's deadly new ray weapon. He had kidnapped Forrest to force him to complete it. Republic cast him again that year in *Federal Operator 99* and the following year, again as a suspect, in *The Crimson Ghost*. The year 1947 saw him featured in *The Black Widow* for Republic, in 1948 he was in Columbia's *Superman*, and in 1949 the veteran actor pulled a "Clutching Hand" act by arranging his own kidnapping and pretending to be the prisoner of the mysterous Recorder in Columbia's *Bruce Gentry*, when he was actually the villain himself. His last serial credit was in 1953 as Professor Edmund Dorn, prisoner on the planet Ergo of electronics villain Dr. Grood in Columbia's *The Lost Planet*. This time he was a genuine pawn again — a fitting climax to his serial career.

The third of the trio of career pawns was William Fawcett, the wiry, wizened little pseudo grouch of an even dozen featured roles in Columbia cliff-hangers, plus an unknown number of supporting parts, one-liners, walk-ons and bits in countless features and television films — ranging from eccentric millionaires to seedy hotel clerks, and including gardners, grandpas and grumpy sourdoughs. In the classic mold of the scientist-inventor-pawn, Fawcett appeared in such Sam Katzman thrillers as the 1949 *Batman and Robin*, in which he played Professor Hammil, an eccentric invalid inventor who was a pawn without knowing it. (The male nurse at his side, holding the professor's life in his hands every moment, was actually the unknown villain, The Wizard.) Others were in *Pirates of the High Seas* as Ben Wharton, beachcomber-witch doctor who learned the secret of the unknown Nazi war criminal, *Blackhawk* as Dr. Rolph, kidnapped inventor, etc., etc., and *Riding with Buffalo Bill* as besieged miner Rocky Ford, who was constantly being captured by the heavies and rescued by hero Bill Cody. A variety of assorted roles included a minor one (Andre in *The Sea Hound*), a major one (the wizard Merlin in *The Adventures of Sir Galahad*) and several diversified ones (a pony express relay station owner in *Cody of the Pony Express*, a railroader in *Roar of the Iron Horse*, a futuristic scientist in *Captain Video*, and a native high priest in *King of the Congo*).

Providing motivation for the principals and suspense for the audiences, the pawn — the citizen whose personal safety often hung in the balance in the struggle between hero and villain — was an invaluable asset to the serial, and emerged as one of its outstanding characterization types.

11

Sons of Adventure

In the constantly moving, fast-paced, bone-crushing momentum of an action serial, the genuine creators of the tension and thrills were the nameless and almost faceless craftsmen who set up and carried out the continuing succession of physically active and highly dangerous mobile and combative sequences supposedly involving the players. Because of the exacting demands for split-second timing and athletic prowess in producing realistic and credible scenes, and the obvious necessity of not endangering the actors who had to keep the story going (and in whom the studios often had large financial investments), there developed early in the movie game a keenly resourceful, rigidly disciplined and expertly skilled breed of motion picture artisans who performed the required feats incognito. They are known as Stuntmen.

It has been no secret that these specially trained and uniquely qualified men and women have substituted for the principal players in scenes involving possible personal danger or requiring some particular skill. There is no shame in it for an actor, even though there have been efforts made from the beginning of motion pictures to conceal the fact from the public so as not to "stain" the image of some important star, or "burst the bubble" of illusion created by a particular film. In most cases, the audiences have benefited from the practice by being able to enjoy more professional and creative scenes than would have been possible utilizing less proficient people for the sake of "authenticity."

Many of the best of this profession either started their careers in serials or—because of their steady output of action—kept their talents honed by working in them. As motion pictures matured technically and the need for more expertly organized and executed action scenes grew, a select few of the outstanding innovators rose to the status of director, and one was recognized with an Academy Award for his contribution to the development of the medium.

Stunts have appealed to audiences and set the motion picture apart from other dramatic forms from the start. In essence, they made stars of Pearl White, Ruth Roland, Helen Holmes and Helen Gibson, who without them would have been just actresses like all the rest. They provided the means of reaching screen immortality to William Duncan, Charles Hutchinson and Joe Bonomo, who would have been "just actors," chewing the scenery for dramatic effect, except for their dashing displays of strength and bravado. In those days of silent films, the actors often did perform their own stunts, but the art was aborning, and with experience came wisdom. By the time of the talkies, only beginners and minor players were doing their own stunts where there was a major element of real danger. It was during the thirties that stunt work began to become specialized.

Silent veterans like Bob Rose, who had doubled for Ruth Roland in airplane stunts, and Richard Talmadge, who had been a leading actor before talkies, led the way toward the intricate, preplanned execution of stunt sequences involving vehicle maneuvers and personal acrobatics, and expert auto and motorcycle stunt rider Alan Pomeroy began the practice of training groups of would-be stuntmen in the techniques he had gained from experience. Young men who found that they worked together well in action sequences began to experiment with new approaches to more broad and graphic styles of screen fighting, many of which are still used today. Such a team was John Wayne and Yakima Canutt, whose contributions to stunt work are legendary. Western star Fred Thomson and veteran stuntman Buddy Mason comprised another. The late thirties and early forties saw the culmination of these experimentations into the concept of the stunt team, manned by expert all-around athletes who could perform most of the feats required by action films, but excelled in one or two particular phases. The most remarkable such team was the group assembled at Republic Pictures during its golden age from 1936 to 1943, out of which came some of the greatest purveyors of thrills and excitement in the history of motion pictures. And today's heirs of the art have learned at their feet.

The graceful and picturesque controlled movement of one's own body—be it through space in a leap or fall or through an intricate fight scene, being dumped from a bucking horse, or diving clear of a colliding vehicle—is the essence of the stuntman's trade. It requires a trained body and an alert mind. The manipulation of animals or vehicles to coincide with that movement requires timing and practice. Richard Talmadge excelled in the former, and Bob Rose in the latter.

Young Talmadge starred in only one sound serial—*Pirate Treasure* for Universal in 1934—but his influence was keenly evident in the work of his contemporaries. As stunt double for Douglas Fairbanks, Sr. (who was a top athlete in his own right and fully capable of performing the feats himself), the agile young man performed such intricate, balanced acrobatic maneuvers on stairs, balconies, rooftops and swinging ropes, drapes and chandeliers, etc., that his contribution to the legendary "swash-buckling" fame of the great Fairbanks was no small part. The same lithe, ballet-like precision marked the later films of Tyrone Power and Errol Flynn and became the model for those doubling for the serial heroes. Particularly adept at this type of graceful motion and split-second timing were Jimmy Fawcett, whose career was cut short by a tragic cycle accident in 1942, David Sharpe, the maestro of the flying leap, who became Douglas Fairbanks, Jr.'s, coach, stunt double and action director for his outstanding film successes during the forties and early fifties, and Jock Mahoney, who darted, dodged and danced his way to stardom.

As a result of his extraordinary ability to design, organize and execute even the most difficult action sequences, Talmadge became one of the top second-unit directors in the business. Called the second unit because of its separate, autonomous nature, this was a group of stunt and action specialists who took that portion of the shooting script describing a particular action scene and went on location to create and film it in its entirety, apart and away from the rest of the company. The film thus produced was later incorporated into the overall picture by the editors. This has become so common a procedure in making movies and television films that more often than not an actor in the regular company does not know what he is supposed to have done until he sees the finished product. One of Talmadge's biggest assignments as a second-unit director was the M.G.M. Cinerama spectacular *How the West Was Won*, which had no less than three of Hollywood's top directors in charge of the various phases — Henry Hathaway for the pioneer sequences, John Ford for the Civil War segment, and George Marshall for the railroad phase.

In addition to the task of doubling for Miss Roland, Bob Rose had also done extremely hazardous stunt work in silent serials for the reluctant Harry Houdini, who felt it would be demeaning for his image if word got out that the greatest escape artist of all time required a substitute. Finally giving in to the obvious economic arguments, the Great Houdini consented to the proxy because of Rose's eminent expertise with cars, boats, trains, planes and vehicles of all kinds. Prior to entering the stunt field in 1917 at the coaxing of great trapeze artist and serial star Eddie Polo, he had been a jockey, and his sense of timing and balance sharpened by that profession stood him in good stead for the new career. Generally accredited with being the first to make death-defying transfers from one moving vehicle to another — and even from one airplane to another without a parachute — Rose became the accepted expert at those delicately timed feats involving men and machines, and remained so for more than half a century. Such great stuntmen as Dick Grace, Wally McDonnell and Paul Mantz (whose tragic death occurred while filming airplane scenes for 20th Century–Fox's *Flight of the Phoenix*) followed Rose's lead in creating the most memorable air, water and ground vehicle action scenes in motion pictures.

Carey Loftin and Harvey Parry gave serials some of their fastest paced mobility and brought fans to the edges of their seats every week with almost unbelievable displays of skill and timing. These were the masters of automobile and motorcycle stunts. Their flawless engineering of human motion with that of machines created moments of breathless bewilderment that are an inseparable part of the peculiar character of serials. Only in rare, isolated cases did feature motion pictures contain the icy fascination of two or more automobiles in frantic chase, hurtling down precarious mountain roads, skidding perilously around hairpin curves and racing neck-and-neck with each other along narrow country roads, threatening every second to suddenly and disastrously slam into each other or go out of control and leap from the road into explosive oblivion. But you could count on it regularly in the Dick Tracy serials. And in *Spy Smasher*, Loftin showed what a motorcycle could do in the hands of an expert. For the Westerns, master teamsters such as Bud Osborne, Terry Wilson and Frank McGrath accomplished the same exciting results with wagons and stagecoaches, plus the third unpredictable element of frenzied, high-strung horses involved. Scenes such as that were not merely planned and carried out. Like the ones involving airplanes and trains, they had to be literally scientifically engineered. And the most demanding of all: they absolutely could not appear contrived.

Loftin, a native of Florida raised on a farm in Mississippi, became a motorcycle addict at a very young age, and as a teenager was performing trick riding in traveling thrill shows. After a hitch in the Marine Corps he wound up in Hollywood, a natural for the rough-and-tumble life of a movie stuntman. That was 1936 and he has thrilled movie audiences for almost fifty years as a stunt driver, double and action director. The slam-bang, no-holds-barred action scenes that provided the title for Stanley Kramer's *It's a Mad, Mad, Mad, Mad World* were filmed under Loftin's supervision, and there were practically no injuries of major consequence. The know-how necessary to accomplish it was the result of years on highways and locations grinding out the steady stream of danger-filled stunts to satiate the hunger for action and excitement of millions of serial fans.

For the medium and close cameras, Harvey Parry created an image which was in direct contrast with the key requirements of a top stuntman. In an automobile, the need for a cool head and steady nerves was absolutely necessary to carry out the split-second execution of a precision maneuver, and Parry was in the same league with Rose and Loftin. But in a nightclub scene, when a light-haired, bleary-eyed drunk bumped into the leading man or tried to wisecrack at the leading lady, you knew that in one minute you were about to see one helluva brawl, for that drunk was likely to be Harvey Parry.

The name of Bud Osborne turned up in the casts of many silent serials as early as 1922. He appeared in Pathé's Ruth Roland starrer *White*

Eagle that year and subsequently in others such as Pathé's *Way of a Man* and Universal's *Fighting Ranger* in 1924, *The Mystery Rider* and *The Vanishing Rider* in 1928, and *The Indians Are Coming* in 1930. Uniquely qualified for stunt work in Westerns, the husky, squint-faced Osborne was a genuine article. Born in Knox County, Texas, he had been a rancher in Indian Territory, a performer and assistant arena director for the 101 Ranch Wild West Show, a member of the original Buffalo Bill shows, and appeared in the first five-reel Western produced by the Thomas H. Ince Co. in 1915. During the silents he appeared in principal roles and performed all the required action stunts himself. In the thirties and forties, like Tom London, George Chesebro, Frank Lackteen and the others, he served in supporting roles and supplied authentic background and stunt work in more Westerns and serials than could be listed. Especially good with wagons and teams, he was a leading expert and mentor for a generation of stuntmen to come. Some of the best Western cliff-hangers produced had the benefit of his services, both as actor and craftsman: *Gordon of Ghost City*, *The Red Rider*, *The Vanishing Shadow* and *Rustlers of Red Dog* for Universal, *The Vigilantes Are Coming* and *Desperadoes of the West* for Republic, and *Perils of the Royal Mounted*, *Roar of the Iron Horse*, *Son of Geronimo*, *The Great Adventures of Captain Kidd*, *The Adventures of Captain Africa* and *Perils of the Wilderness* for Columbia. He was another veteran to participate in both *The Indians Are Coming* and *Blazing the Overland Trail* — the first and last sound serials.

Generally thought of as wagon and stage specialists because of their long association with the television series *Wagon Train*, Terry Wilson and Frank McGrath were top-notch horseback riders as well. McGrath, who played the lovable, irascible Charlie Wooster in the series went back as far as Osborne, and many of the stage and wagon techniques they helped develop were evident in the later work of experts like Wilson, Charlie Roberson, Boyd Stockman, Troy Melton and many others. Wilson, who was Bill Hawks in *Wagon Train*, was typical of the postwar stuntman. Returning from a three-year hitch as a Marine with service at Saipan, Okinawa and China, the California native learned of the opportunity to train under Alan Pomeroy for a stunt job at Warner Bros. studio. One of only a few to finish the training out of more than two dozen starters, he became one of the best free-lance stuntmen in town, specializing in trick riding and wagon stunts. His contemporaries were Bill Catching, Bob Morgan, Paul Baxley, Chuck Roberson, Bill Williams, Chuck Hayward, Charlie Horvath, and on and on.

The story of stunts on horseback could comprise a complete volume alone. The plots of all kinds of action films have revolved around men on horseback — Westerns, desert costume adventures, Oriental thrillers, medieval extravaganzas, Roman Empire and biblical epics — and lent to most of them the dubious tag of "horse opera." One of the prime requisites for the stunt profession was to be a master horseman, and some of the most exacting work ever performed have been scenes involving horses. Scenes have been filmed of everything from plain, furious hard riding to men jumping, leaping, diving and falling from a horse to wagons, stage-coaches, trains, cars, trucks, other horses, or to the ground; jockeying a mount at breakneck speed through rivers, fires, dust storms and thick foliage, off of moving vehicles, across yawning gorges, down steep hill-sides and off of tall cliffs; and mounting them from rocks, balconies and rooftops, at a dead run from the side, top and rear, or from the ground incorrectly up and over to the other side for comedy. With few exceptions, practically all of those doing stunt work have excelled in horsemanship, and have consequently been more or less steadily employed.

Joe Yrigoyen, who was a member of the Republic stunt team of the early forties, and his brother Bill were both expert riders. Especially good at transferring from a saddle to a moving wagon, Joe doubled for stars Gene Autry and Roy Rogers during their reigns at Republic, in addition to providing some outstanding feats for serials.

A former star in his own right and a champion rodeo performer, Kermit Maynard was one of the best horsemen in films during the thirties, doubling for his brother Ken in many of his famous releases, including the Mascot serial *Mystery Mountain.* So alike were the Maynard brothers in action that it was almost impossible to spot a switch.

Jack Williams, Ken Cooper and Jay Wilsey created some memorable moments on horseback for action fans, and John Daheim (billed in supporting roles as Johnny Day) brought his serial experience to good use as an action director in the fifties and sixties, a notable achievement being his supervision of the stunt work in Universal's *Spartacus.* A legion of stuntmen whose faces are still unknown to the public, but whose exploits are part of the fabric of memory in all of us, have gained their experience in chapter films and then used it to provide thrills and excitement in features and television — men like Sandy Sanders, Al Wyatt, Otto and Vic Mazetti, Russ Saunders, Frank McMahon, Bob Woodward, Hal Needham, Jack Perkins, Reg Parton, "Red" Morgan, Ted Mapes, Henry Wills, Dick Farnsworth, Wally Rose, et al.

The high fall — a particularly spectacular visual stunt requiring the utmost in planning and control — was mastered by several top stuntmen including Dick Crockett and Charles Horvath. Different from the high dive in that the protective steamlining of a controlled, poised and rigid positioning must be absent to give the impression of an unexpected emergency jump or accidental plunge, much more careful study had to be given to what twists and turns would be possible before reaching the position desired at the point of impact. Timing was all-important, of course, and usually a dummy weighing the same as the stuntman was employed to plot the course of the fall and get the time down to fractions of a second. The ultimate fall was actually a well-conceived, controlled dive that was engineered to not look like one. The impact point was prepared in several different ways to prevent injury. A natural point was a body of water, but if the fall was to be to earth there had to be provisions made to accommodate the falling body and break the fall. For a short or medium drop, the earth could be loosened sufficiently for the jumper to land and roll in a relaxed tumble. For longer falls, mattresses or cardboard containers (which would break away upon impact but cushion the blow) could be concealed in the scenery, or a fireman's life-saving net or an acrobatic net of the type used in circus trapeze acts could be swung. Whatever the precaution, the key to a successful jump still lay in the ability and timing of the stuntman. Also accomplished at this type of stunt along with Crockett and Horvath, Rose, Roberson and Parry, were Otto Mazetti, Ron Rondell and Saul Gorss.

Gorss, who died in 1966 at the age of 58, was an outstanding stuntman for over thirty years, excelling at all phases of the work. He was especially noted for his agility and swordsmanship. Much of the intricately choreographed swordplay in the Errol Flynn swashbucklers was his work. Like many others successful in the profession, he was good at most things, and better at a few.

Specializing was not necessarily the aim of a good stuntman, but sometimes it developed that certain feats could be brought off more easily or effectively by certain ones. Like actors, they could also be "typed" by directors and casting people, and when the need for their particular talents arose, the call would go out for them. Paul Stader, an all-around stunt technician, began his career in 1937 performing the memorable high dive for Jon Hall in *The Hurricane* and subsequently became a leading water specialist — skin-scuba-snorkel-pressure suit diving as well as high diving. Prior to Gorss and Stader, Olympic performer Harold "Stubby" Kruger, a native of Hawaii who became world-known for his swimming and diving achievements in the twenties, had excelled in both swordsmanship and high diving. Kruger's work in serials had been for Darmour and Republic.

Which brings us to the phase of stunt work that became almost an art in itself — brawls and fistfights. As pointed out, the planning and execution of stunts involving machines and animals, and those involving the laws of physics — dives and falls, etc. — approached the realm of science. On the other hand, the close-quarters hand-to-hand combat of brawls and fistfights required more of an interplay between human beings — action and reaction, initiation and response, give-and-take — and required physical performances often as intricate and dextrous as those of a dancer. The planning and carrying out of fight scenes thus was accomplished by a detailed and painstaking creation of patterns for the movements of the participants and their timed execution of the desired actions. So the wild, slugging fights that seemed to explode in frenzy and send the adversaries moving from one end of a room to the other overturning furniture and equipment and ripping shelves from the walls, racing up and down stairs, ladders and fixtures grappling for weapons or some other advantage, and seeming to be completely out of control and totally vicious, were actually demonstrations of the exquisite but excruciating art we could label prettily as "fantasies for fisticuffs" or the "ballet of the brawl," but which is more properly known as fight choreography.

During the silents and the early days of sound, not so much care was taken with the purely pictorial value of a fight scene. The script called for a fight, so the principals stood head-to-head and slugged it out, and it was enough. Then a new crop of young players like Wayne and Thomson began to display more broad and photogenic techniques in their screen fights. The resulting obviously predictable punches gave the audience the thrill of anticipating a particularly devastating blow and the dubious distinction among juvenile contemporaries of being able to simulate the "style" of a particular hero's fighting. Admittedly not recommended for effective defense in a real-life situation, the wide, sweeping, "telegraphed" punch of a movie slugger was more satisfying to a viewer than the short, choppy blows that would be more effective in a real fight.

After the famous saloon brawl in Universal's 1940 feature thriller *Seven Sinners*, and the classic battle between John Wayne and Randolph Scott (and their stunt doubles) in the 1942 remake of *The Spoilers*, the head-to-head battering match was out. In was the extended, stalk-all-over-the-room, every-blow-a-Sunday-punch fistic duel. And the architects and designers of those two landmark scenes further sharpened their expertise in the technique in serials. The result was a long string of fight and brawl scenes that helped sustain the cliff-hanger through another decade and a half of action and thrills, and established as front-runners in that risky business such pros as Fred Graham, Eddie Parker, Dale Van Sickel, Tom Steele, Ken Terrell, Duke Green, Bud Geary, Al Taylor, Bud Wolfe and John Bagni. These men, along with Fawcett, Loftin and Sharpe, comprised the Republic stunt team begun by Yakima Canutt when that studio was born.

Eddie Parker began work on the master plan for the famous *Spoilers* fight with Alan Pomeroy, but had to leave for other commitments before its final completion. Prior to that time, he had been a top stunt fighter for all three producers of chapter films. One of the first members of the Republic team, he had worked on *Undersea Kingdom*, *The Lone Ranger Rides Again*, *Daredevils of the Red Circle* and *The Mysterious Doctor Satan*, and continued to turn out first-class fights for them throughout the entire era. At Columbia he had doubled for both heroes and villains alike in their first dozen entries, making a particularly formidable adversary as the black-cloaked Spider, doubling for Warren Hull. A big man — six feet four inches tall — Parker became the prime stunt man for Universal's parade of monsters in the forties and fifties — the Frankenstein monster, the Mummy, the hideous Mr. Hyde, the distorted creature in *Tarantula*, the mutant insect man in *This Island Earth* and various other denizens in *The Mole People*, *Monster of the Campus*, and *Bride of the Monster* — after doubling in fights for such serial leading men in the thirties as Buster Crabbe (in all three Flash Gordons, *Red Barry* and *Buck Rogers*) and Dick Foran (*Winners of the West* and *Riders of Death Valley*). To those of us who early recognized the existence and value of expert stuntmen, Parker was easily identifiable when he stepped in for a leading player. His fighting stance was a stalking, flat-footed attack with fists shooting forward from cocked elbows like pistons or horizontal pile drivers. Even cowled and cloaked all over as the "caped crusader," it was possible to spot immediately when Eddie Parker replaced Lewis Wilson for a slugfest in Columbia's *Batman*, because of his unique style. And, instead of distracting from the popularity of the star, the knowledge that he was being doubled by Parker actually enhanced his appeal. Like the Starrett-Mahoney melange to come later, the "savvy" fan felt he was getting two heroes for his money — an acting one and a fighting one.

Fred Graham might just be the "king" of the stunt brawlers. Every studio making films in the forties and fifties utilized his talents at one time or other, and many of them gave him featured acting roles that almost always seemed to lead into or involve a donnybrook of some kind. He was especially memorable at being able to take punishment in a grandiose manner. When given a jarring "haymaker" by the leading man (or most likely his stunt double), the supple Graham jolted his entire frame into a contorted twist that caused shudders up the spines of the audience. And his face formed a grimace of pain so real that it was almost impossible to believe that the blow had only fanned empty air, inches away from any contact with his face.

Also adept at making a slugging match look like the real thing were Duke Green, the former telephone lineman and lifeguard who had doubled some outstanding stunts for Western star Buck Jones in his heyday, Bud Geary, who became well-known to serial audiences as a tight-lipped henchman during the forties, and Kenneth Terrell, the former vaudeville acrobat and tumbler who created some hair-raising sequences in running fights — dashing up ladders, across catwalks and along rooftop edges, swinging from fixtures and beams, and pouncing upon his colleagues from above. Terrell and Jimmy Fawcett had been partners in a vaudeville acrobatic act for 12 years before going into the stunt profession.

Tom Steele and Dale Van Sickel created two of Republic's most famous superheroes in successive 1943 releases, but their names did not appear anywhere in either cast. Both were "stuntman" serials, employing every conceivable action gimmick, and set the pace for all the rest of Republic's cliff-hangers thereafter. In *The Masked Marvel*, released in November of that year, Steele was knocked into a flaming truckload of explosives (a canvas top broke his fall and he leaped to safety), transferred from one racing speedboat to another (only to jump from it before it exploded), was thrown down an elevator shaft (landing atop an ascending elevator), became the target of a careening truck (leaping aside in the nick of time), was shot at point-blank (a heavy had stolen his mask, was shot instead), locked in a trunk and driven over a cliff (jumping from the moving truck at cliff's edge) and attacked by a variety of thugs and hoodlums with guns, knives, axes and furniture — and overcame them all. His superior performance as the masked hero was a tour de force. The very next month, Republic released *Captain America*, with Dale Van Sickel performing much the same repertory of daring feats in the cowl and costume of the patriotic crimefighter as stunt double for leading man Dick Purcell. Directors Spencer Bennet, John English and Elmer Clifton gave free reign to Steele, Van Sickel, Parker, Pomeroy, Graham, Green, Bagni and Terrell, and fight choreography a la *The Spoilers* became a permanent facet of Republic serialmaking.

The tall, lean Tom Steele also began his serial career in *Undersea Kingdom* under the tutorage of Yakima Canutt, and appeared in most of Universal's and Republic's chapter productions from then on. He worked in 46 of the 66 releases of Republic and in more than two-thirds of the entire output of that studio during its quarter century of life. His style of fighting, like Eddie Parker's, was a stalking, aggressive attack, but unlike the heavier Parker, Steele's attack was delivered as a smooth, gliding, almost dance-like rhythm of footwork akin to that of a boxer. Some of the most memorable fights staged for Republic were between Steele and the stockier Dale Van Sickel, and in their own way rivaled the outstanding fights they engineered for the major features.

Dale Van Sickel, a remarkably well-rounded stunt professional, also garnered the respect of his peers and became the first president of the organization formed to represent their interests, ambitions and willingness to serve the community — The Stuntmen's Association of Motion Pictures, Inc. Among its members are to be found the cream of the toughest crop of performers in the entertainment industry — the professional daredevils.

As is true in any area of endeavor, the stunt business has produced its maestros, the handful of men who virtually "wrote the book." Richard Talmadge and Bob Rose are examples. Others are David Sharpe, Cliff Lyons and the compleat stunt artist, Yakima Canutt.

The career of Cliff Lyons (also known as "Tex") is exemplary of the professional potential in stunting, as he rose through the ranks from stunt double to action director. With authentic credentials, Lyons was born on a ranch and raised in the same manner as other Midwest youngsters in the early part of the century. His background led him into a rodeo career during the twenties, when he became a star and picked up his nickname. In the thirties, because of his superb horsemanship, he began doubling for leading Western stars Buck Jones, Ken Maynard, Hopalong Cassidy, George O'Brien, et al. Both as an actor and a stuntman, he appeared in the golden age serials at Republic as well as the other studios. Such was his reputation as a horseman that he became one of the first two or three stuntmen always to appear on any list being made up by the major studios of personnel needed for an outdoor action epic, and doubled the top stars of the day. His ability to learn the tricks of the trade, retain and use them adroitly, and also instruct others in their use, led him more and more into the role of stunt "ramrod," the one to whom the director outlined the desired sequence, and who then organized, assigned and supervised the others in bringing it off. The next logical step was to second-unit director, and from that to the status of full action director, a job he performed so well in such great action spectacles as *The Alamo*.

David Sharpe was a stuntman for virtually all his life. As the St. Louis native grew up in Hollywood, he took an active interest in all athletics, especially those requiring precise timing and physical coordination such as swimming, diving, fencing and tumbling. In the latter he attained U.S. National Championship. Boxing and wrestling, judo and jiujitsu all were challenges to his dexterity, and he mastered them too. The son of a cavalry officer when that division still rode horses, he learned horsemanship from experts. In motion pictures at age 13, he appeared in juvenile roles for Fox, Paramount and Hal Roach studios in the early thirties, and also enjoyed a run in vaudeville as an acrobat, juggler, dancer and musician (piano). In the late thirties as his screen image matured, young Sharpe appeared in several serials at Universal and Republic (including *Buck Rogers, Dick Tracy Returns* and *Daredevils of the Red Circle*) while also stunt doubling other leading players. By that time he had become a vital member of the stunt team at Republic, and assumed its leadership when Yakima Canutt began to broaden his activities in major films like *Gone with the Wind*. During that period from 1939 to 1942, Sharpe acquainted cliff-hanger audiences with a new type of hero — the lithe, graceful, athletic champion who literally "sprang" into action cataclysmically. For example: In Chapter One of *The Mysterious Doctor Satan*, the newly created hero, The Copperhead, returned to the governor's office to do battle with the man who had just assassinated the official. His sudden shot-like dive across a desk at the throat of the murderer jolted the audience with its alacrity and set the pace for one of the best action serials ever released. Doubling for Robert Wilcox, the leap was executed by David Sharpe. As the title character in *The Adventures of Captain Marvel* star Tom Tyler was superb, but when the time came for the fabulous superhero to perform the feat that really set him apart — bodily fly through the air — it was the combined acrobatic artistry of Sharpe and the technical expertise of the special effects men that accomplished it.

Enlisting in the Air Force as a volunteer in 1943, Sharpe rose to the rank of Captain and was discharged after the war holding citations and commendations for his service in the European theater of action. Returning to stunt work, he became one of the most sought-after artisans in the profession as a double, a ramrod, a second-unit director, and personal coach in action techniques for many of the industry's foremost actors. In the sixties, it was a delight to see his work on leading television shows, especially as the "little old lady" who took all the spills and pratfalls during the "Silent Spot" on the Red Skelton Show, a role he took over from another serial veteran, Frankie Darro. For an avid cliff-hanger fan it was gratifying to know that those gems of comedy were the results of the planning of such stunt geniuses as the Daves, O'Brien and Sharpe, along with the versatile Skelton.

It is difficult to imagine what the serial business — yea, even the entire motion picture business — would have been without the stuntmen. I don't even care to speculate. The memories we have as a result of their work attest to the good fortune we have had that they did and do exist and function. And in that profession — as in all others — there was one man who became the lodestar, the guiding light. To his contemporaries in the formulative days, he was the prime innovator; to the studios who benefited from his efforts, he was a master craftsman; and to a successive generation of stuntmen (pros such as Fred Krone, Bob Terhune, Loren James, Howard Curtis, Fred Gabourie, Jr., Buzz Henry, Dick Geary, Bart Andrews, Herbie Kerns, Victor Paul, John Hagner, Dean Smith, Ben Dobbins, Tom Sweet, and his own sons, Tap and Joe, to name a few), he has been model, teacher, mentor, dean and maestro — Number One!

In the spring of 1969, I watched a television promo on the making of a new movie — the type of short film depicting some of the production highlights of an upcoming release intended to whet the potential moviegoer's appetite. The movie being plugged was *Where Eagles Dare*, a World War II picture concerning the rescue of a top Allied officer being held prisoner by the Nazis in a mountaintop stronghold. The scene in the promotion film showed a second-unit crew setting up a sequence in which a Nazi staff car would be attacked and shoved off a mountain road to crash noisily down the side of the mountain. When I recognized the man giving instructions to other members of the crew, I immediately sat upright, and a ticket to the film was thereupon presold. The man was Yakima Canutt, and I reasoned that if he were the action director, there would be some action in the film worth seeing. I was not disappointed.

Enos Edward Canutt was born in Colfax, Washington, and had the nickname "Yakima" (the name of an Indian tribe and also a nearby town in Washington) bestowed upon him during a rodeo career which spanned ten years before, during and after World War I. A natural horseman and athlete, he garnered practically every honor available to a rodeo performer, including World's Champion All-Around Cowboy from 1917 to 1924. It was logical that he would find his way into the young motion picture business, and he starred in silent Westerns until sound ushered in a new type of hero. In silent pictures, ruggedness and stamina were the hall-marks of the purely visual leading man. With sound came the require-ment of a good speaking voice and the desirability of a handsome face to go with it. Yak's hoarse, high-pitched voice and rugged, unpretty appear-ance precluded his success thereafter as a hero, so he turned to playing heavies and stunt doubling for the stars.

During that time he filled in for leading players such as Tom Keene, Lane Chandler and newcomer John Wayne while appearing in supporting roles in Westerns and serials. These included Mascot's *The Lightning Warrior, Shadow of the Eagle* and *The Vanishing Legion*, and Stage and Screen's *The Black Coin* and *The Clutching Hand*. At Mascot and Mono-gram he began his friendship and professional association with John Wayne, and together they developed techniques that became the founda-tion of the modern stunting profession. When Republic was formed out of those two and other small companies, Wayne was their star and Canutt their action expert. Working together, they created the "John Wayne image" of the square-shooting, hard-fighting, hard-riding, hell-bent-for-leather frontier individualist who takes nothing at all from an "ornery sidewinder," but can be totally defeated by a small child or a little old lady.

Applying his know-how at conjuring up and executing exciting, un-expected and unpredictable stunts, Canutt immediately raised Republic serials to the fore with his work in *Undersea Kingdom, The Vigilantes Are Coming, The Painted Stallion, Zorro Rides Again, The Lone Ranger* and others. He also gave Columbia a boost in their fledgling efforts in 1937 and 1938 with outstanding action work in *The Mysterious Pilot* and *The Secret of Treasure Island*. A real daredevil, Yak was the first to execute a leap from the ground to a moving horse and unseat its rider, from a moving wagon to the back of one of the team, and his famous drag scene, in which he is knocked from a stagecoach onto the tongue between the galloping team, suspends himself and drops rigidly between them, allow-ing the horses and coach to pass cleanly over him, grabs the back axle of the wagon and swings to his feet and up to the back of the vehicle, then climbs to the top to again take up the fight. His famous forward flying leap over the neck of a stumbling horse (known as "the Flying W") was another of the almost legendary feats he perfected.

As the years and the imaginative and original stunt work went on, Canutt was elevated to second-unit director on many major films, co-director with Wallace Grissell on *Manhunt of Mystery Island*, and full director of a Sunset Carson Western titled *Sheriff of Cimarron*, the first of several directorial assignments. His forte over the years has been as second-unit director, and as such he has produced in America and around the world some of the most intricate and demanding action sequences ever filmed in spectacles such as *Ivanhoe, Spartacus, Ben-Hur* and the more recent *Where Eagles Dare*.

In April 1967 recognition finally came to a profession and the man who was instrumental in creating it when the Academy of Motion Picture Arts and Sciences voted a special award to Yakima Canutt for his contribution to the motion picture industry. I do not believe there is any shame to admit that a small tear appeared on the cheek of a certain 39 year old grown man (with a ten year old boy lurking inside him) who had known Yakima Canutt since *The Vigilantes Are Coming*, but who had never met him.

12

Masters of Illusion

To place in context the role of the cinematographers and special effects men in creating thrill scenes for serials, there must be the dispensation of any purist requirements for authenticity. Most of the scenes of plush grandiosity, supernatural aptitude or massive destruction were just not possible to create authentically within the budget of a thriller and had to be visually effected. A measure of volunteer gullibility for the finished product was a requisite for the full enjoyment of most inexpensively produced chapter films. The flaw-seekers (self-appointed debunkers) who delighted in catching the filmmakers in an obvious photographic deception, could do so easily enough with some keen attention to lighting and shadows and material textures in the various scenes projected, provided the theatre's equipment was good. But in so doing they deprived themselves of all but the dubious negative pleasure of pointing out the flaw later to others who didn't really want to hear it. Those who "went along" with the deception, even after unwittingly or accidentally noticing it, did so in the spirit that the whole thing was make-believe anyway — like realizing that stuntmen were subbing the principals in a fight scene for better visual effect — so why not relax and enjoy it.

When the special effects were so good that even the debunkers could not spot the substitutions, it was motion picture craftsmanship at its best. And this was true more often than not. Most of the work of the cameramen and special effects technicians was seen but not noticed, and thus became an integral part of the overall illusion that *was* a motion picture. Usually it was the more spectacular, unorthodox efforts (erupting volcanoes, grinding train wrecks, underwater sequences and terrific explosions) that became suspect because of their traumatic effect on a story, or an unexpected human feat like a man flying through the air.

To create the illusion of such an event occurring within the framework of a particular story involving particular characters, many techniques were used. This not being an attempt at a technical treatise, no effort will be made to expose or illustrate those techniques, but to recognize a few that were employed to provide some memorable scenes in action serials.

The fundamental special effect (used to convey perspective or depth to a shot) is the camera angle. Although possibly arguable as a special effect per se, the angle from which a picture is made can definitely enhance the mood and effect of the scene. An upward shot of the hero standing on the edge of a bank (or even a tall box) in a commanding pose gives the impression that he is larger than life and master of all he surveys. What the editor inserts following that shot then becomes in effect that which he supposedly surveys, when in reality he was overlooking only the director, the staff and the crew. A downward shot at a character surrounded by oversized furniture and three walls gives the illusion of smallness and suggests a close, trapped situation. An overhead, straight-down angle suggests great height, even though the camera may be only a few feet above the subjects. And there is no more graphic a picture than a quick close-up of an actor's face showing an emotion or reaction.

Another purely photographic technique — the double exposure — was used effectively to portray the illusion of supernatural spirit activity or to suggest a character's fading into invisibility — a popular device in cliffhangers. Filming the character against a black background and then printing the negative along with one of the intended stage setting resulted in a positive print showing the illusion of a spirit character moving in the desired surroundings. A fade-out of the character portion of the shot suggested his dissolution to invisibility with only the setting remaining empty. This was done effectively in *The Purple Monster Strikes* to give the impression of the Martian monster seeping metaphysically into the inert form of Dr. Layton.

To convey the illusion of movement through a characteristic area, location in surroundings indigenous to some distant place, or performance against a background of specific activities, a technique of rearscreen projection known as the Banning process was used. The actors were placed in front of a huge blank wall screen to act out their parts. Projected onto the screen was a previously filmed picture of the area, the location, or the activities desired for background. Then, when photographed together, the illusion was created that the actors were situated in the scene depicted by the picture behind them. Thus, without leaving the studio, the impression of acting taking place anywhere in the world, or in conjunction with any type of surroundings, could be given. As graphic as it was capable of being, this technique was the easiest to detect because of differences in tone and shadings between the foreground performers and the prefilmed background. One of the most credible examples of the proper use of the process was the Chapter One climax of *Daredevils of the Red Circle*. For long shots of the wild motorcycle dash through the tunnel being inundated with flood waters, a stuntman was used; and for medium close shots of hero Charles Quigley astride the cycle, a direct head-on shot of his gently vibrating but stationary vehicle was made with a film of the onrushing waters projected behind him. His anxious emoting and quick, over-the-shoulder glances provided the human suspense.

The other notable techniques involving "trick" photography were the use of animation and employment of miniatures. Although readily adaptable for action films in the hands of an expert artist, animation was not widely used in the production of serials. Probably the most obvious use in an individual production was that of Columbia's in affording their hero flight in *Superman*. Even though effective — and perfectly acceptable to the devotee — the insertion of animated sequences to depict Superman in flight (and performing some of the totally impossible feats of which he was purportedly capable) was disconcerting. The voluntary gullibility of serial fans was thus richly tested.

A more satisfying technique had already been demonstrated for allowing men to fly in *Darkest Africa* (the batmen of Joba) and *The Adventures of Captain Marvel*, so the attitude of most young fans toward Superman's animation was more of tolerance than appreciation. Through the combined use of miniature figures, life-size dummies attached to unseen wires, and convincing close-up camera angles (shot against the rear-screen process), master special effects creator Howard Lydecker, Jr., had designed and executed the flying man illusion that would again be utilized in *King of the Rocketmen* and subsequent Republic productions. His perfection of miniature figures, devices, vehicles, buildings and even whole cities was recognized by the working industry and raised him to the status of second-unit director on several Republic productions, including *The Fighting Seabees*, a John Wayne epic of 1944.

At once the most potentially effective but most riskily susceptible to detection was the technique of photographing sequences using miniatures and then interspersing them with the medium and close shots involving the actors. By this method, limitless possibilities for wider scope in otherwise financially limited productions were available. Scale model reproductions of needed props and settings could be created at a fraction of the cost of building, buying or renting the real thing — even if it were available — and then either discarding or storing for possible future use at nominal expense to the studio. When expertly done, a good miniature was equally as valuable as the genuine article — and more so in some cases. By their flexibility in the hands of their creators, these reproductions could be manipulated into more pictorially satisfying angles and placements than could real objects. Seeming aerial views of a miniature city, for example, could be simulated simply by photographing downward upon it. To so film a real city would require the precisionary of special aerial equipment, and the result would still not be nearly so controllable. When done less than expertly, detection was more likely (a particularly difficult simulation was depicting smoke coming from the stack of a steamship) but still well worth the risk financially, in view of the intrinsic lack of sensitivity to such things in the juvenile and less sophisticated action fans.

Some classic examples of outstanding miniature work were the barren landscapes and ingenious model spaceships of the Flash Gordon and Buck Rogers epics, the ancient city of Joba in *Darkest Africa*, the rumbling volcano of that film and the later *Hawk of the Wilderness*, the futuristic underworld tower of Unga Khan in *Undersea Kingdom*, and the weird sea monster contrivance in *Haunted Harbor*. The tidal wave inundation of a city supposed to be New York was so vividly created for a 1933 RKO film titled *The Deluge* (and the scenes of destruction so realistic) that they were used many times after as stock shots — notably in *S.O.S. Coast Guard* and *King of the Rocketmen*. The use of miniatures was particularly adaptable to such scenes of violent catastrophe. Miniatures were also used profusely in the blowing up of objects in which the hero was supposedly trapped or detained. One of Republic's most often seen stock shots was the blasting of a miniature barn virtually into smithereens. The little bits and pieces could be seen flying in all directions — a beautiful piece of work.

Working together with the cameramen, the special effects experts created more of the stuff of which nostalgic memories are composed than anyone could realize. The actors gave the story expression, the stuntmen gave it mobility, and the special effects men gave it scope — the stretching of its range from hopeful inception to the full limits of imaginative conception. And the cameramen gave it life. Their work provided the fruition of the efforts of all the others. For the ultimate purpose of them all was to "get it on film," and that was the province of the cinematographer — the cameraman.

The photographer has always received technical credit as is proper, but not so the special effects man. Often, when the requirements for complicated illusions were not great, the camera crew provided them; but when specialists were required, they did not always receive individual credit. It was all in a day's work. Gradually, the value of such specialists was recognized by giving them screen credit, and the names of the men who excelled in the art became known to discerning fans.

In the earliest Columbia cliff-hangers, the photography was handled by the team of Edward Linden and Herman Schopp. Special effects, such as the appearances of the mysterious pirate villain in *The Secret of Treasure Island*, were credited as the work of Ken Peach and Earl Bun. Then, not until 1951 did that studio list special effects credits again. Jack Erickson received credit for his work in *Captain Video* and several subsequent releases. Following Linden and Schopp in succession as photographers of Columbia's late thirties productions were George Meehan and Ben Kline, Allan G. Siegler and John Stuman. From 1940 to 1944, James S. Brown, Jr., filmed 15 productions for producers Larry Darmour and

Rudolph Flothow, turning the job over to Ira H. Morgan upon the arrival at the helm of Sam Katzman. Morgan shot the next 19 releases for Katzman up to 1950, and four more (Columbia's final four) from 1954 to 1956. During the period from 1951 to 1954, Katzman's cameramen were Fayte Brown and William Whitley.

Outstanding lensmen at Universal were Jerry Ash and William Sickner, having filmed most of that studio's chapter films during its last decade of production.

Responsible for Republic's first 20 serials behind the camera was first-rate innovator William Nobles. In collaboration with Edgar Lyons (on the first six) and working solo (for the next fourteen) the former Mascot associate of Nat Levine was one of the best action and Western lensmen in the business. His photographic polish and technique in filming the hectic and furious work of Yak Canutt and company, gained him the reputation of being a major factor in lifting Republic's Westerns and serials far above the quality of its contemporaries, making it the leader in those areas for the next fifteen years. A worthy successor to Nobles was Reggie Lanning, who filmed seven of the studio's next "golden age" releases in the same high calibre as Nobles. In 1942, Bud Thackery photographed *King of the Mounties*, the first of 18 releases for Republic — the largest number credited to a single photographer at that studio. Between then and 1955 when he filmed *King of the Carnival*, the studio's last, he and able cinematographer John MacBurnie accounted for all but eight of the studio's total output. Reggie Lanning shot *The Masked Marvel* in 1943 and William Bradford the same year worked on *Secret Service in Darkest Africa*. Ellis W. Carter lensed four from 1945 to 1951, and that year Walter Strenge and John L. Russell, Jr., each shot one. MacBurnie was credited with *Captain America* in 1944, followed by eight more from 1947 to 1950 and four in 1952 and 1953. His last one was *Canadian Mounties vs. Atomic Invaders*.

Bud Thackery's career is typical of many other veteran cameramen, spanning all three areas of cinematography — silent pictures, talkies and television. He was born in Shawnee, Oklahoma, in 1903 and spent his teens working for the U.S. Agricultural Department and the Dunning Process Co. At the age of 20, he joined First National and worked in various departments, including processing. During the twenties, he also worked for RKO, Universal and other companies. That training led him into a full-time career as a cameraman at Mascot in the early twenties, and from there to chief cameraman at Mascot in the early thirties, and from there to chief cameraman at Republic in 1941. Since then he has photographed every type of motion picture made and is one of the most respected cinematographers in the business. At Universal City Studios, Thackery has supervised filming of some of the leading television series produced, including *Ironside* and *The Name of the Game*.

Almost parallel in chronology is the career of special effects man

Lydecker, the creator of the flying man effect. One of the best technicians in Hollywood — and probably the greatest in miniatures — Howard Lydecker, Jr., was also a graduate of Mascot who became a key member of the Republic production staff and the head of its special effects department. Securing billing credit with the release of *Dick Tracy vs. Crime, Inc.*, in 1941, his name then appeared in the credits of every subsequent Republic serial release except four (which carried the name of his brother, Theodore) as special effects technician. Beginning with *Manhunt of Mystery Island*, the brothers were billed together. So proficient was the work of Republic's special effects department under Howard Lydecker that other film studios and producers contracted for their services. At times the department has had more than four dozen professional scale-model makers working at once. With the advent of television, Republic turned its production facilities to the creation of series films in addition to feature motion pictures. For his work on television films, Lydecker won Emmy awards for exacting miniaturizations for *Voyage to the Bottom of the Sea* and *Lost in Space*. At the time of his death, he had been working on *Tora! Tora! Tora!* the 20th Century–Fox feature about the Japanese attack on Pearl Harbor that triggered World War II. He was supervising the largest assignment of a long and productive career — creation in miniature of the major historic sites of the war: Pearl Harbor, Hickham Field, Scofield Barracks and Tokyo Bay. With the release of that film, the awarding of the movie industry's most prestigious honor, the Academy Award, to another veteran of the cliff-hanger seemed promising.

13

Soothing the Savage Beast

It has been said that the definition of a "highbrow" is a person who can listen to the "William Tell Overture" without thinking of The Lone Ranger. So be it.

However, for many people who were kids during the late thirties and early forties, with no background of family interest in classical music (who otherwise might not have developed and cultivated any such interest), that stirring masterpiece was the musical catalyst that jolted them into an awareness of the exciting and rewarding pleasures of Wagner, Beethoven, Lizst and Rossini. As the official trademark of "the masked rider of the plains," it was truly the "call to arms" of action-loving youngsters and the clarion sound of adventure to millions of not-so-youngsters who also managed to be in earshot of a radio (incidentally, of course) each broadcast day at the appointed hour. Music that could set the heart pounding so excitedly and stir the imagination so expectantly to receive and accept the tale to follow, simply could not go nameless. So we each made it our business to find out what it was, and the knowledge became ours that it was Gioacchino Rossini's "Overture to the Fourth Act of *William Tell.*" Having once made that singular commitment to a piece of classical music, one's attitude toward such music could never again be totally apathetic. Thereafter, upon being similarly stirred by some other composition associated with a cherished excitement, the process would be repeated until a general knowledge of good music had been acquired. And with good music, knowledge is followed almost always by sincere appreciation.

In the days of experimentation with sound, the makers of movies first were concerned with voices and sound effects. After the silents, this seemed sufficient. But soon the desire for richer auditory expression was felt. So, as in the silent days, music again came to the rescue. It was discovered that good music interspersed with the scenes containing dialogue kept the ears of the audience busy at all times, as well as their eyes. The prudent use of well-known classics to bridge those scenes and set moods of romance, comedy, horror and adventure required the establishment of a new profession for films — the music director. It was his job to select the pieces and insert them into the proper places in the soundtrack to enhance the visual and audible action. This was done by the use of phonograph recordings or by performance of a live orchestra. When inserted pieces were replaced by original music written for specific sequences and refined to the changing moods of each scene, the live orchestra became the sole means of musical production, and the musical director became its conductor. Original music thus written for a film is known as the score, and many original scores were composed by the men who were also directors.

Some of the best known classical music selections were thus introduced to the young serial fan, and his ear for original music, although by no means adroitly perceptive, could determine by style if not substance the variations between the different directors. As a "Columbia" gunshot differed from a "Republic" or "Universal" gunshot, so did the sound of the background music vary. Unfortunately, such nuances were not perceived at all by some, but to the ones who did perceive them, another dimension of enjoyment was added decisively.

Charles Previn, a Brooklyn-born Cornell University alumnus, further educated at New York College of Music, was Universal's director of music during the last ten years of their serial production. His profusely effective use of venerable classics interspersed with the musical creations of Frank Skinner, the studio's resident composer (along with added touches of his own), gave that company's chapter films motion and drive that compared with the best evident in their expensive major features. Probably the most remembered were the lively passages used in the Westerns of that time. A combination of music Skinner had written for features such as *Destry Rides Again* (played during the credits with a wild frontier town shoot-up in the background) and the rhythmic passages from Felix Mendelssohn's "The Hebrides Overture (Fingal's Cave)" was employed in practically every Western (series, serial or major feature) released by Universal from 1938 to 1944, and gave them their own unique trademark. *Riders of Death Valley* in 1941 was rich with it, and also sported its own special opening piece — an original song titled "Ride Along," sung by star Dick Foran and his riders as they loped over the trail behind the credits.

Other cherished and revered classics (as well as the stirring fight song of the U.S. Naval Academy) also received Previn's directorial attention and became associated in young minds forever thereafter with Universal's quality-mounted cliff-hangers. The stately strains of "Pomp and Circumstance" was often used to lend majesty to the Forewords, that pyramidic upward stride of words at the beginning of each episode that was the synopsis of previous chapters. Franz Lizst's "Les Preludes," which had already become familiar to young ears as the middle-bridge music of The Lone Ranger radio program, was the opening theme music of *Flash Gordon Conquers the Universe*. Another familiar musical trademark was that of the popular Green Hornet ("The Flight of the Bumblebee" by Rimsky-Korsakov) and it set lips whistling as the opening theme of both Universal serials based on that character. For *The Sea Raiders*, starring the Dead End Kids, Previn incorporated the lively, lilting "Overture to the Barber of Seville," by Rossini, into an exciting background score. And for the opening of the Don Winslow adventures, what else would have been suitable but "Anchors Aweigh?"

The background music for Columbia's first four serials was provided by Abe Meyer, who was a former associate of maestro Hugo Reisenfeld at the Rialto and Rivoli theatres in New York before becoming music supervisor at Columbia. In 1938 he joined the new Music Corporation of America and subsequently became its vice-president in charge of music. Morris Stoloff, the studio's music director, completed the 1938 schedule, receiving music credit for *The Spider's Web*, and Lee Zahler took the baton for *The Flying G-Men* in 1939. From then until 1947, he scored all of the studio's continued pictures except one. *Brenda Starr Reporter* credited Edward Kay for music. From *The Vigilante* in 1947 to the final release, music was then directed by Mischa Bakaleinikoff. Between them, Zahler and Bakaleinikoff scored 51 of the studio's 57 serials. The hallmark of both was a decided Wagnerian influence which gave Columbia's chapter films a darker, more mysterious and portentous aura than the others.

A favorite device of Zahler's to create a feeling of haunting mystery was the use of a sustained violin tremolo passage similar to the fatality theme in Georges Bizet's operatic masterpiece "Carmen," but backed by a rumbling, threatening orchestral vibrato that smacked of Richard Wagner. His musical opening for *Batman* in 1943 was typical of that mood.

As the title and credits for *The Valley of Vanishing Men* were flashed upon the screen, the visual background depicted a scene from the film showing a whip-wielding overseer scowling at the captives working slavishly in the villain's secret mine, and the music was a pounding, pulsating composition that filled the heart with fear and excitement. At that time it was familiar but not known, and haunted the mind. Some time later it was played on a popular radio program featuring the Longines Symphonette and its identification as Wagner's "Ride of the Valkyries" from "Die Walkure" was possible. Even today when it is heard again, it brings to mind what can always be thought of as the "Columbia" sound in serial music.

Republic built the most technically proficent sound recording studio in Hollywood, and its golden age serials were scored there by a procession of top-notch composers and directors. Accordingly, the music in those releases represents the best of what could be described as the "cultural" aspects of the cliff-hangers.

The music in the first half dozen Republic releases was under the direction of Harry Grey, who used excerpts from the classics liberally, as was the custom. The stirring dash-to-the-rescue of the U.S. Naval fleet in Chapter Twelve of *Undersea Kingdom* was made to the accompaniment of "Les Preludes," and the derring-do of The Eagle in *The Vigilantes Are Coming* was augmented by the strains of Ludwig Van Beethoven's "Egmont Overture." In 1937 Raoul Kraushaar, former assistant to Abe Meyer and Hugo Reisenfeld on major feature assignments, took over from Grey and scored *The Painted Stallion* and *S.O.S. Coast Guard*. In the former, the basis for the score was a composition by Reisenfeld titled "Pinto" and a very provocative Indian melody used as the theme for the appearances of "the rider." The latter was sprinkled liberally with excerpts from the "Egmont Overture," "Les Preludes" and Lizst's "Hunnanstadt" (The Battle of the Huns). The next four releases — *Zorro Rides Again, The Lone Ranger, The Fighting Devil Dogs* and *Dick Tracy Returns* — were the beginnings of the golden age at the studio and were scored by Alberto Colombo, leaning more and more on original composition and less on the classics for source material. Of course, in *The Lone Ranger* he was faithful to the familiar "William Tell Overture" and other incidental music established by the radio series, and in *Dick Tracy Returns* employed the moving "Rienzi Overture" by Wagner with telling effect, but in all four his own work was primary.

With *Hawk of the Wilderness* came the first of the five original scores of William Lava. Writing action music with a contagious rhythm — almost in an accelerated march beat — his passages during scenes of relentless action were furiously yet succinctly melodic. After hearing some of them, many a kid who daily reenacted each week's episode in his own backyard (humming aloud breathlessly as he flailed his arms in the fighting style of his favorite hero) found that his humming suddenly had a tune to it as well as a beat — much to his own surprise — and for years to come would be able to recall snatches of a Lava score. So pronounced was his work for *Daredevils of the Red Circle* that passages were reused for the next ten years in Republic feature Westerns. His score for *Zorro's Fighting Legion* (including the Legion's battle song performed by their chorus of voices behind the opening credits each week) is believed by some to be the best ever written for a serial. A reminder of the lilting, bracing scores by William Lava could be perceived in his opening theme for the television series *F Troop* produced at Warner Bros., where he was musical director for a long string of successful series as well as feature motion pictures for a number of years.

The genius of Cy Feuer when writing music for serials in 1940 and 41 was to combine his own composing talents with the theme or mood of a specialistic or traditional melody and thereby establish a new entity — a suite entwining the conventional with the brand-new to form a musical composition as well as a functional background piece. The Oriental motif expressed by the sustained monotone of the drums—as opposed to the usual staccato beat associated with that instrument—gave *Drums of Fu Manchu* an eerie yet exciting flavor. The lighthearted, multioctaval treatment of the "Oh, Susanna" folk melody in *The Adventures of Red Ryder* could stand on its own as a light concerto. After forty years the mounting persistency and relentless rhythm of the fighting and chase music in *King of the Royal Mounted* still cling doggedly to memory. And the subdued but stately background rendition of Canada's beloved "Maple Leaf Forever" in the closing scenes of that serial left a haunting and treasured moment to recall. The original score for *The Mysterious Doctor Satan* was different and unique, transposing almost undetectably from a mood of mounting tension to one of furious, breakneck activity to that of steady, urgent expectancy. The scaling ascendance of the measured, ominous beat climaxed by a pistol shot in the opening scene of Chapter One set the tone for the entire production. Feuer's scores for *The Adventures of Captain Marvel* and *Jungle Girl* were perfectly suited to the fast-paced action and incredible stunts of the former and lusty, primitive setting of the latter. For *King of the Texas Rangers* he started with "Slingin' Sammy" Baugh's former school song (Texas Christian's "Come to the Bower") and developed it into a thrilling, unique score, playing it traditionally during the credits (behind a four-panel montage of the star's sports career) and using it as the basis for action and mood passages throughout the course of the film. His final score for a serial was also keynoted by the opening credits of each chapter. As *Dick Tracy vs. Crime, Inc.*, began each week, a wild dash through city streets at night was depicted as seen from inside an automobile with the cast and credits appearing and dissolving superimposed over the action. The theme by Feuer was a rapid, exhilarating opus somewhat reminiscent of Franz Von Suppe's "Light Cavalry Overture" that drew the audience inexorably into a spirit of high adventure. The subsequent background score maintained that spirit.

The Broadway stage was to benefit from Feuer's talents a decade later. In association with Ernest H. Martin, he became coproducer of some of musical comedy's most illustrious hits during the fifties and sixties: *Where's Charley?*, *Guys and Dolls*, *Can Can*, *The Boy Friend*, *Silk Stockings*, *How to Succeed in Business Without Really Trying*, *Little Me*, *Walking Happy*, and *Skyscraper*, et al.

Following Cy Feuer as music director for Republic serials was Mort Glickman, who performed the job twice. From 1942 to 1944 he scored the final eight of those considered to comprise the golden age, and returned in 1946 to score six more. Continuing Feuer's practice of scoring the openings with vivid thematic music, Glickman led off with a symbolic coup that was nothing less than inspired, according to the impressionable young fans. As its first serial release following Pearl Harbor and the beginning of the war, Republic presented the patriotic hero *Spy Smasher* in one of its most resounding action productions. Already the valiant European underground had adopted as a symbol of victory the international Morse Code designation for the letter *V* (... −), which they used as a password signal until it was detected by the Nazis, and as a victory slogan thereafter. Almost prophetically, the opening and central theme of Beethoven's Fifth Symphony − three rapid notes followed by a lower, sustained fourth one − one of the most stirring and magnificent compositions ever written, provided the perfect parallel to the code symbol, and the symphony became the inspirational anthem for the entire underground movement. Along with a shot of the Statue of Liberty with the *Spy Smasher* cast and credits superimposed over it, Glickman played the opening passages of the famous symphony, and little chills of excitement traversed every spine in the audience. The subsequent passages comprising the total score were expressed in the same grand manner, and testified to Glickman's artistry.

For *The Tiger Woman* and *Haunted Harbor*, Joseph Dubin provided excellent music, following the tradition of Lava, Feuer and Glickman. Richard Cherwin scored the next five from 1944 to 1946, and his colorful passages for the action scenes of *Manhunt of Mystery Island* were outstanding. Morton Scott scored *The Adventures of Frank and Jesse James* in 1948 and was followed by Stanley Wilson, who then matched Mort Glickman in total number of serials scored − 14.

Wilson, who put music to the studio's productions from 1949 to 1953, later became a musical director and supervisor at Universal City Studios, and his subsequent credits spanned the next twenty years, including such well-known television series as *Run for Your Life, Dragnet, It Takes a Thief, Ironside* and *The Name of the Game*.

The studio's final four chapterplays were scored by R. Dale Butts, who contributed scores sprinkled liberally with passages from his predecessors tied together with his own original work. Although good − and, unfortunately, better than the films they augmented − none of these scores could match the brilliance of those earlier ones.

The cliff-hangers music of Previn, Colombo, Zahler, Lava, Feuer and Glickman may not be destined to live forever − as is that of Wagner, Lizst, Rossini and Mendelssohn − but together with that of the masters brought an awareness and wondering that led many a young pragmatist who would never confess to a liking for "long hair" into an appreciation for classical music that he might otherwise never have acquired.

So, if the definition of a highbrow is a person who can listen to the "William Tell Overture" without thinking of The Lone Ranger, then a serial fan was definitely not a highbrow. On the contrary, he was one who now cannot think of The Lone Ranger without hearing in his mind the "William Tell Overture," or The Green Hornet without whistling

"Flight of the Bumblebee," or Flash Gordon without "Les Preludes," or Spy Smasher without Beethoven's Fifth, or Bill Elliott without "Ride of the Valkyries," or the Universal Westerns without "Fingal's Cave." And he is richer for it.

The next time you see a ten-year-old in the yard flailing away in a make-believe brawl and humming in time with the jabs, "Dum de dum dum de dum dum dum de de dum...," listen closely: You must might be hearing the music of the masters.

Top: Johnny Mack Brown (left) and Jack C. Smith in a scene from *The Oregon Trail* (Universal, 1939) which was based on material in the book *The Tie That Binds* by Peter B. Kyne. Bottom: One of the finest brawl stuntmen in the business, Fred Graham takes a punch from Dick Purcell in Republic's *Captain America* (1943).

Top: Allan Lane (right) arrives in the nick of time to save the beautiful Linda Stirling from the cruel fate planned for her by henchman Dale Van Sickel (left) in the Republic serial *The Tiger Woman* (1944). **Bottom:** Helen Talbot and Larry Thompson appear doomed, as villain Stuart Hamblen describes their fate to them, and henchman Anthony Warde prepares an explosive charge in a taut scene from Republic's *King of the Forest Rangers* (1946).

Top: Escape seems impossible for Kay Aldridge in this cliffhanger scene from Republic's *Perils of Nyoka* (1942). **Bottom:** Trapped aboard a burning ship, hero Ralph Byrd struggles to free himself before it's too late in Republic's *Dick Tracy* (1937).

Top: Allan Lane recoils from a vicious attack by Indian heavy Eddie Parker in an action scene from Republic's *Daredevils of the West* (1943). **Bottom:** Kay Aldridge and Clayton Moore are menaced by the gorilla, Satan, in the Republic thriller *Perils of Nyoka* (1942).

Top: John Davidson, henchman lieutenant of The Ghost in Republic's *Dick Tracy vs. Crime, Inc.* (1941), listens intently as his boss issues orders on the telephone to another henchman. **Bottom:** The unknown masked villain prepares an injection for his latest victim, as henchmen Clayton Moore (left) and George Magrill hold him helpless, in Republic's *The Crimson Ghost* (1946).

Top: Faithful ally Charles King (left), in one of his rare appearances as a good guy, plans strategy with hero George Reeves in a scene from Columbia's costume thriller, *Adventures of Sir Galahad* (1948). **Bottom:** Phyllis Isley as Gwen Andrews in Republic's *Dick Tracy's G-Men* (1939) tries to bring in a radio signal for hero Ralph Byrd. Later, as Jennifer Jones, she won an Academy Award for her role in 20th Century–Fox's *Song of Bernadette*.

Top: Buster Crabbe, the most prolific serial hero, starred in nine during a 20-year period. As Captain Silver, above, in Columbia's *The Sea Hound* (1947) he poises for action. **Bottom:** The greatest of all stuntmen was Yakima Canutt, who brought thrills to many serials during the late thirties and early forties, and became one of the most sought-after second-unit directors in Hollywood.

Top: In Republic's *The Painted Stallion* (1937), hero Ray Corrigan had three prestigious sidekicks: (left to right) former western film stars Jack Perrin as Davey Crockett, Hoot Gibson as Wagonmaster Walter Jamison, Corrigan, and Hal Taliaferro (Wally Wales) as Jim Bowie. **Bottom:** Republic's *The Lone Ranger* in 1938 featured two former stars, two future stars, and an ill-fated star as the five heroes — each suspected of being the "real" Lone Ranger. With heroine Lynn Roberts are (left to right) former western star Wally Wales (Hal Taliaferro), future leading man Bruce Bennett (Herman Brix), future star George Montgomery (George Letz), and former silent film star Lane Chandler. Lee Powell (right) was killed in action in World War II. At rear is Chief Thundercloud.

Top: *Secret of Treasure Island* (1938), a modern-day pirate thriller from Columbia, featured Gwen Gaze and Don Terry, who are shown in a desperate battle with a mysterious, ghostly pirate. **Bottom:** Don Terry fights it out with former silent film star Walter Miller in another exciting scene from *Secret of Treasure Island*.

Top: Kirk Alyn as the "Man of Steel" deactivates a squad of The Spider Lady's henchmen in Columbia's super serial, *Superman* (1948). Held helplessly aloft are Terry Frost (left) and George Meeker, while lying subdued on the floor are Rusty Wescoatt (left) and Charles King. **Bottom:** Tom Tyler struggles with a bad guy for possession of a revolver in an action scene from Universal's exciting Mounted Police adventure serial, *Clancy of the Mounted* (1933).

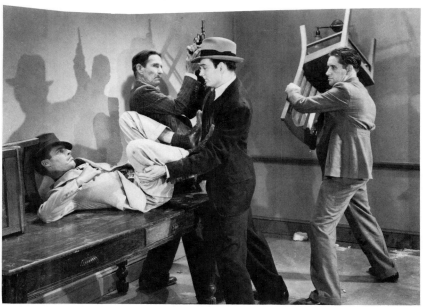

Top: Kane Richmond (center) has his hands full as he defends himself against veteran henchmen Al Ferguson (left) and Stanley Blystone in Columbia's *Brick Bradford* (1948). **Bottom:** Ralph Byrd (light hat) as Dick Tracy battles Charles Middleton (pin stripe) as Pa Stark and two of his henchmen, who are also sons of Stark — Jack Roberts as Dude (on table), and Jack Ingram as Slasher — in Republic's *Dick Tracy Returns* (1938).

Top: Veteran actor Lafe McKee is about to be surprised by Bela Lugosi in Mascot's *The Whispering Shadow* (1933), a 12-chapter mystery serial produced by Nat Levine. **Bottom:** A rare scene from *The Last Frontier*, the only serial produced by RKO Radio Pictures, released in September, 1932. Lon Chaney, Jr., dispatches bad guy Leroy Mason unceremoniously.

Top: An anxious moment for hero Tom Tyler, as he tries to help Gloria Shea in a scene from Universal's aviation adventure, *Phantom of the Air* (1933). **Bottom:** America's number one singing cowboy star, Gene Autry, in his first starring role, as the hero of Mascot's *The Phantom Empire* (1935), forces Frank Glendon to step out of a plane.

Top: Working undercover, hero Bob Steele (third from left) and his sidekick, Guinn "Big Boy" Williams (fourth from left) are faced with exposure in a tense scene from Mascot's *Mystery Squadron* (1933), a 12-chapter air adventure. **Bottom:** *Zorro's Fighting Legion* (Republic, 1939) boasted a whole platoon of hero assistants, as Zorro's legion battled to wrest control of a wealthy gold mine from mystery villain Don Del Oro.

Top: Two of Republic's ace stuntmen play henchmen in this scene from *King of the Rocketmen* (1949). Standing, left to right: David Sharpe, chief henchman Don Haggerty, James Craven as Professor Millard, and stuntman Tom Steele. Seated: House Peters, Jr. and Mae Clarke. **Bottom:** Hero Johnny Mack Brown rescues Louise Stanley from henchmen Jack C. Smith (center) and Charles Stevens in *The Oregon Trail* (1939), a western chapterplay from Universal.

Top: Surrounded by his henchmen, Irving Pichel as the villain Nicolas Zarnoff (with moustache and goatee) strikes a bargain with foreign agents in Republic's *Dick Tracy's G-Men* (1939). **Bottom:** Henry Brandon, as the Oriental arch-villain Fu Manchu, in a standoff with (from left) Olaf Hytten, Tom Chatterton, William Royle and Robert Kellard, in Republic's action-mystery serial, *Drums of Fu Manchu* (1940).

Top: *Brick Bradford*, a 1948 science-fiction serial from Columbia, featured a large metal space chamber that could transport people from Earth to the Moon and back at a moment's notice. **Bottom:** Serial technicians could create what appeared to be great destruction, but with a minimum of damage. This scene is a laboratory explosion from Republic's *King of the Rocketmen* (1949).

Top: Batman and Robin, portrayed by Robert Lowery and Johnny Duncan, survey a mysterious cavern in Columbia's 1949 serial thriller, *Batman and Robin*. **Bottom:** Lyle Talbot as Commissioner Gordon prepares to send up the signal that will summon the dynamic duo in *Batman and Robin*.

Top: The Wizard, an unknown robed villain, issues orders to henchmen Greg McClure (center) and Don C. Harvey, in Columbia's *Batman and Robin* (1949). **Bottom:** The unknown villain known as The Scorpion holds George Pembroke hostage before the momentarily-helpless superhero Tom Tyler in Republic's *Adventures of Captain Marvel* (1941).

Top: Kenne Duncan (left), Iris Meredith and Richard Fiske, aides of the mystery hero "The Spider," are taunted by the voice of the unknown villain "The Octopus," as they face an uncertain doom in a cliffhanger from Columbia's *The Spider's Web* (1938). **Bottom:** A veritable array of Mascot's leading serial "solid citizens" in a scene from *Shadow of the Eagle* (1932). From left: Edmund Burns, Kenneth Harlan, Richard Tucker, Walter Miller, J. Pat O'Malley and Lloyd Whitlock.

Top: Four of Professor Mortis' henchmen members of the "League of Murdered Men," hijack a truck in this scene from Universal's detective serial, *Gang Busters* (1942), adapted from the famous radio program. **Bottom:** Henchmen of Doctor Satan have the upper hand in a scene from Republic's *Mysterious Doctor Satan* (1940). William Newell as Speedy (in striped suit), veteran stuntman Yakima Canutt (to Speedy's left) and C. Montague Shaw (far right) are held at bay by Bud Geary, Lynton Brent, Ken Terrell and Joe McGuinn.

Top: Tom Neal, Frank Lackteen, Frances Gifford and Eddie Acuff in a temple scene from Republic's popular classic, *Jungle Girl* (1941), adapted from a book by Edgar Rice Burroughs. **Bottom:** Stuntman-hero Jock Mahoney questions henchman Rusty Wescoatt, who is being held by Tom London, in Chapter 14 of Columbia's *Cody of the Pony Express* (1950).

Top: *Perils of Pauline,* Universal's 1933 remake of the classic Pearl White cliff-hanger, had Evelyn Knapp in the title role. To her left in this scene in the jungle is supporting player Charles Locher, who later won fame and stardom as Jon Hall. **Bottom:** William Bakewell (foreground) as Ted Richards, trusted aide to hero Commando Cody, and heroine Aline Towne are interrupted by henchmen Clayton Moore (second from right) and Bob Stevenson in a scene from Republic's *Radar Men from the Moon* (1952).

Top: Ralph Byrd (left) stands off a gang of The Spider's henchmen in Republic's 1937 release, *Dick Tracy*. Buddy Roosevelt and Loren Riebe stand closest to Byrd and Al Taylor is at far right. **Bottom:** Lee Van Atta as Billy Norton (right) covers the enemy, while his pal "Crash" Corrigan regains his strength in a scene from Republic's *Undersea Kingdom* (1936). Others, from left: Boothe Howard, Monte Blue, George DeNormand and C. Montague Shaw.

Top: Jean Rogers as Dale Arden anxiously contemplates the unknown fate of herself, Frank Shannon as Dr. Zarkov, and Buster Crabbe as Flash, in Chapter One of Universal's classic serial, *Flash Gordon* (1936). Bottom: Donald Kerr played a very reluctant hero's assistant, a space ship stowaway reporter who found himself headed for Mars and some wild adventures in *Flash Gordon's Trip to Mars* from Universal (1938). From left: Kerr, Buster Crabbe, Frank Shannon and Jean Rogers.

Top: *Undersea Kingdom,* released by Republic in 1936, pitted modern-day hero Ray "Crash" Corrigan against evil forces in a science-fiction kingdom of ancient times — the sunken lost city of Atlantis. Here "Crash" is about to be attacked by C. Montague Shaw, as he attempts to disable one of Unga Khan's robots. **Bottom:** This robot, deactivated by Judd Holdren in Republic's *Zombies of the Stratosphere* (1952), was used many times in that company's serials. Designed by Republic technicians for *Undersea Kingdom* (see above), it underwent various changes in design, but was best known as Doctor Satan's robot, looking as it does here.

Top: A daring fall by one of Republic's stuntmen for a scene in *Government Agents vs. Phantom Legion* (1951). The cardboard boxes in the truck are all empty and will break the fall of the stuntman. **Bottom:** A thrilling sequence from Republic's *Dick Tracy's G-Men* (1939). A stuntman doubling for Ralph Byrd is rescued from a speeding boat loaded with high explosives, just before the boat slams into a barricade and is blown to bits.

Top: *Flash Gordon* (1936), Universal's smash-hit science-fiction serial success, introduced one of the screen's all-time memorable villains — Ming, the Merciless — brought to life by Charles Middleton. **Bottom:** Football great "Slingin' Sammy" Baugh breaks away from would-be captors in an exciting scene from the Republic modern-day western serial, *King of the Texas Rangers* (1941).

Top: Lobby card advertising *Adventures of Red Ryder* (1940), which was adapted by Republic from the comic strip by Fred Harman. **Bottom:** Lobby card for *Dick Tracy's G-Men* (1939), one of Republic's best examples of a true detective serial, based on the newspaper strip by Chester Gould.

Top: Lobby card advertising Chapter 5 of Republic's *Zorro's Black Whip* (1944). If that mask had been taken off, the face of ace stuntwoman Babe De Freest, doubling for The Whip in this shot, would have been revealed. **Bottom:** Rod Cameron starred in two serials for Republic in 1943 — *G-Men vs. the Black Dragon* and *Secret Service in Darkest Africa* — and then made several westerns at Universal. Offered a leading role in a picture starring Yvonne De Carlo, Cameron went on to become a top action star for ten years.

Top: One of the most colorful villains ever to menace a serial was Captain Mephisto in *Manhunt of Mystery Island* (1945), portrayed by the most prolific villain at Republic Studios, maestro Roy Barcroft. **Bottom:** Louise Currie faces danger as the loyal ally of the mysterious hero, played by Tom Steele, in Republic's action-crammed *The Masked Marvel* (1943).

Top: *The Purple Monster Strikes* (Republic, 1945), brought an invader from Mars, portrayed by Roy Barcroft, to clear the way for an invasion of Earth. **Bottom:** Lobby card advertising Columbia's most outstanding serial hit, *Superman*, released in 1948. It was based on the DC Publications feature appearing in *Action Comics* and *Superman* magazines.

14

The Iron Hand with a Velvet Glove

"Lights! Camera! Action! ——Cut! Print it! ——Wrap it up!" — There are expressions that are intrinsically associated with certain professions, the utterance of which create immediate images in our minds: "Play ball!" is a baseball umpire; "Open wide and say ahh!" becomes a doctor; "Where's the fire, buddy?" is asked by no one but a traffic cop; "I object — irrelevant and immaterial," is the language of a lawyer — and these are the cantabile commands of that absolute monarch of a movie set, the director. As the captain of a ship rules unimpeachably on the high seas, so a director reigns on the set. It is he who decides what will be shot — and how. He is the synthesist of script, actors, stuntmen, technicians and musicians. From his mind comes the pragmatic scheme for turning the basic ingredients involved into a finished work. His job is not completed until the production is "in the can" and ready for release.

The director is the catalyst who makes things happen by bringing diverse elements into play with each other, the glue that sticks them together, the emulsifier that retains their individual qualities in the process; he is the interpreter of the writer's words, the teacher of the trade, the professor of the art, and the supervisor of all related activity. It is his decision whether the lighting will be up for bright, forceful direct playing, or down for the shadowy, subtle creation of a mood; whether it is to be a tight scene for controlled dramatic effect, or loose to allow for individual, spontaneous expression; whether a close-up will be used as a gimmick or a tool.

The producer of a film is the arranger and provider of all the elements necessary for a production; the director is the organizer and user of them. So, if a single category of participant could be identified as the "maker" of a motion picture, it would most certainly have to be the director.

The silent film's veteran directors moved into sound, sustained and improved the new techniques, and continued to create most of the serials released by Mascot, Universal and Columbia. At Republic, new talent was developed and, after learning from the veterans, these young men began incorporating their own ideas with the proven ones to provide a new dimension to the genre. After the war, a new crop continued to polish and develop the combined techniques until the advent of television.

Henry MacRae codirected his first serial in 1916 — *Liberty, a Daughter of the U.S.A.*, starring Marie Walcamp and Jack Holt — at Univeral in association with Jacques Jaccard. From then to 1930, his name appeared on a dozen outstanding Universal serials and he had become the studio's top serial director. The foresightedness of the talented, versatile MacRae was largely responsible for Carl Laemmle's decision to commit Universal to a large-scale, full-sound serial epic at a time when the general feeling was that big outdoor films were not conducive to the limitations of sound equipment. The result was *The Indians Are Coming*, which opened the way for a resurgence of the cliff-hanger in the new era. Soon afterwards, MacRae was elevated to the status of producer, and the job of directing the studio's serials became the province of two other tested veterans — Robert F. Hill and Ray Taylor.

Hill had become a director for Universal in 1919 with the release of *The Great Radium Mystery*, and had since directed such stars as Elmo Lincoln, Louise Lorraine, William Desmond, Laura La Plante and Jack Mulhall in a succession of silent thrillers. The Canadian-born crafts-man was also a writer, with a number of screenplays to his credit. At Universal he directed two sound serials — *Spell of the Circus* and *Heroes of the Flames* — and then became associated with Sam Katzman and Victory Pictures for his final cliff-hanger efforts.

Ray Taylor was one of the most prolific of silent directors. Continuing a career begun in 1926 with directorial credit for Universal's *Fighting with Buffalo Bill*, he directed or codirected over half of that studio's 68 sound serials between 1930 and 1946, and also worked for Principal (*The Return of Chandu*), Columbia (*The Spider's Web*) and Republic (*Dick Tracy* and *The Painted Stallion*). About half of that number were credited to him solo, and the others shared with James W. Horne (one), Noel Smith (one), Alan James (four), Ford Beebe (six) and Lewis D. Collins (13). Those with Collins spanned the last five years of Universal serials. Collins, a Baltimore native who had been a juvenile actor and short subjects director, was codirector of only one other serial (*The Mysterious Mr. M*, along with Vernon Keays), with solo credit on none. He was mostly a Western and feature director.

During those same years, Universal also had the benefit of talented craftsmen and artists such as Louis Friedlander, Frederick Stephani, Cliff Smith, Saul Goodkind and John Rawlins for individual or codirecting assignments with Taylor and their other major serial director, Ford Beebe.

Beebe, who had been a writer for silent pictures and associated with

Nat Levine as both writer and codirector, joined Universal in 1935. The former Michiganer, from Grand Rapids, teamed up with Smith, who alone had directed *The Adventures of Frank Merriwell*, for five straight winners — *Ace Drummond, Jungle Jim, Secret Agent X-9, Wild West Days* and *Radio Patrol* — followed by four years of rewarding associations with the others, which led him into the more lucrative career of feature producer for the studio.

While at Mascot, Beebe had received directorial credit for *Shadow of the Eagle* and shared honors with B. Reeves Eason on *The Last of the Mohicans* and *The Adventures of Rex and Rinty*. Along with Eason, Levine had lined up talent such as Richard Thorpe, Ross Lederman, Armand Schaefer, Otto Brower, Albert Herman and Colbert Clark to direct his free-swinging epics. Their valiant efforts with the new demands of sound, a dynamic, ambitious producer, and shoestring-tight budgets, resulted in a phenomenon of the times. Mascot Pictures, which appeared to be always on the brink of bankruptcy, emerged from an inauspicious beginning in the late twenties to become the surviving successor to silent production powers such as Arrow, Rayart, Weiss Brothers Artclass and Pathé; sole worthy competitor to the mighty Universal; and the nucleus of a brand new major production company — the only new one to be formed in the postsilent era.

Richard Thorpe, born Rollo Smolt Thorpe in Kansas, had appeared in vaudeville and musical comedy as a teenager before moving into motion pictures. His association with states-rights producer Levine resulted in four silent serials (three of which included Boris Karloff in the cast) and the Rin Tin Tin, Jr., starrer *The Lone Defender* with sound. A feature director from 1933 on, Thorpe eventually became one of the top directors of all time at Metro–Goldwyn–Mayer, with credits that include such major achievments as *The Great Caruso, Ivanhoe, Prisoner of Zenda, The Student Prince* and *Knights of the Round Table*.

"Breezy" Eason went to Hollywood from Fryors Point, Mississippi, via vaudeville and stock theater. Already a director at the tender age of 22 for the American Film Company, he worked for various major studios (Fox, MGM, Universal) during and following the war years and before his Mascot stint. As either director or codirector he worked on 11 serials for Levine in the early thirties, and a decade later did *The Phantom, Black Arrow* and *The Desert Hawk* for Columbia.

Colbert Clark, known later to many as the producer of Columbia's Durango Kid series, doubled as a writer and director during his Mascot days. The Harvard graduate was credited as codirector on *The Three Musketeers, Fighting with Kit Carson* and *Burn 'em Up Barnes* with Armand Schaefer, and on one each with Albert Herman (*The Whispering Shadow*), Harry Fraser (*Wolf Dog*) and David Howard (*Mystery Squadron*).

Otto Brower directed *The Devil Horse* and shared credit with Eason on *Mystery Mountain* and *The Phantom Empire*. D. Ross Lederman, an expert in chase sequences and trick photography scenes, had been an extra in Mack Sennett comedies and worked as Roscoe "Fatty" Arbuckle's propman. He later became a director and associate producer for Columbia features after directing Tom Tyler and Dorothy Gulliver in *Phantom of the West* at Mascot. Joseph Kane codirected *The Fighting Marines* with Eason at Mascot and the first two to be tagged "Republic" — *Darkest Africa* and *Undersea Kingdom*.

After serving as director, codirector and associate producer on nine Mascot projects, Armand Schaefer, who had also been a Mack Sennett and silent serial alumnus, became a producer at Republic. There, the Canadian-born entrepreneur molded the career of Roy Rogers and other leading Western stars. In the forties he created, in partnership with the famous cowboy star, Gene Autry Productions and became its president, releasing its products through Columbia. When television came, he and Autry joined the tide and formed Flying A Pictures, Inc., and filmed such series as *Gene Autry*, *The Range Rider*, *Annie Oakley*, *Death Valley Days* and *Buffalo Bill, Jr.*, for syndication.

Mascot veteran Harry Fraser, also noted as an outstanding screenwriter, helped get fledgling Columbia serials off the ground by codirecting *Jungle Menace* with George Melford. Having written successful vehicles for leading man Reginald Denny, their association as director and hero on the Frank Buck jungle epic was a natural winner. Louis Weiss was engaged as associate producer. His expertise in producing silent jungle films was invaluable to producer Jack Fier in his first cliff-hanger effort, and he repeated the assignment for *The Mysterious Pilot* and *The Secret of Treasure Island*. For those two, Fier gave the job of directing to Spencer G. Bennet and Elmer Clifton respectively. Bennet was a veteran of silent serials — from as far back as 1920 when he was second-unit director under Bertram Millhauser at Pathé — and Clifton had worked with the Weiss Brothers on two earlier independent releases for Stage and Screen, *The Black Coin* and *Custer's Last Stand*. Mack V. Wright and Sam Nelson then did *The Great Adventures of Wild Bill Hickok*, and Nelson teamed up with Norman Deming for *Mandrake the Magician* and *Overland with Kit Carson*, Fier's last two for the studio. In the meantime, veterans Ray Taylor and James W. Horne (another graduate of silent films, having directed The Little Rascals for Hal Roach and Laurel and Hardy in some of their classics at MGM) had teamed up for *The Spider's Web* and *The Flying G-Men*.

When Larry Darmour became Columbia's serial producer in 1940, Horne was engaged as solo director and performed in that capacity on ten of the 12 Darmour productions released between then and 1943. Spencer Bennet then returned for *The Secret Code* and *The Valley of Vanishing Men*. Rudolph Flothow's five projects as producer — *Batman*, *The Phantom*, *The Desert Hawk*, *Black Arrow* and *The Monster and the*

Ape—credited Lambet Hillyer, former writer and feature director, for the first; B. Reeves Eason the next two; Lew Landers and Howard Bretherton for the last two. Then, under Sam Katzman's production eye, several veteran directors were engaged before Bennet again took over the duties in 1947 to finish out the serial era. Wallace W. Fox, a former newspaper writer and free-lance director, did *Brenda Starr Reporter, Jack Armstrong* and *The Vigilante*. Lesley Selander, who had directed the popular Hopalong Cassidy Westerns for Harry Sherman Productions, directed *Jungle Raiders*. Bretherton codirected *Who's Guilty* with Wallace Grissell. And Derwin Abrahams accounted for four more — *Chick Carter, Hop Harrigan, Son of the Guardsman* and *Tex Granger*. From there on, Bennet was the director of every Columbia serial — at times sharing credit with codirectors such as Thomas Carr (five), Wallace Grissell (two), and Fred F. Sears (one) for brief stints — except one, *The Great Adventures of Captain Kidd*, which was directed by Derwin Abbe and Charles S. Gould.

Spencer Gordon Bennet served as assistant to Pathé's great George B. Seitz in the early twenties following his stints as second-unit director under Millhauser. His previous experience as a stuntman combined with those years with Seitz — during which some of Pathé's greatest thrillers starring Pearl White, Charles Hutchinson, Allene Ray and Edna Murphy were produced — prepared him for a career as one of the best action directors to span the entire serial era. The first production to carry his name as director (following Seitz' departure from Pathé to direct features) was *Play Ball*, starring Allene Ray and Walter Miller, released in July 1925 on the heels of that starring team's first successful venture, *Sunken Silver*, which had been Seitz' last serial. After that, Bennet directed all of the Ray-Miller vehicles, as well as a couple with Gladys McConnell and one with boxing champion Gene Tunney, until 1929 when the team broke up, along with Pathé.

In the sound era, Bennet established two serial careers — at Republic as the successor of the Witney-English team, and as Katzman's ace at Columbia. By actual count of titles, he directed more serials than any other man except Ray Taylor. Those at Republic from 1943 (*Secret Service in Darkest Africa*) to 1947 (*The Black Widow*) were among the best of the entire sound period, next only to the proceeding two dozen golden age classics.

Students of the cliff-hanger are all more or less agreed that the 17 Republic productions directed by William Witney and John English — from *Zorro Rides Again* in 1937 to *Dick Tracy vs. Crime, Inc.*, in 1941 — were the greatest of the sound era, but they don't all agree as to why. Some think it was the tight writing of Davidson, Cox, Shipman, Adreon, Shor and Hall. Others attribute it to the technical finesse of the production crews that gave them the polish and professionalism previously lacking in low-budget efforts. The stunt work of Canutt, Sharpe,

Terrell, and company, is the prime factor to many, as are the brilliant scores of Colombo, Lava and Feuer to those who still recall passages of agitatos and furiosos long since faded away. The one thing there can be no question about is the undeniable perception in the proper use of all those elements possessed by the directing pair. Individually they were good directors — as evidenced by Witney's solo credits on *Spy Smasher, The Perils of Nyoka, King of the Mounties, G-Men vs. the Black Dragon,* and *The Crimson Ghost,* and English's *Daredevils of the West* — and working with other directors were highly effective (Witney with Ray Taylor and Alan James on *The Painted Stallion* and *S.O.S. Coast Guard,* and English with Elmer Clifton on *Captain America*), but teamed together there was a rapport that was unequaled before or since.

Befitting his surname, John English was born in Cumberland, England, and received his education in Canada. His biography states that he was a director of many Republic features and Westerns "since 1942," excluding any mention of his serial work, even though by comparison his feature films were only average or slightly better. William Witney was an Oklahoman from Lawton, who migrated to the West Coast and while a teenager worked as a messenger at Mascot, where he soaked up and retained everything he could learn from Levine, Eason, Schaefer and Clark. From messenger he graduated to the editing department and then became a script supervisor when the studio became Republic. After the codirecting stints with veterans Ray Taylor and Alan James, he was assigned by associate producer Sol Siegel to work with English on *Zorro Rides Again,* and the golden age was born. His career was interrupted by World War II and he served in the U.S. Marine Corps, returning afterward to become one of Republic's most versatile directors of Westerns and low-budget features, experience which gave him preparation for continued work in television.

In addition to the talents of Ray Taylor, who soon returned to Universal, the new Republic also benefited by the presence of "Breezy" Eason and Joe Kane on their first two productions and the versatile Mack Wright, who worked with Taylor on the next two. Wright had been a director since the earliest days of serials when he had tripled as action star, stuntman and one of the youngest directors (in his early twenties) in motion pictures. After codirecting *The Vigilantes Are Coming* and *Robinson Crusoe of Clipper Island* for Republic and the one at Columbia the next year, Wright did not again direct for a serial until 1947, when he teamed up with Walter Eason for Katzman's *The Sea Hound.*

Spencer Bennet's return to Columbia in 1947 opened the way for Fred C. Brannon, his codirector on seven releases the previous two years, to move to full director. He and Yakima Canutt collaborated on Mike Frankovich's remaining two productions (*G-Men Never Forget* and *Dangers of the Canadian Mounted*) and Franklyn Adreon's first one as associate producer (*The Adventures of Frank and Jesse James*). From then on Brannon received solo directorial credit until 1953 when Adreon took over as both associate producer and director for the studio's last five serials. Altogether, the New Orleans native directed or codirected 24 chapterplays for Republic — a prolific achievement.

"The iron hand in a velvet glove" is an expression that has been used to describe the motion picture director, and it is most appropriate to include in that picturesque description those who engineered the action serials. Although less compelled to evoke aesthetically dramatic performances from their actors, they were required to withdraw whatever creative talent there happened to be. And the dramatic acting field had no corner on the likelihood of professional sensitivity. There were prima donnas in all of the various related crafts and occupations involved in the making of a chapter film — including among the animals — and the director had to recognize and deal with them, and somehow bring order from chaos, artistic adhesion from individualistic diversities, a completed motion picture from a conglomeration of talents. To do so required all the drive, persuasion, personality, intelligence, strength, fortitude, patience, understanding and tolerance a human could muster. Directing is the most fulfilling and most challenging role in the performing arts. That is why so many who become involved in them want so much to try it; and why so few succeed.

15

Ascending the Heights

One of the favorite legends in American history is the legend of Abraham Lincoln, who rose from humble Illinois farm boy to the Presidency of the United States. On a far lesser scale, the stories of Horatio Alger used to thrill a generation of less blasé and more naive readers with accounts of boys who starting with nothing, or less, and surmounted seemingly impossible odds to become the industrial and economic giants so admired in this country at that time. Americans have attached a great deal of importance to the existence of a simple or deprived background when judging people who reach the pinnacles of success. It seems more deserved—or more "right"—if the person had obstacles to overcome than if his success came too easy. Nothing more derogatory could be said of a public figure than he "was born with a silver spoon in his mouth" or "had it handed to him on a platter." For success to be valuable, we felt it had to be earned—a feeling that seems to have less credence today—and we had empathy for those who made it.

Motion pictures had a parallel for die-hard action fans. To see one whom we had "discovered" in a favorite serial, Western or "double-bill" feature rise to importance in the industry by hard work and determination gave us a measure of satisfaction that almost amounted to sharing that success. And, when the "cultural snobs" and "literary cynics" would assert about our champion, "Ah, well, he rose above it," we would heartily counter with, "On the contrary, my friend, he rose _from_ it!" For we knew that in the routine, steady grinding out of formula films, and the constant hope to find something new to include in them, an actor learned his trade.

Some former stars of the silent era found in serials and Westerns their best opportunity to continue working when sound came. Action stars such as Walter Miller, William Desmond, Joe Bonomo, Jack Mulhall, William Farnum, Francis X. Bushman, J.P. MacGowan and Francis Ford became the villains and the citizens of sound serials, and the younger actors learned from them. From the learning came experience, and with experience came opportunities. They then went on to become outstanding Western stars, leading romantic players, movie and television personalities, character professionals and even one or two became singularly unique human institutions.

It was easier to be in serials what you already were in some other line, so some of the stars merely embellished careers already begun. Harold "Red" Grange, famed at the University of Illinois as "the galloping ghost" of college football, allowed Mascot to exploit that fame in a 1931 cliff-hanger with his nickname as its title. Ten years later, Sammy Baugh of Texas Christian and the Washington (D.C.) Redskins (a professional football team) repeated history by enrolling his fame as a sports figure and limited acting talent in Republic's *King of the Texas Rangers*. The result was more satisfactory due to the know-how of the new studio's production people.

The same idea was used to good advantage by Nat Levine in casting the fabulous animal trainer, Clyde Beatty, in his two successful serials, and by Jack Fier in securing the equally legendary great game hunter, Frank Buck, for *Jungle Menace*. Fier's second release exploited the popularity of ace aviator Captain Frank Hawks in *The Mysterious Pilot*.

Leading Western stars Ken Maynard, Buck Jones, Tim McCoy and Tom Mix lent prestige to serials, as has already been pointed out, and three young aspirants were boosted into Western stardom by appearances in serials in the thirties.

A career that fits the Horatio Alger legend almost perfectly is that of Gene Autry. A Texan, from Tioga, young Gene was a railroad telegrapher at Sapulpa, Olkahoma, when he was eighteen. The story goes that he taught himself how to play the guitar to while away the hours when he was not at the keys, singing along to amuse himself. A waiting passenger overheard him and encouraged the young man to try a radio and singing career, which he did. As a result of his work on radio and records, he was hired by Mascot in 1934 to make films as one of the first of a new breed of Western hero—the singing cowboy. Among his first featured roles was that of the hero in Nat Levine's fanciful, futuristic serial *The Phantom Empire*. Subsequently at Republic, Autry became the first cowboy star to appear in the list of motion pictures' Top Ten Moneymakers (1939 to 1942), led the Top Ten Western Moneymakers for six years (1937 to 1942), and appeared in that list in ten other years (1936 and 1946 to 1954). During World War II he distinguished himself as one of Hollywood's first volunteers for military service, enlisting in the Army Air Force immediately after Pearl Harbor and rising through the ranks to become an officer. During his hitch he also appeared as an entertainer on U.S.O. tours in addition to his flight duties. Following his return from service, he resumed his film career at Columbia, formed his movie and television production company with Armand Schaefer, and invested in radio and television stations as well, becoming one of the most successful stars in the entertainment business. Oh, yes, the waiting passenger at the Sapulpa station — America's beloved humorist, Will Rogers.

Another football star became a leading motion picture star also, but not in the same fashion as Grange and Baugh. Johnny Mack Brown, top player for the University of Alabama in their bid for Rose Bowl fame in 1926, returned to Hollywood to become a much-in-demand leading man in films of all types — romantic, historic, action, Western and serials. During the early thirties he appeared opposite some of the most glamorous actresses in pictures at MGM, Universal, Paramount, Fox and Warner Bros., and appeared in Mascot's rousing cliff-hanger *Fighting with Kit Carson* as the legendary pioneer hero. At Universal he starred in *Rustlers of Red Dog* (1935), *Wild West Days* (1937), *Flaming Frontiers* (1938) and *The Oregon Trail* (1939), four of the fastest-paced chapter-plays of the era. From 1939 until the mid fifties, Brown starred in a long string of Western adventures at Universal and Monogram that saw him listed 11 times in the list of Top Ten Western Moneymakers and assured for him a place among the all-time Western stars of Hollywood's brightest era.

A serial role created stardom for Gordon Elliott, known to millions as "Wild Bill." Prior to his appearance in the title role of *The Great Adventures of Wild Bill Hickok* in 1938, he had played in supporting roles as a hard-eyed, smooth-talking underworld type in gangster films and a frontier gambler-shyster in Westerns, using his real name. With the showing of the Columbia serial, he subsequently became known for the remainder of his career as the "peaceable man with a gun in each hand" and as that cowboy star who wore his pistols backward. The former was the plaintive credo of the writers' version of the legendary Marshal Hickok, and the latter the manner in which he wore his guns.

(The reason for the unusual practice of wearing the brace of six-shooters with the butts pointed forward was twofold. When I talked with him in 1947, the tall cowboy star told me that one reason for the un-orthodox switch was simply that no one else was doing it that way and it was sure to gain attention as a gimmick. Also, he said that it was actually easier for him to master a quick draw that way than with the guns hanging hammers forward, because of the necessity of first lifting the weapons clear of the holster and then turning them forward with a distinct upward turn of the wrist when drawing from the hammers-forward position. Slung backwards, with holsters tied loosely to his legs, the guns could be snapped out and up in a quick, circular twist-of-the-wrist motion that leveled them into a firing position much faster and more comfortable for him. He then demonstrated the two draws to illustrate what he meant, and for him it certainly appeared easier his way.)

Following that first serial appearance, he starred in a series of Western features and then another cliff-hanger, *Overland with Kit*

Carson, followed by still more features until 1942 when he starred in his final serial, *The Valley of Vanishing Men.* Shortly afterward he moved to Republic to star in a series of Westerns with George "Gabby" Hayes, and then completed two eight-picture series as the comic strip cowboy hero Red Ryder. Looking for an actor to star in several planned major features, Republic chose Elliott to star as a colorful outlaw-hero known as "Spanish Jack" in a top-budgeted epic titled *In Old Sacramento.* His mature, plaintive style—reminiscent of the great William S. Hart—caught on with the public and he starred in nine more important productions at Republic and became a major name in the action field. Ten major Westerns and four detective thrillers at Allied Artists during the fifties climaxed the career that had begun in a serial twenty years before.

Several of the movies' most handsome romantic leading men counted action serials in their list of credits, and four of the most beautiful leading ladies of the forties and fifties escaped the "clutches of death" before falling into the clutching arms of tall dark lovers in major films.

The beginning of Republic's golden age was also the beginning of a career for talented singing star John Carroll. He was perfect for the role of the dashing James Vega in *Zorro Rides Again,* and afterward played the romantic Latin lover in a score of major films. A versatile artist with a kaleidoscopic background, the New Orleans native, born Julian La Faye, studied voice in Italy under Victor Chesnais, circled the world several times, sang in Paris, London, Rome, Vienna and Budapest, worked as a ship's cook, a racecar driver; a barnstorming pilot and a steeplejack, and was a musical comedy performer on stage before his first screen appearance in 1935 in *Hi, Gaucho.* He starred in a number of films at Republic, RKO and MGM, including *The Flying Tigers, Old Los Angeles, Lady Be Good, Rio Rita, Surrender, The Bedside Manner* and *Belle Le Grand.*

The "Latin Lover" with a flair for swashbuckling was also the image of Gilbert Roland—and it was well-founded. The son of Spanish bullfighter Francisco Alonso and given the full name of Luis Antonio Damasco de Alonso when born in Juarez, Mexico, the future screen star was educated in private schools in Mexico before coming to the United States and beginning his movie career under his nom de plume. The list of his pictures cover many spectacular outdoor adventures such as *Captain Kidd, Pirates of Monterey, Ten Tall Men, Apache War Smoke, Underwater* and *Thunder Bay,* and serious dramatic roles in *We Were Strangers, Crisis, My Six Convicts, Glory Alley, The Bad and the Beautiful, The Big Circus* and *The Racers.* Roland's sole venture into cliff-hanging came in 1944 when he was persuaded by Columbia to star in Rudolph Flothow's *The Desert Hawk.* In it he portrayed twin brothers (Kasim, the "rightful" Caliph of Ahad, and Hassan, the ne'er-do-well who secretly kidnapped and replaced him) and also the mysterious "Hawk," who roamed the city and desert thwarting the plots of Hassan and his cohorts in crime—a triple role the agile, athletic Roland handled with aplomb.

A different type of screen lover played cohero to a dog in his one serial outing. As a departure from the career that would establish him as a sophisticated man-of-the-world in romantic comedies for another quarter century, charming Irishman George Brent, who had appeared in a number of silent films as a young leading man, took the hero's role in a serial for Nat Levine in 1931 — *The Lightning Warrior*. Although technically not the star — he shared billing with Rin Tin Tin and child actor Frankie Darro — Brent was the hero, performed the required fights and rescues, and got the girl. And then he resumed his career.

The Flying G-Men, Columbia's sixth continued picture, sported not just one, but two young men who later became major leading men — Robert Paige, who doubled as hero Hal Andrews and the masked champion The Black Falcon, and James Craig, who played G-man John Cummings. That was Paige's only serial credit, but Craig was to appear in *Overland with Kit Carson* and *Winners of the West* before going on to bigger things.

Paige, born John Arthur Paige in Indianapolis, was an alumnus of West Point and a veteran of radio before entering motion pictures. A handsome leading man in the classic mold, his pictures were lighthearted romantic comedies with gorgeous creatures such as Louise Allbritton, Maria Montez, Deanna Durbin, Marguerite Chapman, Ginny Simms and Leslie Brooks.

Leaning more to rugged, outdoor action roles, James Craig (changed from James H. Meador), a Nashville Tennessean and graduate of Rice Institute, built a career as a first-line star in adventure films and "second banana" in romantic features. *Kismet*, *The Heavenly Body*, *Marriage Is a Private Affair*, *Our Vines Have Tender Grapes*, *Northwest Stampede*, *Lost Angel*, *The Man from Texas*, *The Strip*, *Drums in the Deep South* and *While the City Sleeps* are a few of his long list of screen credits.

Blonde and lovely Carole Landis, whose career as a bright, charming sophisticate was terminated by untimely death, had become one of America's favorite screen stars appearing in features such as *One Million B.C.*, after she had performed as the granddaughter of the kidnapped Granville in *Daredevils of the Red Circle*. In that role she also had the distinction of being one of the few female players in serialdom to portray a mystery figure, when it was revealed that she was the black-robed ally of the good guys known as "the Red Circle."

In the cast of *The Lone Ranger Rides Again* was included the name Jinx Falken. It belonged to one of the most photogenic young women ever to grace the serial screen. Born Eugenia Falkenburg in Barcelona, Spain, and educated in Chile, the statuesque beauty had been a famous cover girl for the country's leading model agency, and had adopted the nickname "Jinx" for her career. Following her one serial appearance, she costarred in a bevy of glamorous films for Columbia, including *Two Latins from Manhattan*, *Cover Girl* and *The Gay Senorita*, and became familiar to millions as a radio personality in New York, broadcasting a daily talk show with her husband in the late forties and early fifties.

One of the most talented and versatile — as well as beautiful — actresses to star in films during the past two decades is the fiery brunette with those flashing, expressive eyes — Ruth Roman. Born and educated in Boston, trained in little theatre, the New England Repertory Company and the Elizabeth Peabody Players, the keenly perceptive Miss Roman has portrayed vividly all sorts of characters, from the cynical outlaw queen in *Belle Starr's Daughter* to the patient, understanding wife of a bitter sybarite in *The Bottom of the Bottle*. Her screen debut was as the ethereal benefactor Lothel in Universal's *Jungle Queen* in 1945. The lovely vision of her beauty in that chapter film still haunts many a remembering fan. Later, her name in the cast of a new film or television drama promised a performance filled with intensity and life, and became an event to anticipate. And never did anticipation bring disappointment.

Many of television's leading familiar faces are those that first came to prominence in a cliff-hanger. Stars of action series very much akin to — but more sophisticated than — the serials they used to work in, have taken their places as pioneers of the home screen medium, and many are seen regularly even now. Adventures on land, in the air, at sea and out West are still their forte, and grown-up former fans of the serials are still their audience.

The medium's most durable Western series featured as costars not one, but two veteran performers who had leading roles in continued pictures, and included a third (and until 1969 a fourth) erstwhile serial bad guy in its continuing supporting cast. The kindly but irascible, warmly human but stubbornly noble Doc Adams of C.B.S. Television's *Gunsmoke*, Milburn Stone, appeared in a supporting role in *The Fighting Marines* in 1934, played the hero in *The Great Alaskan Mystery* in 1944 and *The Master Key* in 1945, and wound up his serial career as the villain in *The Royal Mounted Rides Again* later that year. During his motion picture career, Stone appeared in more than a hundred and fifty pictures for various companies in all sorts of roles. For some twenty years he played Doc Adams, a character he was particularly suited to portray. *Gunsmoke* was rife with the history and lore of Kansas in the late nineteenth century. Stone was born in Burrton, Kansas, in 1904 and grew up among men who could recall from personal experiences and memories much of the flavor of those times. He patterned his characterization of Doc after men he had known personally. Doc's reprehensible but well-meaning antagonist in the series — Festus Haggin — is the creation of singer-actor Ken Curtis, former member of The Sons of the Pioneers musical group and star of the 1961 television series *Ripcord*. Curtis fought, leapt and galloped his way through the 1951 Republic serial *Don Daredevil Rides Again* as the dauntless masked hero, whose real identity was that of rancher Lee Hadley, struggling valiantly against villain Roy

Barcroft, who until his death in 1969 often showed up in *Gunsmoke* as the town's general storekeeper. The key supporting role of Sam, the Long Branch Saloon's shotgun-toting bartender, was played by Glenn Strange, whose credits stretch all the way back to Mascot's early days and include *The Hurricane Express*, *Flash Gordon* and *Riders of Death Valley* for random samplings. His face made up as the Frankenstein monster (which he portrayed three times) is perhaps the best known of all the different versions — at least as equally well-known as Karloff's original.

Jackie Cooper, the famous child star with the winsome, pouting look that charmed a generation of moviegoers in films such as *Skippy*, *The Champ*, *Treasure Island* and *Peck's Bad Boy*, appeared as the leader of a group of intrepid youngsters in Universal's twelve-episode *Scouts to the Rescue* in 1938. As an adult, his career has included starring roles in feature films, Broadway plays, two successful television series (*The People's Choice* and *Hennessy*) and culminated in his elevation to head of production at Screen Gems, Inc. From that post he launched into independent production, heading his own company.

Tall, lanky Rod Cameron was seen in numerous dramatic roles in television series such as *The Name of the Game* and *Bonanza*, starred in three syndicated series during the fifties, and racked up a host of major film credits since 1943. That was the year he was featured as the hero in two of Republic's finest patriotic serials — *G-Men vs. the Black Dragon* and *Secret Service in Darkest Africa*. Those appearances launched him into a brief career as a series Western star at Universal, where he subsequently costarred with Yvonne De Carlo in *Salome — Where She Danced* and *Frontier Gal* in 1945 and emerged as a major leading man. For ten years, he starred in outdoor epics for Universal and Allied Artists and was one of Republic's superstars. He then turned to television for the highly successful *State Trooper*, *City Detective* and *Coronado 9* series.

When Universal was casting its hero for the 1945 serial remake of Leslie Charteris' *Secret Agent X-9*, young contract player Lloyd Bridges, who had been playing villains in Charles Starrett Westerns and supporting parts in major films such as *Miss Susie Slagle's*, *Ramrod*, *Canyon Passage* and *Abilene Town*, was selected to portray the American agent who specialized in Oriental assignments. The result was one of the best serials to survive the onrushing demise of the genre at Universal. Bridges moved on to play costarring and feature roles in important films like *High Noon*, *Wichita* and *The Rainmaker*, but his real fame came with television. So popular was he in the expertly produced *Sea Hunt* as a crimefighting skin diver, that his name became synonymous with the sport. Presently he is in great demand as the star of movies and specials made for television.

In the supporting cast of Republic's 1952 *Zombies of the Stratosphere* was included the name of Leonard Nimoy, playing a subvillain named

Narab. With the scaly costume (designed as a Martian invader's uniform) he wore and the garish makeup used to give him an extraterrestrial visage, it was not only difficult to determine what he looked like but impossible to imagine that he would eventually become a major television star. That was accomplished, however, with his emergence in the role of Mr. Spock, an enigmatic half-human, half-robot superior being from an obscure planet in the widely-acclaimed NBC science-fiction series *Star Trek* in the middle sixties. Following its termination, the talented Nimoy moved smoothly into the costarring slot of another very popular series, CBS Television's *Mission: Impossible*, in the role vacated by Martin Landau.

Not only did popular young leading players emerge from serials — or appear in them along the way — so did the outstanding stars of other areas of screen drama. One of the preeminent and most highly respected character actors of the day played a bad guy in a Western chapter film, and three of the superstars of horror films sharpened their talents on the melodramatics of which cliff-hangers were made.

Charles Bickford, a Cambridge, Massachusetts, construction engineer turned burlesque and stage performer, made his screen debut in 1930 as a leading man in *Dynamite*. Then in his forties, his maturity and forcefulness made possible a smooth switch into character roles and a continuing career for three more decades. In 1940 he was engaged by Universal to play in their proposed Million-Dollar super spectacular serial *Riders of Death Valley* as a costar in an all-star cast. His portrayal of Wolf, the renegade outlaw leader who was continually upsetting the well-laid plans of the town-slicker chief villains with ambitions of his own, stands alone as the standard for plain, ornery, gruff meanness in a serial badman. He had little difficulty in stealing the entire film from two leading Western stars (Buck Jones and Dick Foran), three popular Western comic sidekicks (Leo Carillo, "Big Boy" Williams and Noah Beery, Jr.) and an assortment of other "baddies" including Lon Chaney, Jr., Monte Blue and Harry Woods. For a devoted serial addict, that single chapter film role made it very hard to watch him in subsequent masterpieces in features such as *Song of Bernadette*, *A Wing and a Prayer*, *Mr. Lucky*, *The Farmer's Daughter* ("Fish for sale!"), *Fallen Angel* and *Johnny Belinda* without thinking of good old mean Wolf. In 1967 (at the age of 78), he had just recently completed another outstanding performance in *A Big Hand for a Little Lady* and had published his autobiography when the time came for his departure from life.

When Lon Chaney, Jr., played in *Riders of Death Valley*, he had already been in motion pictures for nine years and had appeared in at least four serials, including the only one ever to be produced by RKO. He portrayed the hero — The Black Ghost — in *The Last Frontier* for that studio the same year he made his feature debut in *Captain Hurricane*. Subsequently, he had been billed in supporting roles in *Ace Drummond*, *Undersea Kingdom* and *Secret Agent X-9*. After *Riders of Death Valley*, he starred in one more for Universal—as the hero in 1942's *Overland Mail*—and then graduated into horror features full-time as a result of his performance in the classic *The Wolf Man*. During the forties he became a practitioner in the art of horror characterization in the same league with Lugosi, Karloff and his own father. Two of his finest performances, however, were in straight dramatic, nonhorror roles: big, dumb Lennie in *Of Mice and Men*, and the disabled, disillusioned retired lawman in *High Noon*.

Both Karloff and Lugosi made distinctive marks on the serial as well as motion pictures in general, but it was Karloff who rose to the heights to become the greatest horror films star of all time. A gentle man, according to those who knew him, his real name seemed to fit his private personality best. Born in London in November 1887 and christened William Henry Pratt, the future maestro of the supernatural was educated at Uppingham School and coursed an uneventful childhood and youth which subsequently brought him to America. His first film appearance in this country was in the role of a Mexican bandit in *His Majesty, the American* for United Artists in 1919, and he subsequently appeared in over sixty films in large and small parts, including his four Mascot serial roles— *Vultures of the Sea* in 1928, *The Fatal Warning* and *King of the Kongo* in 1929 (all silent), and *King of the Wild* (a talkie) in 1931—before being cast as the monster in *Frankenstein*. Beginning with the release of that classic, the Karloff legend captured the imaginations of moviegoers and grew into one of Hollywood's true motion picture institutions. For the next nearly forty years, the single word "Karloff" instantly identified a film as potentially a great horror entry, and even following his demise in February 1969 (at the venerable age of 81) it stands as the personification of all that is dark, foreboding and chilling in motion pictures. Such worthy successors as Vincent Price, Peter Cushing and Christopher Lee carried on, still bringing to audiences the special thrill of being submerged for a time in eerie, supernatural surroundings with strange, inhuman things going on, but the ultimate feeling of gothic horror and tragic doom we could experience in movies—without the dreaded expectation of grim reality for our own lives—can best be called up by the mere whisper of the name: *Karloff*.

It is possible that one day the Academy of Motion Picture Arts and Sciences may present a special award to Boris Karloff posthumously for his unique contribution to the medium. It would be proper to do so, for there are few actors who have distinguished themselves as he did—even fewer producers or directors—and recognition of the fact could be a belated rectification of an unfortunate oversight during his life. The Academy does a thorough job of honoring those who give outstanding performances from year to year, but an award to Karloff would most certainly spotlight an extraordinary career that spanned a full half century, and nearly all of the era of the feature motion picture to date.

If such an award were made, it would not be the first for a serial graduate. Three of Hollywood's most prominent Oscar winners labored in the episodic grind as part of their early experience — a sensitive, gifted young woman whose winning role is a classic; a much-beloved three-time winner who portrays crusty-but-likable "old codgers"; and the most famous movie actor in the world.

When the third serial based on Chester Gould's famous detective — *Dick Tracy's G-Men* — was released by Republic in 1939, the part of Gwen, Tracy's girl Friday, was credited to a young actress named Phyllis Isley. Miss Isley was born in Tulsa, Oklahoma, and had graduated from Northwestern University and the American Academy of Dramatic Arts in New York. At the time she was appearing in stock theater and Westerns under her own name. Changing it to Jennifer Jones, she appeared in her first major role as Marie Soubirous in David O. Selznick's *The Song of Bernadette* in 1943 and won the Academy Award for her performance. After having been married to actor Robert Walker (*The Big Clock, See Here, Private Hargrove*, etc.) and becoming the mother of three, she later wed producer Selznick and starred in many of his most prestigious productions: *Since You Went Away, Love Letters, Duel in the Sun, Ruby Gentry, Love Is a Many Splendored Thing* and *A Farewell to Arms*, to name a few.

Walter Brennan is the only actor in the history of motion pictures who has won more than two Oscars. For the best performance by an actor in a supporting role, he won in 1936 for *Come and Get It*, in 1938 for *Kentucky*, and in 1940 for *The Westerner*. Born in Swampscott, Massachusetts, in 1894, the tall, gangling actor is a veteran of military service in World War I and stage theatrics in vaudeville. In movies since 1923, the venerable thespian's facial features early suggested advanced maturity, and he has played middle-aged (i.e. character) roles for most of his long career. In television, Brennan has been the star of no less than three successful series, and at the age of 76 launched into a fourth — *To Rome with Love*. Following up his memorable roles as Grandpa Amos McCoy, a transplanted West Virginia sharecropper living in the rural environs of modern California in *The Real McCoys*, a successful millionaire-with-heart-of-gold in *The Tycoon*, and the tortured, searching father of a wandering gunfighter in *The Guns of Will Sonnett*, he became a costar in the popular John Forsythe series in 1970. Oh, yes, his serial appearance: as a henchman in the 1932 Universal cliff-hanger *The Airmail Mystery*.

And then there is John Wayne himself.

Easily the most prominent alumnus of the cliff-hanger was the most famous movie actor in the world — bar none. A star for over fifty years, leading box office attraction during most of that time, Number One Moneymaker for much of it, eventual Academy Award winner for his role as "Rooster" Cogburn in 1969's *True Grit*, John Wayne was a real "living legend" to the degree that his very name was to a cynical new generation a

cliché, to their immediate predecessors an institution, and to his own
generation a symbol of perpetuity. Star of more than a hundred and fifty
pictures that have grossed nearly a half billion dollars, the man known to
his colleagues as "Duke" was an industry within himself, having been a crew
member, actor, stuntman, director, producer and promoter since switching from all-American football star at the University of Southern California to a job as a prop man at Fox Studios in 1928. His first film was a
production called *Hangman's House* made by John Ford, who became his
lifelong friend and one of the most respected directors in the business.
(Part of the Wayne "legend" is that the only contracts ever negotiated
between Ford and him for their coventures — involving millions of dollars
— were handshakes.)

Ford helped him secure the lead role in the 1930 Raoul Walsh epic
The Big Trail, and Wayne became a star. Following a series of not-too-
important films such as *Girls Demand Excitement, Men Are Like That,
Three Girls Lost* and *Maker of Men*, the young man who was born
Marion Michael Morrison in Winterset, Iowa, 25 years before, turned to
Western roles at Columbia and Warner Bros. and began to establish
himself as a cowboy hero. It was during that time that Nat Levine at
Mascot recognized his potential as a serial hero and secured him for three
of his most outstanding action thrillers: *The Hurricane Express* and
Shadow of the Eagle in 1932, and *The Three Musketeers* the following
year.

Next came the distinction of being the movies' first "singing" cowboy.
In 1933–35, Wayne starred in a series of "horse operas" for Lone Star
Productions, which became a part of the Republic merger in 1935. In one
of these he appeared as "Singing Sandy," with his songs dubbed by a professional singer. Audiences bought the illusion and accepted Wayne as a
"singing cowboy." The next four years saw Wayne starred in a string of
action features for producer Paul Malvern at Universal and at Republic as
a costar of The Three Mesquiteers Western series replacing Robert
Livingston, who had graduated to larger leading roles for the new studio.
Then in 1938 John Ford planned his major epic *Stagecoach* and cast
Wayne in the leading role as The Ringo Kid. The film was released in 1939
and became a milestone in motion picture history. It also established John
Wayne as a major film star. The rest is familiar to all moviegoers, as hit
after major hit starring the compleat he-man of all time packed the
nation's theatres and developed the theatrical legend of John Wayne that
is still going strong today.

(One of the most satisfying incidents to occur in my experience as a
buyer-booker for independent theatres in the Carolinas during the fifties
exemplified the Wayne phenomenon. *Island in the Sky*, a non-Western
film from Warners starring the big man, was released in September 1953
and was booked as tightly as print availability permitted. It was late that
year before I could get it for some of the smaller theatres I booked, and I

grabbed the first dates I could squeeze out of the Warner office in Charlotte. Following its run in one of the small North Carolina towns, the exhibitor was in my office discussing product and I asked him how *Island* had done.

"Terrible," he moaned, "just awful!"

Unbelievingly I asked him just how awful it had done, and he replied, "The damn thing only did 135% of normal business — 135% John Wayne usually does 190% of normal in my town, and that dog did only 135. God, what a beating!"

I breathed a sigh of relief. The only date I had been able to secure for him was Christmas week, the worst week of the year in a small town, when business was excellent if it reached 70% of normal — and he had seen 135. Against his judgment, I booked it for a repeat run nine weeks later and it did 110% of normal on the second run. From then on, we ran all the new Wayne pictures in that town at least twice.)

The story has been the same for forty years in theatres all over the United States. There was no way to know in 1932-33 that the athletic young Lothario who moved like a gazelle but spoke lines like a high school sophomore would become the movie industry's all-time giant at the box office and holder of its most coveted dramatic award, but the crafty and shrewd Nat Levine must have suspected something.

And so did the serial fans, the lovers of action, who took him to their hearts and made him a star. John Wayne's story epitomizes the legend of the working boy who made good. From ten years in the continued pictures and series films (their next of kin), he eventually emerged — not *above* his beginnings, but *from* them — to become the brightest star of them all and the biggest success story in the industry's history.

Epilogue

There has not been a new serial released since 1956; but the serial is not dead. It has changed form and lives on in the guise of television series—more sophisticated, more polished, more respectable and more mature, but nevertheless based on the premise that the audience will return if they are promised more of what they know and like. Critics may question the quality of the old movie serials—and rightly so in many cases—but they cannot question the appeal of their concept. Humans are just naturally curious about what might happen next, and will give their attention to entertainment that withholds a little for later.

Instead of leaving the hero in dire physical peril each Saturday, with the prospect for the audience of a week's suspense before learning how he escapes to carry on to another ordeal, the television adventure shows of today contain all their cliff-hangers within an hour's run. Usually split into four acts, with a number of commercial messages to separate them, the cliff-hanger moments always come just before the commercial "breaks," and the suspense is limited to the 90–180 seconds allotted for the product pitches. Former thrillers such as *The Naked City, The Untouchables, 77 Sunset Strip, Burke's Law, I Spy, Secret Agent* and *The Man from U.N.C.L.E.*, as well as later leaders like *Mission: Impossible, Mannix, Ironside* and *Hawaii Five-0* have all used the cliff-hanger gimmick within an hour's story to sustain interest.

Particularly akin to the serial concept without much pretense—except for making sure that each episode was self-contained, for later syndication purposes—were *The Fugitive, Run for Your Life, The Time Tunnel, Lost in Space* and *The Land of the Giants*. In *Fugitive*, David Janssen played Dr. Richard Kimble, a man convicted wrongly of murdering his wife, who had escaped the police in a train wreck and was on the run to both escape unjust imprisonment and seek out the real killer. Each week there was a different, complete episode, but the central theme kept alive the cliff-hanger concept throughout its run of several years. Likewise, *Run for Your Life* concerned a hero, played by Ben Gazarra, who learned that he was the victim of an incurable terminal disease and had only a short time to live. His efforts to cram a lifetime of experiences into the time left him provided the thread of the various episodes. *The Time Tunnel* and *Lost in Space* left no doubt at all of their serial leanings, closing each weekly show with a brief slide-over into the next adventure, providing a genuine peril for the good guys and ending with the printed title, "Continued Next Week," over the frozen frame depicting the threat. *Mission: Impossible* included in its run several three-part adventures spread over as many weeks which, in total running time, equals the span of a twelve-chapter serial, with 15 minutes allotted for each chapter.

Batman and *The Green Hornet* both followed the same pattern of multipart adventures, but they were designed from the beginning to be revivals-of-a-sort of the old-time action serials to cash in on the camp craze that blossomed temporarily with the one-shot *Batman* showings.

A variation of the *Time Tunnel–Lost in Space* method of identifying outright as cliff-hangers was employed by a short-lived NBC series called *The Outsider* (with Darren McGavin as a tough private eye) that lasted only one season in the late sixties. Each episode began with an action sequence that led to the hero's becoming victim of a violent threat, with a frozen action shot of his peril behind which came McGavin's voice asking in effect, "How did I get myself into a mess like this?" The subsequent episode was designed to flash back and bring the story up to the point of his dilemma, and then show how he got out of it. In less direct fashion, most television series start out with such a "teaser," sometimes delaying the official opening credits as much as seven or eight minutes after the story is fully underway.

Regardless of the particular method used, the point is that most dramatic and adventure series on television use some form of cliff-hanger technique to keep the viewer watching during commercial pauses, or to bring him back to the desired channel. Even the nightly newscasts revert to the "teaser" technique, and this is proper, for it reflects life. To wonder if a particular law will be passed by our legislators, what will happen next on the social or economic scene, when the fighting will stop in a world trouble spot, and whether a handful of brave pioneers will safely return from their voyage to the Moon has been and is the suspense of our time. To wonder about things is to be concerned; to cease to wonder is the beginning of apathy — the slow death of the mind.

As long as this is true, the former serial addict (the "cliff-hanger nut," the "connoisseur of the continued") can watch television and smile, and know that man is still curious — as manifested by his response to today's entertainment styles — about how the events of today will affect the status of tomorrow.

The cliff-hanger is dead. Long live the cliff-hanger!

Filmography

Serials Released from 1930 to 1956
Date shown is the copyright date, or approximate release date, of the first chapter

1930

The Jade Box (Universal, February 25, 1930)
   Director: Ray Taylor. *Cast*: Jack Perrin, Louise Lorraine, Monroe Salisbury, Eileen Sedgwick, Francis Ford, Leo White, Wilbur Mack.
Chapter Titles:

1. The Jade of Jeopardy
2. Buried Alive
3. The Shadow Man
4. The Fatal Prophecy
5. The Unseen Death

6. The Haunting Shadow
7. The Guilty Man
8. The Grip of Death
9. Out of the Shadows
10. The Atonement

The Lightning Express (Universal, April 30, 1930)
   Director: Henry MacRae. *Cast*: Lane Chandler, Louise Lorraine, Floyd Criswell, Jim Pierce, Robert Kelly.
Chapter Titles:

1. A Shot in the Dark
2. A Scream of Terror
3. Dangerous Rails
4. The Death Trap
5. Tower of Terror

6. A Call for Help
7. The Runaway Freight
8. The Showdown
9. The Secret Survey
10. Cleared Tracks

Terry of the Times (Universal, July 17, 1930)
   Director: Henry MacRae. *Cast*: Reed Howes, Lotus Thompson, Sheldon Lewis, John Oscar, William Hayes, Mary Grant, Norman Thom, Kingsley Benedict, Taylor Holmes.
Chapter Titles:

1. The Mystic Mendicants
2. The Fatal 30!
3. Death's Highway
4. Eyes of Evil
5. Prowlers of the Night

6. The Stolen Bride
7. A Doorway of Death
8. A Trail of Treachery
9. Caught in the Net
10. A Race for Love

201

The Indians Are Coming (Universal, August 29, 1930)
  Director: Henry MacRae. *Cast*: Tim McCoy, Allene Ray, Edmund Cobb, Francis Ford, William McGaugh, Bud Osborne, Charles Royal.
Chapter Titles:
  1. Pals in Buckskin
  2. A Call to Arms
  3. A Furnace of Fear
  4. The Red Terror
  5. The Circle of Death
  6. Hate's Harvest
  7. Hostages of Fear
  8. The Dagger Duel
  9. The Blast of Death
  10. Redskin's Vengeance
  11. Frontiers Aflame
  12. The Trail's End

The Spell of the Circus (Universal, October 23, 1930)
  Director: Robert F. Hill. *Cast*: Francis X. Bushman, Jr., Albert Vaughn, Bobby Nelson, Tom London, Monte Montague.
Chapter Titles:
  1. A Menacing Monster
  2. The Phantom Shadow
  3. Racing with Death
  4. A Scream of Terror
  5. A Leap for Life
  6. A Fatal Wedding
  7. A Villain Unmasked
  8. The Baited Trap
  9. The Terror Tent
  10. The Call of the Circus

Fingerprints (Universal, December 16, 1930)
  Director: Ray Taylor. *Cast*: Kenneth Harlan, Edna Murphy, Gayne Whitman, Gertrude Astor, Fletcher Norton, Monte Montague, William L. Thorne.
Chapter Titles:
  1. The Dance of Death
  2. A Fugitive of Fear
  3. Toll of the Sea
  4. The Sinister Shadow
  5. The Plunge of Peril
  6. The Finger of Fate
  7. The Depths of Doom
  8. The Thundering Terror
  9. Flames of Fury
  10. The Final Reckoning

The Lone Defender (Mascot, Unknown)
  Director: Richard Thorpe. *Cast*: Rin Tin Tin, Jr., Walter Miller, June Marlowe, Buzz Barton, Joseph Swickard, Lee Shumway, Frank Lanning, Robert Kortman.
Chapter Titles:
  1. Mystery of the Desert
  2. The Fugitive
  3. Jaws of Peril
  4. Trapped
  5. Circle of Death
  6. Surrounded by the Law
  7. The Ghost Speaks
  8. Brink of Destruction
  9. The Avalanche
  10. Fury of the Desert
  11. Cornered
  12. Vindicated

The Mystery Trooper (Wonder, Unknown)
  Director: Stuart Paton. *Cast*: Buzz Barton, Blanche Mahaffey, Robert Frazer, Al Ferguson, Charles King, William Von Brencken, White Cloud the Horse.
Chapter Titles:
  1. The Trap of Terror
  2. Paths of Peril
  3. Fighting Fate
  4. The Cave of Horror
  5. The House of Hate
  6. The Day of Doom
  7. The Death Trail
  8. The Killer Dogs
  9. The Ghost City
  10. The Lost Treasure

Sign of the Wolf (Metropolitan, Unknown)
Director: Unknown. *Cast*: Rex Lease, Virginia Brown Faire, Joe Bonomo, Jack Mower, Josephine Hull, Al Ferguson, Robert Walker, Edmund Cobb, Harry Todd.
Chapter Titles:

1. Drums of Doom
2. The Dog of Destiny
3. The Wolf's Fangs
4. The Fatal Shot
5. The Well of Terror

6. The Wolf Dogs
7. Trapped
8. The Secret Mark
9. Tongues of Flame
10. The Lost Secret

Across the World with Mr. and Mrs. Martin Johnson (Principal, Unknown)
Director: Martin Johnson. *Cast*: Mr. and Mrs. Martin Johnson.
Chapter Titles: None — Documentary shown in parts

Hunting Tigers in India (Principal, Unknown)
Director: Commander George M. Dyott. *Cast*: Commander George M. Dyott.
Chapter Titles: None — Documentary shown in parts

1931

Phantom of the West (Mascot, January 1, 1931)
Director: Ross Lederman. *Cast*: Tom Tyler, Dorothy Gulliver, Tom Santschi, Kermit Maynard, Joe Bonomo, Tom Dugan, William Desmond, Frank Lanning, Philo McCullough.
Chapter Titles:

1. The Ghost Rides
2. Stairway of Doom
3. Horror in the Dark
4. Battle of the Strong
5. League of the Lawless

6. Canyon of Calamity
7. Price of Silence
8. House of Hate
9. Fatal Secret
10. Rogue's Roundup

King of the Wild (Mascot, March 1, 1931)
Director: B. Reeves Eason. *Cast*; Boris Karloff, Walter Miller, Nora Lane, Dorothy Christy, Tom Santschi, Victor Potel, Arthur McLaglen.
Chapter Titles:

1. Man Eaters
2. Tiger of Destiny
3. The Avenging Horde
4. Secret of the Volcano
5. Pit of Peril
6. Creeping Doom

7. Sealed Lips
8. Jaws of the Jungle
9. Door of Dread
10. Leopard's Lair
11. The Fire of the Gods
12. Jungle Justice

Heroes of the Flames (Universal, March 23 1931)
Director: Robert F. Hill. *Cast*· Tim McCoy, Marion Shockley, Bobby Nelson, Grace Cunard, Gayne Whitman, Joe Bonomo, Bud Osborne, Edmund Cobb, Monte Montague.
Chapter Titles:

1. The Red Peril
2. Flaming Hate
3. The Fire Trap

4. Death's Chariot
5. The Avalanche
6. The Jaws of Death

7. Forests of Fire
8. Blank Cartridges
9. The House of Terror

10. The Depths of Doom
11. A Flaming Death
12. The Last Alarm

The Vanishing Legion (Mascot, June 1, 1931)
Director: B. Reeves Eason. *Cast*: Harry Carey, Edwina Booth, Frankie Darro, Philo McCullough, William Desmond, Joe Bonomo, Edward Hearn, Al Taylor, Lafe McKee.
Chapter Titles:
1. Voice from the Void
2. Queen of the Night Riders
3. The Invisible Enemy
4. The Fatal Message
5. The Trackless Trail
6. The Radio Riddle

7. The Crimson Clue
8. Doorway of Disaster
9. When Time Stood Still
10. Riding the Whirlwind
11. Capsule of Oblivion
12. Hoofs of Horror

Danger Island (Universal, July 9, 1931)
Director: Ray Taylor. *Cast*: Kenneth Harlan, Lucile Browne, Walter Miller, Andy Devine, Beulah Hutton, Thomas Ricketts, William L. Thorne, George Magrill.
Chapter Titles:
1. The Coast of Peril
2. Death Rides the Storm
3. Demons of the Pool
4. Devil Worshippers
5. Mutiny
6. The Cat Creeps

7. The Drums of Doom
8. Human Sacrifice
9. The Devil Bird
10. Captured for Sacrifice
11. The Lion's Lair
12. Fire God's Vengeance

The Galloping Ghost (Mascot, September 1, 1931)
Director: B. Reeves Eason. *Cast*: Harold "Red" Grange, Dorothy Gulliver, Walter Miller, Gwen Lee, Francis X. Bushman, Jr., Tom Dugan, Theodore Lorch, Edward Hearn.
Chapter Titles:
1. The Idol of Clay
2. Port of Peril
3. The Master Mind
4. The House of Secrets
5. The Man Without a Face
6. The Torn $500 Bill

7. When the Lights Went Out
8. The Third Degree
9. Sign in the Sky
10. The Vulture's Lair
11. The Radio Patrol
12. The Ghost Comes Back

Battling with Buffalo Bill (Universal, September 18, 1931)
Director: Ray Taylor. *Cast*: Tom Tyler, Lucile Browne, Rex Bell, William Desmond, Francis Ford, Edmund Cobb, Joe Bonomo, George Regas, Chief Thundercloud, Jim Thorpe.
Chapter Titles:
1. Captured by Redskins
2. Circling Death
3. Between Hostile Tribes
4. The Savage Horde
5. The Fatal Plunge
6. Trapped

7. The Unseen Killer
8. Sentenced to Death
9. The Death Trap
10. A Shot from Ambush
11. The Flaming Death
12. Cheyenne Vengeance

The Lightning Warrior (Mascot, November 1, 1931)
   Director: Armand Schaefer, Benjamin Kline. *Cast*: Rin Tin Tin, Frankie Darro, George Brent, Georgia Hale, Frank Brownlee, Pat O'Malley, Hayden Stevenson, Frank Lanning, Lafe McKee.
Chapter Titles:

1. Drums of Doom	7. The Ordeal of Fire
2. The Wolf Man	8. The Man Who Knew
3. Empty Saddles	9. Traitor's Hour
4. Flaming Arrows	10. Secret of the Cave
5. The Invisible Enemy	11. Red Shadows
6. The Fatal Name	12. Painted Faces

Detective Lloyd (Universal, December 23, 1931)
   Director: Henry MacRae. *Cast*: Jack Lloyd, Lewis Dayton, Janice Adair, Tracy Holmes, Wallace Geoffrey, Muriel Angelus, Shayle Gardner, Emily Fitzroy.
Chapter Titles:

1. The Green Spot Murder	7. The Race with Death
2. The Panther Strikes	8. The Panther's Lair
3. The Trap Springs	9. Imprisoned in the North Tower
4. Tracked by Wireless	10. The Panther's Cunning
5. The Death Ray	11. The Panther at Bay
6. The Poison Dart	12. Heroes of the Law

1932

Shadow of the Eagle (Mascot, February 1, 1932)
   Director: Ford Beebe. *Cast*: John Wayne, Dorothy Gulliver, Kenneth Harlan, Walter Miller, Edward Hearn, Richard Tucker, Lloyd Whitlock, Edmund Burns.
Chapter Titles:

1. The Carnival Mystery	7. Eagle or Vulture?
2. Pinholes	8. On the Spot
3. The Eagle Strikes	9. The Thieves Fall Out
4. Man of a Million Voices	10. The Man Who Knew
5. The Telephone Cipher	11. The Eagle's Wings
6. Code of the Carnival	12. The Shadow Unmasked

The Airmail Mystery (Universal, March 14, 1932)
   Director: Ray Taylor. *Cast*: James Flavin, Lucile Browne, Al Wilson, Wheeler Oakman, Nelson McDowell, Cecil Kellogg, Bob Reeves, Frank Hagney, Walter Brennan.
Chapter Titles:

1. Pirates of the Air	7. The Hawk's Treachery
2. Hovering Death	8. The Aerial Third Degree
3. A Leap for Life	9. The Attack on the Mine
4. A Fatal Crash	10. The Hawk's Lair
5. The Hawk Strikes	11. The Law Strikes
6. The Bridge of Destruction	12. The Mail Must Go Through

The Last of the Mohicans (Mascot, May 1, 1932)
   Directors: B. Reeves Eason, Ford Beebe. *Cast*: Harry Carey, Edwina Booth, Hawkeye, Hobart Bosworth, Junior Coghlan.

Chapter Titles:
1. Wild Waters
2. Flaming Arrows
3. Rifle or Tomahawk
4. Riding with Death
5. Red Shadows
6. Lure of Gold
7. Crimson Trail
8. Tide of Battle
9. Redskins' Honor
10. The Enemy's Stronghold
11. Paleface Magic
12. End of the Trail

Heroes of the West (Universal, May 28, 1932)
Director: Ray Taylor. *Cast*: Onslow Stevens, Diane Duval, Noah Beery, Jr., William Desmond, Martha Mattox, Francis Ford, Philo McCullough, Frank Lackteen.
Chapter Titles:
1. Blazing the Trail
2. Red Peril
3. The Avalanche
4. A Shot from the Dark
5. The Holdup
6. Captured by Indians
7. Flaming Arrows
8. Frontier Justice
9. The Iron Monster
10. Thundering Death
11. Thundering Hoofs
12. The End of the Trail

The Hurricane Express (Mascot, August 1, 1932)
Directors: Armand Schaefer, J.P. MacGowan. *Cast*: John Wayne, Shirley Grey, Conway Tearle, Tully Marshall, J. Farrell MacDonald, Ernie Adams, Glenn Strange.
Chapter Titles:
1. The Wrecker
2. Flying Pirates
3. The Masked Menace
4. Buried Alive
5. Danger Lights
6. Airport Mystery
7. Sealed Lips
8. Outside the Law
9. The Invisible Enemy
10. The Wrecker's Secret
11. Wings of Death
12. Unmasked

Jungle Mystery (Universal, August 5, 1932)
Director: Ray Taylor. *Cast*: Tom Tyler, Cecelia Parker, Noah Beery, Jr., Philo McCullough, Frank Lackteen, Carmelita Geraghty, James A. Marcus, Peggy Watts.
Chapter Titles:
1. Into the Dark Continent
2. The Ivory Trail
3. The Death Stream
4. Poisoned Fangs
5. The Mystery Cavern
6. Daylight Doom
7. The Jaws of Death
8. Trapped by the Enemy
9. The Jungle Terror
10. Ambushed
11. The Lion's Fury
12. Buried Treasure

The Last Frontier (R.K.O., September 5, 1932)
Directors: Spencer G. Bennet, Thomas L. Storey. *Cast*: Lon Chaney, Jr., Richard Neill, Leroy Mason, Francis X. Bushman, Jr., Benny Corbett.
Chapter Titles:
1. The Black Ghost Rides
2. The Thundering Herd
3. The Black Ghost Strikes
4. The Fatal Shot
5. Clutching Sands
6. The Terror Trail
7. Doomed
8. Facing Death

  9. Thundering Doom   11. Driving Danger
 10. The Life Line   12. The Black Ghost's Last Ride

The Lost Special (Universal, October 31, 1932)
 Director: Henry MacRae. *Cast*: Frank Albertson, Ernie Nevers, Cecelia Parker, Caryl Lincoln.
Chapter Titles:

1. The Lost Special	7. The Tank Room Terror
2. Racing Death	8. The Fatal Race
3. The Red Lantern	9. Into the Depths
4. Devouring Flames	10. The Jaws of Death
5. The Lightning Strikes	11. The Flaming Forest
6. The House of Mystery	12. Retribution

The Devil Horse (Mascot, November 1, 1932)
 Director: Otto Brower. *Cast*: Harry Carey, Frankie Darro, Noah Beery, Sr., Greta Granstedt, Barry O'Daniels, Lou Kelly, J. Paul Jones, Al Bridge, Apache.
Chapter Titles;

1. Untamed	7. Battle of the Strong
2. Chasm of Death	8. The Missing Witness
3. Doom Riders	9. The Showdown
4. Vigilante Law	10. The Death Trap
5. The Silent Call	11. Wild Loyalty
6. Heart of the Mystery	12. The Double Decoy

1933

Clancy of the Mounted (Universal, January 19, 1933)
 Director: Ray Taylor. *Cast*: Tom Tyler, Jacqueline Wells, William Desmond, Rosalie Roy, Francis Ford, Earl McCarthy.
Chapter Titles:

1. Toll of the Rapids	7. The Night Attack
2. Brother Against Brother	8. Crashing Timbers
3. Ambuscade	9. Fingerprints
4. The Storm	10. The Breed Strikes
5. A Desperate Chance	11. The Crimson Jacket
6. The Wolf's Fangs	12. Journey's End

The Three Musketeers (Mascot, April 7, 1933)
 Directors: Armand Schaeffer, Colbert Clark. *Cast*: John Wayne, Ruth Hall, Francis X. Bushman, Jr. Jack Mulhall, Raymond Hatton, Al Ferguson, Lon Chaney, Jr., Robert Frazer.
Chapter Titles:

1. The Fiery Circle	7. Naked Steel
2. One for All and All for One	8. The Master Strikes
3. The Master Spy	9. The Fatal Cave
4. Pirates of the Desert	10. Trapped
5. Rebels' Rifles	11. The Measure of a Man
6. Death's Marathon	12. The Glory of Comrades

Phantom of the Air (Universal, May 4, 1933)
Director: Ray Taylor. *Cast*: Tom Tyler, Gloria Shea, William Desmond, Hugh Enfield, Leroy Mason, Sidney Bracey.
Chapter Titles:
1. The Great Air Meet
2. The Secret of the Desert
3. The Avenging Phantom
4. The Battle in the Clouds
5. Terror of the Heights
6. A Wild Ride
7. The Jaws of Death
8. Aflame in the Sky
9. The Attack
10. The Runaway Plane
11. In the Enemy's Hands
12. Safe Landing

Fighting with Kit Carson (Mascot, July 6, 1933)
Directors: Armand Schaefer, Colbert Clark. *Cast*: Johnny Mack Brown, Betsy King Ross, Noah Beery, Sr., Noah Beery, Jr., Tully Marshall, Lane Chandler, William Farnum.
Chapter Titles:
1. The Mystery Riders
2. The White Chief
3. Hidden Gold
4. The Silent Doom
5. Murder Will Out
6. The Secret of Iron Mountain
7. The Law of the Lawless
8. Red Phantoms
9. The Invisible Enemy
10. Midnight Magic
11. Unmasked
12. The Trail to Glory

Gordon of Ghost City (Universal, July 26, 1933)
Director: Ray Taylor. *Cast*: Buck Jones, Madge Bellamy, Walter Miller, Tom Ricketts, William Desmond, Francis Ford, Edmund Cobb, Hugh Enfield, Bud Osborne.
Chapter Titles:
1. A Lone Hand
2. The Stampede
3. Trapped
4. The Man of Mystery
5. Riding for Life
6. Blazing Prairies
7. Entombed in the Tunnel
8. Stampede
9. Flames of Fury
10. Swimming the Torrent
11. A Wild Ride
12. Mystery of Ghost City

Wolf Dog (Mascot, September 30, 1933)
Directors: Colbert Clark, Harry Fraser. *Cast*: Rin Tin Tin, Jr., Frankie Darro, George Lewis, "Boots" Mallory, Fred Kohler, Hale Hamilton, Henry Walthall.
Chapter Titles:
1. The Call of the Wilderness
2. The Shadow of a Crime
3. The Fugitive
4. A Dead Man's Hand
5. Wolf Pack Law
6. The Gates of Mercy
7. The Empty Room
8. Avenging Fangs
9. Wizard of the Wireless
10. Accused
11. The Broken Record
12. Danger Lights

The Perils of Pauline (Universal, October 20, 1933)
Director: Ray Taylor. *Cast*: Evelyn Knapp, Robert Allen, William Desmond, James Durkin, John Davidson, Sonny Ray, Frank Lackteen, Hugh Enfield.
Chapter Titles:
1. The Guns of Doom
2. The Typhoon of Terror
3. The Leopard Leaps
4. Trapped by the Enemy

5. The Flaming Tomb
6. Pursued by Savages
7. Tracked by the Enemy
8. Dangerous Depths

9. The Mummy Walks
10. The Night Attack
11. Into the Flames
12. Confu's Sacred Secret

Mystery Squadron (Mascot, December 22, 1933)
Directors: Colbert Clark, David Howard. *Cast*: Bob Steele, Guinn "Big Boy" Williams, Lucile Browne, Jack Mulhall, J. Carroll Naish, Jack Mower, Robert Frazer, Purnell Pratt.
Chapter Titles:

1. The Black Ace
2. The Fatal Warning
3. The Black Ace Strikes
4. Men of Steel
5. The Death Swoop
6. Doomed

7. Enemy Signals
8. The Canyon of Calamity
9. The Secret of the Mine
10. Clipped Wings
11. The Beast at Bay
12. The Ace of Aces

The Whispering Shadow (Mascot, Unknown)
Directors: Albert Herman, Colbert Clark. *Cast*: Bela Lugosi, Karl Dane, Malcolm MacGregor, Robert Warwick, Ethel Clayton, George Lewis, Henry B. Walthall, Viva Tattersall.
Chapter Titles:

1. Master Magician
2. The Collapsing Room
3. The All-seeing Eye
4. The Shadow Strikes
5. Wanted for Murder
6. The Man Who Was Czar

7. The Double Room
8. The Red Circle
9. The Fatal Secret
10. The Death Warrant
11. The Trap
12. King of the World

Tarzan the Fearless (Principal, Unknown)
Director: Robert F. Hill. *Cast*: Larry "Buster" Crabbe, Jacqueline Wells, Philo McCullough, E. Alyn Warren, Edward Woods, Mathew Betz, Frank Lackteen.
Chapter Titles:

1. The Dive of Death
2. The Storm God Strikes
3. Thundering Death
4. The Pit of Peril
5. Blood Money
6. Voodoo Vengeance

7. Caught by Cannibals
8. The Creeping Terror
9. Eyes of Evil
10. The Death Plunge
11. Harvest of Hate
12. Jungle Justice

1934

Pirate Treasure (Universal, January 9, 1934)
Director: Ray Taylor, *Cast*: Richard Talmadge, Lucille Lund, Walter Miller, Pat O'Malley, William Desmond, Stanley Brassett.
Chapter Titles:

1. Stolen Treasure
2. The Death Plunge
3. The Wheels of Fate
4. The Sea Chase
5. Into the Depths
6. The Death Crash

7. Crashing Doom
8. Mutiny
9. Hidden Gold
10. The Fight for the Treasure
11. The Fatal Plunge
12. Captured

The Lost Jungle (Mascot, March 22, 1934)
   Directors: Armand Schaefer, David Howard. *Cast*: Clyde Beatty, Cecelia Parker, Syd Saylor, Warner Richmond, Wheeler Oakman, Maston Williams, Crauford Kent, Edward LeSaint, Max Wagner.
Chapter Titles:

1. Noah's Ark Island
2. Nature in the Raw
3. The Hypnotic Eye
4. The Pit of Crocodiles
5. Gorilla Warfare
6. The Battle of Beasts
7. The Tiger's Prey
8. The Lion's Brood
9. Eyes of the Jungle
10. Human Hyenas
11. The Gorilla
12. Take Them Back Alive

The Vanishing Shadow (Universal, April 5, 1934)
   Director: Louis Friedlander. *Cast*: Onslow Stevens, Walter Miller, Ada Ince, James Durkin, Richard Cramer, Frank Glendon, William Desmond, Sid Bracey, Beulah Hutton.
Chapter Titles:

1. Accused of Murder
2. The Destroying Ray
3. The Avalanche
4. Trapped
5. Hurled from the Sky
6. Chain Lightning
7. The Tragic Crash
8. The Shadow of Death
9. Blazing Bulkheads
10. The Iron Death
11. The Juggernaut
12. Retribution

Burn 'em Up Barnes (Mascot, June 13, 1934)
   Directors: Colbert Clark, Armand Schaefer. *Cast*: Jack Mulhall, Lola Lane, Frankie Darro, Julian Rivero, Edwin Maxwell, James Bush, John Davidson, Francis MacDonald, James Burtis.
Chapter Titles:

1. King of the Dirt Tracks
2. The Newsreel Murder
3. The Phantom Witness
4. The Celluloid Clue
5. The Decoy Driver
6. The Crimson Alibi
7. Roaring Rails
8. The Death Crash
9. The Man Higher Up
10. The Missing Link
11. Surrounded
12. The Fatal Whisper

The Red Rider (Universal, July 9, 1934)
   Director: Louis Friedlander. *Cast*: Buck Jones, Marion Schilling, Walter Miller, Grant Withers, Margaret Lamarr, Frank Rice, Richard Cramer, J. Frank Glennon, William Desmond.
Chapter Titles:

1. Sentenced to Die
2. A Leap for Life
3. The Night Attack
4. A Treacherous Ambush
5. Trapped
6. The Brink of Death
7. The Fatal Plunge
8. The Stampede
9. The Posse Rider
10. The Avenging Trail
11. The Lost Diamonds
12. Double Trouble
13. The Night Raiders
14. In the Enemies' Hideout
15. Brought to Justice

Law of the Wild (Mascot, September 1, 1934)
   Directors: Armand Schaefer, B. Reeves Eason. *Cast*: Rex, King of Wild Horses,

Rin Tin Tin, Jr., Bob Custer, Ben Turpin, Lucile Browne, Lafe McKee.
Chapter Titles:

1. The Man Killer
2. The Battle of the Strong
3. The Cross-eyed Goony
4. Avenging Fangs
5. A Dead Man's Hand
6. Horse-thief Justice
7. The Death Stampede
8. The Canyon of Calamity
9. Robbers' Roost
10. King of the Range
11. Winner Take All
12. The Grand Sweepstakes

The Return of Chandu (Principal, October 1, 1934)

Director: Ray Taylor. *Cast*: Bela Lugosi, Maria Alba, Clara Kimball Young, Lucian Prival, Dean Benton, Phyllis Ludwig, Bryant Washburn, Peggy Montgomery.
Chapter Titles:

1. The Chosen Victim
2. The House on the Hill
3. On the High Seas
4. The Evil Eye
5. The Invisible Circle
6. Chandu's False Step
7. The Mysterious Island
8. The Edge of the Pit
9. The Invisible Terror
10. The Crushing Rock
11. The Uplifted Knife
12. The Knife Descends

Tailspin Tommy (Universal, October 8, 1934)

Director: Louis Friedlander. *Cast*: Maurice Murphy, Noah Beery, Jr., Walter Miller, Patricia Farr, Grant Withers, John Davidson, William Desmond, Charles A. Browne.
Chapter Titles:

1. Death Flies the Mail
2. The Mail Goes Through
3. Sky Bandits
4. The Copper Room
5. The Night Flight
6. The Baited Trap
7. Tommy to the Rescue
8. The Thrill of Death
9. The Earth God's Roar
10. Death at the Controls
11. Rushing Waters
12. Littleville's Big Day

Mystery Mountain (Mascot, November 30, 1934)

Directors: Otto Brower, B. Reeves Eason. *Cast*: Ken Maynard, Tarzan, the Wonder Horse, Verna Hillie, Syd Saylor, Edward Earle, Edward Hearn, Hooper Atchley, Bob Kortman, Al Bridge.
Chapter Titles:

1. The Rattler
2. The Man Nobody Knows
3. The Eye That Never Sleeps
4. The Human Target
5. Phantom Outlaws
6. The Perfect Crime
7. Tarzan the Cunning
8. The Enemy's Stronghold
9. The Fatal Warning
10. The Secret of the Mountain
11. Behind the Mask
12. The Judgement of Tarzan

The Young Eagles (First Division, Unknown)

Directors: Spencer G. Bennet, Vin Moore. *Cast*: Bobby Ford, Bob Cox, Jim Adams, Jim Vance, Angus McLean, Carter Dixon, Philo McCullough, Frank Lackteen.
Chapter Titles:

1. The Crash
2. Drums of Hate
3. City of the Dead
4. The Bridge of Doom
5. Treasure Trails
6. Fangs of Flame

7. Tropic Fury
8. Wings of Terror
9. The Lost Lagoon

10. Jungle Outlaws
11. Trapped
12. Out of the Sky

1935

Rustlers of Red Dog (Universal, January 7, 1935)
    Director: Louis Friedlander. *Cast*: Johnny Mack Brown, Joyce Compton, Walter Miller, Raymond Hatton, Harry Woods, Frederic Mackaye, William Desmond, Lafe McKee.
Chapter Titles:

1. Hostile Redskins
2. Flaming Arrows
3. Thundering Hoofs
4. Attack at Dawn
5. Buried Alive
6. Flames of Vengeance

7. Into the Depths
8. Paths of Peril
9. The Snake Strikes
10. Riding Wild
11. The Rustlers Clash
12. Law and Order

The Phantom Empire (Mascot, February 23, 1935)
    Directors: Otto Brower, B. Reeves Eason. *Cast*: Gene Autry, Frankie Darro, Betsy King Ross, Smiley Burnette, William Moore, Dorothy Christy, Wheeler Oakman, Warner Richmond.
Chapter Titles:

1. The Singing Cowboy
2. The Thunder Riders
3. The Lightning Chamber
4. Phantom Broadcast
5. Beneath the Earth
6. Disaster from the Skies

7. From Death to Life
8. Jaws of Jeopardy
9. Prisoner of the Ray
10. The Rebellion
11. A Queen in Chains
12. The End of Murania

Call of the Savage (Universal, March 19, 1935)
    Director: Louis Friedlander. *Cast*: Noah Beery, Jr. Dorothy Short, Walter Miller, Harry Woods, Frederic Mackaye, Bryant Washburn, Viva Tattersall, Russ Powell, Grace Cunard.
Chapter Titles:

1. Shipwrecked
2. Captured by Cannibals
3. Stampeding Death
4. Terrors of the Jungle
5. The Plunge of Peril
6. Thundering Waters

7. The Hidden Monster
8. Jungle Treachery
9. The Avenging Fire God
10. Descending Doom
11. The Dragon Strikes
12. The Pit of Flame

The Miracle Rider (Mascot, May 4, 1935)
    Directors: Armand Schaefer, B. Reeves Eason. *Cast*: Tom Mix, Tony, Jr., Joan Gale, Charles Middleton, Edward Hearn, Ernie Adams, Smiley Burnette, Robert Frazer, Wally Wales, Jack Rockwell.
Chapter Titles:

1. The Vanishing Indian
2. The Firebird Strikes
3. The Flying Knife
4. A Race with Death

5. Double Barreled Doom
6. Thundering Hoofs
7. The Dragnet
8. Guerilla Warfare

   9. The Silver Band
  10. Signal Fires
  11. A Traitor Dies
  12. Danger Rides with Death

  13. Secret of X-94
  14. Between Two Fires
  15. Justice Rides the Plains

The Roaring West (Universal, June 26, 1935)
   Director: Ray Taylor. *Cast*: Buck Jones, Walter Miller, Harlan Knight, Muriel Evans, William Thorne, Frank McGlynn, Sr., William Desmond, Tom London, Charles King.
Chapter Titles:

   1. The Land Rush
   2. The Torrent of Terror
   3. Flaming Peril
   4. Stampede of Death
   5. Danger in the Dark
   6. Death Rides the Plains
   7. Hurled to the Depths
   8. Ravaging Flames

   9. Death Holds the Reins
  10. The Fatal Blast
  11. The Baited Trap
  12. The Mystery Shot
  13. Flaming Torrents
  14. Thundering Fury
  15. The Conquering Cowpunchers

The Adventures of Rex and Rinty (Mascot, August 25, 1935)
   Directors: B. Reeves Eason, Ford Beebe. *Cast*: Kane Richmond, Rin Tin Tin, Jr., Rex the Horse, Smiley Burnette, Norma Taylor, Mischa Auer, Harry Woods, Wheeler Oakman, Pedro Regas.
Chapter Titles:

   1. God Horse of Sujan
   2. Sport of Kings
   3. Fangs of Flame
   4. Homeward Bound
   5. Babes in the Woods
   6. Dead Man's Tale

   7. End of the Road
   8. A Dog's Devotion
   9. The Stranger's Recall
  10. The Siren of Death
  11. New Gods for Old
  12. Primitive Justice

Tailspin Tommy in the Great Air Mystery (Universal, October 9, 1935)
   Director: Ray Taylor. *Cast*: Clark Williams, Jean Rogers, Noah Beery, Jr., Delphine Drew, Grant Withers, Bryant Washburn, Helen Brown.
Chapter Titles:

   1. Wreck of the Dirigible
   2. The Roaring Fire God
   3. Hurled from the Skies
   4. A Bolt from the Blue
   5. The Torrent
   6. Flying Death

   7. The Crash in the Clouds
   8. Wings of Disaster
   9. Crossed and Double Crossed
  10. The Dungeon of Doom
  11. Desperate Changes
  12. The Last Stand

The Fighting Marines (Mascot, November 16, 1935)
   Directors: B. Reeves Eason, Joseph Kane. *Cast*: Grant Withers, Adrian Morris, Ann Rutherford, Robert Warwick, Pat O'Malley, George Lewis, Robert Frazer, J. Frank Glendon, Tom London.
Chapter Titles:

   1. Human Targets
   2. Isle of Missing Men
   3. The Savage Horde
   4. The Mark of the Tiger Shark
   5. The Gauntlet of Grief
   6. Robbers' Roost

   7. Jungle Terrors
   8. Siege of Halfway Island
   9. Death from the Sky
  10. Wheels of Destruction
  11. Behind the Mask
  12. Two Against the Horde

The Adventures of Frank Merriwell (Universal, December 17, 1935)
   Director: Cliff Smith. *Cast*: Don Briggs, Jean Rogers, John King, Sumner Getchell, William Carleton, House Peters, Jr., Alan Hersholt, Carla Laemmle, Wallace Reid, Jr.
Chapter Titles:

1. College Hero	7. Monster of the Deep
2. The Death Plunge	8. The Tragic Victory
3. Death at the Crossroads	9. Between Savage Foes
4. Wreck of the Viking	10. Imprisoned in a Dungeon
5. Capsized in the Cataract	11. The Crash in the Chasm
6. Descending Doom	12. The Winning Play

Queen of the Jungle (Screen Attractions, Unknown)
   Director: Robert F. Hill. *Cast*: Reed Howes, Mary Kornman, Dickie Jones, Marilyn Spinner, William Walsh, Lafe McKee, George Chesebro, Eddie Foster, Robert Borman.
Chapter Titles:

1. Lost in the Clouds	7. The Leopard Leaps
2. Radium Rays	8. The Doom Ship
3. The Hand of Death	9. Death Rides the Wave
4. The Natives' Revenge	10. The Temple of Mu
5. Black Magic	11. Fangs in the Dark
6. The Death Vine	12. The Pit of the Lions

The New Adventures of Tarzan (Burroughs-Tarzan, Unknown)
   Director: Edward Kull. *Cast*: Herman Brix, Ula Holt, Frank Baker, Lewis Sargent, Don Costello, Dale Walsh.
Chapter Titles:

1. The New Adventures of Tarzan	7. Flaming Waters
2. Crossed Trails	8. Angry Gods
3. The Devil's Noose	9. Doom's Brink
4. River Perils	10. Secret Signals
5. Unseen Hands	11. Death's Fireworks
6. Fatal Fangs	12. Operator No. 17

The Lost City (Regal, Unknown)
   Director: Harry Revier. *Cast*: Kane Richmond, William Boyd, George Hayes, Claudia Dell, Ralph Lewis, Joseph Swickard, William Bletcher, Gina Corrado.
Chapter Titles:

1. Living Dead Men	7. Spider Men
2. Tunnel of Death	8. Human Targets
3. Dagger Rock	9. Jungle Vengeance
4. Doomed	10. The Lion Pit
5. Tiger Prey	11. Death Ray
6. Human Beasts	12. The Mad Scientist

1936

Darkest Africa (Republic, February 15, 1936)
   Director: B. Reeves Eason, Joseph Kane. *Cast*: Clyde Beatty, Manuel King, Elaine Shepard, Lucien Prival, Naba, Ray Benard, Wheeler Oakman, Edward McWade, Edmund Cobb, Ray Turner.

Chapter Titles:

1. Baru — Son of the Jungle
2. The Tiger Men's God
3. Bat-men of Joba
4. The Hunter Lions of Joba
5. Bonga's Courage
6. Prisoners of the High Priest
7. Swing for Life
8. Jaws of the Tiger
9. When Birdmen Strike
10. Trial by Thunder-rods
11. Jaws of Death
12. Revolt of the Slaves
13. Gauntlet of Destruction
14. The Divine Sacrifice
15. The Prophecy of Gorn

Flash Gordon (Universal, March 18, 1936)

Director: Frederick Stephani. *Cast:* Larry "Buster" Crabbe, Jean Rogers, Charles Middleton, Frank Shannon, Priscilla Lawson, Richard Alexander, John Lipson, Theodore Lorch.

Chapter Titles:

1. The Planet of Peril
2. The Tunnel of Terror
3. Captured by Shark Men
4. Battling the Sea Beast
5. The Destroying Ray
6. Flaming Fortune
7. Shattering Doom
8. Tournament of Death
9. Fighting the Fire Dragon
10. The Unseen Peril
11. In the Claws of the Tigron
12. Trapped in the Turret
13. Rocketing to Earth

Undersea Kingdom (Republic, May 30, 1936)

Director: B. Reeves Eason, Joseph Kane. *Cast:* Ray "Crash" Corrigan, Lois Wilde, Monte Blue, William Farnum, Boothe Howard, C. Montague Shaw, Lee Van Atta, Smiley Burnette.

Chapter Titles:

1. Beneath the Ocean Floor
2. Undersea City
3. Arena of Death
4. Revenge of the Volkites
5. Prisoners of Atlantis
6. The Juggernaut Strikes
7. The Submarine Trap
8. Into the Metal Tower
9. Death in the Air
10. Atlantis Destroyed
11. Flaming Death
12. Ascent to the Upperworld

The Phantom Rider (Universal, June 24, 1936)

Director: Ray Taylor. *Cast:* Buck Jones, Diana Gibson, Marla Shelton, Eddie Gribbon, Joey Ray, George Cooper, Harry Woods, Frank LaRue, Charles King, Tom London.

Chapter Titles:

1. Dynamite
2. The Maddened Herd
3. The Brink of Disaster
4. The Phantom Rides
5. Trapped by Outlaws
6. Shot Down
7. Stark Terror
8. The Night Attack
9. The Indians Attack
10. Human Targets
11. The Shaft of Doom
12. Flaming Gold
13. Crashing Timbers
14. The Last Chance
15. The Outlaw's Vengeance

Ace Drummond (Universal, September 11, 1936)

Director: Ford Beebe, Cliff Smith. *Cast:* John King, Jean Rogers, Noah Beery, Jr., Robert Warwick, Lon Chaney, Jr., Jackie Morrow, James B. Leong, Sr., Hooper Atchley.

Chapter Titles:
1. Where East Meets West
2. The Invisible Enemy
3. The Doorway of Doom
4. The Radio Riddle
5. Bullets of Sand
6. Evil Spirits
7. The Trackless Trail
8. The Sign in the Sky
9. Secret Service
10. The Mountain of Jade
11. The Dragon Commands
12. The Squadron of Death
13. The World's Akin

The Vigilantes Are Coming (Republic, October 2, 1936)
Directors: Mack V. Wright, Ray Taylor. *Cast*: Robert Livingston, Kay Hughes, Guinn "Big Boy" Williams, Fred Kohler, Raymond Hatton, Robert Warwick, William Farnum, Robert Kortman.
Chapter Titles:
1. The Eagle Strikes
2. Birth of the Vigilantes
3. Condemned by Cossacks
4. Unholy Gold
5. Treachery Unmasked
6. A Tyrant's Trickery
7. Wings of Doom
8. A Treaty with Treason
9. Arrow's Flight
10. Prison of Flame
11. A Race with Death
12. Fremont Takes Command

Robinson Crusoe of Clipper Island (Republic, November 19, 1936)
Directors: Mack V. Wright, Ray Taylor. *Cast*: Mala, Rex, Buck, Mamo Clark, Herbert Rawlinson, William Newell, John Ward, Selmer Jackson, John Dilson, John Picorri.
Chapter Titles:
1. The Mysterious Island
2. Flaming Danger
3. Fathoms Below
4. Into the Enemies' Camp
5. Danger in the Air
6. The God of the Volcano
7. Trail's End
8. The Jaws of the Beast
9. The Cave of the Winds
10. Wings of Fury
11. Agents of Disaster
12. The Sea Trap
13. Mutiny
14. Thunder Mountain

Jungle Jim (Universal, December 29, 1936)
Directors: Ford Beebe, Cliff Smith. *Cast*: Grant Withers, Betty Jane Rhodes, Raymond Hatton, Evelyn Brent, Bryant Washburn, Paul Sutton, Frank Mayo, Al Bridge, Henry Brandon.
Chapter Titles:
1. Into the Lion's Den
2. The Cobra Strikes
3. The Menacing Herd
4. The Killer's Trail
5. The Bridge of Terror
6. Drums of Doom
7. The Earth Trembles
8. The Killer Lion
9. The Devil Bird
10. Descending Doom
11. In the Cobra's Castle
12. The Last Safari

The Black Coin (Stage and Screen, Unknown)
Director: Elmer Clifton. *Cast*: Ralph Graves, Ruth Mix, Dave O'Brien, Clara Kimball Young, Constance Bergen, Matthew Betz, Robert Frazer, Snub Pollard, Bob Walker.
Chapter Titles:
1. Dangerous Men
2. The Mystery Ship

3. The Fatal Plunge
4. Monsters of the Deep
5. Wolves of the Night
6. Shark's Fang
7. Midnight Menace
8. Flames of Death
9. Smuggler's Lair

10. Flaming Guns
11. Wheels of Death
12. The Crash
13. Danger Ahead
14. Hidden Peril
15. The Phantom Treasure

The Clutching Hand (Stage and Screen, Unknown)
Director: Albert Herman. *Cast*: Jack Mulhall, William Farnum, Ruth Mix, Rex Lease, Marion Schilling, Reed Howes, Charles Locher, Robert Frazer, Bob Kortman, Tom London.
Chapter Titles:

1. Who Is the Clutching Hand?
2. Shadow
3. House of Mystery
4. The Phantom Car
5. The Double Trap
6. Steps of Doom
7. The Invisible Enemy
8. A Cry in the Night

9. Evil Eyes
10. A Desperate Chance
11. The Ship of Doom
12. Hidden Danger
13. The Mystic Menace
14. The Silent Spectre
15. The Lone Hand

Custer's Last Stand (Stage and Screen, Unknown)
Director: Elmer Clifton. *Cast*: Rex Lease, Frank McGlynn, Jr., Nancy Caswell, Lona Andre, William Farnum, Reed Howes, Jack Mulhall, Ruth Mix, Joseph Swickard.
Chapter Titles:

1. Perils of the Plains
2. Thundering Hoofs
3. Fires of Vengeance
4. The Ghost Dancers
5. Trapped
6. Human Wolves
7. Demons of Disaster
8. White Treachery

9. Circle of Death
10. Flaming Arrow
11. Warpath
12. Firing Squad
13. Red Panthers
14. Custer's Last Ride
15. The Last Stand

Shadow of Chinatown (Victory, Unknown)
Director: Robert F. Hill. *Cast*: Bela Lugosi, Herman Brix, Luana Walters, Joan Barclay, Maurice Liu, Willy Fu, Charles King.
Chapter Titles:

1. The Arms of the God
2. The Crushing Walls
3. 13 Ferguson Alley
4. Death on the Wire
5. The Sinister Ray
6. The Sword Thrower
7. The Noose
8. Midnight

9. The Last Warning
10. The Bomb
11. Thundering Doom
12. Invisible Gas
13. The Brink of Disaster
14. The Fatal Trap
15. The Avenging Powers

1937

Secret Agent X-9 (Universal, February 11, 1937)

Directors: Ford Beebe, Cliff Smith. *Cast*: Scott Kolk, Jean Rogers, David Oliver, Lynn Gilbert, George Shelley, Henry Brandon, Leonard Lord, Monte Blue, Lon Chaney, Jr., Bob Kortman.

Chapter Titles:

1. Modern Pirates
2. The Ray That Blinds
3. The Man of Many Faces
4. The Listening Shadow
5. False Fires
6. The Dragnet
7. Sealed Lips
8. Exhibit A
9. The Masquerader
10. The Forced Lie
11. The Enemy Camp
12. Crime Does Not Pay

Dick Tracy (Republic, March 5, 1937)

Directors: Ray Taylor, Alan James. *Cast*: Ralph Byrd, Kay Hughes, Smiley Burnette, Lee Van Atta, John Picorri, Carleton Young, Fred Hamilton, Francis X. Bushman, Edwin Stanley.

Chapter Titles:

1. The Spider Strikes
2. The Bridge of Terror
3. The Fur Pirates
4. Death Rides the Sky
5. Brother Against Brother
6. Dangerous Waters
7. The Ghost Town Mystery
8. Battle in the Clouds
9. The Stratosphere Adventure
10. The Gold Ship
11. Harbor Pursuit
12. The Trail of the Spider
13. The Fire Trap
14. The Devil in White
15. Brothers United

Wild West Days (Universal, May 20, 1937)

Directors: Ford Beebe, Cliff Smith. *Cast*: Johnny Mack Brown, George Shelley, Lynn Gilbert, Chief Thundercloud, Frank Yaconelli, Robert Kortman, Russell Simpson, Walter Miller.

Chapter Titles:

1. Death Rides the Range
2. The Redskins' Revenge
3. The Brink of Doom
4. The Indians Are Coming
5. The Leap for Life
6. Death Stalks the Plains
7. Six Gun Law
8. The Gold Stampede
9. Walls of Fire
10. The Circle of Doom
11. The Thundering Herd
12. Rustlers and Redskins
13. The Rustlers' Roundup

The Painted Stallion (Republic, June 18, 1937)

Directors: William Witney, Alan James, Ray Taylor. *Cast*: Ray "Crash" Corrigan, Hoot Gibson, Sammy McKim, Leroy Mason, Jack Perrin, Hal Taliaferro, Duncan Renaldo, Julia Thayer, Yakima Canutt.

Chapter Titles:

1. Trail to Empire
2. The Rider of the Stallion
3. The Death Leap
4. Avalanche
5. Volley of Death
6. Thundering Wheels
7. Trail Treachery
8. The Whistling Arrow
9. The Fatal Message
10. Ambush
11. Tunnel of Terror
12. Human Targets

Jungle Menace (Columbia, August 7, 1937)

Directors: George Melford, Harry Fraser. *Cast*: Frank Buck, Reginald Denny,

Sasha Seimel, Esther Ralston, Charlotte Henry, William Bakewell, Clarence Muse, Willie Fung, Leroy Mason.

Chapter Titles:

1. River Pirates
2. Deadly Enemies
3. Flames of Hate
4. One-way Ride
5. Man of Mystery
6. Shanghaied
7. Tiger Eyes
8. The Frame-up
9. The Cave of Mystery
10. Flirting with Death
11. Ship of Doom
12. Mystery Island
13. The Typhoon
14. Murder at Sea
15. Give 'em Rope

Radio Patrol (Universal, August 16, 1937)

Directors: Ford Beebe, Cliff Smith. *Cast:* Grant Withers, Adrian Morris, Catherine Hughes, Frank Lackteen, Jack Mulhall, Tom London, Monte Montague, Mickey Rentchsler, Wheeler Oakman.

Chapter Titles:

1. A Million Dollar Murder
2. The Hypnotic Eye
3. Flaming Death
4. The Human Clue
5. The Flash of Doom
6. The House of Terror
7. Claws of Steel
8. The Perfect Crime
9. Plaything of Disaster
10. A Bargain with Death
11. The Hidden Menace
12. They Get Their Man

S.O.S. Coast Guard (Republic, September, 10, 1937)

Directors: William Witney, Alan James. *Cast:* Ralph Byrd, Bela Lugosi, Maxine Doyle, Herbert Rawlinson, Richard Alexander, Lee Ford, John Picorri, Lawrence Grant, Carleton Young.

Chapter Titles:

1. Disaster at Sea
2. Barrage of Death
3. The Gas Chamber
4. The Fatal Shaft
5. The Mystery Ship
6. Deadly Cargo
7. Undersea Terror
8. The Crash
9. Wolves at Bay
10. The Acid Trail
11. The Sea Battle
12. The Deadly Circle

Tim Tyler's Luck (Universal, November 10, 1937)

Directors: Ford Beebe, Wyndham Gittens. *Cast:* Frankie Thomas, Frances Robinson, Norman Willis, Jack Mulhall, Frank Mayo, Al Bridge, Pat O'Brien, William Benedict, Al Shean, Earle Douglas.

Chapter Titles:

1. Jungle Pirates
2. Dead Man's Pass
3. Into the Lion's Den
4. The Ivory Trail
5. Trapped in the Quicksands
6. The Jaws of the Jungle
7. The King of the Gorillas
8. The Spider Caught
9. The Gates of Doom
10. A Race for Fortune
11. No Man's Land
12. The Kimberley Diamonds

Zorro Rides Again (Republic, December 3, 1937)

Directors: William Witney, John English. *Cast:* John Carroll, Helen Christian, Reed Howes, Duncan Renaldo, Richard Alexander, Noah Beery, Sr., Nigel De Brulier, Robert Kortman.

Chapter Titles:

1. Death from the Sky
2. The Fatal Minute
3. Juggernaut
4. Unmasked
5. Sky Pirates
6. The Fatal Shot
7. Burning Embers
8. Plunge of Peril
9. Tunnel of Terror
10. Trapped
11. Right of Way
12. Retribution

The Mysterious Pilot (Columbia, December 7, 1937)
   Director: Spencer G. Bennet. *Cast:* Captain Frank Hawkes, Dorothy Sebastian, Rex Lease, Guy Bates Post, Kenneth Harlan, Clara Kimball Young, Esther Ralston, Yakima Canutt.
Chapter Titles:

1. The Howl of the Wolf
2. The Web Tangles
3. Enemies of the Air
4. In the Hands of the Law
5. The Crack-up
6. The Dark Hour
7. Wings of Destiny
8. Battle in the Sky
9. The Great Flight
10. Whirlpool of Death
11. The Haunted Mill
12. The Lost Trail
13. The Net Tightens
14. Vengeance Rides the Airways
15. Retribution

Blake of Scotland Yard (Victory, Unknown)
   Director: Robert F. Hill. *Cast:* Ralph Byrd, Joan Barclay, Herbert Rawlinson, Lloyd Hughes, Dickie Jones, Nick Stuart.
Chapter Titles:

1. Mystery of the Blooming Gardenia
2. Death in the Laboratory
3. Cleared Mysteries
4. The Mystery of the Silver Fox
5. Death in the River
6. The Criminal Shadow
7. Face to Face
8. The Fatal Trap
9. Parisian House Tops
10. Battle Royal
11. The Burning Fuse
12. The Roofs of Lime House
13. The Sting of the Scorpion
14. The Scorpion Unmasked
15. The Trap is Sprung

1938

Flash Gordon's Trip to Mars (Universal, February 8, 1938)
   Directors: Ford Beebe, Robert Hill. *Cast:* Larry "Buster" Crabbe, Jean Rogers, Charles Middleton, Frank Shannon, Beatrice Roberts, Donald Kerr, Wheeler Oakman, C. Montague Shaw.
Chapter Titles:

1. New Worlds to Conquer
2. The Living Dead
3. Queen of Magic
4. Ancient Enemies
5. The Boomerang
6. Tree-men of Mars
7. The Prisoner of Mongo
8. The Black Sapphire of Kalu
9. Symbol of Death
10. Incense of Forgetfulness
11. Human Bait
12. Ming the Merciless
13. The Miracle of Magic
14. A Beast at Bay
15. An Eye for an Eye

The Secret of Treasure Island (Columbia, March 2, 1938)
   Director: Elmer Clifton. *Cast*: Don Terry, Gwen Gaze, Grant Withers, Hobart Bosworth, Yakima Canutt, William Farnum, Walter Miller, George Rosener, Dave O'Brien.
Chapter Titles:

1. The Isle of Fear	9. The Pirate's Revenge
2. The Ghost Talks	10. The Crash
3. The Phantom Duel	11. Dynamite
4. Buried Alive	12. The Bridge of Doom
5. The Girl Who Vanished	13. The Mad Flight
6. Trapped by the Flood	14. The Jaws of Destruction
7. The Cannon Roars	15. Justice
8. The Circle of Death	

The Lone Ranger (Republic, March 4, 1938)
   Directors: William Witney, John English. *Cast*: Lee Powell, Herman Brix, George Letz, Lane Chandler, Hal Taliaferro, Lynn Roberts, Stanley Andrews, Chief Thundercloud, William Farnum.
Chapter Titles:

1. Heigh-Yo Sliver!	9. The Missing Spur
2. Thundering Earth	10. Flaming Fury
3. The Pitfall	11. The Silver Bullet
4. Agents of Treachery	12. Escape
5. The Steaming Cauldron	13. The Fatal Plunge
6. Red Man's Courage	14. Messengers of Doom
7. Wheels of Diaster	15. The Last of the Rangers
8. Fatal Treasure	

Flaming Frontiers (Universal, May 12, 1938)
   Directors: Ray Taylor, Alan James. *Cast*: Johnny Mack Brown, Eleanore Hansen, Ralph Bowman, Charles Middleton, Chief Thundercloud, James Blaine, Charles Stevens, William Royle.
Chapter Titles:

1. The River Runs Red	9. Toll of the Torrent
2. Death Rides the Wind	10. In the Claws of the Cougar
3. Treachery at Eagle Pass	11. The Half Breed's Revenge
4. A Night of Terror	12. The Indians Are Coming
5. Blood and Gold	13. The Fatal Plunge
6. Trapped by Fire	14. Dynamite
7. The Human Target	15. A Duel to the Death
8. The Savage Horde	

The Fighting Devil Dogs (Republic, June 9, 1938)
   Directors: William Witney, John English. *Cast*: Lee Powell, Herman Brix, Eleanor Stewart, Montague Love, Hugh Sothern, Sam Flint, Forrest Taylor, John Picorri, Perry Ivins, Carleton Young.
Chapter Titles:

1. The Lightning Strikes	7. The Phantom Killer
2. The Mill of Disaster	8. Tide of Trickery
3. The Silent Witness	9. Attack from the Skies
4. Cargo of Mystery	10. In the Camp of the Enemy
5. Undersea Bandits	11. The Baited Trap
6. The Torpedo of Doom	12. Killer at Bay

The Great Adventures of Wild Bill Hickok (Columbia, July 5, 1938)
Directors: Mack V. Wright, Sam Nelson. *Cast*: Bill Elliott, Carole Wayne, Frankie Darro, Dickie Jones, Sammy McKim, Kermit Maynard, Monte Blue, Roscoe Ates, Reed Hadley, Chief Thundercloud.
Chapter Titles:

1. The Law of the Gun
2. Stampede
3. Blazing Terror
4. Mystery Canyon
5. Flaming Brands
6. The Apache Killer
7. Prowling Wolves
8. The Pit
9. Ambush
10. Savage Vengeance
11. Burning Waters
12. Desperation
13. Phantom Bullets
14. The Lure
15. Trail's End

Red Barry (Universal, August 22, 1938)
Directors: Ford Beebe, Alan James. *Cast*: Larry "Buster" Crabbe, Frances Robinson, Wade Boteler, Edna Sedgwick, Syril Delevanti, Frank Lackteen, Hugh Huntley, Philip Ahn.
Chapter Titles:

1. Millions for Defense
2. The Curtain Falls
3. The Decoy
4. High Stakes
5. Desperate Chances
6. The Human Target
7. Midnight Tragedy
8. The Devil's Disguise
9. Between Two Fires
10. The False Trail
11. Heavy Odds
12. The Enemy Within
13. Mission of Mercy

Dick Tracy Returns (Republic, September 16, 1938)
Directors: William Witney, John English. *Cast*: Ralph Byrd, Lynne Roberts, Charles Middleton, Jerry Tucker, David Sharpe, Lee Ford, Michael Kent, John Merton, Raphael Bennett.
Chapter Titles:

1. The Sky Wreckers
2. The Runaway of Death
3. Handcuffed to Doom
4. Four Seconds to Live
5. Death in the Air
6. Stolen Secrets
7. Tower of Death
8. Cargo of Destruction
9. The Clock of Doom
10. High Voltage
11. The Kidnapped Witness
12. The Runaway Torpedo
13. Passengers to Doom
14. In the Hands of the Enemy
15. G-Men's Dragnet

The Spider's Web (Columbia, October 10, 1938)
Directors: Ray Taylor, James W. Horne. *Cast*: Warren Hull, Iris Meredith, Richard Fiske, Kenne Duncan, Forbes Murray, Don Douglas, Charles Wilson, Marc Lawrence, Lane Chandler.
Chapter Titles:

1. Night of Terror
2. Death Below
3. High Voltage
4. Surrender or Die
5. Shoot to Kill
6. Sealed Lips
7. Shadows of the Night
8. While the City Sleeps
9. Doomed
10. Flaming Danger

11. The Road to Peril
12. The Spider Falls
13. The Manhunt

14. The Double Cross
15. The Octopus Unmasked

Scouts to the Rescue (Universal, November 28, 1938)
   Directors: Ray Taylor, Alan James. *Cast*: Jackie Cooper, Vondell Darr, Edwin Stanley, William Ruhl, Bill Cody, Jr., David Durand.
Chapter Titles:
   1. Death Rides the Air
   2. Avalanche of Doom
   3. Trapped by the Indians
   4. River of Doom
   5. Descending Doom
   6. Ghost Town Menace

   7. Destroyed by Dynamite
   8. Thundering Hoofs
   9. The Fire God Strikes
   10. The Battle at Ghost Town
   11. Hurtling Through Space
   12. The Boy Scouts' Triumph

Hawk of the Wilderness (Republic, December 16, 1938)
   Directors: William Witney, John English. *Cast*: Herman Brix, Mala, Monte Blue, Jill Martin, Noble Johnson, William Royle, Tom Chatterton, George Eldridge, Patrick J. Kelly, Snowflake.
Chapter Titles:
   1. Mysterious Island
   2. Flaming Death
   3. Tiger Trap
   4. Queen's Ransom
   5. Pendulum of Doom
   6. The Dead Fall

   7. White Man's Magic
   8. Ambushed
   9. Marooned
   10. Camp of Horror
   11. Valley of Skulls
   12. Trail's End

1939

Flying G-Men (Columbia, January 24, 1939)
   Directors: Ray Taylor, James W. Horne. *Cast*: Robert Paige, Richard Fiske, James Craig, Lorna Gray, Sammy McKim, Don Beddoe, Forbes Murray, Dick Curtis, Ann Doran, Nestor Paiva.
Chapter Titles:
   1. Challenge in the Sky
   2. Flight of the Condemned
   3. The Vulture's Nest
   4. The Falcon Strikes
   5. Flight from Death
   6. Phantom of the Sky
   7. Trapped by Radio
   8. The Midnight Watch

   9. Wings of Terror
   10. Flaming Wreckage
   11. While a Nation Sleeps
   12. Sealed Orders
   13. Flame Island
   14. Jaws of Death
   15. The Falcon's Reward

Buck Rogers (Universal, February 6, 1939)
   Directors: Ford Beebe, Saul A. Goodkind. *Cast*: Larry "Buster" Crabbe, Jackie Moran, Constance Moore, Anthony Ward, Henry Brandon, Carleton Young, Jack Mulhall, C. Montague Shaw.
Chapter Titles:
   1. Tomorrow's World
   2. Tragedy on Saturn
   3. The Enemy's Stronghold

   4. The Sky Patrol
   5. The Phantom Plane
   6. The Unknown Command

7. Primitive Urge
8. Revolt of the Zuggs
9. Bodies Without Minds
10. Broken Barriers
11. A Prince in Bondage
12. War of the Planets

The Lone Ranger Rides Again (Republic, February 25, 1939)
Directors: William Witney, John English. *Cast*: Robert Livingston, Chief Thundercloud, Duncan Renaldo, Jinx Falken, Ralph Dunn, J. Farrell MacDonald, William Gould, Rex Lease, Ted Mapes.
Chapter Titles:
1. The Lone Ranger Returns
2. Masked Victory
3. The Black Raiders Strike
4. The Cavern of Doom
5. Agents of Deceit
6. The Trap
7. The Lone Ranger at Bay
8. Ambush
9. Wheels of Doom
10. The Dangerous Captive
11. Death Below
12. Blazing Peril
13. Exposed
14. Besieged
15. Frontier Justice

Mandrake the Magician (Columbia, May 2, 1939)
Directors: Sam Nelson, Norman Deming. *Cast*: Warren Hull, Doris Weston, Al Kikume, Rex Downing, Edward Earle, Forbes Murray, Kenneth MacDonald, Don Beddoe, Dick Curtis, John Tyrrell.
Chapter Titles:
1. Shadow on the Wall
2. Trap of the Wasp
3. City of Terror
4. The Secret Passage
5. The Devil's Playmate
6. The Fatal Crash
7. Gamble for Life
8. Across the Deadline
9. Terror Rides the Rails
10. The Unseen Monster
11. At the Stroke of Eight
12. The Reward of Treachery

The Oregon Trail (Universal, May 3, 1939)
Directors: Ford Beebe and Saul A. Goodkind. *Cast*: Johnny Mack Brown, Louise Stanley, Fuzzy Knight, Bill Cody, Jr., Ed LeSaint.
Chapter Titles:
1. The Renegade's Revenge
2. The Flaming Forest
3. The Brink of Disaster
4. Thundering Doom
5. The Stampede
6. Indian Vengeance
7. Trail of Treachery
8. Redskin Revenge
9. The Avalanche of Doom
10. The Plunge of Peril
11. Trapped in the Flames
12. The Baited Trap
13. Crashing Timbers
14. Death in the Night
15. Trail's End

Daredevils of the Red Circle (Republic, June 10, 1939)
Directors: William Witney, John English. *Cast*: Charles Quigley, Herman Brix, David Sharpe, Carole Landis, Miles Mander, Charles Middleton, C. Montague Shaw, Ben Taggart, William Pagan.
Chapter Titles:
1. The Monstrous Plot
2. The Mysterious Friend
3. The Executioner
4. Sabotage
5. The Ray of Death
6. Thirty Seconds to Live
7. The Flooded Mine
8. S.O.S.

9. Ladder of Peril
10. The Infernal Machine

11. The Red Circle Speaks
12. Flight to Doom

Overland with Kit Carson (Columbia, July 21, 1939)

Directors: Sam Nelson, Norman Deming. *Cast*: Bill Elliott, Iris Meredith, Richard Fiske, Leroy Mason, Trevor Bardette, James Craig, Olin Francis, Kenneth Mac-Donald, Francis Sayles, Dick Curtis.

Chapter Titles:

1. Doomed Men
2. Condemned to Die
3. The Fight for Life
4. The Ride of Terror
5. The Path of Doom
6. Rendezvous with Death
7. The Killer Stallion
8. The Devil's Nest

9. Blazing Peril
10. The Black Raiders
11. Foiled
12. The Warning
13. Terror in the Night
14. Crumbling Walls
15. Unmasked

The Phantom Creeps (Universal, July 27, 1939)

Directors: Ford Beebe, Saul A. Goodkind. *Cast*: Bela Lugosi, Robert Kent, Dorothy Arnold, Regis Toomey, Edward Van Sloan.

Chapter Titles:

1. The Menacing Power
2. Death Stalks the Highways
3. Crashing Towers
4. Invisible Terror
5. Thundering Rails
6. The Iron Monster

7. The Menacing Mist
8. Trapped in the Flames
9. Speeding Doom
10. Phantom Footprints
11. The Blast
12. To Destroy the World

Dick Tracy's G-Men. (Republic, September 2, 1939)

Directors; William Witney, John English. *Cast*: Ralph Byrd, Irving Pichel, Ted Pearson, Phyllis Isley, Walter Miller, George Douglas, Kenneth Harlan, Robert Carson, Julian Madison, Ted Mapes.

Chapter Titles:

1. The Master Spy
2. Captured
3. The False Signal
4. The Enemy Strikes
5. Crack-up
6. Sunken Peril
7. Tracking the Enemy
8. Chamber of Doom

9. Flames of Jeopardy
10. Crackling Fury
11. Caverns of Peril
12. Fight in the Sky
13. The Fatal Ride
14. Getaway
15. The Last Stand

The Green Hornet (Universal, November 21, 1939)

Directors: Ford Beebe, Ray Taylor. *Cast*: Gordon Jones, Keye Luke, Anne Nagel, Wade Boteler, Philip Trent, Walter McGrail, John Kelly, Gene Rizzi, Douglas Evans, Ralph Dunn, Cy Kendall.

Chapter Titles:

1. The Tunnel of Terror
2. The Thundering Terror
3. Flying Coffins
4. Pillar of Flame
5. The Time Bomb

6. Highways of Peril
7. Bridge of Disaster
8. Dead or Alive
9. The Hornet Trapped
10. Bullets and Ballots

11. Disaster Rides the Rails   13. Doom of the Underworld
12. Panic in the Zoo

Zorro's Fighting Legion (Republic, December 16, 1939)
Directors: William Witney, John English. *Cast*: Reed Hadley, Sheila Darcy, William Corson, Leander De Cordova, C. Montague Shaw, Edmund Cobb, John Merton, Budd Buster, Carleton Young.
Chapter Titles:

1. The Golden God   7. The Fugitive
2. The Flaming "Z"   8. Flowing Death
3. Descending Doom   9. The Golden Arrow
4. The Bridge of Peril   10. Mystery Wagon
5. The Decoy   11. Face to Face
6. Zorro to the Rescue   12. Unmasked

1940

The Shadow (Columbia, January 1, 1940)
Director: James W. Horne. *Cast*: Victor Jory, Veda Ann Borg, Roger Moore, Robert Fiske, J. Paul Jones, Jack Ingram, Charles Hamilton, Edward Peil, Sr., Frank Larue.
Chapter Titles:

1. The Doomed City   9. The Devil in White
2. The Shadow Attacks   10. The Underground Trap
3. The Shadow's Peril   11. Chinatown at Night
4. In the Tiger's Lair   12. Murder by Remote Control
5. Danger Above   13. Wheels of Death
6. The Shadow's Trap   14. The Sealed Room
7. Where Horror Waits   15. The Shadow's Net Closes
8. The Shadow Rides the Rails

Flash Gordon Conquers the Universe (Universal, February 8, 1940)
Directors: Ford Beebe, Ray Taylor. *Cast*: Larry "Buster" Crabbe, Carol Hughes, Frank Shannon, Charles Middleton, Anne Gwynne, Lee Powell, Roland Drew, Donald Curtis, Shirley Deane.
Chapter Titles:

1. The Purple Death   7. The Land of the Dead
2. Freezing Torture   8. The Fiery Abyss
3. Walking Bombs   9. The Pool of Peril
4. The Destroying Ray   10. The Death Mist
5. The Palace of Horror   11. Stark Treachery
6. Flaming Death   12. Doom of the Dictator

Drums of Fu Manchu (Republic, March 15, 1940)
Directors: William Witney, John English. *Cast*: Henry Brandon, William Royle, Robert Kellard, Gloria Franklin, Olaf Hytten, Tom Chatterton, Luana Walters, George Cleveland, John Dilson.
Chapter Titles:

1. Fu Manchu Strikes   4. The Pendulum of Doom
2. The Monster   5. The House of Terror
3. Ransom in the Sky   6. Death Dials a Number

7. Vengeance of the Si Fan
8. Danger Trail
9. The Crystal of Death
10. Drums of Death
11. The Tomb of the Ghengis Khan

12. Fire of Vengeance
13. The Devil's Tattoo
14. Satan's Surgeon
15. Revolt!

Terry and the Pirates (Columbia, April 3, 1940)
Director: James W. Horne. *Cast*: William Tracy, Granville Owens, Joyce Bryant, Allen Jung, Victor De Camp, Sheila Darcy, Dick Curtis, J. Paul Jones, Forrest Taylor, Jack Ingram.
Chapter Titles:

1. Into the Great Unknown
2. The Fang Strikes
3. The Mountain of Death
4. The Dragon Queen Threatens
5. At the Mercy of a Mob
6. The Scroll of Wealth
7. Angry Waters
8. The Tomb of Peril

9. Jungle Hurricane
10. Too Many Enemies
11. Walls of Doom
12. No Escape
13. The Fatal Mistake
14. Pyre of Death
15. The Secret of the Temple

Winners of the West (Universal, April 30, 1940)
Directors: Ford Beebe, Ray Taylor. *Cast*: Dick Foran, Anne Nagel, James Craig, Tom Fadden, Harry Woods.
Chapter Titles:

1. Redskins Ride Again
2. The Wreck at Red River Gorge
3. The Bridge of Disaster
4. Trapped by Redskins
5. Death Strikes the Trail
6. A Leap for Life
7. Thundering terror

8. The Flaming Arsenal
9. Sacrificed by Savages
10. Under Crashing Timbers
11. Bullets in the Dark
12. The Battle of Blackhawk
13. Barricade Blasted

Adventures of Red Ryder (Republic, June 28, 1940)
Directors: William Witney, John English. *Cast*: Don Barry, Noah Beery, Sr., Tommy Cook, Bob Kortman, William Farnum, Maude Pierce Allen, Vivian Coe, Hal Taliaferro, Harry Worth, Carleton Young.
Chapter Titles:

1. Murder on the Santa Fe Trail
2. Horsemen of Death
3. Trail's End
4. Water Rustlers
5. Avalanche
6. Hangman's Noose

7. Framed
8. Blazing Walls
9. Records of Doom
10. One Second to Live
11. The Devil's Marksman
12. Frontier Justice

Deadwood Dick (Columbia, July 13, 1940)
Director: James W. Horne. *Cast*: Don Douglas, Lorna Gray, Harry Harvey, Marin Sais, Lane Chandler, Jack Ingram, Charles King, Ed Cassidy, Robert Fiske, Lee Shumway.
Chapter Titles:

1. A Wild West Empire
2. Who Is the Skull?
3. Pirates of the Plains

4. The Skull Baits a Trap
5. Win Lose or Draw
6. Buried Alive

7. The Chariot of Doom
8. The Secret of Number Ten
9. The Fatal Warning
10. Framed for Murder
11. The Bucket of Death
12. A Race Against Time
13. The Arsenal of Revolt
14. Holding the Fort
15. The Deadwood Express

Junior G-Men (Universal, July 19, 1940)
Directors: Ford Beebe, John Rawlins. *Cast*: Billy Halop, Huntz Hall, Gabriel Dell, Bernard Punsley, Harris Berger, Kenneth Howell, Cy Kendall, Roger Daniels, Phillip Terry, Russell Hicks.
Chapter Titles:

1. Enemies Within
2. The Blast of Doom
3. Human Dynamite
4. Blazing Danger
5. Trapped by Traitors
6. Traitors' Treachery
7. Flaming Death
8. Hurled Through Space
9. The Plunge of Peril
10. The Toll of Treason
11. Descending Doom
12. The Power of Patriotism

King of the Royal Mounted (Republic, September 20, 1940)
Directors: William Witney, John English. *Cast*: Allan Lane, Robert Strange, Robert Kellard, Lita Conway, Herbert Rawlinson, Harry Cording, Bryant Washburn, Budd Buster, John Davidson.
Chapter Titles:

1. Man Hunt
2. Winged Death
3. Boomerang
4. Devil Doctor
5. Sabotage
6. False Ransom
7. Death Tunes In
8. Satan's Cauldron
9. Espionage
10. Blazing Guns
11. Master Spy
12. Code of the Mounted

The Green Hornet Strikes Again (Universal, October 8, 1940)
Directors: Ford Beebe, John Rawlins. *Cast*: Warren Hull, Anne Nagel, Keye Luke, Wade Boteler, William Hall, Robert Kortman, Jack Perrin.
Chapter Titles:

1. Flaming Havoc
2. The Plunge of Peril
3. The Avenging Heavens
4. A Night of Terror
5. Shattering Doom
6. The Fatal Flash
7. Death in the Clouds
8. Human Targets
9. The Tragic Crash
10. Blazing Fury
11. Thieves of the Night
12. Crashing Barriers
13. The Flaming Inferno
14. Racketeering Vultures
15. Smashing the Crime Ring

The Green Archer (Columbia, November 2, 1940)
Director: James W. Horne. *Cast*: Victor Jory, Iris Meredith, James Craven, Robert Fiske, Dorothy Fay, Forrest Taylor, Jack Ingram, Joseph Girard, Fred Kelsey, Kit Guard.
Chapter Titles:

1. Prison Bars Beckon
2. The Face at the Window
3. The Devil's Dictograph
4. Vanishing Jewels
5. The Fatal Spark
6. The Necklace of Treachery
7. The Secret Passage
8. Garr Castle Is Robbed

9. The Mirror of Treachery
10. The Dagger that Failed
11. The Flaming Arrow
12. The Devil Dogs

13. The Deceiving Microphone
14. End of Hope
15. The Green Archer Exposed

Mysterious Doctor Satan (Republic, December 13, 1940)
   Directors: William Witney, John English. *Cast*: Edward Ciannelli, Robert Wilcox, William Newell, C. Montague Shaw, Ella Neal, Dorothy Herbert, Charles Trowbridge, Jack Mulhall, Edwin Stanley.
Chapter Titles:

1. Return of the Copperhead
2. Thirteen Steps
3. Undersea Tomb
4. The Human Bomb
5. Doctor Satan's Man of Steel
6. Double Cross
7. The Monster Strikes
8. Highway of Death

9. Double Jeopardy
10. Bridge of Peril
11. Death Closes In
12. Crack-up
13. Disguised
14. The Flaming Coffin
15. Doctor Satan Strikes

1941

White Eagle (Columbia, January 4, 1941)
   Director: James W. Horne. *Cast*: Buck Jones, Dorothy Fay, Raymond Hatton, James Craven, Chief Yowlachie, Jack Ingram, Charles King, John Merton.
Chapter Titles:

1. Flaming Tepees
2. The Jail Delivery
3. The Dive into Quicksands
4. The Warning Death Knife
5. Treachery at the Stockade
6. The Gun-Cane Murder
7. The Revealing Blotter
8. Bird-calls of Deliverance

9. The Fake Telegram
10. Mystic Dots and Dashes
11. The Ear at the Window
12. The Massacre Invitation
13. The Framed-up Showdown
14. The Fake Army General
15. Treachery Downed

The Sky Raiders (Universal, January 31, 1941)
   Directors: Ford Beebe, Ray Taylor. *Cast*: Donald Woods, Billy Halop, Robert Armstrong, Kathryn Adams, Edward Ciannelli, Bill Cody, Jr.
Chapter Titles:

1. Wings of Disaster
2. Death Rides the Storm
3. The Toll of Treachery
4. Battle in the Clouds
5. The Fatal Blast
6. Stark Terror

7. Flaming Doom
8. The Plunge of Peril
9. Torturing Trials
10. Flash of Fate
11. Terror of the Storm
12. Winning Warriors

Riders of Death Valley (Universal, March 6, 1941)
   Directors: Ford Beebe, Ray Taylor. *Cast*: Dick Foran, Buck Jones, Charles Bickford, Lon Chaney, Jr., Leo Carillo, Noah Beery, Jr., Guinn "Big Boy" Williams, Jeanne Kelly, Monte Blue.
Chapter Titles:

1. Death Marks the Trail

2. The Menacing Herd

3. The Plunge of Peril
4. Flaming Fury
5. The Avalanche of Doom
6. Blood and Gold
7. Death Rides the Storm
8. Descending Doom
9. Death Holds the Reins

10. Devouring Flames
11. The Fatal Blast
12. Thundering Doom
13. Bridge of Disaster
14. A Fight to the Death
15. The Harvest of Hate

Adventures of Captain Marvel (Republic, March 28, 1941)
Directors: William Witney, John English. *Cast*: Tom Tyler, Frank Coghlan, Jr., Louise Currie, William Benedict, Reed Hadley, Robert Strange, Harry Worth, Bryant Washburn, Kenneth Duncan.
Chapter Titles:

1. Curse of the Scorpion
2. The Guillotine
3. Time Bomb
4. Death Takes the Wheel
5. The Scorpion Strikes
6. Lens of Death

7. Human Targets
8. Boomerang
9. Dead Man's Trap
10. Doom Ship
11. Valley of Death
12. Captain Marvel's Secret

The Spider Returns (Columbia, May 5, 1941)
Director: James W. Horne. *Cast*: Warren Hull, Mary Ainslee, Dave O'Brien, Joseph Girard, Kenne Duncan, Alden Chase, Corbet Harris, Bryant Washburn.
Chapter Titles:

1. The Stolen Plans
2. The Fatal Time-Bomb
3. The Secret Meeting
4. The Smoke Dream
5. The Gargoyle's Trail
6. The X-Ray Eye
7. The Radio Boomerang
8. The Mysterious Message

9. The Cup of Doom
10. The X-Ray Belt
11. Lips Sealed by Murder
12. A Money Bomb
13. Almost a Confession
14. Suspicious Telegrams
15. The Payoff

Jungle Girl (Republic, June 21, 1941)
Directors: William Witney, John English. *Cast*: Frances Gifford, Tom Neal, Gerald Mohr, Trevor Bardette, Eddie Acuff, Frank Lackteen, Tommy Cook, Robert Barron, Al Kikume, Bud Geary.
Chapter Titles:

1. Death by Voodoo
2. Queen of Beasts
3. River of Fire
4. Treachery
5. Jungle Vengeance
6. Tribal Fury
7. The Poison Dart
8. Man Trap

9. Treasure Tomb
10. Jungle Killer
11. Dangerous Secret
12. Trapped
13. Ambush
14. Diamond Trail
15. Flight to Freedom

Sea Raiders (Universal, June 30, 1941)
Directors: Ford Beebe, John Rawlins. *Cast*: Billy Halop, Huntz Hall, Gabriel Dell, Bernard Punsley, Hally Chester, William Hall, John McGuire, Mary Field, Edward Keane, Reed Hadley.
Chapter Titles:

1. The Raider Strikes
2. Flaming Torture
3. The Tragic Crash
4. The Raider Strikes Again
5. Flames of Fury
6. Blasted from the Air
7. Victims of the Storm
8. Dragged to Their Doom
9. Battling the Sea Beast
10. Periled by a Panther
11. Entombed in the Tunnel
12. Paying the Penalty

The Iron Claw (Columbia, August 11, 1941)
Director: James W. Horne. *Cast*: Charles Quigley, Joyce Bryant, Walter Sande, Forrest Taylor, Norman Willis, Alex Callam, James Metcalf, Allen Doone, Edythe Elliott.
Chapter Titles:

1. The Shaft of Doom
2. The Murderous Mirror
3. The Drop to Destiny
4. The Fatal Fuse
5. The Fiery Fall
6. The Ship Log Talks
7. The Mystic Map
8. The Perilous Pit
9. The Cul-de-sac
10. The Curse of the Cave
11. The Doctor's Bargain
12. Vapors of Evil
13. The Secret Door
14. The Evil Eye
15. The Claw's Collapse

King of the Texas Rangers (Republic, October 4, 1941)
Directors: William Witney, John English. *Cast*: Sammy Baugh, Neil Hamilton, Duncan Renaldo, Pauline Moore, Charles Trowbridge, Herbert Rawlinson, Frank Darien, Robert Davis, Monte Blue.
Chapter Titles:

1. The Fifth Column Strikes
2. Dead End
3. Manhunt
4. Trapped
5. Test Flight
6. Double Danger
7. Death Takes the Witness
8. Counterfeit Trail
9. Ambush
10. Sky Raiders
11. Trail of Death
12. Code of the Rangers

Don Winslow of the Navy (Universal, October 24, 1941)
Directors: Ford Beebe, Ray Taylor. *Cast*: Don Terry, Walter Sande, Claire Dodd, John Litel, Kurt Katch.
Chapter Titles:

1. The Human Torpedo
2. Flaming Death
3. Weapons of Horror
4. Towering Doom
5. Trapped in the Dungeon
6. Menaced by Man-Eaters
7. Bombed by the Enemy
8. The Chamber of Doom
9. Wings of Destruction
10. Fighting Fathoms Deep
11. Caught in the Caverns
12. The Scorpion Strangled

Dick Tracy vs. Crime, Inc. (Republic, December 27, 1941)
Directors: William Witney, John English. *Cast*: Ralph Byrd, Michael Owen, John Davidson, Jan Wiley, Ralph Morgan, Kenneth Harlan, John Dilson, Howard Hickman, Robert Frazer, Robert Fiske.
Chapter Titles:

1. The Fatal Hour
2. The Prisoner Vanishes
3. Doom Patrol
4. Dead Man's Trap
5. Murder at Sea
6. Besieged

7. Sea Racketeers
8. Train of Doom
9. Beheaded
10. Flaming Peril
11. Seconds to Live

12. Trial by Fire
13. The Challenge
14. Invisible Terror
15. Retribution

Holt of the Secret Service (Columbia, December 28, 1941)
Director: James W. Horne. *Cast*: Jack Holt, Evelyn Brent, C. Montague Shaw, Tristram Coffin, John Ward, Ted Adams, Joe McGuinn, Ed Hearn, Ray Parsons, George Chesebro.
Chapter Titles:

1. Chaotic Creek
2. Ramparts of Revenge
3. Illicit Wealth
4. Menaced by Fate
5. Exits to Terror
6. Deadly Doom
7. Out of the Past
8. Escape to Peril

9. Sealed in Silence
10. Named to Die
11. Ominous Warnings
12. The Stolen Signal
13. Prison of Jeopardy
14. Afire Afloat
15. Yielded Hostage

1942

Captain Midnight (Columbia, February 15, 1942)
Director: James W. Horne. *Cast*: Dave O'Brien, Dorothy Short, James Craven, Sam Edwards, Guy Wilkerson, Bryant Washburn, Luana Walters, Joseph Girard, Ray Teal, Al Ferguson.
Chapter Titles:

1. Mysterious Pilot
2. The Stolen Range Finder
3. The Captured Plane
4. Mistaken Identity
5. Ambushed Ambulance
6. Weird Waters
7. Menacing Fates
8. Shells of Evil

9. The Drop to Doom
10. The Hidden Bomb
11. Sky Terror
12. Burning Bomber
13. Death in the Cockpit
14. Scourge of Revenge
15. The Fatal Hour

Gangbusters (Universal, February 24, 1942)
Directors: Ray Taylor, Noel Smith. *Cast*: Kent Taylor, Irene Hervey, Robert Armstrong, Ralph Morgan, William Haade, Richard Davies, Joseph Crehan, Grace Cunard, Ralf Harolde.
Chapter Titles:

1. The League of Murdered Men
2. The Death Plunge
3. Murder Blockade
4. Hangman's Noose
5. Man Undercover
6. Under Crumbling Walls
7. The Water Trap

8. Murder by Proxy
9. Gang Bait
10. Mob Vengeance
11. Wanted at Headquarters
12. The Long Chance
13. Law and Order

Spy Smasher (Republic, April 4, 1942)
Director: William Witney. *Cast*: Kane Richmond, Marguerite Chapman, Sam

Flint, Tristram Coffin, Hans Schumm, Frank Corsaro, Hans Von Morhart, Georges Renavent, Robert Davis.

Chapter Titles:

1. America Beware
2. Human Target
3. Iron Coffin
4. Stratosphere Invaders
5. Descending Doom
6. The Invisible Witness
7. Secret Weapon
8. Sea Raiders
9. Highway Racketeers
10. 2700 Degrees Farenheit
11. Hero's Death
12. V ... __

Junior G-Men of the Air (Universal, May 4, 1942)

Directors: Ray Taylor, Lewis D. Collins. *Cast:* Billy Halop, Gene Reynolds, Huntz Hall, Gabriel Dell, Bernard Punsley, Lionel Atwill, Frank Albertson, Frankie Darro, Richard Lane, David Gorcey.

Chapter Titles:

1. Wings Aflame
2. The Plunge of Peril
3. Hidden Danger
4. The Tunnel of Terror
5. The Black Dragon Strikes
6. Flaming Havoc
7. The Death Mist
8. Satan Fires the Fuse
9. Satanic Sabotage
10. Trapped in a Burning 'Chute
11. Undeclared War
12. Civilian Courage Conquers

Perils of the Royal Mounted (Columbia, May 25, 1942)

Director: James W. Horne. *Cast:* Robert Stevens, Nell O'Day, Herbert Rawlinson, Kenneth MacDonald, John Elliott, Nick Thompson, Art Miles, Richard Fiske, Richard Vallin.

Chapter Titles:

1. The Totum Talks
2. The Night Raiders
3. The Water God's Revenge
4. Beware, the Vigilantes
5. The Masked Mountie
6. Underwater Gold
7. Bridge to the Sky
8. Lost in the Mine
9. Into the Trap
10. Betrayed by Law
11. Blazing Beacons
12. The Mounties' Last Chance
13. Painted White Man
14. Burned at the Stake
15. The Mountie Gets His Man

Overland Mail (Universal, June 12, 1942)

Directors: Ford Beebe, John Rawlins. *Cast:* Lon Chaney, Jr., Helen Parrish, Don Terry, Noah Beery, Jr., Bob Baker, Noah Beery, Sr.

Chapter Titles:

1. A Race with Disaster
2. Flaming Havoc
3. The Menacing Herd
4. The Bridge of Disaster
5. Hurled to the Depths
6. Death at the Stake
7. The Path of Peril
8. Imprisoned in Flames
9. Hidden Danger
10. Blazing Wagons
11. The Trail of Terror
12. In the Claws of the Cougar
13. The Frenzied Mob
14. The Toll of Treachery
15. The Mail Goes Through

Perils of Nyoka (Republic, June 27, 1942)

Director: William Witney. *Cast:* Kay Aldridge, Clayton Moore, Lorna Gray, William Benedict, Tristram Coffin, Charles Middleton, Forbes Murray, Robert Strange, John Davidson.

Chapter Titles:
1. Desert Intrigue
2. Death's Chariot
3. The Devil's Crucible
4. Ascending Doom
5. Fatal Second
6. Human Sacrifice
7. The Monster's Clutch
8. Tuareg Vengeance
9. Buried Alive
10. Treacherous Trail
11. Unknown Peril
12. Underground Tornado
13. Thundering Death
14. Blazing Barrier
15. Satan's Fury

The Adventures of Smilin' Jack (Universal, August 21, 1942)
Directors: Ray Taylor, Lewis D. Collins. *Cast:* Tom Brown, Sidney Toler, Marjorie Lord, Edgar Barrier, Rose Hobart, Turhan Bey, Keye Luke, Rico De Montez.
Chapter Titles:
1. The High Road to Doom
2. The Rising Sun Strikes
3. Attacked by Bombers
4. Knives of Vengeance
5. A Watery Grave
6. Escape by Clipper
7. Fifteen Fathoms Below
8. Treachery at Sea
9. The Bridge of Peril
10. Blackout in the Islands
11. Held for Treason
12. The Torture Fire Test
13. Sinking the Rising Sun

The Secret Code (Columbia, September 4, 1942)
Director: Spencer G. Bennet. *Cast:* Paul Kelly, Anne Nagel, Clancy Cooper, Trevor Bardette, Robert O. Davis, Gregory Gay, Louis Donath, Ed Parker, Beal Wong, Jackie Dalya.
Chapter Titles:
1. Enemy Passport
2. The Shadow of the Swastika
3. Nerve Gas
4. The Sea Spy Strikes
5. Wireless Warning
6. Flaming Oil
7. Submarine Signal
8. The Missing Key
9. The Radio Bomb
10. Blind Bombardment
11. Ears of the Enemy
12. Scourge of the Orient
13. Pawn of the Spy Ring
14. Dead Men of the Deep
15. The Secret Code Smashed

King of the Mounties (Republic, October 17, 1942)
Director: William Witney. *Cast:* Allan Lane, Gilbert Emery, Russell Hicks, Peggy Drake, George Irving, Abner Biberman, William Vaughn, Nestor Paiva, Anthony Warde.
Chapter Titles:
1. Phantom Invaders
2. Road to Death
3. Human Target
4. Railroad Saboteurs
5. Suicide Dive
6. Blazing Barrier
7. Perilous Plunge
8. Electrocuted
9. Reign of Terror
10. The Flying Coffin
11. Deliberate Murder
12. On to Victory

The Valley of Vanishing Men (Columbia, December 17, 1942)
Director: Spencer G. Bennet. *Cast:* Bill Elliott, Carmen Morales, Kenneth MacDonald, Slim Summerville, Jack Ingram, George Chesebro, John Shay, Tom London, Arno Frey, Julian Rivero.

Chapter Titles:

1. Trouble in Canyon City
2. The Mystery of Ghost Town
3. Danger Walks by Night
4. Hillside Horror
5. Guns in the Night
6. The Bottomless Well
7. The Man in the Gold Mask
8. When the Devil Drives
9. The Traitor's Shroud
10. Death Strikes at Seven
11. Satan in the Saddle
12. The Mine of Missing Men
13. Danger on Dome Rock
14. The Door that Has No Key
15. Empire's End

Don Winslow of the Coast Guard (Universal, December 22, 1942)
Directors: Ray Taylor, Lewis D. Collins. *Cast:* Don Terry, Walter Sande, Elyse Knox, Philip Ahn, June Duprez, Lionel Royce, Nestor Paiva.
Chapter Titles:

1. Trapped in the Blazing Sea
2. Battling a U-Boat
3. The Crash in the Clouds
4. The Scorpion Strikes
5. A Flaming Target
6. Ramming the Submarine
7. Bombed in the Ocean Depths
8. Blackout Treachery
9. The Torpedo Strikes
10. Blasted from the Skies
11. A Fight to the Death
12. The Death Trap
13. Capturing the Scorpion

1943

G-Men vs. the Black Dragon (Republic, January 16, 1943)
Director: William Witney. *Cast:* Rod Cameron, Roland Got, Constance Worth, Nino Pipitone, Noel Cravat, George J. Lewis, Maxine Doyle, C. Montague Shaw, Forbes Murray.
Chapter Titles:

1. The Yellow Peril
2. Japanese Inquisition
3. Arsenal of Doom
4. Deadly Sorcery
5. Celestial Murder
6. Death and Destruction
7. The Iron Monster
8. Beast of Tokyo
9. Watery Grave
10. The Dragon Strikes
11. Suicide Mission
12. Dead on Arrival
13. Condemned Cargo
14. Flaming Coffin
15. Democracy in Action

Daredevils of the West (Republic, May 1, 1943)
Director: John English. *Cast:* Allan Lane, Kay Aldridge, Eddie Acuff, William Haade, Robert Frazer, Ted Adams, George Lewis, Stanley Andrews, Jack Rockwell, Kenne Duncan.
Chapter Titles:

1. Valley of Death
2. Flaming Prison
3. The Killer Strikes
4. Tunnel of Terror
5. Fiery Tomb
6. Redskin Raiders
7. Perilous Pursuit
8. Dance of Doom
9. Terror Trail
10. Suicide Showdown
11. Cavern of Cremation
12. Frontier Justice

Batman (Columbia, July 16, 1943)
Director: Lambert Hillyer. *Cast:* Lewis Wilson, Douglas Croft, J. Carroll Naish,

Shirley Patterson.

Chapter Titles:

1. The Electrical Brain
2. The Bat's Cave
3. The Mark of the Zombies
4. Slaves of the Rising Sun
5. The Living Corpse
6. Poison Peril
7. The Phoney Doctor
8. Lured by Radium
9. The Sign of the Sphinx
10. Flying Spies
11. A Nipponese Trap
12. Embers of Evil
13. Eight Steps Down
14. The Executioner Strikes
15. The Doom of the Rising Sun

Secret Service in Darkest Africa (Republic, August 6, 1943)

Director: Spencer G. Bennet. *Cast:* Rod Cameron, Joan Marsh, Duncan Renaldo, Lionel Royce, Kurt Krueger, Frederic Brun, Sigurd Tor, Kurt Katch, Ralf Harolde, William Vaughn.

Chapter Titles:

1. North African Intrigue
2. The Charred Witness
3. Double Death
4. The Open Grave
5. Cloaked in Flame
6. Dial of Doom
7. Murder Dungeon
8. Funeral Arrangements Completed
9. Invisible Menace
10. Racing Peril
11. Lightning Terror
12. Ceremonial Execution
13. Fatal Leap
14. Victim of Villainy
15. Nazi Treachery Unmasked

Adventures of the Flying Cadets (Universal, August 20, 1943)

Directors: Ray Taylor, Lewis D. Collins. *Cast:* Robert Armstrong, Bobby Jordan, Johnny Downs, Jennifer Holt, Eduardo Ciannelli, Regis Toomey, Billy Benedict.

Chapter Titles:

1. The Black Hangman Strikes
2. Menaced by Murderers
3. Into the Flames
4. The Door to Death
5. Crashed in a Crater
6. Rendezvous with Doom
7. Gestapo Execution
8. Masters of Treachery
9. Wings of Destruction
10. Caught in the Caves of An-Kar-Ban
11. Hostages for Treason
12. The Black Hangman Strikes Again
13. The Toll of Treason

The Masked Marvel (Republic, November 6, 1943)

Director: Spencer G. Bennet. *Cast:* William Forrest, Louise Currie, Johnny Arthur, Rod Bacon, Richard Clarke, Anthony Warde, David Bacon, Bill Healy, Howard Hickman, Kenneth Harlan.

Chapter Titles:

1. The Masked Crusader
2. Death Takes the Helm
3. Drive to Doom
4. Suspense at Midnight
5. Murder Meter
6. Exit to Eternity
7. Doorway to Destruction
8. Destined to Die
9. Danger Express
10. Suicide Sacrifice
11. The Fatal Mistake
12. The Man Behind the Mask

The Phantom (Columbia, December 24, 1943)

Director: B. Reeves Eason. *Cast:* Tom Tyler, Jeanne Bates, Ernie Adams, Ace the Wonder Dog, Kenneth MacDonald, Frank Shannon, Guy Kingsford, Joe Devlin, John S. Bagni.

Chapter Titles:

1. The Sign of the Skull
2. The Man Who Never Dies
3. A Traitor's Code
4. The Seat of Judgement
5. The Ghost Who Walks
6. Jungle Whispers
7. The Mystery Well
8. In Quest of the Keys
9. The Fire Princess
10. The Chamber of Death
11. The Emerald Key
12. The Fangs of the Beast
13. The Road to Zoloz
14. The Lost City
15. Peace in the Jungle

Captain America (Republic, December 31, 1943)

Directors: John English, Elmer Clifton. *Cast:* Dick Purcell, Lorna Gray, Lionel Atwill, Charles Trowbridge, Russell Hicks, George J. Lewis, John Davidson, Norman Nesbitt, Frank Reicher.

Chapter Titles:

1. The Purple Death
2. Mechanical Executioner
3. The Scarlet Shroud
4. Preview of Murder
5. Blade of Wrath
6. Vault of Vengeance
7. Wholesale Destruction
8. Cremation in the Clouds
9. Triple Tragedy
10. The Avenging Corpse
11. The Dead Man Returns
12. Horror on the Highway
13. Skyscraper Plunge
14. The Scarab Strikes
15. The Toll of Doom

1944

The Great Alaskan Mystery (Universal, April 18, 1944)

Directors: Ray Taylor, Lewis D. Collins. *Cast:* Milburn Stone, Marjorie Weaver, Ralph Morgan, Fuzzy Knight, Edgar Kennedy, Joseph Crehan, Edward Gargan, Martin Kosleck.

Chapter Titles:

1. Shipwrecked Among Icebergs
2. Thundering Doom
3. Battle in the Clouds
4. Masked Murder
5. The Bridge of Disaster
6. Shattering Doom
7. Crashing Timbers
8. In a Flaming Plane
9. Hurtling Through Space
10. Tricked by a Booby Trap
11. The Tunnel of Terror
12. Electrocuted
13. The Boomerang

The Tiger Woman (Republic, May 8, 1944)

Directors: Spencer G. Bennet, Wallace Grissell. *Cast:* Linda Stirling, Allan Lane, Duncan Renaldo, George J. Lewis, Leroy Mason, Crane Whitley, Robert Frazer, Rico De Montez, Stanley Price.

Chapter Titles:

1. The Temple of Terror
2. Doorway to Death
3. Cathedral of Carnage
4. Echo of Eternity
5. Two Shall Die
6. Dungeon of the Doomed
7. Mile-a-Minute Murder
8. Passage to Peril
9. Cruise to Cremation
10. Target for Murder
11. The House of Horror
12. Triumph Over Treachery

The Desert Hawk (Columbia, July 7, 1944)
  Director: B. Reeves Eason. *Cast*: Gilbert Roland, Mona Maris, Ben Welden, Kenneth MacDonald, Frank Lackteen, I. Stanford Jolley, Charles Middleton, Egon Brecher.
Chapter Titles:

1. The Twin Brothers
2. The Evil Eye
3. The Mark of the Scimitar
4. A Caliph's Treachery
5. The Secret of the Palace
6. The Feast of the Beggars
7. Double Jeopardy
8. The Slave Traders
9. The Underground River
10. The Fateful Wheel
11. The Mystery of the Mosque
12. The Hand of Vengeance
13. Swords of Fate
14. The Wizard's Story
15. The Triumph of Kasim

Raiders of Ghost City (Universal, July 28, 1944)
  Directors: Ray Taylor, Lewis D. Collins. *Cast*: Dennis Moore, Wanda McKay, Lionel Atwill, Regis Toomey, Virginia Christine, Joe Sawyer, Edmund Cobb.
Chapter Titles:

1. Murder by Accident
2. Flaming Treachery
3. Death Rides Double
4. Ghost City Terror
5. The Fatal Lariat
6. Water Rising
7. Bullet Avalanche
8. Death Laughs Last
9. Cold Steel
10. Showdown
11. The Trail to Torture
12. Calling all Buckboards
13. Golden Vengeance

Haunted Harbor (Republic, August 18, 1944)
  Directors: Spencer G. Bennet, Wallace Grissell. *Cast*: Kane Richmond, Kay Aldridge, Roy Barcroft, Clancy Cooper, Marshall J. Reed, Oscar O'Shea, Forrest Taylor, Hal Taliaferro, George J. Lewis
Chapter Titles:

1. Wanted for Murder
2. Flight to Danger
3. Ladder of Death
4. The Unknown Assassin
5. Harbor of Horror
6. Return of the Fugitive
7. Journey into Peril
8. Wings of Doom
9. Death's Door
10. Crimson Sacrifice
11. Jungle Jeopardy
12. Fire Trap
13. Monsters of the Deep
14. High Voltage
15. Crucible of Justice

The Mystery of the Riverboat (Universal, October 5, 1944)
  Directors: Ray Taylor, Lewis D. Collins. *Cast*: Robert Lowery, Marjorie Clements, Lyle Talbot, Eddie Quillan, Francis MacDonald, Arthur Hohl, Mantan Moreland.
Chapter Titles:

1. The Tragic Crash
2. The Phantom Killer
3. The Flaming Inferno
4. The Brink of Doom
5. The Highway of Peril
6. The Fatal Plunge
7. The Toll of the Storm
8. The Break in the Levee
9. Trapped in the Quicksands
10. Flaming Havoc
11. Electrocuted
12. Risking Death
13. The Boomerang

Black Arrow (Columbia, October 20, 1944)
Directors: Lew Landers, B. Reeves Eason. *Cast*: Robert Scott, Adele Jergens, Robert Williams, Kenneth MacDonald, Charles Middleton, Martin Garralaga, George J. Lewis, I. Stanford Jolley.
Chapter Titles:

1. The City of Gold
2. Signal of Fear
3. The Seal of Doom
4. Terror of the Badlands
5. The Secret of the Vault
6. Appointment with Death
7. The Chamber of Horror
8. The Vanishing Dagger
9. Escape from Death
10. The Gold Cache
11. The Curse of the Killer
12. Test by Torture
13. The Sign of Evil
14. An Indian's Revenge
15. Black Arrow Triumphs

Zorro's Black Whip (Republic, November 15, 1944)
Directors: Spencer G. Bennet, Wallace Grissell. *Cast*: Linda Stirling, George J. Lewis, Lucien Littlefield, Francis MacDonald, Hal Taliaferro, John Merton, John Hamilton, Tom Chatterton, Tom London.
Chapter Titles:

1. The Masked Avenger
2. Tomb of Terror
3. Mob Murder
4. Detour to Death
5. Take Off that Mask
6. Fatal Gold
7. Wolf Pack
8. The Invisible Victim
9. Avalanche
10. Fangs of Doom
11. Flaming Juggernaut
12. Trail of Tyranny

1945

Jungle Queen (Universal, January 5, 1945)
Directors: Ray Taylor, Lewis D. Collins. *Cast*: Lois Collier, Ruth Roman, Douglas Dumbrille, Edward Norris, Eddie Quillan, Napoleon Simpson, Tala Birell, Clarence Muse.
Chapter Titles:

1. Invitation to Danger
2. Jungle Sacrifice
3. The Flaming Mountain
4. Wildcat Stampede
5. The Burning Jungle
6. Danger Ship
7. Trip-wire Murder
8. The Mortar Bomb
9. Death Watch
10. Execution Chamber
11. The Trail to Doom
12. Dragged Under
13. The Secret of the Sword

Manhunt of Mystery Island (Republic, January 13, 1945)
Directors: Spencer G. Bennet, Wallace Grissell, Yakima Canutt. *Cast*: Richard Bailey, Linda Stirling, Roy Barcroft, Kenne Duncan, Forrest Taylor, Forbes Murray, Jack Ingram, Harry Strang, Ed Cassidy.
Chapter Titles:

1. Secret Weapon
2. Satan's Web
3. The Murder Machine
4. The Lethal Chamber
5. Mephisto's Mantrap
6. Ocean Tomb
7. The Death Trap
8. Bombs Away
9. The Fatal Flood
10. The Sable Shroud

11. Satan's Shadow
12. Cauldron of Cremation
13. Bridge to Eternity

14. Power Dive to Doom
15. Fatal Transformation

Brenda Starr, Reporter (Columbia, January 26, 1945)
 Director: Wallace W. Fox. *Cast*: Joan Woodbury, Kane Richmond, Douglas Fowley, Syd Saylor, Joe Devlin, George Meeker, Wheeler Oakman, Cay Forester, Marion Burns, Jack Ingram.
Chapter Titles:
1. Hot News
2. The Blazing Trap
3. Taken for a Ride
4. A Ghost Walks
5. The Big Boss Speaks
6. Man Hunt
7. Hideout of Terror

8. Killer at Large
9. Dark Magic
10. A Double-cross Backfires
11. On the Spot
12. Murder at Night
13. The Mystery of the Payroll

The Master Key (Universal, April 18, 1945)
 Directors: Ray Taylor, Lewis D. Collins. *Cast*: Milburn Stone, Jan Wiley, Dennis Moore, Alfred La Rue, Maris Wrixon, Addison Richards, Russell Hicks.
Chapter Titles:
1. Trapped by Flames
2. Death Turns the Wheel
3. Ticket to Disaster
4. Drawbridge Danger
5. Runaway Car
6. Shot Down
7. Death on the Dial

8. Bullet Serenade
9. On Stage for Murder
10. Fatal Masquerade
11. Crash Curve
12. Lightning Underground
13. The Last Key

The Monster and the Ape (Columbia, April 20, 1945)
 Director: Howard Bretherton. *Cast*: Robert Lowery, George MacReady, Carole Mathews, Ralph Morgan, Willie Best, Jack Ingram, Anthony Warde, Ted Mapes, Eddie Parker, Kit Guard.
Chapter Titles:
1. The Mechanical Terror
2. The Edge of Doom
3. Flames of Fate
4. The Fatal Search
5. Rocks of Doom
6. A Friend in Disguise
7. A Scream in the Night
8. Death in the Dark

9. The Secret Tunnel
10. Forty Thousand Volts
11. The Mad Professor
12. Shadows of Destiny
13. The Gorilla at Large
14. His Last Flight
15. Justice Triumphs

Federal Operator 99 (Republic, June 4, 1945)
 Directors: Spencer G. Bennet, Wallace Grissell, Yakima Canutt. *Cast*: Marten Lamont, Helen Talbot, George J. Lewis, Lorna Gray, Hal Taliaferro, Leroy Mason, Bill Stevens, Maurice Cass, Forrest Taylor, Jay Novello.
Chapter Titles:
1. The Case of the Crown Jewels
2. The Case of the Stolen Ransom
3. The Case of the Lawful Counterfeit
4. The Case of the Telephone Code

5. The Case of the Missing Expert
6. The Case of the Double Trap
7. The Case of the Golden Car
8. The Case of the Invulnerable Criminal

9. The Case of the Torn Blueprint
10. The Case of the Hidden Witness

11. The Case of the Stradivarius
12. The Case of the Musical Clue

Secret Agent X-9 (Universal, July 30, 1945)
Directors: Ray Taylor, Lewis D. Collins. *Cast*: Lloyd Bridges, Keye Luke, Victoria Horne, Jan Wiley, Samuel S. Hinds, Edmund cobb, Cy Kendall.
Chapter Titles:

1. Torpedo Rendezvous
2. Ringed by Fire
3. Death Curve
4. Floodlight Murder
5. Doom Downgrade
6. Strafed by a Zero
7. High Pressure Deadline

8. The Dropping Floor
9. The Danger Point
10. Japanese Burial
11. Fireworks for Deadmen
12. Big Gun Fusillade
13. Zero Minute

The Purple Monster Strikes (Republic, August 3, 1945)
Directors: Spencer G. Bennet, Fred Brannon. *Cast*: Dennis Moore, Linda Stirling, Roy Barcroft, James Craven, Bud Geary, Mary Moore, John Davidson, Joe Whitehead, Emmett Vogan, Kenne Duncan.
Chapter Titles:

1. The Man in the Meteor
2. The Time Trap
3. Flaming Avalance
4. The Lethal Pit
5. Death on the Beam
6. The Demon Killer
7. The Evil Eye
8. Descending Doom

9. The Living Dead
10. House of Horror
11. Menace from Mars
12. Perilous Plunge
13. Fiery Shroud
14. The Fatal Trial
15. Take-off to Destruction

Jungle Raiders (Columbia, September 14, 1945)
Director: Lesley Selander. *Cast*: Kane Richmond, Eddie Quillan, Veda Ann Borg, Carol Hughes, Janet Shaw, John Elliott, Jack Ingram, Charles King, Ernie Adams, I. Stanford Jolley.
Chapter Titles:

1. Mystery of the Lost Tribe
2. Primitive Sacrifice
3. Prisoners of Fate
4. Valley of Destruction
5. Perilous Mission
6. Into the Valley of Fire
7. Devil's Brew
8. The Dagger Pit

9. Jungle Jeopardy
10. Prisoners of Peril
11. Vengeance of Zara
12. The Key to Arzec
13. Witch Doctor's Treachery
14. The Judgement of Rana
15. The Jewels of Arzec

The Royal Mounted Rides Again (Universal, October 25, 1945)
Directors: Ray Taylor, Lewis D. Collins. *Cast*: Bill Kennedy, Daun Kennedy, Milburn Stone, George Dolenz, Robert Armstrong, Tom Fadden, Paul E. Burns, Addison Richards.
Chapter Titles:

1. Canaska Gold
2. The Avalanche Trap
3. River on Fire
4. Skyline Target

5. Murder Toboggan
6. Ore Car Accident
7. Buckboard Runaway
8. Thundering Water

9. Dead Men for Decoys
10. Derringer Death
11. Night Trail Danger

12. Twenty Dollar Double Cross
13. Flaming Showdown

The Phantom Rider (Republic, October 26, 1945)
Directors: Spencer G. Bennet, Fred Brannon. *Cast*: Robert Kent, Peggy Stewart, Leroy Mason, Hal Taliaferro, George J. Lewis, Kenne Duncan, Chief Thundercloud, Monte Hale, Tom London, Roy Barcroft.
Chapter Titles:
1. The Avenging Spirit
2. Flaming Ambush
3. Hoofs of Doom
4. Murder Masquerade
5. Flying Fury
6. Blazing Peril

7. Gauntlet of Guns
8. Behind the Mask
9. The Captive Chief
10. Beasts at Bay
11. The Death House
12. The Last Stand

Who's Guilty? (Columbia, December 13, 1945)
Directors: Howard Bretherton, Wallace Grissell. *Cast*: Robert Kent, Amelita Ward, Tim Ryan, Jayne Hazard, Minerva Urecal, Belle Mitchell, Charles Middleton, Davison Clark, Sam Flint, Jack Ingram.
Chapter Titles:
1. Avenging Visitor
2. The Unknown Strikes
3. Held for Murder
4. A Killer at Bay
5. Human Bait
6. The Plunge of Doom
7. A Date with Fate
8. Invisible Hands

9. Fate's Vengeance
10. The Unknown Killer
11. Riding to Oblivion
12. The Tank of Terror
13. White Terror
14. A Cry in the Night
15. The Guilty One

1946

The Scarlet Horseman (Universal, January 30, 1946)
Directors: Ray Taylor, Lewis D. Collins. *Cast*: Paul Guilfoyle, Peter Cookson, Janet Shaw, Victoria Horne, Virginia Christine, Danny Morton, Fred Coby, Jack Ingram, Ed Cobb, Cy Kendall.
Chapter Titles:
1. Scarlet for a Champion
2. Dry Grass Danger
3. Railroad Rescue
4. Staked Plains Stampede
5. Death Shifts Passengers
6. Stop that Stage
7. Blunderbuss Broadside

8. Scarlet Doublecross
9. Doom Beyond the Door
10. The Edge of Danger
11. Comanche Avalanche
12. Staked Plains Massacre
13. Scarlet Showdown

King of the Forest Rangers (Republic, February 19, 1946)
Directors: Spencer G. Bennet, Fred Brannon. *Cast*: Larry Thompson, Helen Talbot, Stuart Hamblen, Anthony Warde, Leroy Mason, Scott Elliott, Tom London, Walter Soderling, Bud Geary, Harry Strang.
Chapter Titles:
1. The Mystery of the Towers

2. Shattered Evidence

3. Terror by Night
4. Deluge of Destruction
5. Pursuit into Peril
6. Brink of Doom
7. Design for Murder

8. The Flying Coffin
9. S.O.S. Ranger
10. The Death Detector
11. The Flaming Pit
12. Tower of Vengeance

Hop Harrigan (Columbia, March 24, 1946)
Director: Derwin Abrahams. *Cast*: William Bakewell, Jennifer Holt, Robert Henry, Sumner Getchell, Emmett Vogan, Claire James, John Merton, Wheeler Oakman, Ernie Adams.
Chapter Titles:

1. A Mad Mission
2. The Secret Ray
3. The Mystery Plane
4. Plunging Peril
5. Betrayed by a Madman
6. A Flaming Trap
7. One Chance for Life
8. White Fumes of Fate

9. Dr. Tobor's Revenge
10. Juggernaut of Fate
11. Flying to Oblivion
12. Lost in the Skies
13. No Escape
14. The Chute that Failed
15. The Fate of the World

Lost City of the Jungle (Universal, May 10, 1946)
Directors: Ray Taylor, Lewis D. Collins. *Cast*: Russell Hayden, Jane Adams, Lionel Atwill, Keye Luke, John Miljan, John Eldredge, John Gallaudet.
Chapter Titles:

1. Himalaya Horror
2. The Death Flood
3. Wave Length for Doom
4. The Pit of Pendrang
5. Fiery Danger
6. Death's Shining Face
7. Speedboat Missing

8. Fire Jet Torture
9. Zalabor Death Watch
10. Booby Trap Rendezvous
11. Pendrang Guillotine
12. Jungle Smash-up
13. Atomic Vengeance

The Daughter of Don Q (Republic, June 4, 1946)
Directors: Spencer G. Bennet, Fred Brannon. *Cast*: Adrian Booth, Kirk Alyn, Leroy Mason, Roy Barcroft, Claire Meade, Kernan Cripps, Jimmy Ames, Eddie Parker, Tom Steele, Dale Van Sickel.
Chapter Titles:

1. Multiple Murder
2. Vendetta
3. Under the Knives
4. Race to Destruction
5. Blackout
6. Forged Evidence

7. Execution by Error
8. Window to Death
9. The Juggernaut
10. Cremation
11. Glass Guillotine
12. Dead Man's Vengeance

Chick Carter, Detective (Columbia, July 11, 1946)
Director: Derwin Abrahams. *Cast*: Lyle Talbot, Douglas Fowley, Julie Gibson, Pamela Blake, Eddie Acuff, Robert Elliott, George Meeker, Leonard Penn, Charles King, Jack Ingram.
Chapter Titles:

1. Chick Carter Takes Over
2. Jump to Eternity
3. Grinding Wheels

4. Chick Carter Trapped
5. Out of Control
6. Chick Carter's Quest

7. Chick Carter's Frame-up
8. Chick Carter Gives Chase
9. Shadows in the Night
10. Run to Earth
11. Hurled Into Space

12. Chick Carter Faces Death
13. Rendezvous with Murder
14. Chick Carter Sets a Trap
15. Chick Carter Wins Out

The Mysterious Mr. M (Universal, August 1, 1946)
Directors: Lewis D. Collins, Vernon Keays. *Cast*: Richard Martin, Pamela Blake, Dennis Moore, Virginia Brissac, Danny Morton, Edmund MacDonald, Byron Foulger, Jane Randolph, Jack Ingram.
Chapter Titles:

1. When Clocks Chime Death
2. Danger Downward
3. Flood of Flames
4. The Double Trap
5. Highway Execution
6. Heavier than Water
7. Strange Collision

8. When Friend Kills Friend
9. Parachute Peril
10. The Human Time-bomb
11. The Key to Murder
12. High-line Smash-up
13. The Real Mr. M

The Crimson Ghost (Republic, August 2, 1946)
Directors: William Witney, Fred Brannon. *Cast*: Charles Quigley, Linda Stirling, Clayton Moore, I. Stanford Jolley, Kenne Duncan, Forrest Taylor, Emmett Vogan, Sam Flint, Joe Forte.
Chapter Titles:

1. Atomic Peril
2. Thunderbolt
3. The Fatal Sacrifice
4. The Laughing Skull
5. Flaming Death
6. Mystery of the Mountain

7. Electrocution
8. The Slave Collar
9. Blazing Fury
10. The Trap that Failed
11. Double Murder
12. The Invisible Trail

Son of the Guardsman (Columbia, October 24, 1946)
Director: Derwin Abrahams. *Cast*: Robert Shaw, Daun Kennedy, Robert "Buzz" Henry, Jim Diehl, Hugh Prosser, Leonard Penn, Wheeler Oakman, Charles King, John Merton, Ray Bennett.
Chapter Titles:

1. Outlaws of Sherwood Forest
2. Perils of the Forest
3. Blazing Barrier
4. The Siege of Bullard Hall
5. A Dagger in the Dark
6. A Fight for Freedom
7. Trial by Torture
8. Mark Crowell's Treachery

9. Crushed to Earth
10. A Throne at Stake
11. Double Danger
12. The Secret of the Treasure
13. Into the Depths
14. The Lost Heritage
15. Free Men Triumph

1947

Jack Armstrong (Columbia, February 6, 1947)
Director: Wallace Fox. *Cast*: John Hart, Rosemary La Planche, Joe Brown, Jr., Claire James, Pierre Watkin, Wheeler Oakman, Jack Ingram, Eddie Parker, John Merton.

Chapter Titles:

1. Mystery of the Cosmic Ray
2. The Far World
3. Island of Deception
4. Into the Chasm
5. The Space Ship
6. Tunnels of Treachery
7. Cavern of Chance
8. The Secret Room

9. Human Targets
10. Battle of the Warriors
11. Cosmic Annihilator
12. The Grotto of Greed
13. Wheels of Fate
14. Journey into Fate
15. Retribution

The Vigilante (Columbia, May 22, 1947)
    Director: Wallace Fox. *Cast*: Ralph Byrd, Ramsey Ames, George Offerman, Jr., Lyle Talbot, Robert Barron, Frank Marlo, Hugh Prosser, Jack Ingram, Eddie Parker, George Chesebro.
Chapter Titles:

1. The Vigilante Rides Again
2. Mystery of the White Horses
3. Double Peril
4. Desperate Flight
5. In the Gorilla's Cage
6. Battling the Unknown
7. Midnight Rendezvous
8. Blasted to Eternity

9. The Fatal Flood
10. Danger Ahead
11. X-1 Closes In
12. Death Rides the Rails
13. The Trap that Failed
14. Closing In
15. The Secret of the Skyroom

The Son of Zorro (Republic, June 2, 1947)
    Directors: Spencer G. Bennet, Fred Brannon. *Cast*: George Turner, Peggy Stewart, Roy Barcroft, Edward Cassidy, Ernie Adams, Stanley Price, Tom London, Edmund Cobb, Ken Terrell, Fred Graham.
Chapter Titles:

1. Outlaw County
2. The Deadly Millstone
3. Fugitive from Injustice
4. Buried Alive
5. Water Trap
6. Volley of Death
7. The Fatal Records

8. Third Degree
9. Shoot to Kill
10. Den of the Beast
11. The Devil's Trap
12. Blazing Walls
13. Checkmate

Jesse James Rides Again (Republic, June 2, 1947)
    Directors: Fred Brannon, Thomas Carr. *Cast*: Clayton Moore, Linda Stirling, Roy Barcroft, John Compton, Tristram Coffin, Tom London, Holly Bane, Edmund Cobb, Gene Stutenroth, Leroy Mason.
Chapter Titles:

1. The Black Raiders
2. Signal for Action
3. The Stacked Deck
4. Concealed Evidence
5. The Corpse of Jesse James
6. The Traitor
7. Talk or Die

8. Boomerang
9. The Captured Raider
10. The Revealing Torch
11. The Spy
12. Black Gold
13. Deadline at Midnight

The Black Widow (Republic, July 28, 1947)
    Directors: Spencer G. Bennet, Fred Brannon. *Cast*: Bruce Edwards, Virginia

Lindley, Carol Foreman, Anthony Warde, Ramsey Ames, I. Stanford Jolley, Theodore Gottlieb, Virginia Carroll.

Chapter Titles:

1. Deadly Prophecy
2. The Stolen Formula
3. Hidden Death
4. Peril in the Sky
5. The Spider's Lair
6. The Glass Guillotine
7. Wheels of Death
8. False Information
9. The Spider's Venom
10. The Stolen Corpse
11. Death Dials a Number
12. The Talking Mirror
13. A Life for a Life

The Sea Hound (Columbia, September 11, 1947)

Directors: Walter B. Eason, Mack V. Wright. *Cast*: Larry "Buster" Crabbe, Pamela Blake, Jimmy Lloyd, Ralph Hodges, Spencer Chan, Robert Barron, Hugh Prosser, Rick Vallin, Jack Ingram, Milt Kibbee.

Chapter Titles:

1. Captain Silver Sails Again
2. Spanish Gold
3. The Mystery of the Map
4. Menaced by Ryaks
5. Captain Silver's Strategy
6. The Sea Hound at Bay
7. Rand's Treachery
8. In the Admiral's Lair
9. On the Water Wheel
10. On the Treasure Trail
11. The Sea Hound Attacked
12. Dangerous Waters
13. The Panther's Prey
14. The Fatal Double-cross
15. Captain Silver's Last Stand

G-Men Never Forget (Republic, November 13, 1947)

Directors: Fred Brannon, Yakima Canutt. *Cast*: Clayton Moore, Roy Barcroft, Ramsey Ames, Drew Allen, Tom Steele, Dale Van Sickel, Edmund Cobb, Stanley Price, Jack O'Shea, Barry Brooks.

Chapter Titles:

1. Death Rides the Torrent
2. The Flaming Doll House
3. Code Six-Four-Five
4. Shipyard Saboteurs
5. The Dead Man Speaks
6. Marked Money
7. Hot Cargo
8. The Fatal Letter
9. The Death Wind
10. The Innocent Victim
11. Counter-plot
12. Exposed

1948

Brick Bradford (Columbia, January 5, 1948)

Directors: Spencer G. Bennet, Thomas Carr. *Cast*: Kane Richmond, Linda Johnson, Pierre Watkin, Rick Vallin, Charles Quigley, Jack Ingram, Fred Graham, John Merton, Leonard Penn, Charles King.

Chapter Titles:

1. Atomic Defense
2. Flight to the Moon
3. Prisoners to the Moon
4. Into the Volcano
5. Bradford at Bay
6. Back to Earth
7. Into Another Century
8. Buried Treasure
9. Trapped in the Time Top
10. The Unseen Hand
11. Poison Gas
12. Door of Disaster
13. Sinister Rendezvous
14. River of Revenge
15. For the Peace of the World

Dangers of the Canadian Mounted (Republic, February 17, 1948)
Directors: Fred Brannon, Yakima Canutt. *Cast*: Jim Bannon, Virginia Belmont, Anthony Warde, Dorothy Granger, Bill Van Sickel, Tom Steele, Dale Van Sickel, I. Stanford Jolley, Phil Warren.
Chapter Titles:

1. The Legend of Genghis Khan
2. Key to the Legend
3. Ghost Town
4. Terror in the Sky
5. Pursuit
6. Stolen Cargo
7. The Fatal Shot
8. Fatal Testimony
9. The Prisoner Spy
10. The Secret Meeting
11. Secret of the Altar
12. Liquid Jewels

Tex Granger (Columbia, April 1, 1948)
Director: Derwin Abrahams. *Cast*: Robert Kellard, Peggy Stewart, Robert "Buzz" Henry, Duke the Wonder Dog, Smith Ballew, Jack Ingram, I. Stanford Jolley, Terry Frost, Jim Diehl.
Chapter Titles:

1. Tex Finds Trouble
2. Rider of Mystery Mesa
3. Dead or Alive
4. Dangerous Trails
5. Renegade Pass
6. A Crooked Deal
7. The Rider Unmasked
8. Mystery of the Silver Ghost
9. The Rider Trapped
10. Midnight Ambush
11. Renegade Roundup
12. Carson's Last Draw
13. Blaze Takes Over
14. Riding Wild
15. The Rider Meets Blaze

Superman (Columbia, July 15, 1948)
Directors: Spencer G. Bennet, Thomas Carr. *Cast*: Kirk Alyn, Noel Neill, Tommy Bond, Carol Foreman, Pierre Watkin, George Meeker, Jack Ingram, Terry Frost, Charles King, Charles Quigley.
Chapter Titles:

1. Superman Comes to Earth
2. Depths of the Earth
3. The Reducer Ray
4. Man of Steel
5. A Job for Superman
6. Superman in Danger
7. Into the Electric Furnace
8. Superman to the Rescue
9. Irresistible Force
10. Between Two Fires
11. Superman's Dilemma
12. Blast in the Depths
13. Hurled to Destruction
14. Superman at Bay
15. The Payoff

The Adventures of Frank and Jesse James (Republic, July 26, 1948)
Directors: Fred Brannon, Yakima Canutt. *Cast*: Clayton Moore, Steve Darrell, Noel Neill, George J. Lewis, Stanley Andrews, John Crawford, Dale Van Sickel, Tom Steele, Sam Flint.
Chapter Titles:

1. Agent of Treachery
2. The Hidden Witness
3. The Lost Tunnel
4. Blades of Death
5. Roaring Wheels
6. Passage to Danger
7. The Secret Code
8. Doomed Cargo
9. The Eyes of the Law
10. The Stolen Body
11. Suspicion
12. Talk or Die
13. Unmasked

Congo Bill (Columbia, October 12, 1948)
  Directors: Spencer G. Bennet, Thomas Carr. *Cast*: Don McGuire, Cleo Moore, Jack Ingram, I. Stanford Jolley, Leonard Penn, Nelson Leigh, Charles King, Armida, Hugh Prosser, Fred Graham.
Chapter Titles:

1. The Untamed Beast
2. Jungle Gold
3. A Hot Reception
4. Congo Bill Springs a Trap
5. White Shadows in the Jungle
6. The White Queen
7. Black Panther
8. Sinister Schemes
9. The Witch Doctor Strikes
10. Trail of Treachery
11. A Desperate Chance
12. The Lair of the Beast
13. Menace of the Jungle
14. Treasure Map
15. The Missing Letter

Federal Agents vs. Underworld, Inc. (Republic, November 12, 1948)
  Director: Fred Brannon. *Cast*: Kirk Alyn, Rosemary La Planche, Roy Barcroft, Carol Foreman, James Dale, Bruce Edwards, James Craven, Tristram Coffin, Tom Steele, Dale Van Sickel.
Chapter Titles:

1. The Golden Hands
2. The Floating Coffin
3. Death in Disguise
4. Fatal Evidence
5. The Trapped Conspirator
6. Wheels of Disaster
7. The Hidden Key
8. The Enemy's Mouthpiece
9. The Stolen Hand
10. Unmasked
11. Tombs of the Ancients
12. The Curse of Kurigal

1949

Bruce Gentry (Columbia, February 10, 1949)
  Directors: Spencer G. Bennet, Thomas Carr. *Cast*: Tom Neal, Judy Clark, Ralph Hodges, Forrest Taylor, Hugh Prosser, Tristram Coffin, Jack Ingram, Terry Frost, Eddie Parker, Charles King.
Chapter Titles:

1. The Mysterious Disc
2. The Mine of Menace
3. Fiery Furnace
4. Grade Crossing
5. Danger Trail
6. A Flight for Life
7. The Flying Disc
8. Fate Takes the Wheel
9. Hazardous Heights
10. Over the Falls
11. Gentry at Bay
12. Parachute of Peril
13. Menace of the Mesa
14. Bruce's Strategy
15. The Final Disc

Ghost of Zorro (Republic, April 12, 1949)
  Director: Fred Brannon. *Cast*: Clayton Moore, Pamela Blake, Roy Barcroft, George J. Lewis, Eugene Roth, John Crawford, I. Stanford Jolley, Steve Clark, Tom Steele, Dale Van Sickel.
Chapter Titles:

1. Bandit Territory
2. Forged Orders
3. Robber's Agent
4. Victims of Vengeance
5. Gun Trap
6. Deadline at Midnight
7. Tower of Disaster
8. Mob Justice

9. Money Lure
10. Message of Death

11. Runaway Stagecoach
12. Trail of Blood

Batman and Robin (Columbia, May 26, 1949)

Director: Spencer G. Bennet. *Cast*: Robert Lowery, Johnny Duncan, Jane Adams, Lyle Talbot, Ralph Graves, House Peters, Jr., Eric Wilton, William Fawcett, Leonard Penn, Rick Vallin.

Chapter Titles:

1. Batman Takes Over
2. Tunnel of Terror
3. Robin's Wild Ride
4. Batman Trapped
5. Robin Rescues Batman
6. Target—Robin!
7. The Fatal Blast
8. Robin Meets the Wizard

9. The Wizard Strikes Back
10. Batman's Last Chance
11. Robin's Ruse
12. Robin Rides the Wind
13. The Wizard's Challenge
14. Batman vs. Wizard
15. Batman Victorious

King of the Rocketmen (Republic, June 7, 1949)

Director: Fred Brannon. *Cast*: Tristram Coffin, Mae Clarke, Don Haggerty, House Peters, Jr., James Craven, I. Stanford Jolley, Douglas Evans, Ted Adams, Stanley Price.

Chapter Titles:

1. Dr. Vulcan—Traitor
2. Plunging Death
3. Dangerous Evidence
4. High Peril
5. Fatal Dive
6. Mystery of the Rocket Man

7. Molten Menace
8. Suicide Flight
9. Ten Seconds to Live
10. The Deadly Fog
11. Secret of Dr. Vulcan
12. Wave of Disaster

The James Brothers of Missouri (Republic, October 4, 1949)

Director: Fred Brannon. *Cast*: Keith Richards, Robert Bice, Noel Neill, Roy Barcroft, Patricia Knox, Lane Bradford, Eugene Roth, John Hamilton, Edmund Cobb, Hank Patterson.

Chapter Titles:

1. Frontier Renegades
2. Racing Peril
3. Danger Road
4. Murder at Midnight
5. Road to Oblivion
6. Missouri Manhunt

7. Hangman's Noose
8. Coffin on Wheels
9. Dead Man's Return
10. Galloping Gunslingers
11. The Haunting Past
12. Fugitive Code

The Adventures of Sir Galahad (Columbia, December 22, 1948)

Director: Spencer G. Bennet. *Cast*: George Reeves, Lois Hall, Charles King, William Fawcett, Pat Barton, Hugh Prosser, Nelson Leigh, Jim Diehl, Don Harvey, Marjorie Stapp.

Chapter Titles:

1. The Stolen Sword
2. Galahad's Daring
3. Prisoners of Ulric
4. Attack on Camelot
5. Galahad to the Rescue
6. Passage of Peril

7. Unknown Betrayer
8. Perilous Adventure
9. Treacherous Magic
10. The Sorcerer's Spell
11. Valley of No Return
12. Castle Perilous

13. The Wizard's Revenge   15. Galahad's Triumph
14. Quest for the Queen

Radar Patrol vs. Spy King (Republic, December 28, 1949)
Director: Fred Brannon. *Cast*: Kirk Alyn, Jean Dean, Anthony Warde, George J. Lewis, Eve Whitney, John Merton, Tristram Coffin, John Crawford, Dale Van Sickel, Tom Steele.
Chapter Titles:

1. The Fatal Fog   7. Electrocution
2. Perilous Trail   8. Death Rings the Phone
3. Rolling Fury   9. Tomb of Terror
4. Flight of the Spy King   10. Death Dive
5. Trapped Underground   11. Desperate Mission
6. Wheels of Disaster   12. Day of Reckoning

1950

Cody of the Pony Express (Columbia, March 4, 1950)
Director: Spencer G. Bennet. *Cast*: Jock Mahoney, Dickie Moore, Peggy Stewart, William Fawcett, George J. Lewis, Pierce Lyden, Tom London, Helena Dare, Jack Ingram, Rick Vallin.
Chapter Titles:

1. Cody Carries the Mail   9. Frontier Law
2. Captured by Indians   10. Cody Tempts Fate
3. Cody Saves a Life   11. Trouble at Silver Gap
4. Cody Follows a Trail   12. Cody Comes Through
5. Cody to the Rescue   13. Marshal of Nugget City
6. The Fatal Arrow   14. Unseen Danger
7. Cody Gets His Man   15. Cody's Last Ride
8. Renegade Raiders

The Invisible Monster (Republic, June 8, 1950)
Director: Fred Brannon. *Cast*: Richard Webb, Aline Towne, Lane Bradford, John Crawford, Stanley Price, George Meeker, Keith Richards, Dale Van Sickel, Tom Steele, David Sharpe.
Chapter Titles:

1. Slaves of the Phantom   7. Murder Train
2. The Acid Clue   8. Window of Peril
3. The Death Car   9. Trail to Destruction
4. Highway Holocaust   10. High Voltage Danger
5. Bridge to Eternity   11. Death's Highway
6. Ordeal by Fire   12. The Phantom Meets Justice

Atom Man vs. Superman (Columbia, June 19, 1950)
Directors: Spencer G. Bennet, Derwin Abrahams. *Cast*: Kirk Alyn, Noel Neill, Lyle Talbot, Tommy Bond, Pierre Watkin, Jack Ingram, Don Harvey, Terry Frost, Paul Stader, George Robotham.
Chapter Titles:

1. Superman Flies Again   4. Superman Meets Atom Man
2. Atom Man Appears   5. Atom Man Tricks Superman
3. Ablaze in the Sky   6. Atom Man's Challenge

7. At the Mercy of Atom Man
8. Into the Empty Doom
9. Superman Crashes Through
10. Atom Man's Heat Ray
11. Luthor's Strategy

12. Atom Man Strikes
13. Atom Man's Flying Saucers
14. Rocket of Vengeance
15. Superman Saves the Universe

Desperadoes of the West (Republic, August 17, 1950)
Director: Fred Brannon. *Cast*: Richard Powers, Judy Clark, Roy Barcroft, I. Stanford Jolley, Lee Phelps, Lee Roberts, Cliff Clark, Edmund Cobb, Hank Patterson, Dale Van Sickel.
Chapter Titles:

1. Tower of Jeopardy
2. Perilous Barrier
3. Flaming Cargo
4. Trail of Terror
5. Plunder Cave
6. Six-gun Hi-jacker

7. The Powder Keg
8. Desperate Venture
9. Stagecoach to Eternity
10. Hidden Desperado
11. Open Warfare
12. Desperate Gamble

Pirates of the High Seas (Columbia, October 4, 1950)
Directors: Spencer G. Bennet, Thomas Carr. *Cast*: Larry "Buster" Crabbe, Lois Hall, Tommy Farrell, Gene Roth, Tristram Coffin, Neyle Morrow, Stanley Price, Hugh Prosser, William Fawcett.
Chapter Titles:

1. Mystery Mission
2. Attacked by Pirates
3. Dangerous Depths
4. Blasted to Atoms
5. The Missing Mate
6. Secret of the Ivory Case
7. Captured by Savages
8. The Vanishing Music Box

9. Booby Trap
10. Savage Snare
11. Sinister Cavern
12. Blast from the Depths
13. Cave In
14. Secret of the Music Box
15. Diamonds from the Sea

Flying Disc Man from Mars (Republic, November 30, 1950)
Director: Fred Brannon. *Cast*: Walter Reed, Lois Collier, Gregory Gay, James Craven, Harry Lauter, Richard Irving, Sandy Sanders, Michael Carr, Dale Van Sickel, Tom Steele.
Chapter Titles:

1. Menace from Mars
2. The Volcano's Secret
3. Death Rides the Stratosphere
4. Execution by Fire
5. The Living Projectile
6. Perilous Mission

7. Descending Doom
8. Suicidal Sacrifice
9. The Funeral Pyre
10. Weapons of Hate
11. Disaster on the Highway
12. Volcanic Vengeance

1951

Roar of the Iron Horse (Columbia, May 15, 1951)
Director: Spencer G. Bennet, Thomas Carr. *Cast*: Jock Mahoney, Virginia Herrick, William Fawcett, Hal Landon, Jack Ingram, Mickey Simpson, George Eldredge, Myron Healey, Rusty Westcoatt.
Chapter Titles:

1. Indian Attack
2. Captured by Redskins
3. Trapped by Outlaws
4. In the Baron's Stronghold
5. A Ride for Life
6. White Indians
7. Fumes of Fate
8. Midnight Marauders

9. Raid of the Pay Train
10. Trapped on a Trestle
11. Redskins' Revenge
12. Plunge of Peril
13. The Law Takes Over
14. When Killers Meet
15. The End of the Trail

Don Daredevil Rides Again (Republic, May 23, 1951)
Director: Fred Brannon. *Cast*: Ken Curtis, Aline Towne, Roy Barcroft, Lane Bradford, Robert Einer, John Cason, I. Stanford Jolley, Hank Patterson, Lee Phelps, Sandy Sanders.
Chapter Titles:

1. Return of the Don
2. Double Death
3. Hidden Danger
4. Retreat to Destruction
5. Cold Steel
6. The Flaming Juggernaut

7. Claim Jumper
8. Perilous Combat
9. Hostage of Destiny
10. Marked for Murder
11. The Captive Witness
12. Flames of Vengeance

Mysterious Island (Columbia, August 23, 1951)
Director: Spencer G. Bennet. *Cast*: Richard Crane, Marshall Reed, Karen Randle, Ralph Hodges, Gene Roth, Hugh Prosser, Terry Frost, Rusty West-Coatt, Leonard Penn, Bernard Hamilton.
Chapter Titles:

1. Lost in Space
2. Sinister Savages
3. Savage Justice
4. Wild Man at Large
5. Trail of the Mystery Man
6. The Pirates Attack
7. Menace of the Mercurians
8. Between Two Fires

9. Shrine of the Silver Bird
10. Fighting Fury
11. Desperate Chances
12. Mystery of the Mine
13. Jungle Deadfall
14. Men from Tomorrow
15. The Last of the Mysterious
    Island

Government Agents vs. The Phantom Legion (Republic, August 23, 1951)
Director: Fred Brannon. *Cast*: Walter Reed, Mary Ellen Kay, Dick Curtis, John Pickard, Fred Coby, Pierce Lyden, George Meeker, John Phillips, Mauritz Hugo, Edmund Cobb.
Chapter Titles:

1. River of Fire
2. The Stolen Corpse
3. The Death Drop
4. Doorway to Doom
5. Deadline for Disaster
6. Mechanical Homicide

7. The Flaming Highway
8. Sea Saboteurs
9. Peril Underground
10. Execution by Accident
11. Perilous Plunge
12. Blazing Retribution

Captain Video (Columbia, December 17, 1951)
Directors: Spencer G. Bennet, Wallace Grissell. *Cast*: Judd Holdren, Larry Stewart, George Eldredge, Gene Roth, Don Harvey, William Fawcett, Jack Ingram, I. Stanford Jolley, Skelton Knaggs.
Chapter Titles:

1. Journey into Space
2. Menace of Atoma
3. Captain Video's Peril
4. Entombed in Ice
5. Flames of Atoma
6. Astray in the Stratosphere
7. Blasted by the Atomic Eye
8. Invisible Menace
9. Video Springs a Trap
10. Menace of the Mystery Metal
11. Weapon of Destruction
12. Robot Rocket
13. Mystery of Station X
14. Vengeance of Vultura
15. Video vs. Vultura

1952

King of the Congo (Columbia, January 3, 1952)
Directors: Spencer G. Bennet, Wallace Grissell. *Cast*: Larry "Buster" Crabbe, Gloria Dea, Leonard Penn, Jack Ingram, Rusty Westcoatt, Nick Stuart, Rick Vallin, Neyle Morrow, Bart Davidson.
Chapter Titles:

1. Mission of Menace
2. Red Shadows in the Jungle
3. Into the Valley of Mist
4. Thunda Meets His Match
5. Thunda Turns the Tables
6. Thunda's Desperate Charge
7. Thunda Trapped
8. Mission of Evil
9. Menace of the Magnetic Rocks
10. Lair of the Leopard
11. An Ally from the Sky
12. Riding Wild
13. Red Raiders
14. Savage Vengeance
15. Judgement of the Jungle

Radar Men from the Moon (Republic, January 9, 1952)
Director: Fred Brannon. *Cast*: George Wallace, Aline Towne, William Bakewell, Roy Barcroft, Clayton Moore, Peter Brocco, Bob Stevenson, Don Walters, Tom Steele, Dale Van Sickel.
Chapter Titles:

1. Moon Rocket
2. Molten Terror
3. Bridge of Death
4. Flight to Destruction
5. Murder Car
6. Hills of Death
7. Human Targets
8. The Enemy Planet
9. Battle in the Stratosphere
10. Mass Execution
11. Planned Pursuit
12. Take-off to Eternity

Zombies of the Stratosphere (Republic, July 2, 1952)
Director: Fred Brannon. *Cast*: Judd Holdren, Aline Towne, Wilson Wood, Lane Bradford, John Crawford, Craig Kelly, Ray Boyle, Leonard Nimoy, Tom Steele, Dale Van Sickel.
Chapter Titles:

1. The Zombie Vanguard
2. Battle of the Rockets
3. Undersea Agents
4. Contraband Cargo
5. The Iron Executioner
6. Murder Mine
7. Death on the Waterfront
8. Hostage for Murder
9. The Human Torpedo
10. Flying Gas Chamber
11. Man vs. Monster
12. Tomb of the Traitors

Blackhawk (Columbia, July 24, 1952)
Directors: Spencer G. Bennet, Fred F. Sears. *Cast*: Kirk Alyn, Carole Foreman,

John Crawford, Michael Fox, Don Harvey, Rick Vallin, Larry Stewart, Weaver Levy, Zon Murray, Nick Stuart.

Chapter Titles:

1. Distress Call from Space
2. Blackhawk Traps a Traitor
3. In the Enemy's Hideout
4. The Iron Monster
5. Human Targets
6. Blackhawk's Leap for Life
7. Mystery Fuel
8. Blasted from the Sky
9. Blackhawk Tempts Fate
10. Chase for Element X
11. Forced Down
12. Drums of Doom
13. Blackhawk's Daring Plan
14. Blackhawk's Wild Ride
15. The Leader Unmasked

Son of Geronimo (Columbia, November 5, 1952)

Director: Spencer G. Bennet. *Cast*: Clayton Moore, Eileen Rowe, Rodd Redwing, Tommy Farrell, Bud Osborne, Marshall Reed, John Crawford, Zon Murray, Rick Vallin, Lyle Talbot.

Chapter Titles:

1. War of Vengeance
2. Running the Gauntlet
3. Stampede
4. Apache Allies
5. Indian Ambush
6. Trapped by Fire
7. A Sinister Scheme
8. Prisoners of Porico
9. On the Warpath
10. The Fight at Crystal Springs
11. A Midnight Marauder
12. Trapped in a Flaming Tepee
13. Jim Scott Tempts Fate
14. A Trap for Geronimo
15. Peace Treaty

Jungle Drums of Africa (Republic, December 19, 1952)

Director: Fred Brannon. *Cast*: Clayton Moore, Phyllis Coates, John Spencer, Roy Glenn, John Cason, Henry Rowland, Steve Mitchell, Bill Walker, Don Blackman, Felix Nelson.

Chapter Titles:

1. Jungle Ambush
2. Savage Strategy
3. The Beast-Fiend
4. Voodoo Vengeance
5. The Lion Pit
6. Underground Tornado
7. Cavern of Doom
8. The Water Trap
9. Trail to Destruction
10. The Flaming Ring
11. Bridge to Death
12. The Avenging River

1953

Gunfighters of the Northwest (Columbia, March 18, 1953)

Director: Spencer G. Bennet. *Cast*: Jock Mahoney, Clayton Moore, Phyllis Coates, Don Harvey, Marshall Reed, Rodd Redwing, Lyle Talbot, Tom Farrell, Terry Frost, Lee Roberts.

Chapter Titles:

1. A Trap for the Mounties
2. Indian War Drums
3. Between Two Fires
4. Midnight Raiders
5. Running the Gauntlet
6. Mounties at Bay
7. Plunge of Peril
8. Killer at Large
9. The Fighting Mounties
10. The Sergeant Gets His Man
11. The Fugitive Escapes
12. Stolen Gold

13. Perils of the Mounted Police
14. Surprise Attack

15. Trail's End

The Lost Planet (Columbia, May 7, 1953)
Director: Spencer G. Bennet. *Cast*: Judd Holdren, Vivian Mason, Ted Thorpe, Forrest Taylor, Gene Roth, Michael Fox, Karl Davis, Leonard Penn, John Cason, Nick Stuart.
Chapter Titles:

1. Mystery of the Guided Missile
2. Trapped by the Axial Propeller
3. Blasted by the Thermic Disintegrator
4. The Mind Control Machine
5. The Atomic Plane
6. Disaster in the Stratosphere
7. Snared by the Prysmic Catapult
8. Astray in Space
9. The Hypnotic Ray Machine
10. To Free the Planet People
11. Dr. Grood Defies Gravity
12. Trapped in a Cosmo Jet
13. The Invisible Enemy
14. In the Grip of the De-Thermo Ray
15. Sentenced to Space

Canadian Mounties vs. Atomic Invaders (Republic, June 8, 1953)
Director: Franklin Adreon. *Cast*: Bill Henry, Susan Morrow, Arthur Space, Dale Van Sickel, Pierre Watkin, Mike Ragan, Stanley Andrews, Harry Lauter, Hank Patterson, Edmund Cobb.
Chapter Titles:

1. Arctic Intrigue
2. Murder or Accident?
3. Fangs of Death
4. Underground Inferno
5. Pursuit to Destruction
6. The Boat Trap
7. Flame Versus Gun
8. Highway of Horror
9. Doomed Cargo
10. Human Quarry
11. Mechanical Homicide
12. Cavern of Revenge

The Great Adventures of Captain Kidd (Columbia, September 17, 1953)
Directors: Derwin Abbe and Charles S. Gould. *Cast*: Richard Crane, David Bruce, John Crawford, George Wallace, Lee Roberts, Paul Newlan, Nick Stuart, Terry Frost, John Hart, Marshall Reed.
Chapter Titles:

1. Pirate vs. Man-of-War
2. The Fatal Shot
3. Attacked by Captain Kidd
4. Captured by Captain Kidd
5. Mutiny on the Adventure's Galley
6. Murder on the Main Deck
7. Prisoners of War
8. Mutiny Unmasked
9. Pirate Against Pirate
10. Shot from the Parapet
11. The Flaming Fortess
12. Before the Firing Squad
13. In the Hands of the Mohawks
14. Pirate Gold
15. Captain Kidd's Last Chance

1954

Trader Tom of the China Seas (Republic, January 6, 1954)
Director: Franklin Adreon. *Cast*: Harry Lauter, Aline Towne, Lyle Talbot, Robert Shayne, Fred Graham, Richard Reeves, Tom Steele, John Crawford, Dale Van Sickel, Victor Sen Yung.
Chapter Titles:

1. Sea Saboteurs

2. Death Takes the Deck

3. Five Fathoms Down	8. Native Execution
4. On Target!	9. Mass Attack
5. The Fire Ship	10. Machine Murder
6. Collision!	11. Underwater Ambush
7. War in the Hills	12. Twisted Vengeance

The Man with the Steel Whip (Republic, July 19, 1954)
   Director: Franklin Adreon. *Cast*: Richard Simmons, Barbara Bestar, Mauritz Hugo, Dale Van Sickel, Lane Bradford, Pat Hogan, Roy Barcroft, Stuart Randall, Edmund Cobb.
Chapter Titles:

1. The Spirit Rider	7. Double Ambush
2. Savage Fury	8. The Blazing Barrier
3. Mask of El Latigo	9. The Silent Informer
4. The Murder Cave	10. Window of Death
5. The Stone Guillotine	11. The Fatal Masquerade
6. Flame and Battle	12. Redskin Raiders

Riding with Buffalo Bill (Columbia, November 11, 1954)
   Director: Spencer G. Bennet. *Cast*: Marshall Reed, Rick Vallin, Joanne Rio, Shirley Whitney, Jack Ingram, William Fawcett, Gregg Barton, Ed Coch, Steve Ritch, Pierce Lyden.
Chapter Titles:

1. The Ridin' Terror from St. Joe	9. Into an Outlaw Trap
2. Law of the Six Gun	10. Blast of Oblivion
3. Raiders from Ghost Town	11. The Depths of the Earth
4. Cody to the Rescue	12. The Ridin' Terror
5. Midnight Marauders	13. Trapped in the Apache Mine
6. Under the Avalanche	14. Railroad Wreckers
7. Night Attack	15. Law Comes to the West
8. Trapped in the Powder Shack	

1955

Panther Girl of the Kongo (Republic, January 3, 1955)
   Director: Franklin Adreon. *Cast*: Phyllis Coates, Myron Healey, Arthur Space, John Day, Mike Ragan, Morris Buchanan, Roy Glenn, Sr., Archie Savage, Ramsay Hill, Naaman Brown.
Chapter Titles:

1. The Claw Monster	7. Timber Trap
2. Jungle Ambush	8. Crater of Flame
3. The Killer Beast	9. River of Death
4. Sands of Doom	10. Blasted Evidence
5. Test of Terror	11. Double Danger
6. High Peril	12. House of Doom

King of the Carnival (Republic, May 11, 1955)
   Director: Franklin Adreon. *Cast*: Harry Lauter, Fran Bennet, Keith Richards, Robert Shayne, Gregory Gay, Rick Vallin, Robert Clarke, Terry Frost, Mauritz Hugo, Lee Roberts.
Chapter Titles:

1. Daredevils of the Air
2. Death Takes the Wheel
3. The Trap that Failed
4. Operation Murder
5. The Mechanical Bloodhound
6. Undersea Peril
7. High Hazard
8. Death Alley
9. Cave of Doom
10. The Masked Executioner
11. Undersea Warfare
12. Vengeance Under the Big Top

The Adventures of Captain Africa(Columbia, June 9, 1955)
Director: Spencer G. Bennet. *Cast*: John Hart, Rick Vallin, Ben Welden, June Howard, Bud Osborne, Paul Marion, Lee Roberts, Terry Frost, Ed Coch, Michael Fox.
Chapter Titles:

1. Mystery Man of the Jungle
2. Captain Africa to the Rescue
3. Midnight Attack
4. Into the Crocodile Pit
5. Jungle War Drums
6. Slave Traders
7. Saved by Captain Africa
8. The Bridge in the Sky
9. Blasted by Captain Africa
10. The Vanishing Princess
11. The Tunnel of Terror
12. Fangs of the Beast
13. Renegades at Bay
14. Captain Africa and the Wolf Dog
15. Captain Africa's Final Move

1956

Perils of the Wilderness (Columbia, January 6, 1956)
Director: Spencer G. Bennet. *Cast*: Dennis Moore, Richard Emory, Eve Anderson, Kenneth MacDonald, Rick Vallin, John Elliott, Don Harvey, Terry Frost, Al Ferguson, Bud Osborne.
Chapter Titles:

1. The Voice from the Sky
2. The Mystery Plane
3. The Mine of Menace
4. Ambush for a Mountie
5. Laramie's Desperate Chance
6. Trapped in the Flaming Forest
7. Out of the Trap
8. Laramie Rides Alone
9. Menace of the Medicine Man
10. Midnight Marauders
11. The Falls of Fate
12. Rescue from the Rapids
13. Little Bear Pays a Debt
14. The Mystery Plane Flies Again
15. Laramie Gets His Man

Blazing the Overland Trail (Columbia, August 4, 1956)
Director: Spencer G. Bennet. *Cast*: Lee Roberts, Dennis Moore, Norma Brooks, Gregg Barton, Don Harvey, Lee Morgan, Pierce Lyden, Ed Coch, Reed Howes, Kermit Maynard, Al Ferguson.
Chapter Titles:

1. Gun Emperor of the West
2. Riding the Danger Trail
3. The Black Raiders
4. Into the Flames
5. Trapped in a Runaway Wagon
6. Rifles for Redskins
7. Midnight Attack
8. Blast at Gunstock Pass
9. War at the Wagon Camp
10. Buffalo Stampede
11. Into the Fiery Blast
12. Cave-in
13. Bugle Call
14. Blazing Peril
15. Raiders Unmasked

Index

Note: Most of the pages of this book contain references to four companies that were the leading producers of sound serials (Columbia, Mascot, Republic, and Universal). Please check individual picture titles for page numbers.

G

J

K

M